D1165727

IN PRAISE OF
THE BAAL SHEM TOV
[*Shivhei ha-Besht*]

*The Earliest Collection of Legends about
the Founder of Hasidism*

TRANSLATED & EDITED BY

Dan Ben-Amos & Jerome R. Mintz

JASON ARONSON INC.
Northvale, New Jersey
London

Library of Congress Cataloging-in-Publication Data

Shivḥe ha-Beshṭ. English.
    In praise of the Baal Shem Tov = (Shivhei ha-Besht) : the earliest collection of legends about the founder of Hasidism / translated & edited by Dan Ben-Amos & Jerome R. Mintz.
        p. cm.
    Legends compiled by Dov Baer ben Samuel of Linits.
    Previously published: Bloomington : Indiana University Press, 1970.
    Includes bibliographical references and index.
    ISBN 1-56821-147-3
    1. Ba' al Shem Tov, ca. 1700–1760—Legends. 2. Hasidim—Legends.
3. Legends, Jewish. I. Dov Baer ben Samuel, of Linits. II. Ben-Amos, Dan. III. Mintz, Jerome R. IV. Title. V. Title: Shivhei ha-Besht.
BM755.I8S4413   1994
296.8′332′092—dc20
[B]   93-43456

Manufactured in the United States of America. Jason Aronson Inc. offers books and cassettes. For information and catalog write to Jason Aronson Inc., 230 Livingston Street, Northvale, New Jersey 07647.

Contents

Contents · v

Contents · vii

Contents · ix

PREFACE

SHIVHEI HA-BESHT (*In Praise of the Baal Shem Tov*) has been in print almost continuously for 180 years, a demonstration of the enduring nature of this legendary biography. It was absent during only one short interlude from 1817 to 1848, when the Austrian censor, under pressure from opponents of the Hasidim, prohibited printing the book. The present English translation, the third by as many publishers, is a manifestation of the continuing interest in the work as well as the increasing importance of Hasidism in contemporary Jewish life.

This English translation was the first scholarly edition of *In Praise of the Baal Shem Tov*. It attempted to fulfill one of the major research goals of Jewish studies: the publication of critical editions of traditional texts. More recently the first critical annotated edition in Hebrew appeared, edited by Avraham Rubinstein (*Shivhei Ha-Besht* [Jerusalem: Rubin Mass, 1991]). In the world of scholarship its appearance marks the admittance of the work into the canon of traditional texts, a transition told in biblical metaphor: "The stone that the builders rejected has become the chief cornerstone" (Psalms 118:22).

Just as scholarship of historical Hasidic works has become an integral part of Jewish studies, so too has study of the thriving and not unexpectedly contentious Hasidic community. A new prizewinning work by one of the present editors examines the everyday social and religious experiences of contemporary Hasidim in the New York area (Jerome R. Mintz, *Hasidic People: A Place in the New World* [Cambridge, Mass.: Harvard University Press, 1992]).

We acknowledge with thanks the criticisms made by scholars of our errors of commission and omission. We have incorporated their recommendations into the various editions that have appeared. Some suggestions can be seen in an article by Zeev Gries, "Hasidism: the Present State of Research and Some Desirable Priorities," *Numen* 34 (1987): 97–108, 179–213.

We are delighted that this new edition ensures the availability in English of a classic Hasidic work.

D. B-A and J.R. M.

Translators' Note

The Manuscript

IN THE YEAR 1814 Israel Yofeh, a printer in the town of Kopys in the province of Reissen in Poland, prepared a Hebrew manuscript of Hasidic tales for his press. The tales concerned the life and wonders of the Baal Shem Tov, who had died just fifty-four years before. The Baal Shem Tov had never put his teachings and parables into writing. The essence of his torah or teachings had been written down by his disciples after his death, while tales of his life and deeds had survived primarily by word of mouth. IN PRAISE OF THE BAAL SHEM TOV (Shivḥei ha-Besht) was the first major crystalization of the tales surrounding the Besht and his followers.

The author of the manuscript of tales was Rabbi Dov Ber (also Dob Baer ben Samuel), the son-in-law of Rabbi Alexander the Shohet, who had been the Baal Shem Tov's scribe for eight years.[1] Rabbi Dov Ber had included in the manuscript fifteen tales told to him by his father-in-law, and almost all the other tales in the collection came from sources that the author considered equally reliable. "In each case," Rabbi Dov Ber had written, "I wrote down the name of the person from whom I heard the tale. And praise God, who endowed me with memory, I neither added nor omitted a single detail. All is true and irrefutable. I have not changed a single detail." Except when he was unable to recall his source, each tale began, "I heard this from . . . ."

Israel Yofeh, the printer of Kopys, knew that there were similar manuscripts in circulation, but this was to be the first collection of tales about the Baal Shem Tov to be set in print.[2] Yofeh, himself a follower of Rabbi Shneur Zalman of Lyady (Admor), faithfully prepared the manuscript. However, he could not resist inserting a lengthy account which he had heard from his own master's lips about the early life of the Baal Shem Tov. Rabbi Dov Ber's manuscript version does not properly begin until tale 17.

Being practical as well as pious, the printer also included in his edition a sanction by the local rabbi against anyone else reprinting the book for the next six years. The sanction, however, had little effect since other editions appeared almost immediately in Laszczow and in Berdichev. A Yiddish translation which omitted 40 percent of the original tales but added others not found in the first edition was published in Ostrog. Between 1815 and 1817 four Hebrew editions and three Yiddish translations appeared. Then, in response to the storm of controversy that the Hasidic movement had aroused, the Austrian censor accomplished what the rabbi of Kopys had failed to do: Hasidic works were banned and publication of the book was virtually cut off. Between 1817 and 1848 only two editions of IN PRAISE OF THE BAAL SHEM TOV are known to have appeared, although it is likely that other editions escaped the eye of the censor by being printed without publication dates. Beginning in 1861, however, and continuing up to the present, new editions of the work appeared again in Hebrew and in Yiddish. The best known of the more recent editions in Hebrew, issued first in Berlin in 1922 and later in Tel-Aviv in 1946 and 1960, was prepared by Samuel Aba Horodezky, who rearranged the material in chronological and thematic order.

This Translation

ALTHOUGH SMALL PORTIONS OF IN PRAISE OF THE BAAL SHEM TOV (particularly the opening tales) have been rendered in English and have appeared as parts of collections of Hasidic tales, the present edition is the first complete translation into English.

Hasidic legends, like most traditional tales, have been interpreted and revised by storytellers, novelists, and philosophers. The most famous rendering of Hasidic tales by Martin Buber transformed the tales in accord with Buber's own philosophical beliefs and artistic criteria. Often the Hasidic kernel of thought, as well as customs and details of an earlier generation, became submerged in a new literary narrative. As Buber confessed in later years: "I did not yet know how to hold in check my inner inclination to transform poetically the narrative material."*

This translation consciously avoids reshaping the tales according to contemporary tastes. Such changes do not do justice to the early tale teller and to the reader who may desire to confront the original material on his own. Our responsibility is to provide English readers with the voices of the early narrators in the most accurate and authentic way possible, adding only explanatory notes to clarify the material in its historical context. Interpretations and philosophical enhancement will come as they did in the past—through discussion of the tales by readers and listeners.

The present work follows the original Kopys edition. The present translators have tried to keep faith with Rabbi Dov Ber and the printer of Kopys, even though at times this increased their problems and promised additional difficulties for their readers. The book was composed in two distinct styles, and we have tried to match the spirit of each writer. The sixteen tales added in the beginning by the printer have a distinctly bookish flavor. The Hebrew employed in the original manuscript, on the other hand, is simple and often colloquial. The level of the language of the manuscript is deceptive, however, for the writing is oblique and often awkward. Aside from containing a number of Yiddish words, the Hebrew syntax is often combined with Yiddish language structure. Some of the difficulties noted in the text may have their origin in the erratic nature of oral tradition, or in the corrections made by the printer, or possibly in the author's collation of two different written texts. For example, on occasion the writing passes from third person to first person or from the singular to the plural without notice. It is not always clear who is relating the story. While we have tried to clarify obscure usage, we have also tried to avoid interposing our own standards of order.

Not unexpectedly, the language of the manuscript is sprinkled with phrases from the Bible, Talmud, and Zohar, usually without any indication of their source or even that they are quotations. Whenever possible each phrase has been identified and quoted from a standard English translation (based on the Masoretic text in the case of the Bible).[3] Other problems of translation were created by kabbalistic beliefs and terms. In such cases we have tried to provide an appropriate English equivalent and to skirt the narrow border between translation and interpretation. We have tried to identify the individuals cited in the work; however, in a number of instances, particularly where the characters achieved only local fame, positive identification proved to be impossible.

At times we have made minor editorial changes. Some stylistic uncertainty exists, for example, regarding the identification of individuals cited, and we have often substituted a proper name for a pronoun to ensure clarity. In other ways minor changes have been made: *parasang* was used as the measure of distance in the manuscript because the word had been employed earlier in the Talmud; we have substituted *verst* as it is more in keeping with the eastern European environment. This newest edition also shares some problems with the first edition: in 1814 there was no word in Hebrew for gun and it was called a pipe that fires (151, 26); there is now no exact word for *arrendator*, the feudal tax farmer. In such cases we have let the original terms stand and have provided explanations in the glossary.

In the original manuscript the tales were not titled and numbered, and aside from the use of paragraphs and bold letters, there was no clear division between the tales. These separations often correspond to our division into tales. We have used additional criteria: we indicate the beginning of a new story when the source of the story has changed or when the author makes it clear that he is beginning a new narrative line.

The transliterations of Hebrew and Yiddish words presented a number of irreconcilable linguistic and historical differences. The following system was employed: many Hebrew and Yiddish words are now to be found in Webster's Third International Dictionary, and these spellings were considered as standard; in

general, other spellings follow the rules of transliteration established by the Library of Congress. Names which occur in the
Bible are spelled as they are found in the Masoretic translation
(with the exception of the name Phinehas, which is spelled here
Pinḥas), so that it is Jacob and not Yaʻakow. The names of Talmudic tractates are cited as they appear in the Soncino edition.[4]
The spelling of the names and towns follows that of *The Columbia Lippincott Gazetteer of the World;*[5] in a few instances no
established spelling in English could be found. Problems of con-
sistency were encountered in bibliographical citations as well.
Most often we transliterated the titles of primary sources and
provided an English translation. In some instances, particularly
in the case of secondary sources, authors and editors had already
transliterated Hebrew words in various forms not consistent with
the Library of Congress system. In such instances we retained
the author's transliteration. Similarly, various Hebrew scholars
transliterated their own names according to either German,
Polish, or English spelling. We retain each name as as it appears
in the Library of Congress Catalog and have provided in brackets
the name as it appears in the specific book or article. While the
Hasidim spoke Hebrew with Ashkenazic phonology, the English
spellings of Hebrew words included here use contemporary
Sephardic phonology.

The annotations of the tales refer primarily to material of this
particular historical period or before; we have not usually cited
the countless legends which have appeared in print since the
publication of IN PRAISE OF THE BAAL SHEM TOV. The index of
motifs was prepared by Dan Ben-Amos in 1964 before the present
collaboration began.

The translators would like to acknowledge the aid of many
colleagues. We owe a great debt to Henry A. Fischel of Indiana
University and Joseph Dan of Hebrew University whose criticism and counsel have been of the greatest importance to this
work. Both read the manuscript in its entirety and made many
valuable suggestions. We thank Paula Ben-Amos, who compared
portions of the English translation with the original manuscript.
We also would like to thank Ch. Shmeruk of the Hebrew Uni-

versity, Maria Z. Brooks of the University of Pennsylvania, Heda Jason of Tel-Aviv University and Ishiah E. Trunck of the YIVO Institute for Jewish Research. We thank Kenneth S. Goldstein for preparing the map of eastern Europe.

Lastly, Beryl Eeman has kindly pointed out several errors for correction in the paperback edition.

Introduction

Hasidism

HASIDISM, A PIETISTIC JEWISH MOVEMENT, developed among eastern European Jewry midway in the eighteenth century. The early Hasidim were preachers, shohetim, and rabbis who became identified with the Baal Shem Tov (literally the "Master of the Good Name"), a rabbi and kabbalistic wonder worker whose teachings became the focus of the new movement. The BeShT, as his name was commonly abbreviated, preached a message of pious ecstasy and fervent affirmation, and he renewed religious teachings concerning charity, humility, and selflessness. Tales spread of his power and his piety, and he won an increasing number of followers.

After the death of the Besht in 1760, the more precise religious forms and social organization of Hasidism were shaped by the Great Maggid, Rabbi Dov Ber (also Dob Baer) of Mezhirich (died 1772), Rabbi Jacob Joseph of Polonnoye (died 1782), and other tsaddikim (righteous men, Hasidic leaders) such as Rabbi Aaron of Karlin (1736–72) and Rabbi Shneur Zalman of Lyady (died 1813), who formed dynastic courts and established distinctive patterns of thought, feeling, worship, dress, and custom. These changes drew the Hasidim apart from the followers of the more austere rabbinic tradition, and the Hasidim formed separate congregations in villages and towns throughout eastern and central Europe.

The major focus of Hasidic belief concerned the omnipresence of God in all things and the desire to attain unity with the divine by intense concentration and the abandonment of self. Most striking was the enthusiasm and the intensity which permeated their actions. The pillars of Hasidic teaching are termed kavvanah (concentration), *devekut* (communion with God), and *hitlahavut* (enthusiasm). Other significant Hasidic virtues concerned the attainment of humility and the need to serve the Almighty with joy.

A major source of Hasidic mysticism was Lurianic kabbalism. Isaac Luria (1534–72) and other sixteenth century mystics of Safed provided much of the cosmology, angelology, and demonology of Hasidic belief. The mystics of Safed, too, influenced Hasidic conceptions of the omnipresence of God, the emanations of creation and the unfolding of the coming end, and the complexities of the world of the soul—the dissolutions, transmigrations, and the ultimate union of the soul with God. Yet, whereas the Lurianic Kabbalah appealed primarily to an esoteric audience and to the more learned, Hasidism had its impact among the masses. In Hasidism emphasis was placed on the mystic in relation to the community and on the transformation of the mystic vision into living experience. The mystic visionary became the Tsaddik (or Rebbe)—the righteous leader of the community.

The Hasidic movement stirred new conflicts in the eastern and central European villages, for if Hasidism infused Judaism with new life and spirit, it also threatened traditional roles and values. Talmudic learning, long the touchstone of the pious, occupied a lesser place among the Hasidim; the established forms and hours of the prayers were changed; and the cantor, so prominent in the larger synagogues, was displaced so that any inspired layman could chant the liturgy. The pendulum of community power threatened to swing from the powerful rich and the learned rabbis to the Tsaddikim and their followers. This challenge to entrenched values and the displacement of the social and religious hierarchy alarmed and united the mitnaggedim (literally opponents) of Hasidism and established battle lines in the villages of eastern and central Europe which were to continue into the present century.

In the later development of Hasidism, the Tsaddikim, the saintly leaders who were the descendants of the disciples of the Baal Shem Tov, dominated the communal and religious life. The ways of the Tsaddik as a living incarnation of the Torah were observed, worshiped, and emulated. The court of the Tsaddik became a hereditary institution: the Tsaddik received his spiritual and temporal powers from his lineage; the Hasid, too, generally followed his father by continuing as an adherent of the same rabbinic line. Although IN PRAISE OF THE BAAL SHEM TOV concentrates on the life of the Besht, the work clearly mirrors the early expansion of Tsaddikism. The theoretical workings of the early Hasidim can best be seen in the homilies and sayings of the disciples of the Besht: in the remembered words of the Great Maggid, Dov Ber of Mezhirich, and in the commentaries of Rabbi Jacob Joseph of Polonnoye.* Study of the myth and mysticism of the new movement must focus as well on Hasidic legends, since the telling of tales was (and continues to be) the primary creative expression of Hasidism. Hasidic philosophy was expressed in tale and parable, and the truth of God's ways was pointed out by exempla. Made part of the ritual on the Sabbath and given mystical significance (see tale 194), storytelling became a meritorious deed as well as a pleasurable social ritual. And, as IN PRAISE OF THE BAAL SHEM TOV makes clear, the tales also served as sanctified biographies.

The Life of the Besht in Legend

AS THERE IS LITTLE DOCUMENTATION about the Besht, IN PRAISE OF THE BAAL SHEM TOV stands as the single most important source of his life and his world. Careful analysis, however, is needed to discern the mythical and realistic levels in the book. The tales are the work of many oral narrators and perhaps several written collaborations. They contain both supernatural and realistic elements, and they are based on earlier traditional models as well as on historical events.

One aspect of the book concerns the life cycle of the Besht. There are, however, two slightly different views of the Besht

---

* Rabbi Dov Ber's words were preserved and published by his disciple, Rabbi Solomon of Lutsk, in works such as *Lekutei Amarin (Collection of Sayings)*. Rabbi Jacob Joseph's commentaries appeared in *Toledot Yaakov Yosef (The Generations of Jacob Joseph)* and other works.

presented in In Praise of the Baal Shem Tov. In Rabbi Alexander's account, the Besht appears to have begun as a baalshem (a master of divine names) who wandered from village to village working wonders and providing healing and protective amulets. In these tales the Besht is seen as a popular magician and healer (22), he is considered as a writer of amulets (187), he uses holy names to work miracles (231), and he performs magical transferences (232). Once he exclaims: "I am a besht" (238). However, according to the more literary and stylized version introduced by the printer, the Besht is pictured as a hidden saint who concealed his greatness until he had studied the secret manuscripts of Rabbi Adam and had fully prepared himself in solitude. After revealing himself he was immediately accepted as the mystic leader of the Great Hasidim (15). These differing accounts may have resulted from the desire to make the Besht's past conform to a more acceptable social image than that of a baalshem.

In the tales the Besht is seen to have performed his wonders in the uncertain and dangerous areas of life—healing the sick, exorcising dybbuks (restless souls of dead people), and helping barren women to bear children. The powers attributed to the Besht range from mystic revelation to sympathetic magic: his concentration in prayer could shake the water and make the grain tremble (35, 36, 37), he was able to elevate souls to heaven and to ascend himself to the palaces of heaven (137), and he also possessed the ability to shorten a journey (211, 238) and even to perceive a child's birth and to send a gift of charity before the umbilical cord was cut (234). No mere wonder worker, with the help of God the Besht was said to have mastered the scientific knowledge of medicine (245).

The character of the Besht also endeared him to his followers. He is described as acting with a sense of compassion even when it meant risking his life and his portion of the world-to-come (91). He is depicted as outraged by preachers who vilify and condemn their congregations (165). Though deeply pious, the Besht was aware of the dangers of excessive asceticism (49). He was fearful of being arrogant (88) but hated sham humility:

when a learned rabbi sat at the lower end of a table, the Besht rebuked him, "I despise a man who prides himself on being humble. Come and sit here" (173). On another occasion the Besht disapproved of a rabbi's request to the Almighty that he hear only what was necessary: "If his actions merited this reward, God, blessed be He, would not deprive him of it" (226).

The form of the legends of the Besht is fairly consistent. Customarily, the plots begin with a puzzle, a dilemma, or a calamity. This is often followed by an unsuccessful attempt to solve the problem by a physician, a sorcerer, or a lesser scholar. Then the Besht resolves the situation by means of his supernatural powers. Legends which demonstrate his erudition have essentially the same pattern: he exposes the ignorance of great rabbis and reveals the wisdom of the unlearned. Into this category fall those legends depicting how the Besht won over some of his disciples. In contrast, in those legends where the Besht demonstrates his power of prediction, the plot often centers around someone else, and the Besht has only a passive role in the action. Verification of the prediction customarily concludes the tale.

Many of the tales are local legends which accrued to the Besht. We may also assume that many of the the tales are based on actual events and experiences. On the other hand, several of the tales and many of the motifs in the tales have analogues in international tradition. For example, "The Hour Has Come But Not the Man" is a widely distributed legend known to be associated with a number of rivers and lakes in Europe (see tale 223, note 3).

Storytellers also appear to have patterned the life of the Besht after the scholar-saints of past ages. Features of the life of the Besht, his childhood, marriage, study, and attainment of mystical powers, resemble tales of other sainted figures of Jewish legend such as Rabbi Akiva (about 40 to about 135), Maimonides (1135–1204), Rabbi Judah the Pious (died 1217), and Rabbi Isaac Luria. The Besht's death, too, seems to be based on earlier models. One account indicates that he wasted away from a disease which affected his larynx (114); another version states that his illness was marked by bowel irregularity, a disorder which the righteous are said to suffer at their death (see tale 247, note 4). The death-bed farewell of the Besht and his followers (247) closely resembles the death scenes of Hillel and Yohanan ben Zakkai, rabbis of the first century. The promised return of the Besht in sixty years (147) has parallels to the legends circulating about Shabbetai Tsevi, the false messiah.

Other Historical and Legendary Figures

THE BESHT IS OF COURSE NOT THE ONLY FIGURE to play a part in the narratives. The miraculous story of the Besht's father, Rabbi Eliezer, was appended to the manuscript by the printer. This account is similar to the biblical story of Joseph's adventures in Egypt and its Midrashic elaborations. In addition to the Besht's father, Rabbi Eliezer, there are the mystical Rabbi Adam and his zealous but ill-fated son (5–7). The Besht's wife is depicted as the pious and faithful spouse, as enduring as was Rabbi Akiva's wife in helping her husband prepare himself for his task. Being a woman she is estranged from the brother-hood of the Hasidim, but she learns to appreciate the mystic splendor of their exaltation (61). The Besht's son, unable to assume his father's mantle, is pictured as pathetically inept when his father dies (249). Rabbi Gershon, who appears often among the secondary characters, customarily plays the foil for the Besht. In accounts of the Besht's early years he usually represents the learned and lofty man of the upper class who regards his brother-in-law as an untrustworthy numskull. After the Besht reveals himself, however, Rabbi Gershon becomes one of his ardent admirers. In one tale he says, "I wish I would have the portion of the world that the Besht gains from smoking one pipeful of tobacco" (80). Some members of the holy group surrounding the Besht emerge as individuals as well. The disciples of the Besht often accompanied him in his travels to the villages, but at times even pietists may be playful, as when the Besht followed Rabbi Nahman to prevent him from getting fish for the Sabbath (229). In time other members of the holy group would appear in other cycles of legends, for as indicated in IN PRAISE OF THE BAAL SHEM

Tov, even the least member of the group had the power to help the barren bear a baby boy (222).

Hasidic Beliefs and Customs in the Legends

IN ADDITION TO DEPICTING THE ACTIVITIES OF THE Besht and his followers, the tales portray the life and concerns of the Hasidic Jew in eastern Europe at the turn of the nineteenth century. It is a world structured by the mitzvoth (commandments, duties) in which the faithful are rewarded and lawbreakers are punished by death or by reincarnation in a lower form of life (12, 108, 215, 250). Those who enjoy honest work, such as the simple hose-maker in tale 87, are the foundation of the synagogue. The touchstones of the pious are devout prayer, the giving of charity, and in this later phase of Hasidism, studying the Talmud. When a werewolf terrorized the children, their concern was very pointed: "Some of them became sick, and, heaven help us, could not continue their studies" (4).

If the pious man upheld the synagogue, the woman was the mainstay of the home. She not only bore and tended the children, she often provided for her husband and family by running a small shop or inn, as did the Besht's wife, or by working as a midwife, as did the Besht's mother. Despite her importance, however, she usually had little to do with decision-making, even when it concerned arranging the marriage of her young children: "Is not my husband, thank God, in my house?" questioned such a housewife when asked to betroth her twelve-year-old daughter. "Why should I concern myself with it? He will decide what is best" (75). Her husband did indeed pledge their daughter, although at the time of the wedding he found himself too immersed in his studies to attend the ceremony.

Faithful reflections of the mundane details of daily life, the stories contain the particulars of business arrangements (139) and the precarious circumstances of keeping the *arrendeh*, the privilege received from the master of the estate to mill grain or to distill liquor or to collect taxes (151). The tales also carry the faithful far above the village lanes to heaven, but while the paradise depicted is a complex structure designed by mystic sages, the crowds assembled in the halls of paradise belong to the vision of the poor Hasid struggling for space in the market and a place in the synagogue. In one tale a Hasid finds no more room in paradise than he would at the Rebbe's table. Even when he rushes into the heavenly palace early to get a seat, he is inevitably pushed from his place. Fortunately, he finds a place at the heavenly gate, for he never does manage to sit down inside (152). In the other world one encounters those charged before the Court of Heaven (90), as well as those who, like the excommunicated shohet pitifully naked but for a kerchief, wander in demonic form between Gehenna and paradise (209). The tales furnish the panorama of village life, the visions and dreams of the afterlife, and a portfolio of faces from the small town, the *shtetl*, and from the other world.

Two hostile supernatural worlds confronted the pious: the world of supernatural evil inhabited by Satan, and that of the demons spawned by base thoughts, accidental sexual emissions, and unholy liaisons. The Jews were vulnerable to the powers of Satan when they commited sins, for then he could prevent their prayers from ascending to heaven. While Satan was situated above, the less powerful and often pixyish demons prowled closer at hand in attics and passageways and they occasionally inhabited a human form. To survive one had to be well armed with prayer, amulet, and the use of the holy name (162). Demons could be exorcised by a holy man and cast out into uninhabitable places. The more powerful Satan could be foiled by absolute devotion and by intense prayer.

The feudal world of Jew and gentile, administered by oppressive governors, masters of estates, and priests, held terrors as frightening as the spawn of supernatural creatures. Jew and gentile were the chattel of their masters, who could do to them as they pleased; in addition the Jews were the victims of unfavorable edicts restricting their legal rights, their residence, and choice of occupation. They were plagued as well by false accusations of ritual murder (235). But like Satan, the masters of the estates and the priests could be made to feel the power and the cunning of the Besht. The gentile peasants who appear in the tales, on the other hand, generally appear less threatening than their masters (with the exception of the lawless Haidamaks*). The peasants often perform the difficult manual tasks of hauling horses from the mud or of pushing a loaded wagon to town (126). In one tale set in the other world the Besht wins an appeal for a gentile sentenced to gather wood for those in Gehenna (166); on the other side of the scale, two tales note that there is an accusation in heaven that the Jews in the villages do not treat the gentiles fairly, a circumstance that the Besht remedies by acting kindly to a gentile woodcutter (236). But no matter how correct relations might be, the world of the Jew and gentile was sharply divided (189, 192), and those who breached the separation and became intimate could expect to be considered as pariahs (138).

If the tales are rich in saintly miracles and supernatural happenings, they also abound in earthy observations. At times there is a juxtaposition of piety and profanity. In the middle of the night when a visiting rabbi awoke and saw the glow emanating from the holiness of the Besht, he first thought that the stove was on fire and awoke his wife to get water to put it out. "Don't be so modest," she chides him. "You have water to put out the fire." On another occasion when the Besht left the synagogue, the worshipers thought that he had gone to urinate, although actually he had left in order to trick a priest into having an accidental sexual emission (239). In a counterpoint of sentiment and linguistic ritual the pious could curse the anti-Semite, "May he fall to the bottom and break his bones, God forbid." They could take delight, too, in telling of the anti-Semite who found human dung in his pocket and whose hand could be cleansed only by having a Jew urinate on it (5).

The tales also provide some delightfully ingenuous moments. On one occasion, the Besht advised operating on a sick girl for piles; the narrator later tells us, however, that she proved to be pregnant (59). Another time the Besht advised a Hasid against divorcing his wife because she had not borne him a son. "You will

---

* Ukrainian bands, hostile to the Poles and the Jews, who were active chiefly in the regions of Kiev and Podolia in the eighteenth century.

have children," he promised. Indeed, the prophecy was fulfilled: the man's spouse died and he raised a family with his second wife (212). The Besht's eminent practicality is also revealing. In order to check on the results of a bloodletting that he had advised, he says: "I can see from afar, but send a messenger anyway" (27). The Hasidim too did not like to take chances. In one tale about a false charge of ritual murder the Besht assured the accused that they would be cleared. The Hasidim bribed the doctor anyway: "Thank God no charge resulted from this" (60).

Like most collections of legends, In Praise of the Baal Shem Tov contains historical evidence; however, in Hasidic perspective, history appears governed by religious faith and by righteous men. One tale, for example, tells of a journey made by Rabbi Eliezer Rokeaḥ to the Holy Land (169). There is evidence that such a journey did indeed take place, probably as the result of internal friction in the Jewish community; the Hasidim, however, explain that Rabbi Eliezer went in order to bring the Messiah. Most of the historical accounts are given from the personalized view of the villager who counts the passage of time in local happenings, in the flight from marauding soldiers, in miracles wrought and prophesies fulfilled (217, 213). These tales tell more of the world view of the Hasidic faithful than of the actual passage of events.

The tales contain a feast rich with the details of Hasidic life, and like the Jews hastily fleeing for their lives, we have summarily strained the soup from the meat (210). The full meal awaits the reader.

ABBREVIATIONS

B.	Babylonian Talmud	Lam.	Lamentations
Dan.	Daniel	Lam. R.	Lamentations Rabbati
Deut.	Deuteronomy	Lev.	Leviticus
Deut. R.	Deuteronomy Rabbah	Lev. R.	Leviticus Rabbah
Ecc.	Ecclesiastes	Num.	Numbers
Exod.	Exodus	Num. R.	Numbers Rabbah
Exod. R.	Exodus Rabbah	Prov.	Proverbs
Ezek.	Ezekiel	Ps.	Psalms
Gen.	Genesis	Sam.	Samuel
Gen. R.	Genesis Rabbah	Song. R.	Song of Songs Rabbah
Is.	Isaiah	Song.	Song of Songs
Jer.	Jeremiah	Y.	Yerushalmi (the Palestinian Talmud)
Josh.	Joshua		
Judg.	Judges	Zech.	Zechariah

THE PRINTER'S PREFACE

THE PRINTER SAID: After I received these holy
scriptures about the wonders of God which He revealed through
His holy servants—since with the help of God there is no generation without famous tsaddikim *for the Lord will not forsake His
people for His great name's sake**¹—I realized the many great
benefits which would result from them, especially because it is
written in the book that the Besht said that when one relates the
praises of the tsaddikim it is as if he concentrates on *Ma'aseh
Merkavah*.² It is easy for the wise to understand his reasoning,
especially since *one higher than the high watcheth*.³

I heard, moreover, from the people of the Holy Land, that the
first time there was a plague in the Holy Land, God forbid, the
holy Rabbi Menaḥem Mendel, blessed be the memory of this
righteous and holy man,⁴ locked himself in his home with a
minyan. During all the time that they were secluded their prayers
were successful. However, on the holy Sabbaths he did not say
torah at the third meal as was his custom; instead, he used to sit
at the dinner table with his companions who hearkened to his
voice.⁵ There was an old man with him, one of the Besht's disciples, who told stories in praise of the Besht. One time, the rabbi,
the Maggid, blessed be the memory of this righteous and holy
man, appeared in the dream of Menaḥem Mendel and said to him:
"Are you not my disciple? Why do you not tell stories in my
praise also?" So he agreed to tell stories in praise of our Great
Rabbi during the third meal. When Menaḥem Mendel began to

* Biblical verses are italicized; quotations from any other source appear
within quotation marks.

relate the wonders of the Great Maggid, the old man began to tell about the Besht, as was his custom. Menaḥem Mendel did not let him continue, and immediately realized that he would be punished for it. Indeed, it happened that after the meal he became sick with an intestinal disease. In a few days he passed away. This is the end. The profundity of these things is easily understood.

We are quite aware that these tales certainly do not contain even one thousandth of the greatness of our old father, the Besht, may his merit protect us, amen. We heard awesome things about his greatness and grandeur from *Admor,* may his soul rest in heaven, which he wrote in the preface to the book *Likutei Amarim.*[6] The rabbi, our rabbi and teacher, Menaḥem Mendel who is mentioned above, wrote from our Holy Land in these words: "Thus it was that the word of God was given to the Baal Shem. He was the one. None of the ancients were like him, nor will there be any like him upon earth, and so on."[7]

I realized all the benefits that would result from this printing. And as we know, the book *Shivḥei ha-Ari,*[8] God bless his memory, was also printed. There his disciple Rabbi Ḥayyim Vital, God bless his memory, also testified that it did not contain even one thousandth of his greatness. Nevertheless, *and mine ear received a whisper thereof.*[9]

I understood the greatness and the intensity of the desire of those who wished to copy down these holy scriptures. However, I was aware that this manuscript was full of mistakes, and certainly if it had been copied over and over the errors would have increased in number until the meaning of the sentences would have been almost unrecognizable, and so I took great pains to rid it of error. Therefore, I gathered my strength to set it on my printing press and to proofread it as carefully as I could. Nevertheless, I could not avoid making some mistakes. As it is written, *who can discern errors?*[10] We ask for forgiveness and atonement from God, and may the merit of the Besht and his holy disciples protect me and my descendants forever, and may God, blessed be He, allow me to be one of His innocent and true worshipers. Let it be so. AMEN.

THE WRITER'S PREFACE

I SAID TO MYSELF, Let me explain *with the roll of a book which is prescribed for me*[1] so that the reader will not question my decision or wonder what brought me to write meaningless narratives. I do so especially because there are some people who say in ridicule,[2] "Why does he keep quiet?" But *if it concerneth the scorners He scorneth them.*[3] As for the others who say, "Your silence is better than your words!" *there is no speech, there are no words*[4] to answer their harsh and evil slander, especially since each accuser has a different style of attack. Therefore, I said to myself, "The Judge is my true *witness in the sky*[5] that it is not my intention to be haughty, God forbid, nor to *exercise myself in things too great or in things too wonderful for me*[6] nor to make a name for myself in the world as a great person." I have another reason to justify my doing this, and I will partially reveal it. I heard these tales from the rabbi, the famous great light, Rabbi Gedaliah, God bless his memory,* who said that he heard them from the famous Hasid, our teacher Shmeril, God bless his memory, the preacher of the holy community of Zwierzchowka.[7] According to my opinion if all the signs, the marvels, and the famous miracles and their revelation are beyond a person's comprehension, he should cling to belief alone. I myself have noticed as well that in the time between my youth and my old age every day miracles have become fewer and marvels have begun to disappear. This happens because of our many sins.

* Rabbi Gedaliah of Ilintsy was one of the major sources from whom the author obtained these traditions. The writer refers to him also as "the rabbi of our community."

In earlier days when people revived after lying in a coma close to death, they used to tell about the awesome things they had seen in the upper world. As it is mentioned in the Gemara, "You saw a clear world,"[8] and there are other tales like it in the Gemara. Likewise, my father-in-law, our teacher Alexander, God bless his memory, told about a man who had been lying in a coma in the holy community of Bershad.[9] It was in the time when the sect of Shabbetai Tsevi, may his name be blotted out, was stirring.[10] That man was shown several places in the books in which some rabbis had erred and were almost led astray by that sect. He was ordered to tell the rabbis the exact meaning of those portions. In his days there were also mad people who injured themselves with stones during the reading of the Torah, and who used to reveal people's sins to them and to tell them which of their sins would cause their soul to wander restlessly. I know that in my youth in the village where I studied with a teacher, poor people once came to the heder* and were given a meal. Among them there was a woman possessed by an evil spirit, but they did not realize it. The teacher began to study the portion of the Torah with the children, but when he had recited two or three verses the evil spirit threw the woman down, and her husband came and asked the teacher to stop his instruction because the contaminated spirit could not stand anything holy. When he stopped teaching she rose and sat at her place. Because of all these things, many repented and the faith in the heart of each Jew was strengthened. Now, because of our many sins, the number of pious people is lessened *and those that look out shall be darkened in the windows.*[11] Because of our many sins the faith has decreased and heresy has been spread in the world. We should not write evil about the people of God, and God, blessed be He, will forgive me for this.

Therefore, I was careful to write down all the awesome things that I heard from truthful people. In each case I wrote down from whom I heard it. Thank God, who endowed me with memory, I neither added nor omitted anything. Every word is true, and I did

* Elementary religious school.

not change a word. I wrote it down as a rememberance for my children and their children, so that it would be a reminder for them and for all who cling to God, blessed be He and His Torah, to strengthen their faith in God and his Torah and in the tsaddikim, and so they would see how His Torah purifies the souls of its students so that a man can reach higher stages. As our rabbis, God bless their memory, said: "A man should always look forward and say: 'When will my deeds reach the degree of the deeds of my patriarchs, Abraham, Isaac, and Jacob.' "[12]

The reader should realize that I wrote all this not as history nor as stories. In each tale he should perceive His awesome deeds. He should infer the moral of each tale, so that he will be able to attach his heart to the fear of God, the beliefs of the sages, and the power of our holy Torah. It was in my mind to write after each story the moral and belief which should be inferred from it, but I was afraid lest I say too little, God forbid, and so I have let each one learn from the tales according to his value and his capacity. The small and the great will find what fits them. I said to myself that since I am writing this for my sons anyway, I will let the rest of the Jews enjoy it as well, and God, blessed be He, will grant us favor and help us to merit Israel. I told my descendants to give them to everybody.

For every reader *I will utter dark sayings concerning days of old. That which we have heard and known, and our fathers have told us, we will not hide from their children, telling to the generation to come the praises of the Lord, and His strength, and His wondrous works that He hath done. For He established a testimony in Jacob, and appointed a law in Israel, which He commanded our fathers, that they should make them known to their children; that the generation to come might know them.*[13] *A watcher and a holy one came down from heaven.*[14] Blessed be He, the creator of the sparks of light which are the souls of the pious ones, who together are the soul of the light of the world, the holy light. They are Rabbi Israel Besht and his companions. He was a spark of Rabbi Simeon ben Yoḥai.* I heard from the son of Rabbi

---

* A second century Tanna, the traditional author of the Zohar.

Jacob from Medzhibozh, who is called Rabbi Yakil, that once his father led him to the beth-hamidrash, and the Besht was praying before the ark. His father said to him in these words: "My son, observe him closely. There will not be one like him in the world until the coming of the Messiah, as he is the spark of Rabbi Simeon Ben Yohai and his companions." There is also a story in the book concerning his brother-in-law, Rabbi Gershon of Kuty and the Besht, who brought about an ascension of his soul during minhah in order to raise many other souls.[15] And as it is written in the book *'Ets Hayyim,* in the "gate" of the Sabbath, chapter eight, "Moses our teacher, may he rest in peace, was quick to raise the souls of living and dead every holy Sabbath eve."[16] From this story it is evident that he was also the likeness of the soul of Moses our teacher, may he rest in peace. Look up the story within. What is known does not require proof.[17]

· · ·

The printer said: "Since in the manuscripts from which I have copied these tales the sequence of events and the revelation of the Besht—may his merit protect us, amen—are not in the right order, and because I heard everything as it came from *Admor,* whose soul rests in heaven,* in the proper order and with the correct interpretation, I will print them first as I heard them from his holy lips,and after that point in the story I will include what has been written in the manuscripts."**

* Probably Rabbi Shneur Zalman of Lyady (1747-1813), a disciple of the Great Maggid, Rabbi Dov Ber of Mezhirich, and the founder of Habad Hasidism.
** The printer does not carry out his plan. He presents *Admor's* tale but inserts analogous and supplementary versions from the manuscript. See tales 2, 5-8.

1] *Rabbi Eliezer*

RABBI ELIEZER, OUR TEACHER, THE FATHER OF THE BESHT, LIVED IN THE STATE OF WALACHIA NEAR THE BORDER. HE AND HIS WIFE WERE OLD. ONCE BANDITS CAME TO THE CITY AND CAPTURED HIM, BUT HIS WIFE MANAGED TO ESCAPE TO ANOTHER TOWN. SHE WAS SO POOR THAT SHE BECAME A MIDWIFE[1] AND IN THIS WAY EARNED HER LIVING.

RABBI ELIEZER'S CAPTORS TOOK HIM TO A REMOTE COUNTRY WHERE THERE WERE NO JEWS AND SOLD HIM. RABBI ELIEZER served his master faithfully. His master liked him and *he appointed him overseer over his house*.[2] He asked his master to allow him to observe the Sabbath and to rest on that day,· and his master granted his request. And it came to pass that he remained there a long time. He wanted to escape and save himself, but a dream came to him: "Do not be too hasty, since you must still remain in this country."

It came to pass that his master had dealings with the king's viceroy and as a gift he gave him the rabbi, our teacher, our rabbi, Eliezer. He lavished praise on him and extolled him. As soon as he came to the home of the king's viceroy, he found favor in his eyes and was given a special chamber in which to stay. He had no duties to perform at all, except that when the king's viceroy came home Rabbi Eliezer would welcome him with a bowl of water to wash his feet, since this was the custom accorded great men of state. During all that time he studied the Torah and prayed in his special chamber.

Once the king became embroiled in a great war and he sent for his viceroy to counsel him on tactics of attack and defense. Because it was difficult for the viceroy to grasp the actual situation, he did not know what to say. The king stormed with rage because the viceroy could not help him in this time of trouble. The king's viceroy went home dejected. When he arrived, Rabbi Eliezer, the rabbi, our rabbi and teacher, welcomed him as usual with a bowl of water, but the king's viceroy rejected it and lay down on his couch in a troubled mood. Rabbi Eliezer said to him: "My master, why are you so troubled? Please tell me."

The king's viceroy scolded him, but Rabbi Eliezer was a faithful servant to his master and wanted him to be treated justly. He endangered his life and repeatedly urged him until the king's viceroy was forced to tell him what had happened. And he said to his master: *"Do not interpretations belong to God?*[3] *The Lord is a man of war*.[4] I will keep fasts[5] and I will ask the Lord, blessed be He, for this secret since He is a revealer of secrets."[6] And he asked a dream-question and it was answered.[7] All the tactics of war were revealed and clearly explained to him.

The next day he came to his master and told him the advice

that had been revealed to him from heaven. The king's viceroy was very pleased with the information and he joyfully hastened to the king. And he said, "Oh, my master, this is the advice I have to give." And he answered every question.

When the king heard all the viceroy's words, he said: "This is marvelous advice. It is not from a human mind—unless it comes from a holy man who had inspiration from *gods whose dwelling is not with flesh*[8] or from one who had contact with the Evil Spirit. Since I know that you are by no means a godly man, you must be a sorcerer." The king's viceroy was forced to confess the truth and tell him what had happened.

1a] *Rabbi Eliezer, A Second Version*

(IN THE MANUSCRIPTS IT IS WRITTEN IN THESE words: Once the king sailed with his army to attack a fortress. When they came to the fortress, the king scoffed at it and said, "Look, the day is almost gone. The fortress is small. We'll sleep here overnight, a short distance away, and early tomorrow instead of bothering all our men, we'll send a small force to conquer it."

Rabbi Eliezer was also a sailor on one of the boats. It was revealed to him in a dream that he should go and tell the king not to make light of this battle, for if the king did so, he and all his army would be lost. Iron pillars were planted in the sea all around the city to overturn invading boats, and it was impossible to land there except by way of the channel leading to the entrance of the city. Signs marking the channel were revealed to him so that they would not take the wrong course.

The king and all his troops arose eagerly early in the morning and began to wake up the sailors so that they would man the boats. Rabbi Eliezer did not want to sail, and he said, "I have to tell the king a secret." They immediately shaved him and changed his clothes and then he was taken to the king in a small boat. He told the king what had been revealed to him from heaven. He said to the king: "If you don't believe me, send a small boat manned by convicts and see what their fate will be." And the king did so,

When the boat reached the point where the pillars were placed, it overturned and everyone on board was lost.

The king said, "What do you advise me to do now?"

The rabbi told him: "There is a straight channel which is the entrance to the city and through which the people sail back and forth." He showed him the signs of this channel. They did as he suggested, and the king succeeded in conquering the fortress. That is the end of this version.)

2] *Rabbi Eliezer and the Viceroy's Daughter*

THE KING ELEVATED HIM AND MADE HIM HIS BATTLE commander, for he perceived that *the Lord was with him* and that all that he did prospered.[1] He won every battle that the king sent him to fight. During this time Rabbi Eliezer became concerned about what would happen to him, and he thought that it might be the time to flee to his native land. It was then revealed to him from heaven: "You must still remain in this country."

Then it happened that the viceroy died, and since Rabbi Eliezer had found favor in the king's eyes the king appointed him as his advisor. He also gave him the viceroy's daughter as his wife. Yet with God's help, the rabbi did not touch her. He devised various ways to avoid remaining at home, and even if by chance it so happened that he was at home, he refrained from touching her.

It so happened that no Jew was allowed to live in that country. When they found a Jew, there was only one verdict—that he be put to death. It had been so for several years. Once, his wife asked him, "Tell me, what fault do you find in me that you do not touch me and you do not make me your wife?"

He said to her, "Swear to me that you'll not reveal this to anyone, and I'll tell you the truth." She swore to him, and he told her: "I am a Jew."

She immediately sent him home with a rich treasure of silver and gold. But on the way thieves robbed him and he lost everything that he possessed.[2]

3] *The Birth of the Besht*

WHILE HE WAS ON HIS JOURNEY, ELIJAH THE Prophet revealed himself to him and said: "Because of the merit of your behavior a son will be born to you who will bring light to Israel,[1] and in him this saying will be fulfilled: *Israel in whom I will be glorified.*"[2]

He came home and with God's help he found his wife still alive. The Besht was born to them in their old age, when both of them were close to a hundred. (The Besht said that it had been impossible for his father to draw his soul from heaven until he had lost his sexual desire.)

The boy grew up and was weaned. The time came for his father to die, and he took his son in his arms and he said, "I see that you will light my candle,* and I will not enjoy the pleasure of raising you. My beloved son, remember this all your days: God is with you. Do not fear anything." (In the name of *Admor*, I heard that it is natural for a son and a father to be closely bound, for as our sages, God bless their memory, have said: "The talk of the child in the market place is either that of his father or of his mother."[3] How much closer then are ties between parents and children who are born to them in their old age. For example, Jacob loved Joseph because he was born to him in his old age, and the ties between them were very great, as it is said in the holy Zohar.[4] And it was true here. Although the Besht was a small child, because of the intensity and sincerity of the tie, the words were fixed in his heart.)

4] *The Besht's Education and Youth*

AFTER THE DEATH OF HIS FATHER THE CHILD GREW up. Because the people of the town revered the memory of his

---

* The candle seems to refer to the flame lit by one's son to mark the anniversary of the death of a parent. Buber's translation imparts a somewhat different meaning to this passage: "I see that you will make my light shine out." *Tales of the Hasidim*, I, 36.

father, they favored the child and sent him to study with a melamed.* And he succeeded in his studies. But it was his way to study for a few days and then to run away from school. They would search for him and find him sitting alone in the forest. They would attribute this to his being an orphan. There was no one to look after him and he was a footloose child. Though they brought him again and again to the melamed, he would run away to the forest to be in solitude. In the course of time they gave up in despair and no longer returned him to the melamed. He did not grow up in the accustomed way.[1]

He hired himself out as the melamed's assistant, to take the children to school and to the synagogue, to teach them to say in a pleasant voice, "Amen, let His great name be blessed forever and to all eternity,[2] kedushah,[3] and amen." This was his work—holy work with school children whose conversations are without sin. While he walked with the children he would sing with them enthusiastically in a pleasant voice that could be heard far away. His prayers were elevated higher and higher, and there was great satisfaction above, as there was with the songs that the Levites had sung in the Temple. And it was time of rejoicing in heaven.

And Satan came also among them.[4] Since Satan understood what must come to pass, he was afraid that the time was approaching when he would disappear from the earth.[5] He transformed himself into a sorcerer. Once while the Besht was walking with the children, singing enthusiastically with pleasure, the sorcerer transformed himself into a beast, a werewolf. He attacked and frightened them, and they ran away. Some of them became sick, and, heaven help us, could not continue their studies.**

Afterwards, the Besht recalled the words of his father, God bless his memory, not to fear anything since God is with him. He took strength in the Lord, his God, and went to the householders of the community, the fathers of the children, and urged them to return the children to his care. He would fight with the beast and kill it in the name of God.

* A teacher.
** Literally, "heaven help us, the continual offering would be abolished." See B. 'Arakin 11b–12a.

"Should school children go idle when idleness is a great sin?" They were convinced by his words. He took a good sturdy club with him. While he walked with the children, singing pleasantly, chanting with joy, this beast attacked them. He ran toward it, hit it on its forehead, and killed it. The next morning the corpse of the gentile sorcerer was found lying on the ground.

After that the Besht became the watchman of the beth-hamidrash. This was his way: while all the people of the house of study were awake, he slept; and while they slept, he was awake, doing his pure works of study and prayer until the time came when people would awaken. Then he would go back to sleep. They thought that he slept from the beginning until the end of the night.

5] *Rabbi Adam and the King's Banquet*

I HEARD THE FOLLOWING FROM RABBI SAMSON, THE rabbi of the holy community of Raszkow, the son of the rabbi of the holy community of Polonnoye. Once there was a man who was called Rabbi Adam.[1] He was the one from whom the Besht received the manuscripts. Rabbi Adam had found these manuscripts containing the hidden secrets of the Torah in a cave.[2]

Once this Rabbi Adam invited the kaiser to come to a banquet and the kaiser promised that he would come. Rabbi Adam lived in a very small house. The feast he intended to serve was one that he had perceived that one king was preparing for another. The preparation had taken two years so that the host could build great palaces. He had constructed a staircase of expensive decorative glass called crystal, beside which ran a small canal in which fish swam back and forth in the water. He prepared table settings of silver and gold, and arranged for food, drink, and servants to honor the visiting king. A date was set for the king to come to the banquet. On that day Rabbi Adam invited the kaiser to dinner. And the kaiser and all the ministers of the court went to the banquet of this Rabbi Adam.

Among these ministers was one who violently hated the Jews.

He wanted to persuade the kaiser that if he attended the dinner it would disgrace him, since, as the minister knew, Rabbi Adam had neither palace nor banquet. The kaiser paid no attention and went. While they were on their way, the minister again tried to convince the kaiser to return to the court but was ignored. Nevertheless, the kaiser sent one minister to see if the banquet preparations had been made and if there was room in Rabbi Adam's house. The messenger returned and said that Rabbi Adam had a small house just as before. The kaiser continued on his way in spite of that, and when he drew near to Rabbi Adam's city, he sent another messenger, who returned with the same information. But when the kaiser came to the street on which Rabbi Adam lived, he saw great palaces and a large courtyard, and he entered the courtyard with all his ministers and servants. Immediately all his servants took the horses to the stables, while palace waiters did the tasks to which they were appointed. All of the palace waiters were mutes. The kaiser's court partook of all the delicacies, and Rabbi Adam said to them: "Eat and drink as much as you like, only let none of you take any of the table settings."

Afterwards, Rabbi Adam said: "Every one who has a wish should say to me—'I want this or that'—and then put his hand in the pocket of his coat, and he will find what he wished for." The kaiser was first. He wished for something and found it in the pocket of his coat. All the ministers did the same. When it was the turn of the minister who was a Jew hater, he wished for something as well. Rabbi Adam told him: "Put your hand into your pocket." When he put his hand in his pocket, he dirtied his hand and he took it out filthy with human dung. There was a terrible stink and the kaiser ordered him to be removed. He washed his hand with water, but it did not do any good, and he appealed for mercy to Rabbi Adam. Rabbi Adam said to him: "If you swear never to be a Jew hater it will be all right. If not, your hands will be filthy all your life." He swore, and Rabbi Adam told him: "There is only one remedy for you—a Jew must urinate on your hands. You will wash in it and this will help you." And so it happened.

The kaiser took two glasses from one table setting and concealed them in his breastpocket. After the kaiser went away all the palaces disappeared, and nothing was missing except those two glasses and what they had eaten and drunk. When the world's newspapers announced the extraordinary event—the disappearance of the palace and the table settings and their return intact except for the missing two glasses and all the food and drink—the kaiser sent a letter to the king in which it was written: "I have a Jew who brought us to your palace and we ate the dinner that you prepared. As a sign I return to you your two glasses."[3]

6] *The New Coat of Rabbi Adam's Wife*

ONCE THE WIFE OF RABBI ADAM SAID TO HIM, "How long will we suffer this poverty?"

And he told her, "What is your wish? You can go to the closet and take any coat that you wish from the rod." She went to the closet and took the coat that she liked from the rod and brought it into the house. But he urged her to return the coat. He said to her: "It is better for us to endure poverty in this world."[1] And she returned the coat.

7] *The Secret Manuscripts and Rabbi Adam's Son*

RABBI ADAM PREPARED A DREAM-QUESTION: TO whom should he hand down his manuscripts? He was told to hand them down to Rabbi Israel ben Eliezer of the city of Okopy.[1] Before his death he commanded his only son: "I have manuscripts here which hold the secrets of the Torah. But you do not merit them. Search for the city called Okopy and there you will find a man whose name is Israel ben Eliezer. He is about fourteen years old. You will hand him the manuscripts for they belong to the root of his soul.* If you will be fortunate enough to study with him, then so much the better."

And so it happened that after our teacher Rabbi Adam passed away, his only son, a distinguished, eminent scholar, perfect in every virtue, traveled with a wagon and horses from one city to another until he arrived at the city of Okopy. He stayed with one of the elders of the community,[2] who asked him: "Where do you come from and where are you going? Collecting money doesn't seem to be your object."

He answered him, "My late father, God bless his memory, was a well known righteous man, and before he passed away he ordered me to marry a wife here in the holy community of Okopy. I must fulfill his will." Immediately the whole city was in an uproar, and several marriages were proposed to him because he was admired by everyone. And he settled a marriage contract with a wealthy man.

After his wedding he began to search for the man that he was seeking. But he found only Israel, who was an attendant in the beth-hamidrash. After watching him closely he realized that his outer appearance did not reveal his inner qualities. Perhaps this was the person he was seeking. He said to his father-in-law: "There's so much confusion here in your house that it's hard for me to study. Please have a small partition prepared for me in the beth-hamidrash where I'll be able to study regularly. 'The prayer is to be recited where there is song.'[3] " His intention was to be with Israel all the time in order to learn his true character. His father-in-law did not hesitate to fulfill this request because he was very dear to him. He commanded the Besht to serve his son-in-law, the rabbi, and promised to pay him for this. And he did so.

Once, at night, when everyone was asleep, Rabbi Adam's son pretended that he also was asleep. He watched the Besht rise and study and pray at his customary place. He observed this happening once and then again. During the third night, while standing and studying, the Besht fell asleep. The son of Rabbi Adam got

---

* In Lurianic mysticism the root of each soul is found in holy *sefirot*. The nature of each soul corresponds to the portion of the divine world in which it originally resided.

up and took one folio of the manuscripts, put it before the Besht, and then again pretended to be asleep. When the Besht woke up and saw the folio in front of him, he was deeply stirred. He studied it and then concealed it in the inner fold of his garment.

The son of Rabbi Adam did the same thing again during the following night, until he had made certain that this was the man that his father had commanded him to hand over the manuscripts. He called him over and said: "My master and father, God bless his memory, left me these manuscripts and ordered me to give them to you. Here they are before you. But please, my master, let my soul be dear to you and allow me to study with you."

He answered him: "I grant you this on one condition: that no one besides you will know about it and you will not reveal it by your behavior. You must continue to order me to serve you as you did before." And so it was.

Afterwards, the Rabbi's son told his father-in-law: "I desire more seclusion. If it is possible, obtain a separate house for me outside the city where I can study the Torah and pray." And he did so. He asked his father-in-law to hire the boy, Israel, to stay with him and to serve him whenever he would need to send a message. And he did so because Rabbi Adam's son was a very respected man. When the people of the community saw that our teacher Israel was studying with Rabbi Adam's son, they said that it was probably on account of Israel's father that Rabbi Adam's son came here to care for Israel. It seemed to them that Israel was behaving in the right way. And so they gave him a wife; however, the days of this wife were numbered and she died.

When they went to their house of solitude, they studied the Gemara, the commentary of *Rashi*, the tosaphoth,* the writings of the legal codifiers, and all the Holy Scriptures. In the above mentioned manuscripts there was both Divine Kabbalah and Practical Kabbalah.[4] Once, Rabbi Adam's son asked the Besht to bring down the Prince of the Torah[5] to explain something to them and the Besht refused him and said, "If we err, God forbid, in our kavvanah it can be dangerous. We lack the ashes of a red heifer."[6] But Rabbi Adam's son urged him every day until he

* These are critical and explanatory glosses of the Talmud.

could not refuse him. They fasted *hafsakah** from one Sabbath to the other, and they properly immersed themselves in the ritual bath; and at the end of the holy Sabbath, they concentrated on some particular kavvanoth. Immediately, the Besht shouted, "Oh! We made a mistake. The Prince of Fire** will descend and will probably burn the whole town. Now, since you are regarded by everyone as a pious man, go immediately to your father-in-law and to the others in the city and tell them to save themselves, because the town will soon be in flames." And so it happened. Then all the people thought of Rabbi Adam's son very highly and considered him a holy man and a miracle worker.

After a long time he again urged the Besht to bring down the Prince of Torah, but the Besht refused. But he urged him for several days until the Besht felt compelled to do his will. They kept *hafsakah* fasts as they did before. On the night of the holy Sabbath, when they concentrated on certain kavvanoth,[7] the Besht cried: "Oh! Both of us are condemned to death tonight because of what we have done. There is one way we can escape. If we can gather strength to stand and concentrate on the kavvanoth the entire night without sleeping a wink, then the verdict will be postponed.[8] Sleep is of the nature of death,[9] and if we but doze, God forbid, the Evil One will overcome us and control us completely." They remained awake the whole night. Before the morning light, Rabbi Adam's son could not restrain himself and he dozed a little. When the Besht saw this he ran to him quickly and made a loud noise, but Rabbi Adam's son suddenly fainted. They tried to awaken him but it was no use. They buried him with great honor.

8] *The Besht's Marriage*

After that the Besht took another path. He left there and went to a community near the holy community of

---

* A type of fasting which is not supposed to be broken with a meal at the end of the day.

** The angel Gabriel is known as the Prince of Fire. See Louis Ginzberg, *The Legends of the Jews* (Philadelphia, 1909), I, 140; VI, 202; and B. Pesaḥim 118a; and Song R., 3, 11:5.

Brody, where he became a successful melamed. Since he was a
very eminent scholar and a man of great wisdom, he found favor
in the eyes of everyone, and all the affairs of the community were
decided by him. When there was a quarrel between people, they
came to him and he would give them his decision. Both the guilty
and the innocent agreed with him because in his great wisdom he
appealed directly to their hearts, so that all were satisfied.

Our master, Rabbi Gershon of Kuty, was head of the rabbinical court in the holy community of Brody.* His father, our
master Abraham,** had a law-suit to settle with one of the people
in the community where the Besht was staying, so he went there.
He asked his opponent to travel with him to the holy community
of Brody to settle the issue between them according to the law of
the Torah. But the man said to him: "There is with us here a
teacher, eminent in the knowledge of Torah, who is a righteous
judge. Whenever a case is brought before him both sides agree
completely with his decision because he clearly explains the verdict. Let us go to him and present our arguments, and, sir, if you
are not satisfied with his decision, then I will go with you to the
holy community of Brody." He accepted his advice and they
went to him. When our master and rabbi, Rabbi Abraham, came
before the Besht, he immediately was inspired with the holy
spirit*** and perceived that his daughter was to be the future wife
of the Besht. At that time it was the custom of great scholars that
when a worthy guest came he would give an explanation of a

* During that period there were four juridical courts in Brody. Rabbi
Gershon might have been a member of one of these courts; however there
is no evidence that he was the head of any of them. Yet he was known
to be a learned person, and contemporary documents mention him as a
cantor in the beth-hamidrash of Brody. See Nathan Michael Gelber, *The
History of the Jews in Brody*, Hebrew (Jerusalem, 1955), pp. 51, 71, 332.
A biographical study of Rabbi Gershon was done by Abraham J. Heschel,
"Rabbi Gershon of Kuty, his Life and Immigration to the Land of Israel,"
Hebrew, *Hebrew Union College Annual*, XXIII, pt. 2 (1950–51), 17–71.

** Samuel A. Horodezky points out that since the second name of
Rabbi Gershon was Abraham, it was unlikely that his father would have
the same name. European Jews do not name their children after their
fathers while the latter are alive. See *Shivḥei ha-Besht* ["In praise of the
Baal Shem Tov"] (Tel-Aviv, 1960), p. 185.

*** In Judaism the concept of the holy spirit (*ruaḥ ha-kodesh*) refers,
among other things, to the prophetic spirit, or inspiration.

difficult passage. And so the Besht clarified a complex point in the *Rambam** with great subtlety. He continued to do so until Abraham's soul became attracted to the Besht's soul and their souls were in accord.

Afterward, the two opponents presented their arguments before him, and there were many disagreements and conflicts. After about an hour the Besht rendered a truthful and just decision. Rabbi Abraham was in awe of the Besht and loved him very much. In the meantime he found out that the Besht was marriageable and needed a wife. Our master and rabbi, Rabbi Abraham, had a divorced daughter, and he came to the Besht secretly and said to him, "I have heard, sir, that you are in need of a wife. Perhaps you, sir, would be willing to make a match with my daughter?"

He answered: "I am willing, but since in this community many of the leaders favor me, we shall have to conceal the matter so that no one will know of it. I don't want to insult them since they have always helped me and improved my position. If you wish, sir, we will arrange the engagement contract between ourselves. I require one other thing from you. You must make the match with me, and not with my knowledge of Torah and my wisdom. I do not want you to exaggerate my virtues in any way. You should write simply '*Mar* Israel, son of *Mar* Eliezer.' " Since their souls were in accord Rabbi Abraham agreed to all the demands, and they signed the engagement contract without noting either their learned titles or the name of the place. The matter was not revealed to anyone.

When our rabbi and master, Rabbi Abraham, returned to his home, he fell sick on the way of a disease from which he never recovered, and he passed away. They informed his son, the great rabbi, our rabbi and master, Gershon of Kuty, who was in the holy community of Brody. He came to grieve for his father according to the law of the Torah. He received all his father's

---

* Abbreviation of Rabbi Moses ben Maimon, Maimonides (1135–1204) a medieval Jewish philosopher and codifier. His major halakic work is *Mishneh Torah* ("Second Torah"), and Jews often refer to it by the name of the author himself rather than by title.

papers and among them he found the engagement contract, showing that his father had made a match between his daughter, Rabbi Gershon's sister, and some man whose name was Israel. He was amazed that his father, who was a famous man, could make a match with a person of low rank, and, moreover, with someone whose background and family lines were unknown. He told it to his sister, and she answered: "If our father thought the match was proper, we shouldn't doubt his decision."

The Besht waited until he finished his term of teaching, and then he went to the householders of the community and said: "I am returning to my old place." They urged him to stay and promised him more gifts and money. But he had other intentions and he did not listen to them.

He disguised himself by putting on clothes like those worn by loafers. He put on a short coat and a broad belt, *he changed his demeanour*[1] and manner of speech, and he went to the holy community of Brody to the house of the rabbi, our master and rabbi, Rabbi Gershon.

There were two rabbinical courts supervised by Rabbi Gershon which were holding sessions in his house, and Rabbi Gershon examined the cases that were brought before them. The Besht was standing at the door. Our rabbi and master, Rabbi Gershon, thought that he was a beggar. He took a coin with the intention of giving it to him, and the Besht told him, "I have a secret to tell you." They went to a room and the Besht showed him the engagement contract and said: "Give me my wife."

When the rabbi saw the man, his dress, and heard his language, he was astonished and frightened at what his father, God bless his memory, had done. He called his sister and told her the whole situation.

She return[ed] answer to[2] him: "Since our father has arranged this, we should not reverse the decision. It is surely God's will and perhaps a virtuous child will be born from the marriage."

They agreed and appointed a time for the wedding ceremony. Before the wedding took place the Besht said that he wanted to speak with his bride, as the saying of our rabbis, God bless their memory, goes.[3] He talked with his bride secretly and told her the truth, the why's and wherefore's of the whole situation. He made her swear that she would not reveal anything, even if she would undergo many periods of great poverty.

After the wedding, our rabbi and master, Rabbi Gershon, wanted to study with him in the hope that the Besht would learn something, but the Besht concealed his knowledge and pretended to be unable to learn. The Rabbi said to his sister: "Really, I am disgraced by your husband, and if you want to divorce him, it is acceptable to me. If not, I will buy you a horse, and you may go and lodge with him wherever he will lodge. I cannot bear this shame."

She agreed to this proposal and they wandered about the country. The Besht arranged for a place in which she could live, and he secluded himself in the great mountains. She made her living in this way: two or three times a week she came to him with a horse and wagon; he would quarry clay, and she would cart it to town. In this way she made her living.

The Besht fasted *hafsakah* for long periods. When he wanted to eat he dug a small pit and put in flour and water, which was then baked by the heat of the sun. This was his only food after fasting. All these days he was in solitude.

9] The Besht and the Robbers

The mountains were immense. Between them was a deep ravine, and the sides of the cliffs were steep. Once the Besht was walking deep in meditation. There were robbers standing on the other mountain. When from afar they saw him walk to the edge of the mountain engrossed in his meditations, they said, "He will probably fall to the bottom and break his bones, God forbid." When he came near the edge, the other mountain moved towards him and the ground became level. He continued to walk and the two mountains were divided behind him as they were previously. On his return, when he came to the edge, one mountain moved toward the other and it became flat. And so it happened several times during his walking back and forth. The robbers saw that he was a holy man and that God was with him, and they made peace with him. They came to him and told him what they had seen, and they said: "With our own eyes we saw that you are a holy man. We appeal to you to pray for us so that God will make us successful in our chosen path of endeavor, for which we are sacrificing our lives."

The Besht told them: "If you swear to me that you will not hurt nor rob a Jew, then I will do as you ask." They swore to him. From that day on if there was any quarrel or disagreement among them, they came to him and he arranged a compromise.

10] *The Vengeful Robber*

ONCE TWO ROBBERS CAME TO HIM FOR JUDGEMENT. One of them did not like the sentence pronounced by the Besht. He said in his heart: "When the Besht is awake, it is impossible to do any evil to him; but when he is asleep, I will fulfill my wish to kill him." And this is what he tried to do. When the Besht was sleeping the robber came to him and lifted his axe to cut off the Besht's head. Immediately the axe was snatched from him, he could not tell by whom, and he was cruelly beaten. He received cuts and welts. All the breath was beaten out of him, and he almost lost the power of speech.

The Besht woke up and saw the beaten man before him, smeared with blood, and covered with wounds and bruises, and he asked him: "Who are you and who did this thing to you?" But the robber did not have the power to tell him anything. The Besht went on his way, and the next day when the robber recovered a little bit, he told the Besht all that had taken place.

11] *The Besht's Journey to the Holy Land*

(ONCE THE ROBBERS CAME TO HIM AND SAID, "SIR, we know a short way to the Land of Israel through caves and underground passages. If you wish, come with us and we'll show you the way." He agreed to go with them. While they were on their way they came to a wide ditch full of water, mud, and mire. They crossed it on a board which was extended from one bank to the other. While crossing it they leaned on a pole which they stuck into the mud. The robbers went first. When the Besht wanted to step on the board he saw there *the flaming sword which turned every way*,[1] and he turned back since there would have been great danger for him if he had crossed.[2] And the Besht said in his heart: "There is surely a reason why I have come to this place."

On his way back he met the frog mentioned above.)*

12] *The Besht and the Frog*

THERE ARE PEOPLE WHO SAY THAT ONCE THE RABBI** entered into deep meditation. He was absorbed in his thoughts for three days and three nights, and he was not aware that he was walking. Then he realized that he was in a vast desert, remote from his own place. He was surprised that he had wandered to this desert, and he thought that his wandering was probably not without meaning. While engrossed in his thoughts, there appeared before him a frog that was so large he could not tell what kind of creature it was. He asked the frog, "Who are you?" And the frog replied that he was a scholar who had been reincarnated as a frog. (The Besht said: "You are indeed a scholar!" and with this pronouncement he greatly elevated his soul.)

The frog told him that it had been five hundred years since he

* Tales 11 and 12 are two versions of a story which narrates the encounter of the Besht with the frog. Tale no. 11 appears within parentheses in the original text, probably indicating that it constitutes a secondary version which supplements the one obtained through the *Admoric* tradition. The printer apparently has made a mistake or he has shifted the order of tales 11 and 12.

** The Besht. He is referred to as a rabbi in a few of the tales. See for example tales 17, 32, 214, 215, 218, 225, 227, 233, 234.

had been transformed into a frog, and although Rabbi *ha-Ari*,* God bless his memory, had redeemed all the souls, because of the severity of his crimes he had been expelled to a place without people so that no one could redeem him.**

The Besht asked him: "What was your crime?" He said that once he neglected to wash his hands properly and that Satan accused him before God of his transgression. Satan had been told that it was impossible to indict him for a single sin; however, "since one transgression draws in its train another transgression,"[1] if Satan could trap him into committing another transgression, then the first would also be considered. But if he would remember God and not commit a second transgression then the first sin would be cleared. Satan had tested him again and had caused him to stumble, and so he had failed the trial. This had happened a second, and then a third time, until he had broken almost all the commandments of the Torah. Sentence had been passed to reject his repentence. Despite all this, if he would have knocked at all the gates of repentence, he would have been accepted, since we know that in the case of the Other One*** a heavenly voice said, "*Return O backsliding children*[2] except the Other One.*" This was the punishment for his sin: to reject him. But if he had persisted and repented they would have accepted him since there is nothing which can stand in the way of repentance.[3] Satan led him astray, and he became so great a drunkard that he did not have time to meditate and to repent. He committed all the sins

---

* Rabbi Isaac Luria (1534–1572) was the major figure of the kabbalistic school at Safed, Palestine. The doctrine of redemption has a central place in his mystical thought. For a discussion of its different aspects, see Gershom G. Scholem, *Major Trends in Jewish Mysticism* (New York, 1961), pp. 268–86.

** According to the Safed school of mysticism the transmigration of the soul into another form of nature (such as that of an animal, a plant, or an inanimate object) was a particularly dreadful form of punishment. See Scholem, pp. 281–84.

*** Elisha ben Avuyah, a Tanna of the second century who became a heretic. Consequently the rabbis never called him by name but referred to him as *Aḥer*, "the Other One." See B. Ḥagigah 14b, 15a–b; Ḳiddushin 39b; Y. Ḥagigah 2.1, 77b.

that there are in the world. Since the cause of the sins was the first one, his neglect to wash his hands, when he died he was transformed into a frog, a creature which lives in water. He was consigned to a place where human beings do not live, because whenever a Jew might pass by or make some kind of blessing, or think some good thought, he could by that means *bring forth the precious out of the vile.*[4]

The Besht redeemed his soul and elevated it, and the body of the frog lay dead.

13] *The Besht Serves as Rabbi Gershon's Coachman*

AFTER THE BESHT HAD SPENT SEVEN YEARS IN SOLITUDE in the mountains, the time approached when he was to reveal himself.[1] He went with his wife to the holy community of Brody to his brother-in-law, our master and rabbi, Rabbi Gershon. When they came to him he greeted them, and asked: "Where have you been?"

His sister *return*[ed] *answer to*[2] him: "We wandered from village to village and were beset with many troubles."

He was filled with pity for her, so he settled them near his house and took the Besht as his personal servant.

Once he went on a journey and he took the Besht along as his coachman. In the course of the journey our master and rabbi, Rabbi Gershon, fell asleep, and the Besht drove the horses into a marsh filled with mud and mire from which it was impossible to pull them free. Just then his brother-in-law, Rabbi Gershon, woke up. He realized that they were in serious trouble. He thought that the Besht was a simpleton, and he feared that if he sent him to the village to find some gentiles to haul out the horses, he would wander wherever he pleased. He preferred to go and find help himself. He was forced to climb from the wagon into the mire and he walked to a certain village. He was returning with several people to pull the horses from the mud when he looked up and saw the Besht coming towards him. He asked: "Who pulled you out?"

He answered: "I struck the horses just once and they simply walked out."

Our rabbi and master, Rabbi Gershon, said: "It is impossible to obtain even this service from him. He is good for nothing."

14] *The Besht Reveals Himself*

AFTER THAT OUR MASTER AND RABBI, RABBI GER-shon, rented a place for the Besht in a certain village where he would be able to earn a living. And there he achieved perfection. He built a house of seclusion in the forest. He prayed and studied there all day and all night every day of the week, and he returned home only on the Sabbath. He also kept there white garments for the Sabbath. He also had a bathhouse and a mikveh. His wife was occupied with earning a living, and God blessed the deeds of her hand and she was successful. They were hospitable to guests: they gave them food and drink with great respect. When a guest came she sent for the Besht and he returned and served him. The guest never knew about the Besht.

It was the Besht's custom when he came to the city for Rosh Hashanah to remain there for the entire month. Once during the intermediate days of Sukkoth, our master and rabbi, Rabbi Gershon, noticed that he was not putting on tefillin. It was his custom to pray by the eastern wall of the synagogue. And he asked him: "Why don't you put on tefillin today?"

He answered: "I saw in the *Taich** books that he who puts on tefillin during the intermediate days is sentenced to death."**

The rabbi became very angry that the Besht followed the customs that are written in the books from Germany. There was no telling what the result would be. He went with him to the rabbi of the community so that the rabbi would admonish him.

* "Deutsch," old Yiddish, the language in which popular books of exempla were written.

** The Hasidim, following the Kabbalah and in opposition to the custom which prevailed among the Jewry of Galicia, did not put on tefillin during the intermediate days of holidays. For a discussion of the dispute concerning this problem see Aaron Wertheim, *Laws and Customs of Chassidism*, Hebrew (Jerusalem, 1960), pp. 79–81.

They considered the Besht to be a pious man, but as the saying goes, "an uncultured person is not sin-fearing."[1]

The rabbi was a very righteous man. When they came to the rabbi's house, Rabbi Gershon kissed the mezuzah,* but the Besht put his hand on the mezuzah without kissing it, and our master and rabbi, Rabbi Gershon, became angry with him over this as well.

When they entered the rabbi's house the Besht put aside his mask and the rabbi saw a great light. He rose up before the Besht. Then the Besht resumed the mask and the rabbi sat down. And this happened several times. The rabbi was very frightened since he did not know who he was. Sometimes he seemed to be a holy person and at other times he seemed to be a common man. But when our master and rabbi, Rabbi Gershon, complained to him about the tefillin and the mezuzah, the rabbi took the Besht aside privately and said to him: "I command you to reveal the truth to me." And the Besht was forced to reveal himself to him. But the Besht commanded him in turn not to reveal anything that had transpired.

When they came out the rabbi said to our master and rabbi, Rabbi Gershon: "I taught him a lesson, but I think he would not knowingly commit a fault against our customs. He has acted in innocence." Then the rabbi examined the mezuzah and they discovered that it had a defect.

15] *The Besht Reveals Himself to the Sect of the Great Hasidim*

When the time for him to reveal himself approached, it happened that one of the students of our master and rabbi, Rabbi Gershon, went to him. On Tuesday he stayed

---

* A small parchment placed in a metal or wooden case and nailed in a slanting position on the doorpost. Inscribed on one side of the parchment are Deut. 6:4–9 and 11:13–21, inscribed on the other side, and visible through an aperture is the name of God, *Shaddai*, Almighty. The inscription on the parchment must be done with utmost care by a qualified person only, and any fault with the writing makes the mezuzah defective.

with the Besht, who received him with great honor, and after dinner the guest said: "Israel, prepare the horses for me so that I can leave immediately." The Besht harnessed the horses to the wagon.

Afterwards, the Besht said: "What would happen if you, sir, stayed here over the Sabbath?" The visitor laughed at him. But he had gone only half a verst* when one wheel broke. He returned and replaced it with another wheel and started off again. The second time something else broke, and he had to stay over on Wednesday and Thursday as well. On Friday other things happened to him and he finally had to remain at the village for the Sabbath. He was very unhappy about it and wondered what he would do there with the peasant. In the meanwhile he was surprised to see the Besht's wife prepare twelve loaves of hallah, and he said to her, "What need have you for twelve loaves of hallah?"**

She answered him: "What does it matter if my husband is a simple man; he is still observant. Since I saw my brother saying the kiddush[1] blessing over the twelve loaves of hallah, I prepare them in the same manner for my husband."

He asked her if they had a bathhouse, and she answered, "Yes, we have, and we have a mikveh*** also."

He said: "What need do you have for a mikveh?"

She answered: "My husband is an observant man and he goes daily to the mikveh."

Nevertheless, the guest was sad because of his delay there. Soon it came time to pray the Minhah[2] and he said, "Where is your husband?"

"He is in the field with the sheep and the cows," she said. He prayed minhah and the Reception of the Sabbath[3] and the Maariv[4] by himself.

---

* About two-thirds of a mile.

** Baking twelve loaves of hallah for the Sabbath was a custom introduced in the Ukraine and Galicia, Poland, by Hasidic rabbis who were following kabbalistic teachings. See Wertheim, *Laws and Customs of Chassidism*, pp. 150–51.

*** A bathing place for ritual purification.

The Besht did not return home for a time as he was praying in his house of seclusion. When he came home he changed his manners and dress and speech, and he said: "Good Sabbath!" He said to his guest: "See. I said that you would remain here for the Sabbath and here you are."

The Besht stood at the wall to make it appear as if he were praying. After that the Besht said to himself that if he were to make the kiddush himself with his customary special devotion,[5] the guest would realize the truth. Therefore, he honored his guest by asking him to make the kiddush. They sat down at the table to eat, and in the way of peasants his wife sat next to him. They ate the evening meal with joy and good feeling, but the guest could not remove the sadness from his heart. The Besht said to him: "Rabbi, let us hear some Torah from you." On that Sabbath the reading of the Torah was the portion of Exodus, and so in a simple way the guest related to him the story of the Egyptian exile under the rule of the Pharoah. Then they made the bed for their guest near the table, and the Besht slept next to his wife.

At midnight the guest awoke and saw a large fire burning on the oven. He ran to the oven because he thought that the wood on the oven was burning. He saw that it was a great light—then he was hurled backward and he fainted. They revived him and the Besht said: "You should not have looked at what is not permitted you." The guest marveled at what had happened.

In the morning the Besht went to pray in his house of seclusion as usual and afterwards he returned home joyfully with his head held high. Inside the house he walked back and forth singing *Asader le-S'udata*,[6] and he made Kiddusha Rabbah[7] in his customary way with wonderful devotion. In the course of the meal he asked the guest to say torah but the guest was perplexed and did not know what to say. He cited a phrase and interpreted it. The Besht responded: "I heard another interpretation of this phrase." After the meal he went to his house of seclusion and after Minhah he returned and revealed himself. He said torah and revealed such secrets of the Torah that no one had ever heard before. They prayed Maariv and he made the Havdalah[8] in his usual fashion. Afterwards, he commanded his guest to go to our master and rabbi, Rabbi Gershon, but he was not to reveal anything. He was to go instead to the Sect of the Great Hasidim in the town,* and also to the rabbi of the community, and say these words: "There is a great light living near your community, and it will be worthwhile for you to seek him out and bring him to the town."

When all the Hasidim and the rabbi heard these things, they decided that it must refer to the Besht. They recalled their questions about him, which now seemed clear. All of them went to his village to invite him to come to town. The Besht had foreseen what would happen and he went toward the town as they were going out to see him. When they encountered each other they all went to a place in the forest where they made a chair out of the branches of trees. They placed him on the chair and they accepted him as their rabbi. And the Besht said torah to them.

Up to this point I heard the unfolding of these events in the name of *Admor*, may his soul rest in heaven. The other events and miracles that occurred I shall print according to the manuscripts that I obtained.

16] *The Besht Locks up the Secret Manuscripts*

THE BESHT HAD SEALED RABBI ADAM'S MANUSCRIPTS[1] in a stone in a mountain. When he said some sceret words the stone opened and he placed the manuscripts inside. Then it closed. He placed a watchman there. The rabbi of our community said

* At that period Brody was a center for study which attracted well known rabbis who clustered around the *Klaus*, the beth-hamidrash. The term the "Sect of the Great Hasidim" refers to these well known rabbis. Benzion Dinaburg suggests that among them were some who were inclined toward Hasidism, and he conceived these members to be the historical nucleus for this legend. See his article "The Beginning of Hassidism and Its Social and Messianic Elements," Hebrew, *Zion*, IX (1944), 187–97. Nathan Gelber, on the other hand, points out that the leaders of this group opposed the Besht. He regards this incident as historically impossible. See, *The History of the Jews in Brody*, Hebrew, pp. 109–110.

that when the Preacher of Polonnoye[2] was old he said: "I have the power to take the manuscripts from there since I know their hiding place, but because it was the Besht who sealed them up, I do not want to take them." He said, "It was only the fifth time that those manuscripts had been revealed." He said, "They were in the hands of Abraham the Patriarch, may he rest in peace, and in the hands of Joshua, the son of Nun, but I do not know the others."

17] *The Beginning of the Writer's Manuscript*

I HEARD ABOUT THE BEGINNING[1] FROM MY FATHER-in-law, God bless his holy memory, who was none other than our teacher Alexander Shohet, who a few years prior to the coming of the famous Hasidic scribe, Rabbi Tsevi, was for eight years a scribe for the holy pious rabbi of the exile, our teacher and rabbi, Rabbi Israel Besht of Medzhibozh. Afterwards both of them served as scribes because the Besht's affairs grew too big for one scribe to handle. Later, my father-in-law became a shohet since he had "the pain of bringing up children."[2] The Besht gave him a place in the holy community of Whitefield,[3] and after that he became a shohet in the holy community of Berdichev. In his old age the Besht gave a letter to my father-in-law for the rabbi, the great light of the holy community of Nemirov, the author of the book *Toldot Ya'akov Yosef,** and he became a shohet in the holy community of Nemirov.

* He is Rabbi Jacob Joseph of Polonnoye (died 1782). After the death of the Besht, he became one of the main leaders of the Hasidic movement. He wrote several books, the first of which was *Toldot Ya'akov Yosef* ["The Generations of Jacob Joseph"] (1st ed.; Korets, 1780), in which he presented the teachings of the Besht. See monographs about him by Samuel H. Dresner, *The Zaddik, the Doctrine of the Zaddik According to the Writings of Rabbi Yaakov Yosef of Polnoy* (London, New York, Toronto, 1960), and by Gedalyah Nigal, *Leader and Community*, Hebrew (Jerusalem, 1962).

18] *Fingernails*

SEVERAL TIMES I HEARD RABBI JACOB JOSEPH OF Polonnoye, God bless his holy memory, say to my father-in-law, chidingly, at the third meal* of the Sabbath: "Remember what the Besht told you: 'Once I went up to paradise and many Jewish people accompanied me. The closer I came to paradise the fewer people there were that followed me, and when I came to the tree of life¹ very few people had remained with me. And, Sendril, I saw you also among them, but you lagged behind.' "

The nails on my father-in-law's right hand had not fully grown. Two nails on one finger had grown together; one began at the top of the finger and the other one started at the knuckle. The two nails were separated by the flesh of the finger. He cut the upper nail every Saturday night so that there was nothing left of it. The lower one grew up to the top of the finger, became separated from its root, and began to grow.

How did he get this thing? It all began when the Besht once sent him to exorcise a madman. During the night while he was sleeping the spirit frightened him. In his thoughts he saw the image of his hand, and on every single finger of his hand he saw that holy names were written. I have seen the picture of such hands in books. He slapped the spirit on the cheek, but he hit the wall so that all his fingernails bled and then fell from his fingers. From that day on his fingernails grew in the manner described above.

The Besht immediately came to him and said: "You were frightened. Do not be afraid. Have no fear."

* The eating of three meals on the Sabbath was already required by the rabbis in the Talmudic period. See B. Shabbath 118a-b. The third meal had become a public institution among the kabbalists, but it acquired particular social religious significance among the Hasidim. The meal itself, which consisted mainly of fish, was minimal. This was an occasion for the rabbi to say his torah and for the followers to tell stories and sing songs. It took place in the late afternoon. The twilight contributed to the social and mystical atmosphere. See Wertheim, *Laws and Customs of Chassidism*, pp. 151–53, and Jacob S. Minkin, *The Romance of Hassidism*, 2nd ed. (New York, 1955), pp. 328–30.

19] *The Besht's Seclusion*

Now I will relate the great events, which I heard from my father-in-law, God bless his memory, concerning how the Besht was revealed.

He lived in a small village and made his living by keeping a tavern. After he brought brandy to his wife he would cross the river Prut and retire into seclusion in a house-like crevice that was cut into the mountain. He used to take one loaf of bread for one meal and eat once a week. He endured this way of life for several years. On the eve of the holy Sabbath he used to return home. His brother-in-law, Rabbi Gershon of Kuty, thought him to be an ignorant and boorish person, and he used to try to persuade his sister to obtain a divorce from him. But she refused since she knew his secret but did not reveal it to anybody.[1]

20] *The Besht Exorcises a Madwoman*

Once the besht came to a town where there was a madwoman who revealed to everyone his virtues and vices. When the Besht, God bless his holy memory, came to the town, Rabbi Gershon asked the righteous rabbi, the head of the court of the holy community of Kuty, the righteous rabbi, the great light, our master and teacher, Moses, to take the Besht to this woman. Perhaps he would take to heart her reproaches and return to the proper path. And all of them went to her.

When the rabbi of the holy community of Kuty entered, she said: "Welcome to you who are holy and pure." She greeted each one according to his merits. The Besht came in last and when she saw him she said: "Welcome, Rabbi Israel," although he was still a young man. "Do you suppose that I am afraid of you?" she said to him. "Not in the least, since I know that you have been warned from heaven not to practice with holy names until you are thirty-six years old."[1]

The Besht was very modest.[2] And the people asked her: "What did you say?"

She repeated her words to them until the Besht chided her and said: "Be quiet. If not, I will appoint a court to release me from my vow of secrecy, and I shall exorcise you from this woman."[3] She began to implore him, "I will be quiet." The Hasidim who accompanied him said that they would permit him to break his vow and urged him to exorcise the spirit from the woman. The Besht asked them not to grant him permission since the spirit was very dangerous, but they insisted. Then the Besht said to the spirit: "Look what you have done. My advice to you is to leave this woman without causing any difficulty and all of us will study on your behalf." And he asked the spirit for his name.*

He answered: "I cannot reveal it before the others. Let the people leave here and I will reveal it to you." Otherwise, it would have shamed his children who were living in the town. When the people left, he revealed his name to the Besht. My father-in-law, blessed be his memory, also knew him. He had become a spirit only because he had mocked the Hasidim of the community of Kuty. Then the spirit released himself from that woman without causing any trouble.[4]

From that time on they did not let the Besht stay in that village. A certain *arrendator* hired him as a melamed for his children. My father-in-law, God bless his memory, told me that the *arrendator* who accepted him as a melamed told him that he had only one house for him, but it was thought to be inhabited by impure spirits. The Besht said that he would live in it. The Besht assigned the attic to the demons, God forbid, and when they laughed he scolded them and they became silent.

21] *The Besht's Prayer Produces Rain*

THERE WAS A TIME WHEN THERE WAS NO RAIN. THE gentiles took out their idols and carried them around the village according to their custom, but it still did not rain. Once the Besht

---

* The knowledge of the name of the person is required for conducting a proper prayer and study session for the redemption of his soul.

said to the *arrendator:* "Send for the Jews in the surrounding area to come here for a minyan."* And he proclaimed a fast.¹ The Besht himself prayed before the ark,² and the Jews prolonged the prayer.

One gentile asked: "Why did you remain at prayer so long today? And why was there a great cry among you?" The *arrendator* told him the truth—that they prayed for rain—and the gentile mocked him sharply, saying, "We went around with our idols and it did not help. What help will you bring with your prayers?"

The *arrendator* told the words of the gentile to the Besht, who said to him: "Tell the gentile that it will rain today." And so it did.³

22] *The Besht Cures a Madman*

AFTERWARDS THE BESHT MOVED TO THE HOLY community of Tlust, and he was a melamed there as well. At first he could not assemble a minyan in his home, and so he gathered around him a group of people and prayed with them. He was so poor that he wore only a short, woolen winter coat, and his toes stuck out through the holes in his shoes. He used to go to the mikveh before praying, even in the month of Tevet.** While he was praying, perspiration drops the size of large beans would fall from him. Later on, several sick people came to him, but he refused to see them. Then once a madman or a madwoman was brought to him and he refused to see him. That night they told him that he was already thirty-six years old, and in the morning he calculated his age and found that they were correct. He saw that madman and cured him. He left teaching and accepted my father-in-law, God bless his memory, as his scribe. And people came to him from everywhere.

---

* The quorum of ten adult men required for holding liturgical services.
** Approximately corresponds to January.

23] *The Besht Exorcises Demons from a House*

Once an *arrendator* from a small town came to the Besht. The *arrendator* was bewitched. Anything left inside his house, in a utensil, or even money in his pocket, was reduced to half overnight. He went to the Besht, and the Besht ordered his scribe to write protective amulets for all his rooms.[1] And he returned with the *arrendator* to his home. When they arrived at the house the Besht collected all the amulets on the table and then he went to the market. The members of the household saw the spirit whirling like a whirlwind from corner to corner until it quit the house. There was a big fenced yard around the house which had a small gate. When the Besht went to his inn, it seemed to him that there was a huge Cossack at the gate. The closer he came to the yard the smaller the demon[2] became, and when he came very near the demon disappeared. The Besht placed protective amulets there. The people of the house told him how the spirit had whirled around and then left the house. He searched in the bed, in the rooms, and between the barrels which were there, because this was his way of driving the demon from his hiding places. Then he returned home.

Immediately, a gentile woman, the miller's wife, came to the *arrendator* in tears, and she said to the *arrendator* in Russian: "I am smart, but you are smarter." It was because the spirit had gone to her house sullen and angry. "I was not at home and he killed two snakes."[3]

24] *The Innkeeper's Death*

An *arrendator* who had bad luck came to the Besht as well. The Besht saw the Angel of Death dancing behind him. He strongly warned him to repent of his sins: "Why do you pursue the affairs of this world? It would be better for you to repent and correct your ways."

The man suspected that the Besht wanted some money. He offered him some coins, but the Besht refused to take them. When the *arrendator* left, the Besht said: "The fool. He will die today or tomorrow, and he worries about his luck."

His brother-in-law, the rabbi, our teacher, Rabbi Gershon, scolded him and said: "Why did you speak evil against a Jew?"

He answered him: "What can I do about it if you are blind and did not see the Angel of Death following behind him." And the Besht went home.

At that time the brother-in-law of the Besht, our rabbi and teacher, Jacob,[1] was a widower, and he went on a journey to be remarried. He was accompanied by this same *arrendator*, since both of them had to go the same way.

They slept overnight at an inn neighboring the village of the *arrendator*. The *arrendator* ordered a fine dinner. Rabbi Jacob did not want to eat meat, and they gave him dairy food at the end of the table. The *arrendator* mocked him. Afterwards they went to sleep. During the night the *arrendator* awoke with a severe headache and he cried out. He asked that someone say the rite of confession with him. Since there was no one else to say the confession with him, Rabbi Jacob said the prayer and the *arrendator* chanted the confession after him. Rabbi Jacob wondered about it. Then the *arrendator*'s wife left him alone, saying, "Perhaps he'll sleep for a while and then he'll feel better." But in a little while she looked at him and saw that he was dead.

Then Rabbi Jacob returned home to tell that indeed we are blind.

25] *The Besht Attracts Followers*

THIS EVENT HAPPENED WHEN THE BESHT TRAVELED to the town of Kribush.[1] The head of the court of justice in that town was the Hasid, Rabbi Aba, who later became the head of the court of justice in the holy community of Whitefield.[2] The head of the court of justice had as his guest a relative by marriage, and both of them were arguing about a mishnah.* When the Besht came they did not go out to welcome him, and he came in and said, "God be with you. What is it that you are discussing?"

They showed him a different mishnah, and he said: "I know that actually you were debating about another mishnah. Still, how did you interpret it?" He pointed out to them that there was a complicated problem in that mishnah, and he told them its meaning. Then he traveled for about a verst and stopped to graze the horses in the field.

They began to talk with each other: "How did we interpret this mishnah?" They immediately hired a wagon and pursued him. They found him in the field and stopped there. And from that time on Rabbi Aba traveled to the Besht for one Sabbath every single month.

Once he observed the Sabbath in the Besht's house. During the reciting of Maariv he made a mistake and began to say, "Thou favorest men." When he came home the Besht said: "Very well, rabbi of Kribush, go ahead and pray "Thou favorest men."[3]

When the Besht came to the holy community of Whitefield, the head of the court of justice was a certain tsaddik whose name was Rabbi Ḥayyim. The Besht prayed in the field along the way and when he arrived in the town, they were still praying in the synagogue. He went to listen to the kedushah and stood in the synagogue vestibule. The Besht told the gabbai to remove the candlestick on the wall opposite the rabbi and he did so. When the rabbi moved away from his place after the prayer, he noticed that the candlestick opposite him was not there and he inquired about it. They told him that the Besht was standing in the synagogue vestibule. Immediately after kedushah he went out to him and asked him about it.

The Besht said: "You had a wayward thought in your prayer because of this candlestick."

(Opinions are divided about this matter. Some people say that the scribe played with a dog while enscribing this candlestick; others say that he was a thoroughly wicked person.)

* A paragraph of the Mishnah, the post-biblical compilation of Jewish oral law.

26] *The Besht and the Physician*

THE MAGGID OF KRIBUSH WAS VERY FAMOUS. HIS
name was Rabbi Abraham Podlisker. He was a great and famous
tsaddik. Once there was no satisfactory slaughtering knife, and
they sent for shohetim from several communities, but none of
them could provide a satisfactory knife.[1]

Once the Besht came to them and they said to him: "The
guest is very welcome, but we have nothing to offer him." They
explained the circumstances. He said that he would provide them
with a knife, and he did so and they were satisfied. They slaughtered the animals and they ate. He promised to send them a
shohet, and he sent them my father-in-law, God bless his memory,
and he became rich there.[2]

My father-in-law, God bless his memory, told me that while
he was there, the pious Rabbi Abraham Podlisker lived there for
several years until his death. When Rabbi Abraham Podlisker
became very sick, he sent for the Besht who stayed with him for a
long time trying to cure him. When the Rabbi's son saw that the
Besht's healing did not have any effect upon him they sent to the
holy community of Ostrog for a doctor to come to Whitefield.
The Besht realized that the doctor was coming, and he said to
Rabbi Abraham Podlisker: "I am going away from this place
since the doctor of the holy community of Ostrog is coming
here." The rabbi had not known about it, and he urged him not to
go away. The Besht stayed there overnight because of the rabbi's
repeated pleas. The Besht said that the doctor was staying overnight two versts from the town.

The doctor had already threatened the Besht. He said: "When
I see the Besht I will kill him with my gun."

In the morning the Besht hurried to leave, but the sick rabbi
detained him until the doctor came to the town. Then the Besht
said: "Well, the doctor has arrived in town." He said goodbye to
the rabbi, climbed on the wagon and went away. When he passed
by the inn where the doctor was staying, he stepped down from
the wagon, entered the house, and greeted the doctor.

The doctor asked him: "Where did you learn about medicine?"

He answered: "God, blessed be He, taught me." And he went home.

The sons of the sick rabbi brought the doctor to their father, but whatever he prescribed they told him, "The Besht already prescribed it for him." The doctor went away disappointed. Then the sick rabbi complained to his sons: "What have you done? The Besht did not cure me, but when he came into my room I knew that the Shekinah* accompanied him. When the doctor entered, it seemed as if a priest had entered."

27] *The Besht Predicts a Need for Bloodletting*

AFTER RABBI ABRAHAM PODLISKER PASSED AWAY, they accepted as the head of the court Rabbi Aba, of the holy community of Kribush. I will write a story about him as well. It is a story about the Besht which I heard from one man of our community whose name is Rabbi Isaac Aizik the Hasid, the son of the rabbi of the holy community of Brahin, who heard it from his father. I have, however, a secret reason of my own for not writing down the essence of what happened.

The rabbi of the holy community of Brahin visited the rabbi of Whitefield during that winter, and he showed him letters from the Besht which contained these words: "This winter you will return from a journey, and you will find a great tumult in the yard of your house. A crowd of men, women, and children will be there, and you will faint from fear. When they awaken you, tell them to let blood from two veins at once.[1] Send a special messenger immediately to inform me about that tumult. Even though, thank God, I can see from afar, nevertheless, send me a letter by messenger. So said Israel Besht." That is all. I do not want to reveal the heart of the story.

* Divine Presence.

28] *Rabbi Gershon, the Besht, and the Zohar*

I heard this from the great light, the hasid of our community, our master and teacher, Rabbi Gedaliah. Once the Besht borrowed a copy of the Zohar from the rabbi of the holy community of Kuty. On his way back home he encountered his brother-in-law, Rabbi Gershon, who asked him: "What do you have under your arm?"

He did not want to tell him. Rabbi Gershon climbed down from the wagon, took the Zohar from under his arm, and said in wonder: "*You* need the Zohar?"

After that Rabbi Gedaliah said that the Besht came to the city to pray in the beth-hamidrash. In his prayer he sighed deeply. After the prayer, Rabbi Moses, the head of the court of that holy community, asked him: "Why did I hear a deep sigh from you during the prayer?" And he persuaded him to explain.

The Besht told him: "The truth is that it was a sigh from the heart." He said: "The mezuzah is defective."

The rabbi found that indeed it was as he said. He gave the Besht the copy of the Zohar and blessed him so that he would not encounter Rabbi Gershon.

29] *Elijah the Prophet Reveals Himself to the Besht*

I heard this from Rabbi Gedaliah. Once the Besht had neither matzoth nor meat for Passover. He harnessed his donkey to the wagon and went on his way to the villages. He slaughtered animals, and he brought back flour and meat for the Passover. When he came home he told his wife: "See to it that the flour is removed from the wagon."

But it rained and the flour became hametz.* She told her

* Leaven. Dough kneaded from flour and water and allowed to become sour. During Passover, in commemoration of the Exodus, when the Jews could not wait until their dough had leavened, only unleavened food is allowed.

husband. He examined his slaughtering knife and went to the villages in the other direction, and again he brought back flour for the holiday.

Near his home he had to climb a high mountain. The horse could not pull the wagon, and so he helped the horse draw the load. Halfway up the mountain the horse died. He was afraid to leave the flour unprotected and so he had to pull the wagon all by himself. He exhausted his energy, and he stood beside the wagon weeping, crying aloud to God, blessed be He. And while he wept, he fell asleep. Elijah, God bless his memory, came to him in a dream, and this was the first revelation of the prophet to the Besht.[1]

Elijah said to him: "Your tears satisfied God and your prayer was accepted. I will send you a gentile who will take your wagon with the flour to your home."

As soon as he awoke from his sleep, a gentile came along with a wagon and horses and said: "Israel, tie your wagon to mine and I'll pull you to your home."

When they came to the Besht's home, the gentile said to him: "How much will you give me for skinning your horses's hide?" And he gave him a sixer.*

After that another gentile came who bought the skin for four golden coins** and the buyer told him: "See that you use this money to dress yourself and your wife for the coming holiday."

Sometime later a caravan of merchants brought a stock of marten furs. That winter the Besht rented his house of seclusion in the village from a gentile, and the Besht's wife went to her husband to ask him whether or not she could buy the furs. He told her: "You can buy them. It is like abandoned property since all of them will be killed by robbers." And she bought the furs with the four golden coins. He made a coat for himself and a dress for his wife for the holiday.

When the *arrendator* from whom the Besht rented the tavern saw how the Besht dressed himself and his wife, he suspected that

---

* A Polish currency. Its value varied from six to twelve groschen.
** Zloty, literally in Polish, a "golden coin." It was equal to thirty groschen.

he was buying brandy from some other place. He complained about the Besht to Rabbi Gershon,[2] saying: "With all due respect, if he does not admit what he has done and pay me what I have lost, I will have him beaten in the manor house."

Rabbi Gershon, God bless his memory, told him: "I will be severe with him."

When the Besht came to the town he admonished him, and the Besht said: "That never happened, God forbid."

Rabbi Gershon said: "Where did you get the money to dress up yourself and your wife?"

He answered him: "God gave it to me."

He said: "Why does God not give it to me?"

He answered: "He does not give it to you, but He does give to me."

He said: "Be careful lest the *arrendator* inform on you in the manor house and you will be beaten."

He said: "I am not afraid of him."

What finally happened was that the *arrendator* wanted to inform on him, but he died.

30] *The Stolen Horse*

I HEARD FROM MY FATHER-IN-LAW, GOD BLESS his memory, that the Besht had a horse, but it was stolen from him. Rabbi Gershon was chiding him about it when suddenly the Besht exclaimed: "The horse will be returned to me."

Rabbi Gershon ridiculed him, and every time that he came to the town he teased him and said: "Israel, has the horse been returned to you?"

The horse was missing for about a year. Finally, a gentile came riding by on the back of that horse and he knocked on the window to ask for a light for his pipe. The Besht recognized his horse and he said: "That is my horse."

The man got off the horse at once and returned it to him.[1]

31] *The Besht Reveals Himself to Rabbi David of Kolomyya*

I HEARD ABOUT THIS EVENT FROM RABBI GEDALIAH and from my father-in-law.

Rabbi David, the maggid of the holy community of Kolomyya, traveled around collecting Hanukkah money.* He wandered off his path and came to the Besht's house at the time of the lighting of the candles. The Besht was in his house of seclusion. Rabbi David asked the Besht's wife where her husband was, and she answered that he had to go to the *arrendator* to help water the stock.

The maggid said: "What can I eat here?"

She answered: "My husband slaughtered a chicken. Examine the knife, and if you find it satisfactory I will cook the chicken."

He examined the knife and found it satisfactory.[1]

The pious woman went and told it to her husband, and he returned home pretending that he came from the *arrendator*. He served Rabbi David as the humble serve the great. He himself prepared the bed for Rabbi David, and he arranged a glass of water and a chamber pot. The Besht lay with his wife in the same bed, like a peasant. In the middle of the night the Besht arose.[2] I heard that generally he slept but two hours. He sat at the base of the oven, and he did whatever he did in secret.

The maggid, Rabbi David, woke up and saw a great light beneath the oven, and he thought that the logs on the oven had been kindled and were burning. He began to wake up his wife: "Hannah, Hannah, there's a fire burning on the oven!"

She answered him: "I'm a woman. Before I can dress and cover myself with a shawl, the fire will become stronger, God forbid. Don't be so modest. You have water to put out the fire."

So he took the chamber pot with the waste water and went to put out the fire. When he came to the oven he saw the Besht

* A collection of money for charity before the Hanukkah holiday.

sitting there and there was light shining above him. The rabbi told me personally that the light shone above the Besht like a rainbow. When the maggid saw that he fainted. Hannah had to rouse the Besht to revive the maggid from his faint.

In the morning the maggid, Rabbi David, said: "This is what I saw. Tell me what it was."

He answered: "I do not know. I recited the Psalms. Perhaps in concentrating I became connected with God, blessed be He, and that is what it was."

But Rabbi David insisted, and the Besht revealed himself before him. From that day on Rabbi David, the maggid, went to the Besht on every occasion to listen to his torah.

When his friends heard his torah they said: "Where did you get it from?"

He answered: "From a certain poor, ragged man."

From that time on, whenever Rabbi David heard Rabbi Gershon admonish the Besht harshly, he would say simply: "Leave him alone. He is wiser than you are."

The Besht had forbidden him to reveal anything.

32] *The Melamed's Dream*

IN THE HOLY COMMUNITY OF MEDZHIBOZH THERE was a rich man who was not in sympathy with the Besht, and he employed a melamed for his children, a very learned man, knowledgeable in every way, who also kept away from the Besht. And the rabbi* wanted very much to attract him to the worship of God, since good fortune was waiting for him. But the Besht wondered how it would come about as the melamed kept far away, especially since his employer watched him very carefully.

Once on a Friday night, the melamed dreamed that he was strolling all over the holy community of Medzhibozh, and he saw a wonderful palace, which was elaborately decorated in every conceivable way. He was fascinated by it, and he could not have

* The Besht. See tale 12, n. 1.

his fill of staring at it. The more he looked the more wonderful things he saw. Afterwards, he realized that all this decoration was carved into the building itself, which made it all the more amazing, considering the splendor of the craftsmanship and the design. And when he took pains to concentrate on the beauty of the craftsmanship, he was astonished because every minute space contained wisdom and skill as had never before seen in the whole world. His heart perceived the great wisdom, and he was attracted to it with all his soul. And he told himself that since the outside of the palace was so ornate the inside would be even more so. Indeed it must be incomparable. When he approached the window to look inside, behold, he saw the Besht and his entire holy group seated around the table, and the Besht was saying torah. He was filled with excitement and he wanted to reach the innermost section of the building. He ran toward the door, but when he wanted to get in the attendant pushed him aside and did not let him enter. He felt deeply grieved. Nevertheless, in spite of all this, his strong desire to listen to the living words of God was so great that he stood at the window and heard all the Besht's holy words.

He woke up and it was a dream. He began to repeat the torah that he had heard, and it was sweeter than honey. He repeated it twice and three times, but since it was only midnight he fell asleep again.

In the morning when he got up from his bed, he realized that he still remembered the dream very clearly, but the torah had slipped from his mind altogether. He grieved about the loss until he was so beset with despair that he did not know how he managed to pray. At breakfast he sat bewildered.

His employer said to him: "Why is this day different from any other? If you had a bad dream we will change it to a good dream before three people who will say 'All Merciful!' "*

---

* According to the Babylonian Talmud a person who had a bad dream should gather three men and say to them, "I have had a good dream." They should reply to him, "Good it is and good may it be. May the All Merciful turn it to good." See B. Berakoth 55b, and also Trachtenberg, *Jewish Magic and Superstition* (New York, 1939), pp. 247–48.

He did not answer a word.

Perhaps he would have gone to the Besht by himself, but he recalled that in the dream the servant had rebuffed him, and he was afraid that it would be so in reality as well and that he would endure disgrace and shame. And he grieved greatly all day.

At the third meal the Besht ordered: "Go to the house of that wealthy man and tell the melamed to come here." They were greatly amazed by it.

When the messenger opened the door and said to the melamed, "The Besht invites you, sir, to come to him," he immediately leaped over the table and ran without his overcoat like a madman. Then he heard all the torah that he had heard at night, and he immediately fainted.

When he caught his breath again the Besht said to him jokingly: "If you had heard new things, you would have reason to be so excited, but this is not new since you heard all this last night."

And he understood that what had happened was from God, and he followed the Besht wholeheartedly and he became a truly righteous man.

33] The Delayed Homecoming

In that same holy community there was a certain great merchant who was one of those who were still opposed to the Besht. This merchant had an only son who was wise and who excelled in learning and in other virtues. The only son used to go to Breslau to buy merchandise, and this trip usually lasted four weeks. Once he did not return for more than ten weeks. There was no news from him at all, and his family was very worried about him.

His mother, the merchant's wife, said: "Why do you harden your heart against the Besht. Everyone from the four corners of the earth goes to him, and he helps them. You refuse to go to his home to ask his advice and inquire about our son. This is a serious matter."

But he did not pay any attention. As the days passed she urged him repeatedly until he was forced to do his wife's will.

On the evening of the holy Sabbath he went to the Besht and said: "Our rabbi, it is more than ten weeks since our only son went to Breslau. We had not had any news from him, and we do not know what has happened to him."

The Besht immediately ordered the book of the Zohar to be brought to him, and he opened it and looked into it. He said: "With the help of God your son is alive and well. This coming Sabbath he will stay in a village which is one verst from our town."

The merchant could not believe his words. How could that be? Their yearnings and their anguish were not unknown to their son. Certainly he did not care about the expense and could have paid what was asked for a wagon in order to return home for the Sabbath. Nevertheless, just to be certain, he sent a gentile to that village and ordered him to remain there until nightfall. Perhaps his son would arrive just before dark.

At night the gentile returned and said that *there was no voice nor any that answered*[1] his call. "Nothing has been heard or seen of your son."

Then the merchant said to his wife: "That is exactly what I said before. His words are empty promises."

But this is what actually happened. His son's wagon had broken several times on the road, and he arrived at the village at midnight. Immediately after the close of the holy Sabbath he came home. Then the merchant realized that all the Besht's words were righteous and honest. He went to the Besht and asked his forgiveness since he had slandered him, and he told him the whole story.

The Besht said to him: "You fool. Is it not true that with the light which the Holy One, blessed be He, created during the six days of creation, one could see from one end of the world to the other. This light He hid for the righteous in the time to come. Where did He hide it? In the Torah.[2] Therefore, when I open the book of the Zohar I see the whole world, and with the help of God I do not err in what I see."

34] *The Besht's Trembling in Prayer*

I HEARD THIS FROM OUR TEACHER AND RABBI, RABBI Falk, the famous Hasid from Chechelnik, who heard it from Rabbi Abraham, the head of the court in the holy community of Dubossary, who was formerly the cantor in the beth-hamidrash of the holy community of Medzhibozh.

Once they had to say the Hallel, since it was either the first of the month or during the intermediate days of Passover.[1] Rabbi Abraham was reciting Shaharith before the ark, and the Besht was praying in his usual place. It was his custom to pray before the ark beginning with the Hallel. During the voiced eighteen benedictions,[2] the Besht trembled greatly as he always did while praying.[3] Everyone who looked at the Besht while he was praying noticed this trembling. When Rabbi Abraham finished the repetition of the prayer, the Besht was still standing at his place and he did not go to the ark. Rabbi Wolf Kotses, the Hasid, looked at his face. He saw that it was burning like a torch. The Besht's eyes were bulging and fixed straight ahead like those of someone dying, God forbid.

Rabbi Ze'ev* motioned to Rabbi Abraham and each gave his hand to the Besht and led him to the ark. He went with them and stood before the ark. He trembled for a long time and they had to postpone the reading of the Torah until he stopped trembling.

35] *The Besht's Trembling in Prayer: A Second Version*

IN ADDITION, I HEARD FROM THE RABBI OF THE HOLY community of Polonnoye, the author of the book *Tolodot Ya'akov Yosef*, that a large barrel of water was standing near where the Besht was praying, and everyone saw that the water was rippling. The Shekinah hovered over him and as a result the earth

* Rabbi Ze'ev Kotses; Ze'ev means "Wolf" in Hebrew.

trembled. As it is written, *the Lord descended upon it in fire . . .
and the whole mount quaked greatly.*[1] But the earthquake was
not noticeable except as it was seen in the water.

36] *The Besht's Trembling in Prayer: A Third Version*

I HEARD ALSO FROM THE MAGGID, OUR TEACHER,
Elijah, God bless his memory, that when he came for the first time
to the Great Maggid of the holy community of Mezhirich, the
Great Maggid told him the following story:

"Once, on a holiday—I do not know whether it was the first
day of Passover or the eighth day of Sukkoth—I had to say the
blessing for either rain or dew.* The Besht was praying before
the ark with great enthusiasm. I already knew from his best
disciples that he used to utter a great cry and pray louder than
anyone else."

The rabbi, the Great Maggid, could not stand it since he was
very sick. He left and entered a small room in the beth-hamidrash
where he prayed alone. Before the Musaf the Besht entered the
small room to put on his kittel.** The Maggid said that he realized that the Besht was inspired by the Shekinah, and that he was
not in this world. When the Besht put on his kittel it was wrinkled
around his shoulders. The Great Maggid grasped the kittel in
order to straighten it, and when he touched the Besht he himself
began to tremble. He held the table that was there and the table
began to tremble with him as well. The Besht went away, but
this kept on until he prayed to God, blessed be He, that He free
him from this trembling since he could no longer endure it.

* A special prayer for rain (*geshem*), is recited after the second benediction in the Musaf service on the eighth day of Sukkoth, "He causes the
wind to blow and the rain to descend." On the first day of Passover, dew
(*tal*) substitutes for rain in accordance with the seasonal change in Israel.
Therefore, the Musaf services of these days are known by the names of
geshem or *tal*, respectively.

** A white robe worn by the officiant at the Musaf, Additional Service,
on the first day of Passover and the eighth day of Sukkoth.

37] *The Besht's Trembling in Prayer: A Fourth Version*

I HEARD ALSO FROM THE HASID, RABBI DAVID Forkes from Medzhibozh, that once while the Besht was traveling he prayed near the eastern wall in a house. There were barrels full of grain that were placed at the western wall, and you could see that the grain was shaking.

38] *A Sincere Prayer*

I HEARD THIS FROM RABBI DAVID FORKES AS WELL, though not directly from him, that while he was a shohet in the holy community of Tulchin he used to observe the Sabbath there. Rabbi David of the village of Khladevkeh had arranged a betrothal party, and he sent wagons for all the in-laws. Our teacher, David the maggid, also traveled to the betrothal party, and on the way he told this story. When the people of the community arrived, they told it to me.

Once early on the morning of Yom Kippur, the Besht did not come to the beth-hamidrash to pray as is the custom. He delayed until the people were in despair, and they postponed the beginning of the prayer. After a long while he arrived and sat at his place. He rested his head on the stand. Then he raised his head and laid it down again, raised it up and laid it down again several more times. After that he gestured that they should pray before the ark, and Rabbi David went to pray there as he did during the Days of Awe. When he approached the ark the Besht began to shame him in front of all the people in the community, saying: "Lewd old man, where are you going?" He heaped shame and scorn upon him for half an hour.

Rabbi David became upset and wanted to go away from the reader's stand. "Perhaps, God forbid," he thought, "he sees an ugly sin in me." The Besht scolded him and said: "Stand up." And Rabbi David began to pray and to cry, and he babbled incoherently. He could only cry out and sob since his heart was completely broken. Afterwards, at the conclusion of Yom Kippur, Rabbi David, the maggid, God bless his memory, went to the Besht and said to him: "Our rabbi, what ugly sin did you see in me, God forbid?"

The Besht answered him: "I did not see anything in you, God forbid. But just at dawn I saw Satan blocking the path where all the prayers pass in order to take them himself, God forbid. I said to myself, 'Why would I pray and hand him all the prayers, God forbid?' Therefore, I delayed my praying. Thank God, I cleared one path for the prayers to pass through where Satan would not be able to catch them. But I was afraid that Satan would enter your heart, God forbid, and would spoil my efforts. So I broke your heart to protect you from having wayward thoughts, and then afterwards I ordered you to pray."[1]

39] *The Besht's Trembling in Prayer: a Fifth Version*

I HEARD THIS ALSO FROM THE HASID, THE RABBI, our teacher Gedaliah, God bless his memory. Once the Besht prayed Minhah in a certain village in a granary in which there were many barrels full of grain. While he was praying his trembling made the barrels dance. As it is written: *The Lord descended upon it in fire . . . and the whole mount quaked greatly.*[1] And, thanks to God, I saw in him an image of the soul of Moses, God bless his memory.

40] *The Dream of Rabbi Joseph Ashkenazi*

I HEARD MORE FROM THE ABOVE-MENTIONED RABBI Falk, who at the time of the flight[1] went into exile in the Crimea with Rabbi Joseph Ashkenazi, the Besht's hazan.* Rabbi Falk heard this from Rabbi Joseph and I heard it from him.

Once Rabbi Joseph dreamed that he saw a certain Hasid who

* Cantor.

had passed away and was survived by a young talented son who was being pushed into a marriage of low degree. The Hasid appeared in Rabbi Joseph's dream and asked him to go to his wife and to tell her on his behalf not to make this match. He insisted that she make a match with the first person to come to her home that day. Afterwards, he saw in his dream an image of an altar to which the dead man ascended. He saw him put his head between his knees and began to cry the selihah. "Answer us, God, answer us. Answer us, our Father, answer us,"[2] and so on throughout the alphabet. After that he said:

> Answer us, O God of our fathers, answer us.
> Answer us, O God of Abraham, answer us.
> Answer us, O revered of Isaac, answer us.
> Answer us, O mighty one of Jacob, answer us.
> Answer us, O compassionate one, answer us.
> Answer us, O king of the chariots, answer us.[3]

Then he ascended to heaven.

In the morning Rabbi Joseph went to the Besht and told him the dream. The Besht said to him: "Do you think it was a dream that you had? Not at all. It was a vision that you saw. I saw it as well and it became a reality before my eyes. The altar was that on which the angel Michael sacrifices the souls for God, blessed be He."[4]

Rabbi Joseph asked him: "Why did he say those verses of "Answer us"?

The Besht replied that the Angel of Souls could not ascend from one world to the other except by the prayer 'Answer us.' "

Rabbi Joseph asked him: "Why did he say this version?"[5]

The Besht answered that this is the version that they use in heaven. The Besht sent for the deceased's wife and told her about the match.

41] *The Besht in the Messiah's Heavenly Palace*

I heard still more from Rabbi Falk. One Yom Kippur Eve the Besht perceived a serious charge brought against the Jews that the oral tradition[1] would no longer be theirs. He greatly grieved the whole Yom Kippur Eve. Toward evening when everyone in the town came to him to receive his blessing, he blessed only one or two and said: "I can do no more." He did not bless them because of his sorrow. He went to the synagogue and preached harsh words to them, and he fell upon the ark and cried: "Woe! They want to take the Torah from us. How will we be able to survive among the nations even half a day?"

He was very angry with the rabbis and said that it was because of them, since they invented lies of their own and wrote false introductions.* He said that all the Tannaim and Amoraim were brought before the heavenly court. Afterwards he went to the beth-hamidrash and said other harsh words, and then they prayed the Kol Nidre.[2] After Kol Nidre he said that the charge had become more severe. Since he, himself, always led Neilah,[3] he urged all the leaders of prayer to hurry throughout the day so that he would be able to pray the Neilah prayer while it was still broad daylight. Before Neilah he began to preach in harsh words and he cried. He put his head backward on the ark, and he sighed and he wept. Afterwards he began to pray the silent eighteen benedictions, and then the voiced eighteen benedictions. It was always his custom during the Days of Awe not to look at the holiday prayer book since the rabbi, Rabbi Yakil of Medzhibozh, used to prompt him from the holiday prayer book, and he would repeat after him. When he reached the words "Open the gate for us" or "Open the gates of Heaven,"[4] Rabbi Yakil spoke once and then twice, but he did not hear the Besht repeating after him and he fell silent. The Besht began to make terrible gestures, and he bent backwards until his head came close to his knees,[5] and everyone feared that he would fall down. They wanted to support him, but they were afraid to. They told it to Rabbi Ze'ev Kotses, God bless his memory, who came and looked at the Besht's face and motioned that they were not to touch him. His eyes bulged and he sounded like a slaughtered bull. He kept this up for about two hours. Suddenly he stirred and straightened up. He prayed in a great hurry and finished the prayer. At the conclusion of Yom

---

* Unfortunately we could not clarify the meaning of these sentences to our satisfaction. The "false introductions" which are mentioned in the text may refer to introductions to books which the rabbis gave to new authors.

Kippur all the people came to greet him, since this was always the custom. They asked him what was the outcome of the charge. He told them that during the Neilah prayers he found he could pray, and he moved from one world to another without any hindrance during the silent eighteen benedictions.

"In the spoken eighteen benedictions I also continued to move until I came to one palace.⁶ I had but one more gate to pass through to appear before God, blessed be He. In that palace I found all the prayers of the past fifty years that had not ascended, and now, because on this Yom Kippur we prayed with kavvanah, all the prayers ascended.⁷ Each prayer shone as the bright dawn. I said to those prayers: 'Why did you not ascend before?' "

"And they said: 'We were instructed to wait for you, sir, to lead us.' "

"I told them: 'Come along with me.' And the gate was open."

He told the people of his town that the gate was as large as the whole world.

"When we started to accompany the prayers, one angel came and closed the door, and he put a lock on the gate."

He told them that the lock was as big as all of Medzhibozh. "And I began to turn the lock to open it, but I could not do it. So I ran to my rabbi⁸—who is mentioned in the book *Toldot Ya'akov Yosef*,*—and I said: 'The people of Israel are in great trouble and now they will not let me in. At another time I would not have forced my way in.' "

"My rabbi said: 'I shall go with you and if there is a possibility to open the gate for you I shall open it.' And when he came he turned the lock, but he could not open it either. Then he said to me: 'What can I do for you?'

"I began to complain to my rabbi. 'Why have you forsaken me at such a troubled time?'

"And he answered: 'I do not know what to do for you, but

---

* Rabbi Jacob Joseph of Polonnoye mentioned in his book *Toldot Ya'akov Yosef* (Medzhibozh, 1817) p. 27a, that Ahijah the prophet of Shiloh was the teacher of the Besht. According to Jewish tradition he was also the teacher of Elijah. See *Y*. 'Erubin 5.1, 22b. Concerning the piety of Ahijah, see Ginzberg, *The Legends of the Jews*, IV, 180, VI, 305, 317.

you and I will go to the palace of the Messiah. Perhaps there will
be some help there.'

"With a great outcry I went to the palace of the Messiah.
When our righteous Messiah saw me from afar he said to me,
'Don't shout.' He gave me two holy letters of the alphabet.

"I went to the gate. Thank God, I turned the lock and opened
the gate, and I led in all the prayers. Because of the great joy
when all the prayers ascended, the accuser became silent, and I
did not need to argue. The decree was canceled and nothing
remained of it but an impression of the decree."*

I remember the great tumult that that impression caused in the
world since several people sent their books to the state of Walachia. That charge was made because of the sect of Shabbetai
Tsevi,** may his name be blotted out. The bishop of the town
of Kamenets burned two volumes of the Talmud. The rabbi of
our community said that the bishop forcibly took the books of the
Talmud from the *arrendator* of his village. He paid him for the
Talmud and placed them in a bonfire. Because of our many sins
they were completely burned. Thank God that the bishop was
injured as he stood in front of the fire. They took him to the town

---

* In the original text the terms רשימה מהגזרה, *Reshimah meha-gzerah*,
are used. The word *reshimah* is associated with the Lurianic conception of
reshimu, according to which a residue of divine light remains in the primeval space created by the withdrawal of God into Himself, which was
necessary for the act of creation. See Scholem, *Major Trends in Jewish
Mysticism*, pp. 260-64, and Tishby, *The Doctrine of Evil*, pp. 21-25. In
the present context the word *reshimah* implies a residue of the decree.

** Shabbetai Tsevi (1625-76) (also spelled Sabbatai Zevi, Shabbetai
Tzevi, Shabtai Tsevi), originally of Smyrna, Turkey, regarded himself as
the Messiah. With the aid of his prophet Nathan of Gaza he aroused messianic expectations among the world Jewry. After his conversion to Islam
(1666), his movement collapsed; however, many of his followers secretly
continued to believe in him. This caused a great schism among the European Jews. Some scholars believe that there is evidence that some of his
followers were linked with the Hasidic movement. See Isaiah Tishby,
"Between Sabbetanism and Hasidism," Hebrew, *Kenesset*, IX (Tel-Aviv,
1945), 268-338. The Hasidim emphatically declared their animosity to
Sabbetianism. For a critical biography of the False Messiah, see Gershom
Scholem, *Shabbetai Tsevi and the Shabbetianic Movement in His Life
Time*, Hebrew, 2 vols. (Tel-Aviv, 1956-57); and *Major Trends in Jewish
Mysticism*, pp. 287-324.

of Kamenets, but they failed to bring him there alive. That wicked person died on the road. Afterwards there was a debate before the bishop of the holy community of Lvov,. but he was struck by fear of the Torah and he did not condemn the Jews. All of that wicked sect were converted to Christianity since the bishop shamed and disgraced them greatly by shaving one earlock and half of each one's beard to make it known that they were neither Jews nor gentiles. They converted because of the disgrace.[9]

42] *The Palace of the Bird's Nest*

Once the rabbi, the Hasid, our rabbi and teacher Menaḥem Nahum of Chernobyl was in our town, and he told this story to the people. I came in the middle of the story, and I heard his version which contained some changes and something new—that the Messiah said to the Besht, "I do not know whether you will open the gate, but if you do redemption will certainly come to Israel." He said further that this was the gate of the palace of the Bird's Nest through which no one has ever passed save the Messiah, as it is said in the holy Zohar.[1] He said that he heard God's voice saying to him: "What can I do with you since I must fulfill your will?"

43] *The Besht and his Guests*

The rabbi of our community explained that the Besht was still upset, and he was so angry with the guests that they left his home. After that his wife scolded him for being angry with the guests. The Besht leaned over the table and said: "I am ready to accept your rebuke." And after that he sent a messenger to apologize to the guests, and in the morning he prayed in public.[1]

44] *The Wailing of the Shekinah*

I HEARD FROM THE RABBI OF OUR COMMUNITY
that concerning those who converted, the Besht said that the
Shekinah wailed and said: "As long as the member is connected,
there is some hope that it will recover, but when the member is
cut off there is no repair possible."* Each person of Israel is a
member of the Shekinah.

45] *The Destruction of Balta*

I HEARD FROM THE FATHER-IN-LAW OF RABBI
Falk, the cohen, the Hasid, Rabbi Shmeril, the maggid of the holy
community of Virchivkeh,[1] that once the Besht observed the
Sabbath in the holy community of Balta. The Besht said that at
some time that town would be destroyed. After that it would be
reconstructed and become a prominent city for the Jews. It
would then stand until the coming of the redeemer, may he come
soon, amen.

The rabbi of our community explained how the Besht came to
say this. There were great market fairs in the holy community of
Balta. There were many gentiles, Ishmaelite** and Kedarite***
merchants, and others from the rest of the nations. The merchants
were hurrying with their wagons at the time of the third meal
while the Besht, God bless his memory, said torah, and the tumult
confused him. He was angered and he said: "Why do you hurry,
Balta? Trouble awaits you."

I heard from that same Rabbi Shmeril that one year before the
flight[2] there was a war between the Ishmaelites and the Greeks in
which the town and its neighboring villages were destroyed,
along with the town of Chechelnik and its neighboring villages.

* He refers to the Frankists who converted to Christianity. See tale 41,
n. 8.
** Turks, Muslems.
*** Tartars.

Nothing remained in Balta but a small house surrounded by a fence.

46] *Rabbi Gershon Imitates the Besht*

I HEARD FROM THIS SAME RABBI FALK THAT WHEN Rabbi Gershon of Kuty traveled abroad from the Land of Israel[1] in order to arrange the marriage of his son, he said to himself: "Since I crossed the sea, thank God, I will take this opportunity to go to my brother-in-law, the Besht, God bless his memory."

He came to him on the eve of the holy Sabbath. The Besht stood up to pray Minhah, which he had prolonged until the appearance of the stars.[2] Rabbi Gershon was also praying from the prayer book of *ha-Ari*, God bless his memory. It was his custom to read two verses of the Bible and then one in translation.[3] After that he asked for pillows and he lay down to rest. On Sabbath Eve at dinner time, Rabbi Gershon asked his brother-in-law, the Besht: "Why did you prolong your prayer so much? I too prayed with kavvanoth. Then I read a portion of the Bible, two verses in the original and one in translation, and I had to lie down to rest. And you stood and trembled, making your gestures and motions." He wanted to induce the Besht to talk.

The Besht remained quiet and did not say a word. He repeated his question again.

Then the Besht answered him: "When I reached the words, 'Quicken the dead,' "—and Rabbi Falk did not know if he referred to the words, "Thou quicken the dead" or "quickenest the dead with great mercy,"[4]—"I concentrated on the *yiḥudim** and souls by the thousands and the tens of thousands came to me. I had to talk with each one of them, the most important ones first, and find out why he was rejected from his portion of heaven.

---

* The *Yiḥudim* are special mystical formulae which constitute divine names. The doctrine underlying these formulae was developed by Ḥayyim Vital (1543–1620), the disciple of the Ari, in his book *Sha'ar ha-Yiḥudim* (Lemberg, 1855). Concerning this concept, see also R. J. Zwi Werblowsky, *Joseph Karo, Lawyer and Mystic*, Scripta Judaica, IV (Oxford, 1962), pp. 72–73.

I would redeem him and pray for him and elevate him. There were so many that if I wanted to elevate all of them I would have to stand for the eighteen benedictions for three years. But when I heard the herald proclaim 'The holy is sanctified,' then it was impossible to elevate more souls and I stepped back from the eighteen benedictions."

Rabbi Gershon said to him jokingly, "Why do they not come to me?"

The Besht answered him: "If you stay with me for the next Sabbath, I will write down the kavvanoth, and they will come to you as well." And so he did.

The next Sabbath Eve when the Besht concluded kaddish before the prayer, Rabbi Gershon started to pray as well. The Besht had not yet begun his prayer, since he knew that Rabbi Gershon would not be able to stand it and would be frightened. In the meantime he fixed his watch and sniffed snuff until Rabbi Gershon passed the place of the kavvanah. When Rabbi Gershon concentrated on that kavvanah and saw the multitude of the dead coming to him like a great flock of sheep, he fell down in a faint. Then the Besht woke him up and told him to go to his home.

At night, around the table at dinner time, the Besht asked him: "Why did you faint?"

He answered him: "When I concentrated on the kavvanah the dead came to me in droves."

Then the Besht said jokingly to his followers, "Hit him so he will not laugh at the Besht."

47] *Rabbi Jacob Joseph Recognizes the Greatness of the Besht*

I HEARD THIS FROM THE FAMOUS HASID, THE WISE rabbi of the holy community of Polonnoye, who was the head of the court in the holy community of Shargorod. When he had heard that the Besht had come to the holy community of Mohilev, since then he was not yet a Hasid, he had said to himself: "I will go there also."

He traveled so that he would come to the Besht before the morning prayers on Friday. When he arrived he saw that the Besht was smoking a pipe. This seemed strange.

"Afterwards, during the prayer, I wept as never before in my life, and I realized that it was not my weeping.

"Later, when the Besht traveled to the land of Israel, I was left desolate until he returned.[1] Then I began to travel to him and remained for some time with him. The Besht used to say that it was necessary to elevate me. After I had been with him for about five weeks, I asked, 'When, sir, will you elevate me?' "

48] *Rabbi Jacob Joseph Is Expelled from Shargorod*

The rest of the account I learned from the rabbi of our community, our rabbi and teacher, Gedaliah, God bless his memory. He told me that he heard from the rabbi of Polonnoye that the Preacher was the first to follow the Besht. He came on Sabbath Eve to Jacob Joseph in the holy community of Shargorod, and he asked the rabbi if he could stay with him over the Sabbath. The rabbi did not refuse him. The Preacher asked him if he could have a minyan in his house to pray. The rabbi gave him permission to do so, but he himself went to the synagogue. On the Sabbath when the Preacher went to preach, he asked the rabbi to come to the sermon, and his sermon portrayed the rabbi thoroughly from head to toe. The rabbi said to himself: "He must be a prophet—otherwise how would he know my thoughts?" And so he joined him. The rabbi immediately asked the leaders of the community to come to the third meal, and they were surprised since they knew that he was not one of the Hasidim. But later on when the rabbi persisted, the people of the city began to quarrel with him, and they became his worst enemies. The controversy increased more and more, until they banished him from the city on a Friday and he had to observe the Sabbath in a village.[1]

The Besht was not far away. When he perceived the whole affair he said to his followers: "Let us go to such and such village.

I know that the rabbi of the holy community of Shargorod is in great sorrow. We will be with him to observe the Sabbath and ease his sorrow." And so they did.

The Preacher was with them as well. On the Sabbath after the Musaf prayer the Preacher watched the rabbi grieving. He said to him: "Do not feel sorry. I heard a herald announcing that one of your enemies will be killed. Another will die while on the road. And the entire town will be burned down."[2]

When the Besht heard these words he shouted at the Preacher and said: "Fool. *You*, too, hear heralds?" And the preacher became quiet.

The rabbi went to the holy community of Raszkow and they accepted him as a rabbi for the second time.[3] It was there that he undertook upon himself many acts of repentence. He was very rich and had about sixty thousand [golden coins], and he distributed all his wealth. He returned all the fines that he had received and all the fees from transactions about which there was the slightest doubt. He threatened with excommunication any one from whom he had received money improperly who would not come to him to take back the money. As a result he became a poor man.[4]

49] *The Ascetic Fasting of Rabbi Jacob Joseph*

I HEARD FROM THE RABBI, OUR TEACHER AND RABBI, the maggid of the holy community of Nemirov, Joel,* whose tomb is in the land of Israel in Jerusalem—let it be reconstructed soon in our days—that once he traveled with the rabbi of the holy

* Rabbi Joel was the rabbi of Nemirov until 1752 when Rabbi Jacob Joseph of Polonnoye accepted this post. In an interesting historical analysis, Isaac Schiper identifies Rabbi Joel of Nemirov with the Rabbi Joel Baalshem mentioned in *Solomon Maimon, Autobiography*, trans. J. C. Murray (London, 1954), p. 170. Schiper asserts that Rabbi Joel Baalshem was considered to be the founder of the Hasidic movement by the court of the Great Maggid, Rabbi Dov Ber of Mezhirich. See his article "The Image of Rabbi Israel Baal Shem Tov in Early Hasidic Literature," Hebrew, *Hadoar*, XL (1960), 525-32, 551-52.

community of Raszkow to the holy community of Medzhibozh. He came to the holy community of Bar, where they prayed in the inn with a minyan. At the end of the prayer the rabbi left unnoticed, and later they went to look for him. They found him leaving a certain house. They asked the owner of the house: "What did the rabbi want in your home?"

He did not want to tell them as the rabbi had ordered him not to reveal it. The important people that were there with the rabbi became angry with him and forced the silversmith to tell them the truth. The silversmith said: "I am now taking revenge on him. When he dwelt in the holy community of Raszkow he fined me two red coins. Now he has given me his Sabbath tallith until he returns from his trip and redeems it."

The people ordered him to renounce the debt of two red coins immediately and to return the tallith. He returned it, but the rabbi refused to accept it until the silversmith promised him with a handshake that he forgave him wholeheartedly. Then the rabbi accepted the tallith.

This is the manner in which the rabbi fasted the *Kanah* repentance:* He used to fast daily, and in each month he fasted once from one Sabbath to the other. No one of the household knew about his fast except a young girl, the daughter of his sister, who alone brought him food. She had to deliver the food at a particular time and place and then remove it so that it would not become known to anyone else of the household. In this way he fasted for five years.

This happened when he fasted from Sabbath to a Sabbath during the sixth year. During a journey the Besht heard a herald: "Rush to him immediately since today he will lose his mind."

He hurried to him in such a great rush that a horse worth ten red coins died on the way. The Besht said to the rabbi: "My horse worth ten red coins has died because of you. This will be your atonement." The rabbi immediately ate, and later he listened to the Besht.

I have a letter that the Besht sent to the rabbi. The address

* The penance of *Kanah* consists of daily fasting for six years, and avoiding anything that comes from living animals for supper.

written on the outside of the letter is as follows: "From the holy community of Medzhibozh to the great community of Nemirov. Send these words like lightening to the cohen, head of the court of the community. Fortress and mighty tower, wonderful rabbi, performer of miracles, brilliant sage, our teacher of the holy community and head of the court, Joseph the Cohen."

And this is the body of the letter:

"To my beloved, the rabbi, the great light, the crown of this generation, famous in piety, perfect and wonderful sage, performer of miracles who is attached to my innermost heart and who is closer to me than a brother, our teacher, Joseph the Cohen, I received your letter at the conclusion of the Sabbath and saw that in the first two lines you, sir, said that you must fast. I am deeply upset at your words, and let me add that *by the decree of the watchers*[1] and God and His Shekinah, you should not place yourself in this danger. This is the way of melancholy and sadness, and the Shekinah does not inspire through sadness but only through the happiness of doing mitzvoth. As it is known to you, sir, these are things that I have taught repeatedly, and they should be close to your heart and in the thoughts that bring you to this melancholy. Let me advise you, *the Lord is with thee thou mighty man of valour;*[2] every single morning while you are studying contemplate the letters with utmost devotion in worship of your Creator and God will be with you. With the help of God, blessed be His name, they will sweeten the charges against you in their source and the pressure of the charges here will be reduced. *Hide not thyself from thine own flesh.*[3] You should not, God forbid, fast more than is required and is necessary. If you listen to me God will be with you. With these words let me shorten my letter and say farewell. Always wishing you well, Signed: Israel Besht. Best wishes to your only son, the famous rabbi, my friend, his honor, our teacher, Samson, and his heir, who is a friend of our rabbi and teacher, Herts, may his light endure. Best wishes to all of them together and to each of them respectively."

50] *Rabbi Jacob Joseph Observes the Sabbath in Shargorod*

I heard from the rabbi of our community, our teacher, Gedaliah, God bless his memory, that the rabbi, Jacob Joseph, wanted to go to the Holy Land on several occasions, but the rabbi, the Besht, told him not to go. He said to him: "This will be an omen for you. Every time that you have the desire to go to the Holy Land you will know for certain that there are accusations against the city, God forbid, and that Satan is distracting you so that you will not pray for the city. Therefore, when it occurs to you to go to the Holy Land, pray instead for the city."

Once the rabbi went to the Besht for the Sabbath, and he had to pass through the town of Shargorod. He was very angry with the people of the town, and he did not want to stop there.* However, since he had to give fodder to the horses, he was forced to stop. He did not leave the wagon and he said: "As soon as they finish eating we will go on."

But when they entered the inn it started raining heavily, and they could not continue. The rain did not stop, and so he had to remain there overnight against his will. In the morning it did not stop raining, and the rain kept increasing until Thursday. When the rabbi realized that the rain was not stopping, he said: "Perhaps it is your wish, O God, that I observe the Sabbath here and then the rain will stop."

And so it was that the rain stopped immediately. He prayed for the town the whole Sabbath.

The Besht perceived that the rabbi observed the Sabbath in the holy community of Shargorod. The Besht knew that the rabbi was very angry at the town, and he said to his followers with a smile: "Look. The rabbi of the holy community of Raszkow observed the Sabbath in the holy community of Shargorod," and he continued smiling.

After the Sabbath, the rabbi came to the Besht, who shook his

---

* The community leaders of Shargorod expelled Rabbi Jacob Joseph after he began to associate with the Besht. See tale 48.

hand and laughed. The rabbi said to the Besht: "Rabbi, why are you laughing?"

He said to him: "Because you spent the entire holy Sabbath in Shargorod."

He answered: "Indeed, this was the case." And he wept and clung to the Besht like an only son. He told him that he was forced to remain there for the Sabbath because of the rain.

Then the Besht told him: "Did you think that the Preacher was lying, God forbid, when he said he heard a herald's voice?* The reason I became angry at him was that he revealed it. If he had not pronounced the words of the herald, on that Sabbath I would have completely revoked the punishment decreed for the town. As it turned out, I could not ask for more than a reprieve. The entire city will not be burned at one time. Instead, first one end of the city will be burned and then the other end, until it will be completely destroyed."

And so it happened. The city caught fire several times. Those who were destined to be murdered were killed in the community of Uman at the time of the flight, God forbid, and those who were doomed to death by plague died in the plague two years after the flight.** They had a reprieve of about twenty years or more. I know because the rabbi was the head of the court of the holy community of Nemirov for sixteen years before the flight, except for the time that he was in Raszkow, which was several years before.

51] *The Protective Prayers*

LET ME WRITE A LITTLE IN PRAISE OF THE RABBI when he was the head of the court in the holy community of Nemirov, one year after the flight. It was my custom that when I

---

* See tale 48.

** During the spring and the summer of 1768, the Haidamaks raged in the Ukraine, within the Kiev region, murdering Jews and Poles. Many people fled for their lives and about twenty thousand Jews and Poles were murdered in Uman, an important town in this region. Shargorod is about 100 miles west of Uman. See Dubnov [Dubnow], *History of the Jews in Russia and Poland* (Philadelphia, 1916-20), I, 180-87. This event is mentioned also in tales 40, 45, 51, 171, 210.

put on the tefillin of Rabbenu Tam,* I was afraid to do so publicly since I was still young. When I reached the parts "Happy are they" and "A redeemer will come to Zion,"¹ I used to go into a large house which was empty during the time of the prayer since they prayed in a room near the small house. Only the gabbai was in the house. Once he went to the market to buy provisions. I entered the house and put on the tefillin of Rabbenu Tam. And so I was delayed. In the meantime they finished the prayer, and the rabbi, God bless his memory, entered his home, and he looked here and there and realized that no one was there.

I asked him: "Our rabbi, what are you looking for?"

He said to me: "You are walking around with tefillin." I immediately removed the tefillin from my head, and he said: "Go to the beth-hamidrash and see whether they have finished the prayer." I went and they were still praying "Happy are they" and "A redeemer shall come to Zion." I returned to his house and did not find him, as he had taken off his tefillin and gone to relieve himself. I waited for him. When he returned to the house and asked me, I said that they had finished the prayer, since I imagined that indeed they had. He began to put on the tefillin, and I knew that he was about to go to the beth-hamidrash. I went before him and found that someone was standing before the ark reciting the Psalms as if asleep. I knew that the rabbi would be irritated by this, as he used to compare the genital union to the spoken covenant:² just as it is impossible to procreate with an inert organ in the genital union, so it is impossible to create with a mute organ in the spoken covenant. The rabbi ordered all the synagogues in the community to recite the psalm, *Happy are they that are upright in the way*³ especially the verse starting with the letters N-E-M-I-R-O-V and R-E-N-D S-A-T-A-N,⁴ combined with the name

* There are two sets of tefillin which differ from each other in the order of the Biblical portions written on the scrolls within the cubes. One was arranged according to *Rashi*, Rabbi Shelomoh Yitshaki (1040–1105), and the other according to Rabbenu Tam, Jacob ben Meir (1100–1171), who was *Rashi's* grandson. Customarily, most Jews put on the tefillin according to *Rashi*; however, some pietists put on either both of them at the same time or one after the other. Since this was a sign of great piety, it was not done in public.

Y-A-H-W-E-H. And before that they were to recite chapter eighty-three. They would say every day after prayer, "May it be the will of our fathers."[5]

When the rabbi came to the beth-hamidrash and heard the recitation of the psalms, he became angry and he said: "I cannot endure you any more. Each of you is thinking all kinds of thoughts about me. I warn you. Do not make light of the Kedarites.

From there he went to the synagogue, and his anger subsided. He alluded briefly to various matters. If I had not heard his words in the beth-hamidrash I would not have been able to understand what he meant. During the day he gathered the school children in the synagogue and ordered them to recite ninety-one times: *Let the graciousness of the Lord our God be upon us.*[6] Before Minhah they heard that on the previous night the Kedarites had advanced half a verst nearer Tulchin. They were a large number and they were close to Nemirov. Thank God, the Ishmaelites sent a pasha after them and the Kedarites retreated.

52] *The Asceticism of Rabbi Jacob Joseph*

I heard from a certain person whose name is Rabbi David, who dwelt at that time in Shargorod, that one day before the event just related, Rabbi Mordecai of that holy community ordered the people to send a special messenger to the rabbi of the holy community of Nemirov asking him to pray about the Kedarites. They appointed a messenger and ordered him to go very early in the morning.

In the morning, the rabbi said: "The rabbi of the holy community of Nemirov does not need a messenger. He knows already. God will save His people, Israel, from trouble and affliction, amen."

Let me write a little bit about his way of life. He used to study every day wrapped in a tallith and tefillin. Before eating he studied a portion of seven pages of Talmud, and even during the meal between dishes he did not stop reciting his studies. After eating he slept but very little. He arose from his sleep and put on tefillin and studied until Minhah. He studied a good deal during the night as well. There was not a single night, summer and winter, Sabbath and holy day, in which he did not wake at midnight. He worked to ransom fugitives and gave a great deal to charity.

At home he lived in poverty and oppression. Once his son complained, and he answered him: "It is written in the *Midrash Samuel*, 'Let the poor be members of thy household.'"[1] He performed his studies, his prayers, and every holy deed with such force that his flesh trembled.

53] *The Voyage of Rabbi Gershon*

I HEARD FROM MY FATHER-IN-LAW, GOD BLESS HIS memory, that Rabbi Gershon, the Hasid, the rabbi, our teacher and rabbi, swam in the sea while his ship was sailing. I asked my father-in-law how Rabbi Gershon was permitted to subject himself to such great danger, and he could not answer me. When Rabbi Gedaliah visited us I recalled the problem and asked him about it, and he told me:

Once I was sitting on the step in front of the house with the Hasid, the rabbi, our teacher and rabbi, Rabbi Tsevi from Kamenets, and I asked him about this matter and he answered me: "On this very step I sat with Rabbi Gershon, and I asked him in these words: I heard that you swam in the sea while your ship was sailing. How were you allowed to endanger yourself in such a way?"

"He smiled and answered me: 'What is wrong?' All the sailors swim in the sea. The ship has a leather net which hangs in the sea. There is a leather ladder on which they climb up and down to swim in the net. But let me tell you, I did not swim in that net. This is what I did. I perceived that there were charges against the vessel, and I wanted to immerse myself in the water in order to cancel the charges. And it happened that they came to a certain island and anchored the ship, and all the passengers went out for a walk. I said to myself, "Now is the right time to immerse myself in the water." I took off my clothes, stored them in the hold of the ship, and I jumped into the water and stayed there. While I was in the water the ship started moving. When I got out of the water I saw that the ship had gone. I said to myself: "What can I do? If I go to the island, I am naked, and I will not be able to pronounce a single holy word. Moreover, I have nothing to drink or eat." I said, "I shall pursue the ship and overtake it."[1] I was confident that I was a good swimmer since once I saved a Jew who was drowning in the Dnestr half a verst away. And so I set off. I swam after the ship and overtook it. But since the ship was high and slippery because of the coating of pitch, I did not have anything to hold onto. I shouted but my voice was not heard over the noise of the ship. The ship sailed farther away and I swam with all the strength within me. This happened several times until I was very frightened and began to drown, struggling up and down in the water. I could not say a word, even to make my confession. I thought in my heart: "I will both drown and be denied heaven, which is like committing suicide." Immediately, someone appeared on the ship and saw me. He put out a small boat. He pulled me out of the water, brought me to the ship, and threw me into it. I went down to the stern of the boat and lay there for about two hours. I was vomiting because of all the water that I had swallowed. I lay there until I rested a little, and then I put on my clothes and I said to myself: "I should reward the man because of the favor that he did me so that he will not enter paradise because of me." I took a purse full of money and I looked for an Ishmaelite all over the boat, but there was none there. I said to myself: "Probably it was Elijah the Prophet." ' "[2]

54] *Rabbi Gershon's Sin*

I HEARD THE FOLLOWING FROM THE RABBI OF OUR community. It happened that the Besht saw an impression[1] of adulterous acts committed by his brother-in-law, Rabbi Gershon.

He was surprised and felt great sorrow. He was ashamed to bring it up; nevertheless, he spoke to him about it.

Rabbi Gershon answered him: "You are a liar!" And he hit the Besht.

The Besht said to him: "Wait until tomorrow because I still see the charge of adultery hanging over you."

That night, the Besht, in his *yiḥudim*, saw what Rabbi Gershon had done. The following day he said to him: "You took upon yourself a vow of abstinence from your wife, and I heard in heaven that the *Rambam* interpreted it and said: 'It is as if he said of his wife that she is as his mother.' Although it is not a binding vow, the impression of accidental emission, which you attempted to absolve by fasting from Sabbath to Sabbath, was raised against you. Moreover, because you did not keep your vow of abstinence, the impression against you became more severe so that I perceived it as adultery."

Rabbi Gershon confessed the truth. He did not keep his vow of abstinence because he wanted to go to the Holy Land and his wife would not agree since he would be away from her. Therefore, he did not keep abstinent. Both of them worked to redeem this act until they succeeded. From that union was born the maggid of the holy community of Ladyzhin,[2] about whom the Preacher of the holy community of Polonnoye said that he never experienced an accidental emission.[3]

55] *Prayers for Rain in Jerusalem*

I HEARD THE FOLLOWING FROM THAT MAGGID. ONCE Rabbi Shalom* from the Land of Israel[1] decreed a fast because of the lack of rain in Jerusalem. He was an important and pious man, and he ordered all the people to gather in a certain synagogue in Jerusalem to pray in a group. He sent for Rabbi Gershon and

* Rabbi Shalom Shar'abi, a Yemenite kabbalist who lived in Jerusalem in the middle of the eighteenth century. See A. Bension, *Sar Shalom Shar'abi*, Hebrew (Jerusalem, 1930), and Scholem, *Major Trends in Jewish Mysticism*, p. 328.

asked him to pray before the ark. It is the custom in Jerusalem that whoever prays before the ark has to deliver a moralizing sermon. It is the custom of the preachers there to give exact quotes from the Gemara, the Midrash, or Bible, and they are shamed if they make any changes in the text.

Rabbi Gershon prepared himself for this sermon by rehearsing the text several times so that he could quote the words exactly. He did not sleep the whole night, and by dawn his throat was sore. He said to his son, Rabbi Leib: "My voice is gone. Go to Rabbi Shalom and tell him that I cannot pray."

As a result the group dispersed and each one prayed in his customary place of worship. Rabbi Shalom prayed in the bethhamidrash which he usually attended. Someone else went to pray before the ark. During the recitation Rabbi Shalom heard that Rabbi Gershon had regained his voice. Immediately after the silent prayer, he ordered the person who was praying to leave the stand and to let Rabbi Gershon stand there and pray the eighteen benedictions aloud and to recite the selihoth.[2]

Rabbi Gershon went to the ark. After the eighteen benedictions he started reciting the selihoth. He said the opening lines, but he immediately stepped back from the ark and refused to continue reciting the selihoth.

Rabbi Leib, his son, asked him why he did that.

He answered him, "I recited the opening lines very fluently, and I felt that if I had continued saying the selihoth it would have started raining immediately. I was afraid of my arrogance, and therefore I did not pray. I knew that after that it would rain for two or three days in a row."

And so it was.

56] *A Quarrel in Safed*

I ALSO HEARD THE FOLLOWING FROM RABBI PINḤAS, the melamed who was formerly a maggid. I believe that the event took place in the community of Safed. The rabbi of that holy community, who is called hakam in their language,[1] was a very good man who liked Rabbi Gershon.

Once Rabbi Gershon said to that hakam: "I ran out of money and I had to borrow for Sabbath expenses."

One very cold day Rabbi Gershon wore an outer jacket made of heavy cotton, and he went to the beth-hamidrash to pray. After the prayer the men lingered in the beth-hamidrash, each one studying his daily portion. Rabbi Gershon walked back and forth in the beth-hamidrash. He was sniffing snuff, and as he drew his handkerchief out of his coat pocket, a small locked purse fell out of his coat. There were five sixers in this purse. In the Holy Land they are unfamiliar with this kind of purse. The hakam saw the purse fall from Rabbi Gershon's pocket, and he picked it up and felt it on the outside since he could not open it. He felt the five coins that were in it, and he thought that they were five red coins. The hakam wondered why Rabbi Gershon would lie. They are very strict there about lying.

He began to talk with Rabbi Gershon: "You, sir, borrowed money for Sabbath expenses because you, sir, did not have money."

He answered: "Indeed this is the case."

The hakam said to him: "You, sir, are lying."

And he said: "I spoke the truth." They repeated the argument. One said one thing and the other said the opposite. In the middle of the quarrel the hakam leaped to the holy ark and swore that Rabbi Gershon was lying. Rabbi Gershon jumped up and excommunicated the hakam.[2]

The hakam removed his shoes and went home. He gathered everyone together and related the case. He showed them the purse, which they too felt, and they agreed that it contained five red coins. He cried out: "Not only did he lie, but he also excommunicated me."

The people of the community went to Rabbi Gershon and asked him: "Why did you excommunicate our hakam?"

He answered: "Because he took a false vow."

They showed him the purse and said: "Look. There are five red coins here."

Rabbi Gershon said: "Why did he not open the purse before he made his vow?"

They answered: "He could not open it."

He said to them: "He should have broken the purse to see what is in it. These coins, much like my other silver objects—my silver myrtle and silver utensils—are not in currency here."

The hakam apologized to Rabbi Gershon who then removed the ban from him.

Then a letter came to Rabbi Gershon from the Besht in which he had written: "I perceived that you were tried in a palace in heaven, and they wanted to sentence you to death, God forbid. Why were you impudent to the rabbi, the head of the court? I wanted to go to the palace and defend you, but they barred the door before me and I could not enter there. I called out, 'God O God, whatever he did was for Your sake.' And a voice proclaimed: 'Let him be since he did it for the sake of the Lord of hosts.' Nevertheless, they sentenced you to be blind for one month, because a blind person is as though he were dead.[3] From now on do not be so strict."

Rabbi Gershon wrote to the Besht: "I cannot understand how this happened. The story is indeed true, but how did you see the trial before the actual deed was committed?"

The date on which the Besht wrote was on his letter.

57] *Rabbi Lipeh Quarrels with Rabbi Gedaliah*

I HEARD A SIMILAR STORY FROM THE RABBI OF OUR community, that Rabbi Lipeh, God bless his memory, from the holy community of Chmielnik, quarreled with the rabbi of that holy community about a certain problem. One forbade something while the other permitted it. When Rabbi Lipeh[1] visited the Besht on Rosh Hashanah, the Besht said during the dinner: "Today I saw that they sentenced a scholar to death because he was impudent toward the rabbi, the head of the court of his community."

Rabbi Lipeh understood that the Besht was talking about him, and he began to weep.

The Besht said to him: "Do not be afraid. I have already prayed for you, and they commuted your sentence.

58] *The Mocking Song*

I HEARD MORE FROM RABBI PINHAS ABOUT THE period of Rabbi Gershon's stay in the Holy Land. It is an old custom there to filter the water used for cooking and drinking because their water collects in cisterns, and worms and mosquitoes are frequently found it it. Rabbi Gershon's wife did not know about this, and she did not filter the water, since in her country it was not then the custom to do so. The wives mocked her and composed a mocking song. They laughed at her in the synagogue, and she came home weeping bitterly.

"Why did you bring me to a distant place where they make fun of me?"

Rabbi Gershon pacified her and said: "Show me the woman who composed this song."

She showed him that woman on her way from the synagogue. Rabbi Gershon spat and said in wonder, "What is this? Is this woman able to talk?" And that woman became dumb.

59] *The Sick Girl*

I HEARD THIS FROM MY SON, OUR TEACHER, *Mar* Leib, may he have a long life. Once Rabbi Hirsh, the son-in-law of Rabbi David, the great light, the head of the court of the holy community of Ostrog, observed the Sabbath with us. Rabbi Aizik was the brother-in-law of Rabbi Herts,* and the son of Rabbi David. On the conclusion of the Sabbath his son, Rabbi Herts, told a story which he had heard from Rabbi David.

Our rabbi and teacher, Aizik, the rabbi's son, had a young daughter, thirteen years old, who was married. She became sick.

---

* *Hirsh* and *Herts* are used here interchangeably. The name is a Yiddish translation of the Hebrew Tsevi, deer (in German *Hirsch*).

When the Besht was in the holy community of Zaslavl, they showed him the sick girl. He ordered them to call a nurse the next day to put leeches on her, and he told them to operate on her for piles.

The wealthy man, our rabbi and teacher, Aizik, was afraid to rely on the Besht. He inquired of the physician of the duchess of that community, who told him that piles can be found even among young girls. When he came home he sent for the nurse.

The Besht stayed with Rabbi David, who formerly was the head of the court of the holy community of Ostrog. Rabbi Hirsh, the rabbi's son-in-law, went with the Besht to Rabbi Aizik's house through the passageway where the horses were quartered. The Besht went from one horse to the other. He looked them over, tapped them, and he decided that he liked one horse in particular. He said to me: "Herts, is it possible to sell me this horse?"

Rabbi Herts answered that he did not know.

They entered the house. The Besht said to Rabbi Aizik: "Sell me that horse."

He answered him: "Our rabbi, it is written *'Thou shalt not covet.'*"[1]

He said to him: "You idiot. I covet nevertheless."

But he still did not want to sell it to him.

Afterwards, the Besht saw the nurse, and he said to Rabbi Aizik: "Isn't there some other woman in town you could have called besides this gluttoness creature?"* This woman was a person of some importance in the town. She operated on the piles, but in spite of that the girl did not recover.

The Besht went home and Rabbi Aizik took his daughter to the Kedarites in the community of Konstantynow. When the Besht heard about it, he went to Konstantynow himself and said to Rabbi Aizik angrily: "You too would do this to me?"

Rabbi Aizik promised him to return home, although actually he did not mean to do so. But when Aizik saw that the Kedarites were not able to improve his daughter's condition, he went back home with her.

---

* In Hebrew הבולעת הזה. The exact meaning of this word in this context is not entirely clear. The translation is one possible solution.

Once near the Sabbath she became extremely weak and our rabbi and teacher, Rabbi David, made a loud outcry and gathered melamedim to recite the Psalms. They gave her another name and blessed her.[2] He sent a letter to Medzhibozh by a gentile messenger, who would be able to travel on the Sabbath, asking the Besht to pray for her. The gentile arrived at Medzhibozh on the holy Sabbath after the reading of the Torah and before the Musaf prayer.[3] At the end of the Sabbath the Besht ordered his scribe to write a letter and to give it to the gentile. The letter said: "Written at the conclusion of the holy day. I received the letter before Musaf. So I prayed for her aloud, but I did not get any response —not a word or even half a word. I do not know what has happened to me, unless she has been blessed with a new name. In that case, let me know the name immediately."

At last it was learned that the girl was pregnant, and she recovered after she gave birth.

Some time later the Besht came to the holy community of Zaslavl, and Rabbi Aizik said to him: "You knew of the need to call a nurse, and you knew that she had a new name, why couldn't you also tell that she was pregnant?"

He answered him: "Do you think that she really was pregnant? She conceived from my prayer and from your father's prayer."

The letter that the Besht sent was in Rabbi Jacob of Yampol's handwriting.

60] *The Blood Libel*

THERE IS ANOTHER STORY ABOUT THE BESHT WHEN he stayed in the community of Zaslavl and observed several Sabbath days there. In the course of that time a dead gentile was found in the field and brought to town. There was a plot to accuse the Jews. They went to the duchess and said to her that the Jews killed him. The duchess was frightened, as her husband, the duke, had died a dishonorable death on the highway because he had martyred Jews through false accusations.[1] Therefore, she said: "It is impossible to sentence anyone to capital punishment without investigating the matter and definitely establishing that the Jews killed him."

When the Jews of the city learned about it, they trembled with fear, and they sent Rabbi Aizik to the inn where the Besht was staying to inform him about it. The Besht was standing with one foot on a stool and one foot on the ground.[2] Rabbi Tsevi the scribe was reciting the Zohar before him. The Besht was repeating after him, and he was in such great rapture that his face glowed. When Rabbi Aizik came to the threshold of the house, the Besht motioned to him to go away, and so he did. Their fear increased and they sent him a second time, but the Besht motioned to him to go away again. Finally, they urged Rabbi David to go himself to the Besht, since he would not put him off as he was an elder and a respected person. Rabbi David went to the Besht.

The Besht told him: "I do not hear them talking about it at court at all."

Once on another occasion, on the Sabbath at midday after the meal, the Besht was reclining on a chest, his head resting on his hand. His followers were standing around him. He cocked his ear as if he wanted to listen, and he said that they are talking at court about this accusation. He said: "Heat the mikveh for me immediately."

He went to the mikveh and came back and said: "Do not worry. There is nothing to fear at all." Then the leaders of the community sent their spokesman to the court where he heard the gentiles complain to the duchess about the murdered gentile. She ordered her physician to examine the dead man to find out whether or not he died a natural death. The leaders of the community were afraid to rely on the Besht alone, and they gave the physician thirty red coins. Thank God no charge resulted from this.

The head of the court of the holy community of Zaslavl was the brother-in-law of Rabbi David and he asked the Besht: "Why didn't you inform the Jews about the murdered man before he was found so that they would not be afraid when they found him in the field."

The Besht answered them: "I prayed about it in the mikveh, and I asked why this thing was concealed from me at first. They answered that this was to punish me for neglecting to fully eulogize a certain scholar whose name was Rabbi Ḥayyim of Brody."* The Besht said to the rabbi of the holy community of Zaslavl: "Do you think that I do not know that several times you hid yourself under the benches in the bathhouse and in other places?"

And the Rabbi of Zaslavl admitted it was true.

61] *The Dance of the Hasidim*

I HEARD THIS UPON THE ARRIVAL OF THE RABBI OF the community of Nemirov. Once on Simhath Torah** the followers of the Besht were happy, dancing and drinking a lot of wine from the Besht's cellar.[1]

The Besht's pious wife said: "They will not leave any wine for the blessing of the kiddush and Havdalah,'" and she entered the Besht's room and said to him: "Tell them to stop drinking and dancing since you will not have any wine left over for the kiddush and Havdalah."

The Besht said to her jokingly: "Well said. Go and tell them to stop and go home."

When she opened the door and saw that they were dancing in

---

* Horodezky identifies him with Rabbi Ḥayyim Tsenzer of Brody, who was one of the leading rabbis of the group of scholars who centered around the beth-hamidrash of that town. However, if this identification is correct, this quotation of the Besht is the product of folk tradition since Rabbi Ḥayyim Tsenzer died in 1783, twenty-three years after the passing of the Besht himself. Ḥayyim Tsenzer opposed the Besht, yet the Besht compared him to the important Tanna Rabbi Yoḥanan ben Zakkai. See tale 241. About the relationships between the Besht and Rabbi Ḥayyim Tsenzer, see Gelber, *The History of the Jews in Brody*, pp. 63, 109, 330–31, 334.

** Literally "the rejoicing of the Torah," a holiday celebrating the conclusion of the annual public reading of the Torah. It takes place on the eighth day of Sukkoth. For a monograph about its historical development and diversified forms of celebration, see A. Yaari, *The History of Simhath Torah*, Hebrew (Jerusalem, 1964).

a circle and that flames of fire were burning around them like a canopy, she herself took the pots, went to the cellar, and brought them as much wine as they wanted.

After a while the Besht asked her: "Did you tell them to go?" She said to him: "You should have told them yourself."

62] *The Great Maggid and the Besht*

I HEARD FROM THE RABBI OF THE HOLY COMMUNITY of Derazne, who formerly was the head of the court in the holy community of Pavlysh, the story of how the rabbi, the Great Maggid, was attracted to the Besht.* The Maggid fasted from one Sabbath to another seven or eight times successively, and he became seriously ill. Once, Rabbi Mendel of the holy community of Bar came to the community of Torchin, where he stayed with an elder of the community. The Maggid lived in a small house, which was attached to that of the elder. Rabbi Mendel entered the passageway of his host and he heard the Maggid studying with a pupil. The Maggid's explanations appealed to him. He entered the room and he saw that the Maggid was very sick. He said to him: "Have you not heard that there is a Besht in the world? You, sir, should go to him and he will cure you."

* Rabbi Dov Ber of Mezhirich (d. 1772). (In *The Columbia Lippincott Gazetteer of the World*, the name of his town is spelled Mezhirichi. The spelling employed in this work is more widely known in Hasidic literature.) After the death of the Besht he became one of the two leading rabbis of the Hasidic movement. Under his leadership, Hasidism acquired many more followers. His relationship with the Besht is not clear. He rarely mentions the Besht's name in his sermons, and even when he does he never refers to him as "my teacher," as does Rabbi Jacob Joseph of Polonnoye. Dubnov suggests that Rabbi Dov Ber conceived of himself as an independent Hasidic leader rather than as a disciple of the Besht. See *History of Hasidism*, p. 93. Isaac Schiper develops an elaborate theory which makes Rabbi Dov Ber a disciple of Rabbi Joel Baalshem rather than the Besht. See his article, "The Image of Rabbi Israel Baal Shem Tov," Hebrew, *Hadoar*, XL (1960) 525–32, 551–52. In this light the following story has a polemic value since it emphasizes the indebtedness of Rabbi Dov Ber to the Besht, and not to any other personality.

The Maggid answered: "It is better to seek God's protection than to put one's trust in a human being."

When Rabbi Mendel came to the Besht, he praised the Maggid and said: "I have been to the community of Torchin and I saw there a holy vessel."

The Besht said: "I have known of him for several years and I long for him to come to me."

There are several versions of how the Maggid came to the Besht.[1] But I heard that his relatives pressed him to go to the Besht. When he came to the Besht he found him sitting on his bed studying, and he shook his hand. The Maggid asked the Besht to cure him.

The Besht scolded him and said: "My horses do not eat matzoth."

The Maggid began to perspire from weakness. He went outside and sat on the step in front of the house in order to rest. He saw a very young man, and he called him over and said to him: "Please go to the Besht and tell him: "Why do you not follow the phrase: *Love ye therefore the stranger?*"[2]

The young man was Rabbi Jacob of Annopol. He felt pity for the Maggid and so he went to the Besht. He was afraid to talk with him, and so he wisely managed to go to the end of the house and then immediately turned back to leave. On his way out he said: "There is an unhappy man sitting in front of the house and he asked me to ask you, sir, why you have not fulfilled the phrase: *Love ye therefore the stranger?*" And he left the house.

The Besht immediately gathered ten men and went to the Maggid to appease him. He wanted to cure him with words. I heard from Rabbi Gershon of the community of Pavlysh that the Besht visited him daily for about two weeks and sat opposite him and recited Psalms. After that the Besht said to him: "I wanted to cure you with words alone since this is an enduring remedy, but now I have to cure you with medication." The Besht gave him an apartment and for each Sabbath he gave him twelve golden coins for his expenses.

Rabbi Jacob of Annopol and Rabbi Elijah visited him often.

Sometimes they argued about problems in the Gemara and in the tosaphoth.

The Maggid could not go to the Besht because he was so weak. After a little while he began to recover, and he used to go to the Besht to sit at his table. Once he fainted and they tried for half a day to revive him. The Besht went three times to the mikveh, and he sent for a certain man who lived three versts away in order to buy from him a precious stone, a diamond, for thirty red coins, and they ground the stone and gave it to the Maggid to drink.

After that Rabbi Jacob and his friend came to visit him and they asked him why he had fainted, but he did not answer them at all. They asked the people of the household whether he had left the house during that night. They said, "He went outside and stayed there, and when he returned home, he began to feel faint. They asked him where he had been.

He said, "The Besht sent his gabbai to me at midnight. I found the Besht sitting with a small candle on his head. He was dressed in a coat of wolf fur turned inside out, and he asked me whether I had studied Kabbalah. I answered that I had. A book was lying in front of him on the table and he instructed me to read aloud from the book. The book was written in short paragraphs, each of which began: "Rabbi Ishmael said: 'Metatron, the Prince of Presence, told me.' "³ I recited a page or half a page to him.

"The Besht said to me: 'It is not correct. I will read it to you.' He began to read, and while he read he trembled. He rose and said: 'We are dealing with *Ma'aseh Merkavah*⁴ and I am sitting down.' He stood up and continued to read.

"As he was talking he lay me down in the shape of a circle on the bed. I was not able to see him any more. I only heard voices and saw frightening flashes and torches. This continued for about two hours. I was extremely afraid and that fear caused me to feel faint."

And let me, the writer, say that it seems to me that that was the way his torah was revealed to him. I heard from the Hasid, the rabbi of the holy community of Polonnoye, that he received his

soul's torah from the Besht amidst thunder and lightning. Moreover, he said that this revelation was accompanied by musical
instruments, as it is said in the holy Zohar. But I have not seen in
the Zohar any mention of musical instruments accompanying the
giving of Torah.[5] I did hear from the rabbi this explanation: "As
all the Israelites received the Torah as one people in the same way
the Besht received it as an individual."

Once, after the Besht's followers asked him the meaning of a
sentence in the Zohar and he explained it to them, they asked the
Maggid, God bless his memory, the same question, and his explanation amplified the answer of the Besht. They told this to the
Besht and he said: "Do you think that he learned the Torah by
himself?"

When the Maggid, God bless his memory, was ready to leave
the Besht, the Besht blessed him. Afterwards, the Besht bent his
head for the Maggid to bless him, but the Maggid refused. So the
Besht took the Maggid's hand and put it on his head and the
Maggid blessed him.

This is as far as it goes.

63] *The Death of Rabbi Eliezer Rokeaḥ*

I HEARD THIS FROM RABBI JOEL, THE MAGGID OF
the holy community of Nemirov, who always visited with Jacob
Joseph, the rabbi of the holy community of Polonnoye, while he
was in the holy communities of Raszkow and Shargorod. In
Nemirov he told me that once the Besht observed the Sabbath in
Shargorod.

"At the conclusion of the Sabbath, after the Havdalah, he used
to tell what he had envisioned during the Sabbath. He said that he
perceived that Rabbi Eliezer had died in the holy community of
Amsterdam on the previous Sabbath, which was the Sabbath
when the reading of Genesis begins.* I asked him the cause of his

---

* Rabbi Eliezer Rokeaḥ (born 1665), originally of Brody, became the
rabbi of the Ashkenazic community in Amsterdam in 1735. Because of
intrigues within the community, he immigrated to the Land of Israel and

death, and he told me that two men from Poland had scorned him on Simhath Torah. (Rabbi Joel refused to tell their names.) They said to him in these words: 'Here you are a community leader, but in Poland you would not have been worthy of being even the rabbi of the tailors.'

"And he willed himself to die. 'But I will take revenge on them with plague and war, God forbid.'

"I asked him, 'What will you do about your wife?'

"He answered: 'I will take her from them.'

"I forgot to ask him whether he meant alive or that she would die also.

"That year the son of the rabbi of the holy community of Polonnoye returned and his father asked him: 'What is Rabbi Eliezer doing?'

"He said: 'He passed away.'

"He asked him whether he had passed away on the Sabbath when the reading of Genesis begins or later.

"He said: 'How did you know? No one has come from Amsterdam before me.'

"He said: 'We knew on the following Sabbath when the portion of Noah was read. The Besht told us.'

"The rabbi's son was surprised.

"Rabbi Jacob Joseph asked his son about Rabbi Eliezer's wife, and his son answered that Rabbi Abraham Shverdlik from Jerusalem came and took her to Jerusalem. He asked about the opponents of that rabbi, and his son said that they were weakened by the plague, God forbid, and that the people expelled them into the fields and the Ishmaelites came and killed them."

64] *The Book* Ḥemdat ha-Yamim

AGAIN ON THE VERY SAME SABBATH, THE BESHT SAID that he perceived that they would print a new book during that year. He still did not know the name of the book since they had

---

arrived there in June 1740. He died in 1742 in Safed, and not in Amsterdam as the text states. See Gelber, *The History of the Jews in Brody*, pp. 50–54. See also tale 169.

not yet given it a title. The author of this book was a member of the sect of Shabbetai Tsevi, may his name be blotted out. *For the lips of a strange woman drop honey,*[1] may her name be blotted out. The style will be attractive and it will lure many people. Because of our many sins it will contaminate the world, God forbid.

When the book was published Rabbi Jacob Joseph bought a copy, as the title was new to him. When the Besht came to him and saw the book lying on the table, he opened the door and said: "The book lying on your table is condemned."

The rabbi asked: "Which one is it?"

He pointed to it with his finger. This was the book *Ḥemdat ha-Yamim* ("Joy of the Days").[2] They wrapped it in a filthy rag and put it under the table.

65] *The Dream of Rabbi Jacob Joseph*

RABBI JOEL TOLD ME THAT ONCE THE RABBI* SAW IN his dream that one member of his minyan had been converted to Christianity. The rabbi awoke trembling with fear. He sent someone to wake up the others in the minyan, and he saw that all of them, thank God, were faithful. He asked them: "Perhaps one of you has secretly committed a crime, God forbid." And he told them of his dream.

One pious man, Rabbi Eliezer of Tomashpol, answered: "I don't know of anything I did wrong, but before I went to bed I looked through the book, *Ḥemdat ha-Yamim.*

66] *The Besht and Shabbetai Tsevi*

RABBI JOEL TOLD ME, IN ADDITION, THAT SHABBETAI Tsevi came to the Besht to ask for redemption. Rabbi Joel said in these words: "The *tikkun*[1] is done through the connection of soul with soul, spirit with spirit, and breath with breath."[2] The Besht

* Rabbi Jacob Joseph of Polonnoye.

began to establish the connection moderately. He was afraid as Shabbetai Tsevi was a terribly wicked man. Once the Besht was asleep, and Shabbetai Tsevi, may his name be blotted out, came and attempted to tempt him again, God forbid. With a mighty thrust the Besht hurled him to the bottom of hell. The Besht peered down and saw that he landed on the same pallet with Jesus.

Rabbi Joel said that the Besht said that Shabbetai Tsevi had a spark of holiness in him, but that Satan caught him in his snare, God forbid. The Besht heard that his fall came through pride and anger. I was reluctant to write it down, but nevertheless I did so to show to what extent pride can be dangerous.

67] *Rabbi Isaac Drabizner*

I HEARD THIS STORY ALSO FROM RABBI JOEL. RABBI Isaac Drabizner was accepted as a maggid in the great and holy community of Orekhov, and he remained there for a few weeks. It so happened that a butcher owed money to the tax collector. While the tax collector was away, his wife confiscated the butcher's possessions—even his pillows and cushions. The butcher's wife came in tears to Rabbi Isaac to complain. Rabbi Isaac sent word to the tax collector's wife ordering her to return all that she had confiscated, but she did not obey him. Rabbi Isaac cursed her and immediately her baby died.

When her husband returned from his journey she told him the story and said: "A maggid, just appointed, cursed me, and the child died immediately."

Rabbi Isaac went to his home in the community of Ostrog, since he was a maggid there for Rabbi Yozpa. The leaders of the community sent wagons for him so that he would come to the community of Orekhov with all his family.

What did the tax collector do? He sent a letter by special messenger in which the following was written: "If he has not yet moved, he should remain where he is. If he is on his way he should return home, because even if he comes here, he will be forced to leave this place."

Rabbi Isaac wrote to him in reply: "I will come to the community when they carry your bier toward me."

And so it was. When Rabbi Isaac passed through the city gate they were carrying the dead tax collector on his bier, although they were not able to pass through the gates with his body.

The tax collector had a large family. They kept their hate toward the maggid hidden in their hearts since they were afraid of him. "Strife is compared to an opening made by a rush of water that widens as the water presses through it."[1]

The feud intensified and anyone who tried to harm the maggid suffered death. Rabbi Itsik, who was the head of the court there and who later became the head of the court in the community of Brody and then in the community of Hamburg, also took part in the feud. But because Rabbi Ezekiel, the head of the court of the community of Tomashpol, was a relative of Rabbi Itsik, he wrote him that, for the sake of heaven, he should make peace with Rabbi Isaac because he was like a consuming fire. So he made peace with him.

Once a great bolt of lightning hit the synagogue during the afternoon prayer and killed two men, one at the eastern wall and the other in the vestibule. The people of the city came to Rabbi Isaac and said: "Our rabbi, you have killed some of God's people."

He answered and said: "The one who was killed at the eastern wall died because of the feud. The one who was killed in the vestibule died because of a false oath that he made in the community of Brody for three red coins. During the prayer he was holding them in his hand and playing with them."

They found the three red coins in his hand.

68] *Perjury*

I HEARD THIS FROM THE RABBI OF OUR COMMUNITY. Two litigants brought a case before Rabbi Isaac. He ordered one of them to swear under oath, and the man agreed. The other litigant shouted, "Take the oath!" He was very bitter since he knew very well that his opponent had lied.

Rabbi Isaac said: "Why do you urge him to take the oath? Usually if anyone lies to me one of his descendants will die. Then he will regret his false oath, confess the truth, and live."

And so it happened. One of his descendants died, and he regretted his action and confessed the truth.

69] *The Oxen of Rabbi Barukh*

I HEARD FROM THE RABBI OF OUR COMMUNITY that during the war with the Greeks,* Rabbi Jonah of Kamenka, Rabbi Barukh's brother, sent oxen to be sold in the villages. They heard that the Greeks robbed Rabbi Jonah's oxen. Rabbi Barukh sent oxen as well, and he was afraid lest they would rob his oxen also. So Rabbi Joseph of Kamenka was sent to the Besht, and he found him washing his hands before the meal. The Besht told Rabbi Joseph of Kamenka to wash his hands also. After the blessing over the bread, the Besht said: "Why did they not consult me when they started out? I would have watched over them." Then the Besht opened the Zohar. He scrutinized it for a minute and said: "I see that Rabbi Barukh's oxen are still alive. They were not stolen."

Rabbi Joseph asked the Besht: "Is this written in the Zohar?"

The Besht answered: "This is what our sages of blessed memory said about the Biblical verse, *And God saw the light that it was good*.[1] They said that the light was good for concealment, since in the light of the first six days it was possible to see from one end of the world to the other. Where did God hide the light? He hid it in the Torah. What he said to the righteous people of that time was meant for future righteous people as well. Anyone who has the merit to find the hidden light in the Torah is able to see the whole world from one end to the other.[2] Do you think

* Ukrainians.

that I saw only the oxen? While I was looking I saw what happened in the holy community of Amsterdam."[3]

He told Rabbi Joseph about the event, but I did not hear it.

70] *The Stolen Halter*

Once the Besht wanted to begin a journey, but since it was the time for the blessing of the new moon,[1] he delayed until nightfall. One of his followers who accompanied him to bless the new moon wanted to look back, but he was stopped by the Besht. He said: "Someone has stolen the halter from the horses." The horses were harnessed to the wagon in order to start out immediately after the blessing of the new moon. The person who stole the harness did so because he did not have money for the Sabbath expenses."

After the blessing of the new moon the gabbai began to shout: "Who stole the halter?"

The Besht said to him: "Do not shout. The thief pawned the halter with a certain person. Take eighteen groschen and go to him and redeem it. And do not publicize the matter."

71] *The Shohet Who Was a Drunkard*

In a certain place there lived a shohet who was a frivolous person and a drunkard. One morning, after the prayer, the rabbi of the holy community of Polonnoye called him aside into another room and said to him: "I saw the Besht and he told me several times the judgement given concerning a shohet. I cannot tell exactly what took place, although he told me also how gentile butchers were judged, but they were particularly strict with the shohet. He told me what to look for to catch a shohet neglecting a certain law." And so it happened.

The rabbi, God bless his memory, was very careful not to cut off the livelihood of any person unnecessarily, and because of that the shohet had always made a living. But when I caught him the rabbi ordered the court to assemble to take testimony from the butcher and determine if according to the evidence and the law of the Torah he should be removed from his post. The butcher gave his testimony and they removed him.[1]

72] *The Death of Rabbi Abraham, the "Angel"*

IT HAPPENED THAT WHEN RABBI ABRAHAM, THE son of the rabbi, the Great Maggid, was accepted as a maggid in the holy community of Fastov the intermediary was Rabbi Menaḥem Nahum, the famous Hasid of the holy community of Chernobyl. I heard this from Rabbi Joel of Prot'hur, who learned it when he celebrated the Passover with Rabbi Nahum in the holy community of Porivosts.[1]

The day after Yom Kippur a messenger from Rabbi Abraham came to Rabbi Nahum and told him that Rabbi Abraham had begun to grow weak during Yom Kippur, and by the time of Neilah he had stopped speaking. They asked him whether to call for Rabbi Nahum. He nodded his head yes, and so they sent for him. In the meanwhile, he passed away.*

Rabbi Nahum went to the mikveh because he said to himself: "I will pray for him in my place."

It was learned that he passed away prior to Sukkoth, but they did not tell it to Rabbi Nahum. During the intermediate days** one person innocently revealed to Rabbi Nahum that Rabbi Abraham had died. Rabbi Nahum began to strike his head against the wall. He wept bitterly for about two hours, and they could not calm him down until they took him in their arms and carried him to the sukkah and said: "Rabbi, remember that it is a holiday today."

* Rabbi Abraham was known for his extreme asceticism. The Hasidim called him the "Angel," in regard to his great piety. He died at the age of 36 in 1776.
** The days between the first day and the last day of Sukkoth. The intermediate days have few restrictions in contrast to the requirements imposed on the holy days.

He stopped sobbing, and he began to speak in praise of Rabbi Abraham: "Once I was in the holy community of Annopol, and I asked him if he saw his father.

"He answered: 'Yes.' "

"I asked whether he appears in his dreams or when he is awake. And he answered: 'He comes to me in my dreams. He talks with me and afterwards I wake up, and he talks with me while I am awake.' "

Rabbi Abraham told Rabbi Nahum that there was at that time a wealthy man who had caused him grief several times. Rabbi Joel refused to reveal the name of that wealthy man. "I complained to my father, and my father said to me: 'I will summon him.' "

"And I asked him: 'To what place will you summon him?' "

"And he said, 'To your beth-hamidrash.' "

"He sent my servant, whose name was Rabbi Filt, to him. Rabbi Filt was at that time in the state of Polesye about sixty versts away from Annopol. He came to the house of the wealthy man and knocked on the door and said: 'Open the door for me.' "

"The wealthy man recognized his voice and he wondered about this, and he said to himself: 'But didn't he leave his home?' Immediately, he answered himself. 'Perhaps he came home in the evening.' So he gladly shook his hand, and they asked each other how they were.

"Then Rabbi Filt said: 'There is no time to waste since the rabbi summons you.'

"He said to him: 'What are you talking about? Is not our rabbi dead and passed on to the next world?'

"Rabbi Filt said to him: 'Nevertheless, he calls you.' And he went with him.

"When the wealthy man came to the beth-hamidrash of Rabbi Abraham, he saw that the Maggid was sitting at the head of the table, dressed as he was when he was alive. The Maggid said to him: 'Do you think that because I am not here you may do whatever you wish? Therefore I show you now that I am sitting here.'

"The wealthy man began to find excuses and reasons for his actions. But the rabbi did not want to listen, and he said to him:

'Go away from me. Go away from me.' And he rebuked him: 'Filt, take him home.' And he took him to his home.

"When they arrived at his home Rabbi Filt told him: 'Go in since I have to return.'

"When the wealthy man entered his home, he fainted. There was a great outcry and all his neighbors gathered around him. They revived him and asked him why he had fainted, and he told them the whole story. They said to him: 'Let us go to Rabbi Abraham.'

"All of them went to Rabbi Abraham. When he saw them he smiled and said: 'Probably my father summoned him.'

"They asked him: 'How did you know?'

"He answered: 'My father told me that he would.' "

73] *Rabbi Abraham as a Sandek*

RABBI NAHUM TOLD FURTHER THAT RABBI ABRAHAM was in the city of Fastov, and he isolated himself completely. No one was able to see him. Rabbi Nahum had praised him before the townspeople, and they longed to see him. Once there was a berith. They accorded Rabbi Nahum all the honors at the berith, and they asked Rabbi Abraham to be the sandek of the baby. He was accustomed to prolonging his prayer, and they waited for him a long while. Many people had gathered in the synagogue in order to see him, but when they were told that Rabbi Abraham was finally coming to the synagogue they became frightened and only twenty people remained there. He came running to the synagogue, and the rabbi of the community moved aside as he thought that Rabbi Abraham was going to take his place. Rabbi Abraham came in and sat in the rabbi's place. He rested his head on the reader's stand. They brought the baby to the pulpit, and he continued to rest his head.

They said to the shammash: "Go and tell him that they brought the baby." But he refused to go because he was frightened. They asked other people to go and tell him, but no one wanted to go. In the meantime, Rabbi Abraham himself appeared on the pulpit.

Rabbi Nahum said: "When he appeared I was so frightened that the knife fell from my hand, and I had to snatch it by the blade. I was so frightened that until today I do not remember whether I recited the blessings for the berith. I let him take my place for the blessing of the *metsitsah*.*

When Rabbi Nahum came home he sat in silent wonder. Twice his gabbai brought him coffee, but he refused it and pushed it aside. The gabbai insisted that he drink, but he answered him: "Fool. How is it possible to drink coffee after you witness someone worshipping God in such a way."

74] *Rabbi Abraham as a Mohel*

(WE HEARD THAT *Admor*,** MAY HIS SOUL REST IN heaven, said that our rabbi and teacher, Menaḥem of Chernobyl, was the sandek, and the rabbi, our rabbi and teacher, Abraham, God bless his memory, was the mohel. When he said the blessing of the berith, his awe and trembling were so profound before the greatness of God that the knife fell from his hand. After that the rabbi, our rabbi and teacher, Menaḥem, asked him about the nature of that great awe, and he answered: "It is amazing to me that it is possible to ask such a question.")

75] *The Wife of Rabbi Abraham*

I HEARD FROM THE RABBI, OUR TEACHER MENAḤEM, that he heard the following from the daughter-in-law of the rabbi, the Great Maggid, the wife of our rabbi and teacher Abraham. When the Great Maggid's son, our teacher, Abraham, God bless

---

* The sucking of the blood from the penis after the berith.
** Rabbi Shneur Zalman of Lyady was Rabbi Abraham's close friend. Both of them studied under Rabbi Dov Ber, the Great Maggid.

the memory of the righteous, became a widower, the Great Maggid called two leaders of the community to him and said: "It is my request that you go to the holy community of Kremenets and arrange for my son, may he have a long life, to marry the daughter of the rabbi, our teacher, Faivel, the author of the book *Mishnat Hakhamim.*[1] Then bring her here."

They immediately did as he said. They prepared a good wagon with horses and put on fine clothes to enhance the grandeur of their rabbi, and they started out on their way. When they reached that community they took lodgings at an inn. After they rested from the journey, immediately after prayer, they went to the house of the rabbi, our rabbi and teacher Faivel. It was the custom of that rabbi not to trouble himself with the worldly problems of earning a living, but instead to engage himself in studying the Torah the whole day and the night as well. His wife was the one who had to concern herself with earning a livlihood. So when they came to his house, his wife was returning from the synagogue, and she greeted them and said: "My brethren, where did you come from?"

They said: "From the holy community of Mezhirich."

She said: "What are you doing here? Do you have some negotiation to arrange or something else?"

They told her the story. "Our great rabbi sent us to propose the marriage of your daughter and his son, who recently became a widower."

She laughed at them since she did not know the rabbi and had never heard his name. Moreover, the girl was only twelve years old, and it had never occurred to her to seek marriage proposals. After hearing the offer repeated many times, the idea registered in her mind, and she said: "Is not my husband, thank God, in my house? Why should I concern myself with it? He will decide what is best."

They sent for him at the beth-hamidrash. He came home, and they discussed the proposal with the rabbi, our rabbi and teacher, Faivel, until it was settled to his liking. They immediately ordered that a scribe be brought in to write the betrothal contract, mazal tov. When they began to write the contract, the Great Maggid's emissaries said: "Write down *as it liketh you in the king's name*,[2] except it is impossible to delay the date of the marriage."

They argued: "But our rabbis, God bless their memory, said that one should grant a girl twelve months after her betrothal.[3] Besides, it did not even occur to us to marry her off in the near future. She has no clothes or a bridal gown."

They answered: "We don't mind that at all, but it is absolutely impossible to postpone the date of the wedding. She must return with us immediately." And since this had come from God, they accepted it also.

It was agreed that the rabbi, our rabbi and teacher, Faivel, would stay at home so that he would not stop his studies, and the bride and her mother would travel to the wedding. They rented another good wagon and horses for her and they all departed.

During the journey the mother wondered how they had allowed themselves to be talked into it. They came to the holy community of Rovno, and all the people of the city, from the youngest to the eldest, men, women, and children, welcomed them and greeted the daughter-in-law of the Great Rabbi. Then they felt better about the match. After that, upon arriving at the outskirts of the holy community of Mezhirich, they were greeted by so many men and children that they had to proceed very slowly. As they entered the town, all the women came out to greet them, and when they arrived in front of the rabbi's house, he and his son came out to welcome them. After that they went to the inn.

The wedding party lasted seven joyous days. They satiated themselves with endless discussions of the Torah. After the wedding party, Rabbi Abraham's mother-in-law, returned home with great joy, since she had never heard nor seen anything like it.

The rabbi became very fond of his bride. It came to pass that one day she dreamed that she entered into a spacious hall in which a supreme council of venerable elders was seated, and they wanted to take her husband from her. She cried out to them and argued her plea before the court. Then she woke up and realized that it was a dream, but she did not tell anyone. Even when she was with the rabbi she did not tell him. The second night she also dreamed the same thing, and again she did not tell a soul. The third night she dreamed the same dream, and she pleaded with them for a long time until at last they said to her: "Very well. Because your arguments are true, we will let you have him for twelve years as a gift."

The next day when she came to the rabbi he congratulated her and blessed her for the true plea which prolonged his time for twelve years. Indeed this was what happened to him.[4]

It came to pass after several years that the Great Maggid died and ascended to heaven. In spite of this, whenever they were in trouble or need he came to her in a dream and told her what to do.

Once, on a Friday night he appeared to her in a dream and said: "Tell your husband to switch apartments with you or at least to put his books in your room."

In the morning she told it to her husband but he did not pay any attention. He said to her: "Why did he tell it to you and not to me?" Because of our many sins his room was burned during the night and all his books were lost.

After that the rabbi, our rabbi and teacher, Rabbi Abraham, journeyed to the capital. When he came to the holy community of Fastov, they welcomed him with great honor and accepted him as a rabbi. They set his salary and then they sent a messenger to his wife so that she would arrive in time for the Days of Awe. Just when they arrived, the rabbi, the Great Maggid, appeared to her in a dream and told her not to travel with those wagons to the holy community of Fastov. In the morning she refused to accompany them. The tsaddikim, our teacher, Meshulam Zusya, and our teacher, Judah Leib Cohen were distressed. They wanted her to travel there in order to fulfill the wish of the tsaddik, her husband, but she did not pay any attention to them. A short time later, because of our many sins, the holy ark, Rabbi Abraham, was taken away from that community. They sent a messenger to the holy community of Annopol. The tsaddikim were ashamed to face Rabbi Abraham's wife because she had perceived the future better than they had. They concealed the news from her. They revealed it only to her son, the rabbi, our rabbi and teacher, Shalom, who was then a small boy, so that he would be able to say kaddish and say it in such a way that his mother would not find out. But with her great wisdom, she wondered about the eagerness of her son to arise early in the morning to go to the synagogue, something he was not accustomed to do. When she left the synagogue she leaned against the wall of the beth-hamidrash to listen if her son was saying the kaddish for orphans, but she could not hear it clearly. After the prayer she sought to question him: "Why do you conceal your words? I was behind the wall, and I heard you say the orphan's kaddish." Then he had to reveal the truth, and she mourned her husband.

After the seven days of mourning had passed, she went to the holy community of Fastov to take her husband's possessions. When she came there, they welcomed her with great honor. On that Sabbath they held a dinner for her at the inn, and all our people ate there out of respect to her and in order to console her. But she could not be consoled. At the third meal almost all the people of the city gathered there and sang songs as usual. She, filled with sorrow and sadness, sat on a high couch next to the innkeeper's wife. She dozed and she dreamed. In her dream she saw a huge, beautifully decorated hall. She opened one door and her husband, the rabbi, our teacher, Abraham, came into the house shining like the sun at noon and very happy. And after him came several venerable old men.

He said to them, "Sit down my rabbis." They sat around the table. He said to them, "Here is my wife, may her days be long. She has a grievance against me because I maintained extreme abstinence. Her complaint is just. I ask her forgiveness before you."

She said: "I forgive you with all my heart."

He said to them further: "The Torah allows that she marry with another husband, especially since she is only a girl of twenty-four, and I can not prevent her from doing so. But if she agrees not to marry anyone else, I pledge to fulfill all her needs. And before she returns home, each of her children will be assured of a good life."

Consoled by his words, her face at once lost its angry expression.

When she returned home, her sons and daughters immediately received marriage proposals. God sent His blessing in the deeds of her hand, and she made a respectable living from the store that she had, so that her needs were fulfilled. When it was necessary, her father-in-law appeared to her in a dream and told her what she should do.

Many years later, the wife of the great rabbi, our teacher, Menaḥem of Chernobyl, died, and he wanted to take the widow of Rabbi Abraham as his wife. He consulted with her son, the rabbi, our teacher, Shalom, may his days be long, who was the bridegroom of his daughter, and since he was young it also seemed to him to be a good idea. Rabbi Menaḥem sent Rabbi Shalom to talk with his mother. On his way the rabbi, our teacher and rabbi, Shalom, had a dream in which he saw a large, beautifully decorated hall. His father, the rabbi, God bless the memory of the righteous, was standing at the door of the hall, with his two hands stretched to the roof, crying out in a loud voice: "Who is he who dares to enter into my hall?" He awoke and realized the seriousness of the matter, and he returned home in peace.[5]

76] *The City of Adultery*

THE GREAT RABBI, OUR TEACHER, DOV OF MEZHI-rich, God bless his memory, once ordered his disciple, the rabbi, our teacher, Aaron of Karlin,* to go home by way of a certain community, and he did as he was told. When he came to that certain city he looked in his traveling bag and realized that he had forgotten his tallith and tefillin. Rabbi Aaron had never prayed with borrowed tallith and tefillin, and so he sent somebody to a store to buy a tallith and have fringes sewn on it. He himself went to a scribe to buy tefillin. When the scribe handed him the tefillin

* Rabbi Aaron of Karlin was the founder of the Karliner dynasty. He died in 1772 at the age of 36. See Wolf Rabinowitsch, *Lithuanian Hassidism from its Beginning to the Present Day*, Hebrew (Jerusalem, 1961), pp. 9–23, and his essay, "Karlin Hasidism," *YIVO, Annual of Jewish Social Science*, V, (1950), 123–51. Karlin is a small town near Pinsk.

the rabbi cried: "Yesterday he slept with a married woman and today he sells tefillin. Confess, wicked man!"

The man admitted his sin. His confession led to an investigation, and they found many men and women who were contaminated by sin. It was necessary to have more than a hundred divorces.

In one case there was a problem that he could not cope with, and he had to go back to the Great Rabbi, our teacher and rabbi, Dov. When he came to him it was the rabbi, our teacher and rabbi, Dov, who recounted all the circumstances, and he also discussed the case about which Rabbi Aaron had doubts regarding the practical application of the law.

Before the rabbi, our teacher and rabbi, Aaron, returned to that holy community a second time, the Great Rabbi told him: "The rabbi, our teacher, Menahem Mendel,[1] will accompany you, since he speaks Polish. Take white Sabbath clothes with you." And so they did.

On the way the rabbi, our teacher and rabbi, Menahem Mendel, said: "The purpose of our trip is only to arrange divorces, so what need have we to speak Polish? And why do we need the white clothes? Undoubtedly our rabbi must have perceived in his mind that the wicked people have regretted their confessions and have slandered us to the governor of the town."

Indeed, so it was. Upon their arrival at the town the governor ordered policemen to bring them immediately to him. He wanted to cause trouble for them. The wicked men hid themselves in another room of the governor's house. When they came to the governor dressed in their white clothes, they found favor in his eyes. He received them with great honor, and he told them to sit down with him.

While they were talking, the governor said to them: "Why are you rabbis concerned with this place?"

The rabbi, our teacher and rabbi, Menahem Mendel, said: "Since the rabbi, our rabbi and teacher, Aaron, is a godly man, he perceived that there are heavy charges against your city. It is actually condemned to destruction because the inhabitants are evil and have sinned against God, especially regarding adultery.

Several women have to be divorced.* We came to you since you are the governor of the city, and you must care for its well being."

As they were talking the governor recalled the words of the wicked men, and he ordered them to appear and to speak with the rabbis. Immediately, the rabbi, our teacher and rabbi, Aaron, shouted at them in a loud, angry voice, and they had to confess all their sins before the governor. The governor ordered them to divorce their wives and treated them with great severity.²

77] *The Advice of the Great Maggid*

IN ONE HOLY COMMUNITY THE PEOPLE OF THE city endured many trials and were oppressed by the governor until they could bear it no more. They consulted among themselves and decided that they had no other way but to send a messenger to the duke who was about eighty versts away. They chose two of their leading citizens. One was a venerable old man, and the other was a young man. The people of the community warned them that for the sake of heaven they must travel quickly. Their contract with the duke was coming to an end, and if they would be even one day late the situation would be beyond repair.

The holy community of Mezhirich was along their way. They arrived there on Sunday morning and stayed at an inn where they prayed. Meanwhile the innkeeper asked them about their business and their destination. They told him the whole affair. The innkeeper said: "My advice is that you go to our Great Rabbi and ask his holy counsel."

Although the old man was a little reluctant to take this advice, the younger man liked the idea, and he persuaded the old man to go with him to the rabbi. And so they did.

On their arrival at the rabbi's house they found that there were many others who wanted to enter the inner sanctum of the court. They were there for several hours until they found the rabbi's gabbai, and they told him that they wished to see the rabbi.

* According to Jewish religious law divorce is mandatory when a woman commits adultery.

The gabbai went to the rabbi and then answered them on his behalf that they should stay there overnight, and that he would give them an answer the next day. This delay was difficult for the old man to accept as the time was very short and they needed to be on their way. Nevertheless, they agreed to stay there overnight.

After prayer the next day they went to the rabbi, and again they waited a long time until the attendant arrived. The gabbai went to the rabbi a second time and then answered them on his behalf that they should stay there another night. This made matters worse. They greatly regretted having gone to the rabbi. They had to wait until Tuesday. When they came to the rabbi's court on Tuesday, word was sent from the rabbi that they should not take the customary road, but should travel instead on another road which was terribly winding. The old man became very angry with his companion because their delay had been for nothing. Nevertheless, they accepted the advice and took the road designated by the rabbi. As they were traveling, embittered because of the delay, the sky darkened and it began to rain. It was a torrential downpour. During the storm they went astray, and they were very upset. They traveled on until they came to a village. They had caught cold from the rain and the wind, and they decided to remain there overnight. They gave their horses to a gentile to graze during the night, and they ordered him to return them early in the morning.

The following morning they arose early. They completed their prayers, and they found that the horses had not yet been brought. They were very upset because of the time they had lost, as they were afriad that the date set by the contract had passed. In the meantime the gentile came and said that the horses had been taken to the governor's court because they had trespassed onto his land. They asked the innkeeper to go and ask for the horses. The innkeeper said that he would certainly not go to the governor because not only would he surely not return the horses, but he would even have him cruelly beaten, as this was what usually happened. They wanted to pay the innkeeper for his bother in going there, but he refused to go under any circumstances, as "he values his life more than his money."[1] Very depressed, they were forced to go to the governor themselves.

When they arrived at the court they saw an attendant whom they recognized as the servant of their duke. Since the attendant had visited their community with the duke several times, he recognized them and knew that they were from a well known community.

They asked the attendant: "What are you doing here?"

He answered: "I am here with the duke."

They were filled with joy and accompanied him to the duke. When the duke saw them he was pleased and asked them where they were going. They told him the entire problem. They settled the affair in the best possible way, and the duke gave them written approval. They told him further: "Our horses were caught by the governor." The duke sent for the governor and had him return their horses to them at once.

They returned home with great joy a few days before the time limit, and they realized that from the very beginning to the end it had been decreed by God.

78] *The Prayers of the Hasidim*

THIS IS WHAT WAS HEARD FROM THE HOLY RABBI, our teacher, Zusya of Annopol,* who heard it from his brother, the rabbi, our teacher, Elimelekh, blessed be the memory of the righteous.**

Once Rabbi Elimelekh ascended to heaven and met there the author of *Hesed le-Abraham,**** who asked him: "Rabbi, look,

* Known as Meshulam Zusya (died 1800).

** Rabbi Elimelekh (1717–86) of Lizensk, a small town near Jaroslaw, was a disciple of Rabbi Dov Ber of Mezhirich, and after the death of the Great Maggid he became the leader of the Hasidim of Galicia and Poland. His main book is *No'am Elimelekh* ("Elimelekh's Delight") (Lvov, 1788). See Dubnov, *History of Hasidism*, pp. 178–88.

*** Several books that bear that title. This may be a reference to the work of Abraham Azulai (1570–1643), who was born in Fez, Morocco, with the help of God I wrote ten holy essays which are very highly considered in paradise. Tell me why is there so much excitement in heaven concerning your motions during prayer? Tell me what deeds you have done since we can not comprehend the depth of its meaning."

79] *The Two Brothers*

The holy rabbi, Rabbi Shmelka, and his brother, our teacher, Pinḥas, may their souls rest in heaven, were both asked at the same time to fill the rabbinical position by the holy community of Frankfurt am Main and the holy community of Nikolsburg. Since the holy community of Frankfurt am Main was a larger and more respected community than that of Nikolsburg, the people of the communities could not decide who would take the rabbinical chair in Frankfurt am Main, and who would be in Nikolsburg. They said that they would leave it to the two rabbis to settle it between themselves.

Although the rabbi, our teacher, Shmelka, God bless his memory, was older than his brother; nevertheless, because of his great humility, he said that his brother, Rabbi Pinḥas, was more worthy than he was of the rabbinical position of the holy community of Frankfurt am Main. And Rabbi Pinḥas considered his elder brother to be greater than himself. Both of them agreed that before they would depart from the Great Rabbi, the Maggid of the holy community of Mezhirich, they would ask his holy counsel. They would do whatever he decided. In addition they wanted to ask him about a saying from the Zohar which they could not understand. When they came to the rabbi the brothers began to argue, one with the other, about who would enter first, since each of them maintained that the other was the greater man.

Immediately, the rabbi, the Maggid, said the following: "The

---

and emigrated to Hebron, Palestine, in the beginning of the seventeenth century. While residing in Gaza he wrote his kabbalistic work, *Ḥesed le-Abraham* (Amsterdam, 1685).

rabbi of the holy community of Nikolsburg will go first since he is the elder brother."

When they came in the rabbi told them a story about the customs of a governor regarding his slaves and his palaces. When he finished the story he told them to leave in peace, and they did not ask him about the saying from the Zohar. When they came to their inn they thought about it, because he certainly had a reason for telling them the story. They realized that it was a parable from which they would clearly understand the saying from the Zohar.

80] *Sounding Out the Nature of the Besht*

I HEARD FROM THE RABBI OF OUR COMMUNITY, Rabbi Gedaliah, God bless his memory, that the Hasid, Rabbi Jehiel, the head of the court of the holy community of Kovel, sent a certain person, a scholar and a wise man, to sound out the nature of the Besht. He became ill on the way. When he came to the inn in the holy community of Medzhibozh, he lay down on the oven, and he felt very warm. The Besht sent Rabbi Gershon, his brother-in-law, to him. He sat with him on the oven, saying torah to him. Afterwards, Rabbi Gershon said to him: "Come with me to the afternoon prayer."

On the way the man felt that he had recovered from his illness and he thought that Rabbi Gershon was the Besht. He asked him: "Are you the Besht?"

Rabbi Gershon answered him: "Ay! Ay! Ay! I am the rabbi. I wish I would have the portion of the next world that the Besht gains from smoking one pipeful of tobacco."

Rabbi Jehiel became an adherent of the Besht.

81] *The Lithuanian Jew and the Besht*

I HEARD THIS FROM MY BROTHER-IN-LAW, OUR teacher Mordecai, who heard it from Rabbi Jehiel of Kovel.

Once the Lithuanians sent someone to sound out the nature of the Besht. He stayed as a guest with Rabbi Jehiel and ate with the Besht. When he heard the Besht's prayer on the eve of the holy Sabbath, it appealed to him very much. After the prayer he went with the Besht to his home. When the Besht came home he became angry with his servant and began shouting at him. He told him to go to the stable immediately because a horse was strangling.

The servant pleaded with him and said: "My lord, I will go right away."

The Besht shouted at him again and wanted to hit him. The servant went and saved the horse.

The guest was surprised by the anger of the Besht, and he said to himself: "After such prayer how could he care for one horse so much as to shout at his servant, especially on the Sabbath."

In the morning he heard the Besht's prayer and it pleased him; nevertheless, this reservation haunted him. After the Sabbath when he wanted to return home he revealed it to Rabbi Jehiel, and then he went on his way. Rabbi Jehiel told the Besht about it.

The Besht became angry and said: "Who are they to examine me? I'll tell you what happened. A Jew was traveling on the road on the eve of the holy Sabbath, and evening fell upon him. He could not reach a settlement in time for the Sabbath. It occurred to him to turn off the road into the field and observe the Sabbath there. A thief came and began to hit him and wanted to kill him. This Jew was very coarse and I had no contact with him except through an animal. I frightened my servant, and the more I frightened him the more the thieves were frightened, until they refrained from killing the man. You will see that they will soon bring him to the town." And so it was.

82] *The Besht and Rabbi Sa'adyah Gaon*

I heard from my father-in-law, God bless his memory, that the Besht said about himself that he was a reincarnation of our Rabbi Sa'adyah Gaon. I told it to the rabbi of our community and he said that he knew that the Besht had diligently studied the books of Rabbi Sa'adyah Gaon.*

83] *The Besht's Sermon*

ONCE, PEOPLE ASKED THE BESHT TO PREACH TO them after prayer. And he did so. While he preached he moved and trembled as if in prayer, and he inserted in his sermon, "God O God, it is known and revealed to you that I do not preach this sermon for my honor (but for the honor of my father's and my mother's families). I know many things and I can do many things, but there is not a person to whom I can reveal them."[1]

84] *The Besht Banishes Demons*

I HEARD FROM THE RABBI OF OUR COMMUNITY AND also from the rabbi of the holy community of Polonnoye that in the holy community of Zbarazh two demons were seen in the women's section of the synagogue. The women were so frightened that they had to leave the synagogue.

Rabbi Ḥayyim, the maggid of our community, went to sit in the synagogue. The demons appeared while he was studying and he banished them. So they went and entered into his two children. Rabbi Ḥayyim sent for the Besht.

The Besht went to sleep in his house of seclusion with *Mar* Tsevi, the scribe. He told them to bring the children to his sleeping quarters. And they did. When they went to bed, the Besht's couch was placed at the head of the table, and the scribe slept next to the Besht's head. They were not yet asleep when the demons came to the house. They stood at the door and mocked the Besht's way of singing "Come my beloved."[1] The Besht rose and sat on his bed. He said to the scribe: "Have you seen them?"

* Sa'adyah Gaon (about 892 to 942), a medieval Jewish philosopher and codifier.

The scribe saw them also, but he tucked his head under the Besht's pillow and said: "Leave me alone."

When the demons finished mocking him they went toward the children. The Besht jumped from his couch and scolded them, saying, "Where are you going?"

They were not afraid and they said: "It is none of your business." They began to mock him again and to sing the Besht's melody "Come my beloved."

The Besht did whatever he did, and the two demons fell down and could not get up. They began to appeal to him, and he said: "See to it that the children recover immediately."

One of them said: "What is done is done, since their internal organs are injured. We came to finish them off. It's their luck that you, sir, were here."

He asked them: "How and why did you go to the synagogue?"

They answered: "Because the cantor who used to sing in the synagogue, the one with the bass voice, was a great adulterer. He purposely attracted the women with his singing. He thought about them and they thought about him, and from these thoughts we were created, two demons, a male and a female. We live in the synagogue."

The Besht gave them a place at a certain well where human beings did not go.

85] *The Rabbi's Wife in Labor*

THE HASID, RABBI JOSEPH OF ZORNISZIZA,[1] WHO is called Rabbi Joseph Melamed, visited our town, the holy community of Ilintsy. At that time I was not in good health and I could not remain with him. I was able only to greet him. I did not hear this from him, but my friends heard it and they told it to me.

Our teacher and rabbi, Joseph, always held other people's money for them. He also kept the money of Rabbi Hayyim. At that time there was a change of currency, and they quarreled as a result of it. Rabbi Joseph said: "Let us go to the Rabbi and Maggid, and he will propose a compromise."

They went to the Rabbi and Maggid, and he suggested a solution. The rabbi's wife went home and Rabbi Joseph remained with the Maggid. The Maggid said to Rabbi Joseph: "The wife of Rabbi Ḥayyim is beyond hope."

The next day she felt birth pains, and she knew that she was going to have a difficult delivery. She sent for Rabbi Joseph and said to him: "Please, sir, forgive me for asking you, but go to the Maggid and ask him to redeem my soul." In doing this she was following the instructions given her by the Maggid.

Rabbi Joseph said to her that he would go to the Maggid if she gave him the key to the strongbox so that he could take as much money as he liked. If she did not agree then he could not go. She gave him the key and a handkerchief, and he took one hundred and sixty golden coins and went to the Maggid.

The Maggid said to him: "Why do you come to me? Did I not tell you her situation?"

Rabbi Joseph said: "She gave me the key and control over all her money."

The Maggid immediately sent for Rabbi Mikhel, God bless his memory, and for Rabbi Leib Cohen, God bless his memory, and for Rabbi Joseph, and he asked them to go to the mikveh. The Maggid was then still able to walk on his feet, but he could not get into the water. The three of them went and the Maggid went with them. The three entered the mikveh and the Maggid stood over them. They remained under the water, and when they rose up the Maggid said: "You have not yet succeeded."

They immersed themselves in the water in this way several times. Rabbi Joseph, God bless his memory, said: "The Maggid wanted to teach me the kavvanoth, but it was better that I acted out of innocence."

They stayed in the water for a long time, and Rabbi Joseph, who was an old man, caught cold. He said: "God, O God, give the rabbi's wife as a gift to me. If not, I am in danger."

Afterwards, the Maggid ordered them to get out of the mikveh. "Thank God, you have succeeded. The rabbi's wife will live, and she will give birth to three babies." He noted how many males and how many females, but I do not remember. Before that the Maggid ordered that they go to the mikveh and prepare a dish with many herbs so that he could warm himself after the mikveh. After he ate, the Maggid said that he would hide himself so that they would not find him, because there would be a great tumult. He also locked the door behind him and did not let anyone in until she gave birth to the babies and he saw that she would live.

86] *The Church That Caught Fire*

I ALSO HEARD FROM RABBI MEIR OF ANNOPOL that Rabbi Joseph Melamed lived in a city, the name of which I forget, and his house was next to a house of idolatry.* Once the Besht came to his city and saw his house next to the house of idolatry, and he said: "In this house lives a pious man."

When Rabbi Joseph came to welcome him the Besht asked him: "Why do you live next to a house of idolatry?"

He answered him: "I am a very poor man. If I had money I would move to another place."

Not long after, the house of idolatry burned down, and the governor did not allow them to rebuild another one there.

87] *The Hose-Maker*

I ALSO HEARD FROM RABBI MEIR THAT IN THAT town there lived a worker who made stockings. He used to pray regularly in the synagogue, summer and winter, and if there were less than ten people in the synagogue he would pray alone. Once, when the Besht was in that town, as he was smoking his pipe before prayer, he looked through the window and saw the worker going to the synagogue. He was stunned and he said to the householder: "Go outside and inquire about the man who just went by carrying a tallith and tefillin."

The householder went out to see and he said: "It is a certain worker going to the synagogue."

The Besht told him to fetch the man. The householder said to

* A reference to a church.

the Besht: "It's an insane idea, and he certainly wouldn't want to come."

The Besht kept quiet. After prayer he sent for the worker and asked him to bring four pairs of stockings. He came and brought the stockings with him. The Besht asked him: "How much is a pair of stockings?"

He told him: "Each pair costs a golden coin and a half."

The householder said to him: "Perhaps you'll take one golden coin for a pair?"

The man did not say a word.

The Besht told the householder to stop bargaining, but he said nevertheless: "Perhaps you'll sell a pair for less than a golden coin and a half."

The worker answered him: "If I had wanted to sell for less I would have asked a lower price right at the start."

The Besht paid him for four pairs of stockings and then he asked him: "What do you do?"

He said: "I work at my trade."

The Besht asked: "How do you conduct your business?"

He said: "I do not make less than forty or fifty pairs of stockings. I put all of them in a big tub with hot water and then I step on them until they are ready."

He asked him: "How do you sell them?"

He answered: "I do not leave the door of my house. The shopkeepers come to my home and buy from me. In turn, they bring me wool which they have bought for me, and I pay them some profit for their bother. I came to you, sir, simply out of respect to you. I do not leave my house but to go to the synagogue. If there is a minyan there, I pray with the congregation. If there is not a minyan then I pray alone at my place."

The Besht asked him: "If you need money to pay for the weddings of your sons, what do you do?"

He answered: "God, blessed be He, helps me somehow in my trade, and I arrange marriages for my sons."

The Besht said to him: "What do you do very early in the morning?"

He said: "I make stockings at that time as well."

He asked him: "How do you recite the Psalms?"

He said to him: "I repeat what I can say by heart."

The Besht said about him that he is the foundation of the synagogue until the coming of the Messiah, may he come soon in our days, amen, selah.*

From this we can see the greatness of the person who enjoys honest work.[1]

88] *The Sin of Pride*

I HEARD THIS FROM RABBI AARON OF THE HOLY community of Medzhibozh when he told it to the rabbi of our community. Once the Besht went to the holy community of Brody and slept overnight in a place near there. During the night the Besht became frightened and his knees knocked against each other. The noise awoke Rabbi Tsevi, the scribe, from his sleep.

The scribe said to him: "Why are you afraid?"

The Besht told him. "My rabbi** came to me and he asked me: 'Who is more worthy, you or Abraham our father, may he rest in peace?'

"I asked him, 'What is the point of such a question?'

"He said to me: 'You will go to the holy community of Brody, and they will honor you greatly. If, God forbid, you do not resist, you will lose all the merit that you have earned until now.'

"I became very frightened."

When he came to the holy community of Brody the wealthy men of the community welcomed him dressed in their finest raiment. He began to play with the horses, stroking them with his hands in the manner of one familiar with animals.

Now you know the extent of the Besht's fear of sin.***

* Concluding word in certain Psalms and liturgy. Originally it probably provided some liturgical or musical directions such as pause, interlude, or elevation of voice. Here it is used as an emphatic term.

** Ahijah, the prophet of Shiloh. See tale 41.

*** The Besht feared the sin of pride. He played with the horses and thus behaved like a commoner or even a wagon driver, who had very low status in the community.

89] *Two Hasidim Visit Hell*

I HEARD THIS FROM RABBI ZELIG OF THE HOLY community of Letichev. This story is not about the Besht; nevertheless, I include it here because from this story we can learn the fear of heaven.

This story is about a young man who was a relative of Rabbi Zelig. In a dream he saw himself in a field with two Hasidim. They said to each other: "Let us go and visit Gehenna and see what they are doing there."

They went. They arrived at Gehenna, and they saw a large gate. They opened it and saw that this was not Gehenna. While entering it they realized that one of the Hasidim had disappeared. They opened the second gate and realized that this too was a corridor. The second Hasid disappeared and the young man remained alone. He argued with himself about whether or not to enter, and he decided: "Since I am here I will go in." He saw that this was Gehenna. A man with a tallith and tefillin was standing at the gate. The man asked him: "What are you doing here and where are you from?" The young man was from Medzhibozh, but the people from Medzhibozh always used to say that they were from the holy community of Bar, since their community was near there. So he said to him: "I am from the holy community of Bar, and I came to see Gehenna." He saw burned corpses, each of them like a *brand plucked out of the fire*,[1] placed in great piles like sheaves on the threshing floor.

That man said to him: "Since you are from the holy community of Bar, go to the other side of that pile and you will see a young man lying there who is also from the holy community of Bar."

He felt very embarrassed because the man was considered to be very respectable. He returned to the gate and saw that the corpses were lying there quite still, and they were not being punished. He asked the man who was standing at the second gate: "Why do they not punish the wicked today?"

The man answered him: "From your question I can tell that

you did not say "Arise and come"[2] in Maariv, and therefore you forgot that today is the first of the month."

Indeed so it was. After that he asked him to let him go out.

He said: "I will not let you out by any means."

He asked him again and he said: "Let me out. I'm a respectable man."

He said to him: "What kind of righteousness is it when while you collect alms you have evil thoughts?" And he told him his thoughts.

He said: "I had to pay tuition in order to study."

The man began to purse his lips and he said: "That is very, very nice; nevertheless, I cannot let you go out."

He appealed to him and begged for mercy.

He said to him: "I advise you to hide under my tallith. The Prince of Gehenna[3] will soon come here in a great storm. They will open the gate and you can slip through and escape."

When the sound of the Prince of Gehenna was heard from afar, the corpses began to tremble violently and he hid himself under the tallith. When the Prince of Gehenna arrived the man opened the gate, and the young man slipped out. He swallowed a little bit of the wind of the storm and he began to cough in his esophagus. His coughing woke him up.

From that day on he suffered with a cough for a whole year, and he died of it. The man from the holy community of Bar whom he saw in Gehenna lived on for two years after this event.

90] *The Court in Heaven*

I heard further from Rabbi Zelig, who heard from Rabbi Shneur, the son of the tsaddik, our teacher, Moses who was a maggid in the holy community of Raszkow, that he, Rabbi Shneur, saw in the holy community of Ladimir[1] a manuscript of the rabbi who wrote the book, *Toldot Ya'akov Yosef*.[2] There it is written that the author had a dream that he entered a palace in paradise. It was so magnificent that he could not get his fill of looking at it, and he remained there attracted by the great beauty of the palace.

While he was there he saw Satan entering the palace in the form of a dog.[3] He informed against a villager before a court holding a session there by saying: "It is true that he studies constantly. And he gives charity. But I have a charge to make against him. He has lived in his village for several years and each year he robs the gentiles." And Satan presented the court with the total amount. The members of the court scolded Satan as one scolds a dog and he ran away.

When the rabbi heard the charge, it hurt him very much. He did not want to leave there until he heard the ending.

In about half an hour Satan came a second time and presented his charge again. They scolded him a second time and again he ran away. Then he returned a third time and stood before the court and said: "Masters of the world. I brought a charge before the court, and you do not pay any attention to my words."

A proclamation from above was heard that they should issue a verdict, and they wrote down their decision. The *arrendator* was to decide between these two choices: either the master of the village was to confiscate all his possessions and imprison the man and his family or one of his descendants would convert to Christianity. Satan took the written verdict in his mouth and went away.

The rabbi woke up from his nap. He felt sorry for the *arrendator* because he loved him very much, especially as he had heard Satan himself commend him. He sent for the *arrendator* and told him what he had seen. The *arrendator* decided that it was better that the noblemen of the village take everything that he had and imprison himself and the members of his household rather than have one of his descendants depart from his religion, God forbid.

And so it was that the master of the village took everything that he had and put him and his family in prison. The rabbi had to go around and collect money to ransom the prisoners, and he redeemed the man and his family. From this a man can see that one should refrain from robbing the gentiles, since, as it is written in the books, Satan collects it back from one's holy merits, God forbid.

91] *The Besht and the Angel of Death*

I HEARD FROM THE RABBI OF OUR COMMUNITY that Rabbi Leibush of the holy community of Mezhirich visited the Besht for the Days of Awe. Before Rosh Hashanah he became sick. The Besht was busy curing him on the eve of Rosh Hashanah and the entire night as well, and he did not see any sign of death, God forbid, at all. When he went to the beth-hamidrash at the time for prayer, Rabbi Leibush became faint and felt very weak. They tried to tell the Besht, but they were afraid to shout and he did not hear them. When Rabbi Isaac of the holy community of Mezhirich saw that the Besht did not respond, he shouted to him in a loud voice.

The Besht answered: "Why didn't you tell me?" And he hurried home and found the Angel of Death standing at the head of the bed. The Besht scolded the Angel of Death severely, and he ran away. The Besht then held Rabbi Leibush by the hand and he recovered immediately. He led him to the beth-hamidrash, as he was afraid to leave him at home lest the Angel of Death return, God forbid.

After that the Besht said that because of what had happened they wanted to reject him from both this world and the next world. He said that he did it only because it had happened so quickly. He had not seen any signs of death earlier. "When I saw the Angel of Death I suddenly felt grief-stricken and I acted."

92] *The Repentant Rich Man*

I HEARD FROM THE RABBI OF OUR COMMUNITY THAT in the holy community of Mezhirich there was a man who was modestly wealthy. When he reached his old age he thought in his heart: "What have I done in my life? What will become of me? I wasted all my days on vanity and emptiness without studying the Torah and without doing good deeds." And he did not know what to do.

It occurred to him to give charity secretly. So every day he put one taler[1] in the sack containing the tefillin of Rabbi Isaac.

Rabbi Isaac found the coins once and then a second time, and he said to himself: "Who is putting coins into my sack of tefillin?" And he asked the shammash of the beth-hamidrash, "Watch who touches my sack of tefillin during prayer. And do not reveal it to anyone but me." The shammash watched, and he saw the man touch the sack of tefillin and the tallith of Rabbi Isaac. After prayer he told Rabbi Isaac who it was. Rabbi Isaac began to become friendly with him, and he taught him the six orders of the Mishnah. Each chapter of the Mishnah that Rabbi Isaac taught, the man repeated with him several times until he knew it fluently. Then he studied another chapter with him until they finished with all the chapters of the Mishnah. In this manner he studied with him *Ein Ya'akov*[2] as well. By the time they finished *Ein Ya'akov* and the Mishnah, the man was somewhat of a scholar. He studied religious books and moral books and the Zohar, and he became a member of the Mishnah study group.[3] He continued to study until the day of his death.

Before his death he became ill and Rabbi Isaac went to visit him. He forced the man to shake hands and promise that he would return and appear to him from time to time.

The custom in that city was that near the time of death, when the soul was about to depart, the members of the Mishnah study group would come and study the Mishnah. During the thirty-day mourning period after his death, they studied, and they finished all of the Mishnah for his soul. After the thirty day period he appeared to Rabbi Isaac, who asked him: "Where is your resting place?"

He said: "My resting place is among the righteous ones in paradise." And he added, "I corrected all but one of my misdeeds during my lifetime, and the Mishnah group corrected it for me by their study."

He used to appear before him from time to time. Rabbi Isaac used to ask him for interpretations of the sayings of the Zohar, and he would reveal to him how they would study a particular saying in paradise. Once Rabbi Isaac revealed to someone else an interpretation that he was told, and he did not appear to him for a long time. Nevertheless, he had to come because of the pledge on which they had shaken hands. When he appeared Rabbi Isaac asked him: "Why did you delay so long in returning?"

He answered: "Because you revealed to other people the interpretation of the saying."

Rabbi Isaac said: "From now on I will not reveal it to anyone. Just appear to me without any delay."

He used to come and go. Once it happened that he was late again. When he appeared Rabbi Isaac asked him: "Why are you late now? I have not revealed anything to anyone."

He said: "Know that they have uplifted me to the higher worlds, and it distresses me to descend from those worlds to this world. As a result, I was delayed, but I was forced to appear because of our pledge. I would like to ask you, sir, to release me from that pledge on which we shook hands."

And he released him from the pledge.

93] *The Defective Tefillin*

I HEARD STILL MORE FROM THE RABBI OF OUR community. Once the son of Rabbi Joseph Yozpa of the holy community of Ostrog was accepted as the head of the court of the holy community of Polonnoye, and he brought a rabbinical judge along with him in order to be able to challenge the Preacher, God bless his memory. On the Sabbath the Preacher prayed before the ark. Rabbi Isaac heard the judge cursing the Preacher during the prayer, but he did not say a word to him. After the prayer, on the Sunday following the Sabbath, Rabbi Isaac said: "I heard you curse the Preacher, our rabbi, quite clearly." And they quarreled.

While they were quarreling Rabbi Isaac looked at him and said: "You are wearing defective tefillin."

They took the tefillin from the judge's head. They removed the verses of the Torah, and they were found to be defective. The judge made an effort to correct them according to the *Shulḥan Arukh*,[1] and Rabbi Isaac showed him that he was ignorant and did not know the law. The judge fled from the town in shame.[2]

94] *The Tefillin Written by Rabbi Isaac*

IT HAPPENED ON ANOTHER OCCASION THAT RABBI Isaac perceived the condition of the tefillin on the head of a certain man. Before Rabbi Isaac's death he was confined to his home because of his weakness, and he gathered a minyan at his house. One member of the community who prayed there used to remain afterwards to study. I believe that his name was Rabbi Beirekh. Rabbi Isaac looked at him and said: "Beirekh, I see a defect in your tefillin."

Rabbi Beirekh removed them from his head and gave them to Rabbi Isaac to examine. He found that they had been defective from the time they were written down. He had had the tefillin since his bar mitzvah, and because they were from a good scribe, he had kept them. At that time he was about sixty years old. He was very bitter that all his life he had not properly performed the mitzvah of putting on tefillin. He urged Rabbi Isaac to write the verses for the tefillin for him, and Rabbi Isaac promised that he would do so. But because of his weakness he postponed it from one day to the next until finally he wrote the verses from the Torah for the tefillin.

Afterwards, he went home and said to him: "Not only have I not written such tefillin before, but no one has done so since the time of Ezra."

About two hours later he passed away from this world. This was Rabbi Isaac, the brother of Rabbi Joseph of Kamenka.

95] *The Righteous Woman*

I heard a story from the rabbi of our community about Rivaleh the Pious, the mother of the brothers Rabbi Joseph and Rabbi Isaac, whose house was in the holy community of Satanov.

Once the Besht went to that holy community, and as he neared the town he perceived a light over one of the townspeople. He remained still and he saw that that light hovered above a woman.

When he arrived in the city the important people there came to welcome him. The Besht said to them: "You should be ashamed. I saw a light hovering above a woman rather than a man." And he asked the people of the city: "Do you know the woman over whom such a light would hover?"

They said to him: "Certainly this is the woman called Rivaleh the Pious."

He wanted to send for her, but the people said: "The invitation is unnecessary, for she will surely come by herself to ask alms from you, sir, because she busies herself with charitable deeds."

The next day after prayer the Besht said: "I can see her approaching, and she has made up her mind not to take less than forty golden coins from me. You will see what I am going to do to her."

The woman came and said to the Besht: "There are several poor sick people in our community. I hope that you, sir, will give a generous gift."

He gave her one sixer. She did not utter a word, and just motioned that she did not want to take it. So he put before her another sixer, and she still did not accept it. He said to her: "Who nominated you to be a collector of charity and to steal from the charity fund?"

She did not utter a syllable in reply, and she was not offended. These words did not make any impression on her because she held firmly to the traits of humbleness and humility. She considered herself as lowly as sand. She did not leave him until he had given her forty golden coins.

Toward evening she returned to him and said: "There is a doctor who is very sick. Pray that he live because he is in critical condition."

He said: "There will be one less adulterer in this world."

She said: "Who says that he is an adulterer?"

He said to the people who stood there: "Do I speak the truth?"

They said: "It is the truth."

She answered: "He's the sort of person who has never seen a paint brush in a tube.[1] Furthermore, he is ignorant and does not know the severity of the sin. If he had known the seriousness of the crime he would not have committed it."

Actually the Besht had heard the accusation about him in heaven, and had repeated the accusation before her so that she would be able to commend his merits. The appeal that she made was accepted above and the doctor recovered from his sickness.

When she visited her husband's grave she would rap with her stick on the grave and say these words: "Hershel, Hershel, go before the throne of God and pray that your sons will be poor so that they will not go astray from God's way."

96] *The Righteous Woman and her Sons*

ONCE, RIVALEH THE PIOUS' TWO SONS, RABBI ISAAC and Rabbi Joseph, came to her for the Sabbath to fulfill the mitzvah of honoring their mother, and they arrived on Thursday. The people of the town came to welcome them. They recognized some old friends, and the affection between them was reawakened.

The following day after prayer Rivaleh the Pious set the table and offered food to her sons. She sat at the table with them and said: "My children, there is one thing that I would like to ask you to do for me."

They said: "We will certainly do everything that you tell us."

She said to them: "Shake hands with me as a promise that you will fulfill my wishes."

They said to her: "Mother, how can you doubt us?"

She said: "Perhaps I want to ask a great thing of you, and I am afraid that you will not fulfill my wishes."

They pacified her about not shaking hands, and they promised to do her will.

She said: "Please go on your way immediately and do not observe the Sabbath here. God, blessed be He, gave me sons so that I shall have pleasure in the next world and not in this world."

They said to her: "Is it possible that the townspeople will let us leave here on the day before the Sabbath?"

She said to them: "Send your wagons outside the town, and I will lead you through the backyards so that the townspeople will not see you." And so they did.

97] *The Blessing of Rabbi Pinḥas*

I heard from Rabbi Samuel the leader,[1] as he was telling it to the rabbi, that he and Rabbi Ber, son of Bunim, were traveling before Rosh Hashanah to redeem prisoners, and they came to the Great Maggid. The Maggid wanted them to stay for the holiday, but they refused, saying: "We have to redeem prisoners for the coming Rosh Hashanah."

They went on their way and they came to Rabbi Pinḥas. He wanted them to stay, but they refused him also for the same reason. Rabbi Pinḥas said: "Rabbi Samuel, you return home and redeem prisoners. Rabbi Ber, you remain here." But Rabbi Samuel did not want to leave Rabbi Ber behind. Rabbi Pinḥas said: "Rabbi Ber has to stay here because he does not have children."

Rabbi Samuel said: "I too have the same need."

He said to him: "You will return on the coming Simhath Torah." And Rabbi Ber remained there for Rosh Hashanah.

Before the holiday Rabbi Ber became ill and could not go to the synagogue to pray on Rosh Hashanah. Rabbi Pinḥas came

home in order to read the Torah aloud, and he asked Rabbi Ber
to come up to the Torah. They dressed him and led him to the
Torah scroll, and after the second blessing he recovered. Furthermore, a daughter was born to him in that year, and she was the
daughter-in-law of Rabbi Pinḥas. Rabbi Samuel came on Simhath
Torah, and during that year a daughter was born to him as well.

98] *The Besht's Combat With a Witch*

I HEARD FROM MY FATHER-IN-LAW, AND ALSO FROM
the rabbi of our community, that once, when the Besht was still
living in the inn in the village, they needed rain and he prayed for
rain. There was a witch who had a demon and she used sorcery to
prevent it from raining, but the Besht's prayer set aside her sorcery. The demon told her that the Besht had spoiled her sorcery.

The witch went to the Besht's mother and said to her: "Tell
your son to leave me alone; otherwise, I will put a spell on him."

His mother thought that the quarrel between them concerned
some debts for brandy, and she said to him: "My child, don't
bother with that gentile woman because she is a witch."

He said to his mother: "I am not afraid of her." And he
continued on his way and prayed for rain.

The witch went to his mother a second time, and after that she
sent her demon against him. But when the demon came to him he
could not approach within four steps.

The Besht told him: "How dare you come to me? Return
immediately and do harm to that gentile woman through a small
glass window." And so he did. Afterwards the Besht imprisoned
him in the forest so that he would never be able to move from
there.

When the Besht became famous he traveled with some people
through that forest. He stopped and went into the forest. He
peeped in and saw the demon sitting in his prison, and he laughed
a great deal. They asked him why he was laughing, and he told
them this story.[1]

99] *A Choice of Punishment*

I HEARD THIS FROM RABBI JOEL WHO WAS A MAGGID in the holy community of Nemirov. Once the Besht was traveling on the road and he heard a herald from above: "I am going to punish you in one of two ways: either the Haidamaks will attack you and rob you of your money," and he carried about two hundred red coins, "or you will have a high fever." I forgot the third possibility.

The Besht wanted to save the money because he had great debts at home, and so he chose the high fever. And so it was.

He came to the holy community of Shargorod on the eve of the Sabbath, and he became very weak because of the fever. Nevertheless he went to the beth-hamidrash and prayed before the ark. The prayer was like a leaping flame. After the prayer he was so weak that they supported him under his shoulders and led him to the inn. He told them to bring him a very good wine. After one glass he recovered immediately. He said jokingly: "This wine is so good it would be worth it to be sick another hour for a second glass."

100] *The Revenant*

I HEARD THIS FROM RABBI FALK, THE HEAD OF THE court of the holy community of Chechelnik. Once, at the conclusion of the Sabbath, the Besht ordered his stepfather's son-in-law, Rabbi Joseph Ashkenazi,* to read him from *Ein Ya'akov* while he lay on the bed and listened. At one place the Besht said torah concerning a saying in the *Ein Ya'akov*. Then Rabbi Joseph con-

* The exact relation between the Besht and Rabbi Joseph Ashkenazi is not clear from the text. In tale 40 he is mentioned as the Besht's cantor. If the present reading of the text is correct, this is the only reference in the book which implies that the Besht's mother remarried. This is, of course, a possibility, since we are able to infer from tales 4 and 98 that she lived some years after the death of the Besht's father.

tinued to recite the *Ein Ya'akov*, and during the reading Rabbi Joseph envisioned a maggid, whose name was also Rabbi Joseph, who had passed away about three-quarters of a year before that time. He saw him entering the house dressed in Sabbath clothes and wearing a hat, and he said aloud: "A good week to our rabbi." He carried a stick in his hand and he walked as if he were alive.

When Rabbi Joseph saw him he became very frightened and the book of *Ein Ya'akov* fell from his hand. The Besht passed his hand over Rabbi Joseph's face, and Rabbi Joseph Ashkenazi saw the dead man no more.

The Besht said to him: "Take a candle in your hand and stand on the side." He used to say: "One candle hurts the eyes and so do three, but two candles are kind to the eyes."

Rabbi Joseph stepped aside, and the dead man remained with the Besht for about half an hour or more. Rabbi Joseph Ashkenazi saw the Besht talking with him. Then the Besht called to Rabbi Joseph Ashkenazi in these words: *"Deutsch,** come over here." He went over to him and recited more of the *Ein Ya'akov*.

During their study the Besht began to chide him, and he said: "Why were you frightened? Did Rabbi Joseph the maggid slaughter a *deutscher* like you while he was alive so that you were afraid of him after his death?"

Rabbi Joseph asked him: "Why was I privileged to see him?"

The Besht said to him: "Because you read aloud to me, and I recited before you, and my words purified you. We were united as one, and because of that, you were able to see him. If your mind had been stronger, you would have heard what he said to me, and you, too, would have been able to ask him whatever your heart wished. Moreover, you would have been made known to him, and you would be able to envision him at any time."

Rabbi Joseph grieved about this matter very much because seeing the soul of a righteous man is at the level of prophecy, as it is said in the book *Sha'arei Kedusha* of Rabbi Ḥayyim Vital.[1] Rabbi Joseph asked the Besht why he had come and what his

* The Besht refers to his name Ashkenazi, which means the "German" in Hebrew.

needs were, and the Besht told him that he came because it was necessary for him to come.

101] *The Redemptions of Sparks*

I HEARD THIS FROM RABBI JACOB, THE HEAD OF THE court in the holy community of Smela, who heard it from his father, Rabbi Meir Harif, God bless his memory. Once the Besht came to the rabbi of the holy community of Polonnoye. I am not sure whether it happened in the holy community of Nemirov or in the holy community of Shargorod. The Besht came a few days prior to the Sabbath, and he did not eat during all those days. The rabbi urged him to eat, but he answered: "Please excuse me from eating because there are great sparks here and it is difficult to redeem them.* When I do not redeem them they are dangerous and kill men. Therefore, I do not want to eat."

At the conclusion of the Sabbath he ordered food brought before him and he ate. After the meal he called aside the rabbi, God bless his memory, and he said: "Know that it was revealed to me from heaven that in the villages around the city there are two melamdim who carry some of the sparks that I have to redeem. From heaven it was made to appear that the men would believe themselves to be sick so that they would come to the city to be cured. Station your servant at the city gate so that he may bring them to you. Have pity on them and do not give them any respect and honor. I want you, sir, to promise me to advise them to come to me to be cured. Urge them to go to the mikveh because they will be reluctant to go there as they believe themselves to be sick. Tell them that I like people to come to me pure from the mikveh. Lend them shirts and coats for the Sabbath because they are poor. On the Sabbath they should dine with the householders and not

---

* The sparks of light were scattered in the world after the breaking of the vessels. Elevating or redeeming these sparks from the lower depths (*tikkun*) is one of the main functions of the tsaddik according to Lurianic mysticism and Hasidic thought. See Scholem, *Major Trends in Jewish Mysticism*, pp. 265–68, 330; and Dresner, *The Zaddik*, pp. 148–221.

with you, sir. Whisper in my ear when they come to the beth-hamidrash even though I will be praying the eighteen benedictions."

And so they did. After the meal they came to the rabbi's house, but they did not give them even a cup of mead. And so it was in the morning as well. They ate at the third meal and then they gave them mead.

After the Havdalah the Besht was filled with joy, and he took his tobacco pipe and went to the small house where he slept. The rabbis wanted to go after him as well. The two melamedim came and asked him to let them into the Besht's room.

He said to them: "Come with me," and they entered with the rabbi.

The Besht said to the rabbi: "They do not need a remedy. The shirts and the coats are to be given to them as presents. Let them go in peace."

And the melamedim were not aware of a single thing.

102] *The Reader's Stand of Rabbi Samson*

I HEARD FROM THE RABBI OF OUR COMMUNITY that the Besht did not want to go to the holy community of Annopol. He said: "There is nothing for me to do there since Rabbi Samson of that holy community has already corrected whatever was necessary."

Once Rabbi Gershon, the Besht's brother-in-law, stayed there over the Sabbath, and then he returned and said to the Besht: "Rabbi Samson's great light illuminated my thoughts."

The Besht said: "Do not fool yourself."

Once they sent for the Besht and asked him to come to that community. During the meal the Besht sat opposite the window. He opened the window and he looked through it constantly.

Rabbi Joseph of Kamenka wondered about it and wanted to know the reason why he looked through the window so often. What was he doing? When the Besht turned away from the window Rabbi Joseph closed it. When the Besht wanted to look through the window he opened it, and Rabbi Joseph closed it again. He did this a third time until the Besht scolded him and said: "Who is closing this window?"

Rabbi Joseph said: "I am. The cold gets into the house through the window. Besides, why do you open it every time?"

He said: "Do you not see Rabbi Samson's reader's stand shining from the earth to heaven?" They told me that at that time there was a dump there, and Rabbi Samson's beth-hamidrash had stood on that spot.

He said: "Today I understand what Rabbi Gershon, your brother-in-law, meant."

103] *The Dismissed* Arrendator

I heard that there was an *arrendator* who lived near the holy community of Medzhibozh. Another man came and paid more for the *arrendeh* and the first *arrendator* was dismissed from the village. He was in debt to the master of that village, but he did not have sufficient money to pay the debt. Both the master and the new *arrendator* forbade the people to let the man leave the village to go anywhere. In spite of that, the former *arrendator* traveled to see the Besht. When the new *arrendator* learned about it he reported it to the master, saying, "The former *arrendator* went to a sorcerer to enchant you."

The master was angry with him and placed his son in prison.

The *arrendator* did not find the Besht at home because he was in the holy community of Kamenka. He followed him to that town, but he did not find him there because the Besht had gone home. He followed after him and caught up with him on the road.

The Besht said to him: "What can I possibly do for you while I am traveling? Follow me to my home."

On their way the Besht perceived that the master had placed the *arrendator*'s son in prison. He said: "We do not have time to waste."

They came to a river, and the Besht immersed himself in it.

Coming out from the river he said to him: "Return home, and immediately upon your arrival in the village go to the manor house."

And so he did. When the master saw him through the window he was frightened lest he be hurt by his magic, and he chased the son away from the prison. He sent his servant to drive the *arrendator* and his family away from the village. And so it was. Then the master sent a letter to the governor of the holy community of Medzhibozh containing a serious complaint about the Besht in these words: "There is a sorcerer in your town."

The governor answered him: "See to it that you make the utmost effort to appease the Besht because he is not a sorcerer. If you do not appease him, heaven will punish you."

The master immediately sent a wagon with chickens and all sorts of flour to appease the Besht.

104] *The Besht's* Devekut

I HEARD FROM THE RABBI OF THE HOLY COMMUNITY of Polonnoye that because of his devotion the Besht could not communicate with people. His words lacked order. His well-known rabbi* had taught him to recite each day the chapter of *Happy are they that are upright in the way*[1] and other special psalms. He revealed to him wisdom[2] by which he could talk with people and continue his devotion. He used to recite these psalms every day.[3]

105] *The Besht Resuscitates a Child*

I HEARD FROM RABBI PESAH, THE SON OF RABBI Jacob of Kamenka, that while the Besht was traveling he came to a city, and a herald told him that he should stay as a guest in a certain house. He came to that house, and they refused to receive him as a guest because the son of the householder was seriously

* Ahijah of Shiloh, see tale 41.

ill. The Besht sent his scribe to the house, and the woman said: "How is it possible for you to stay here overnight?" Don't you see that the boy is sick and I am in great sorrow." And she cursed the Besht.

The householder did not dare interfere. He went out to appease the Besht and told him that it was impossible to stay there. The Besht promised that if he remained with him as a guest the boy would live, and so he was received in the home.

The Besht went immediately to the mikveh and he perceived that the boy's condition was poor. He ordered that no one remain in the house. Everybody went to another house. He ordered his scribe to leave the house as well. He would call him to ask for wine for the kiddush since this took place on the eve of the holy Sabbath.

The Besht remained alone with the boy. He prayed Minhah near him. He remained awake long into the night.

The scribe was afraid that the Besht would endanger himself, God forbid, by his great efforts in praying for the sick boy, since it was a dangerous situation. The scribe went to the door and slowly opened it, and he heard the Besht saying to the boy's soul: "Enter this body. You must enter it because I can not swear a false oath."

The scribe did not know whether the boy was dead or still alive. The boy had a little bit life in him. The scribe went away from the door, and after a short while he returned and entered. He found the Besht lying on the floor with his arms and legs stretched out.

The Besht stood up and said: "I told you, didn't I, to enter the boy's body?" And he shouted: "Hirsh, bring me wine for the kiddush." He ate with the scribe, and he did not sleep the entire night. In the morning he gave the scribe instructions and medicines, and then he went to pray in the beth-hamidrash.

The boy's mother gathered that the child had recovered, and she began to sob. The scribe heard her and asked: "Why are you crying?"

She said to him: "How can I not cry after I cursed such a pious man."

He answered her: "Do not cry. My rabbi is a good man and he will forgive you."

When the Besht returned from prayer he also heard her crying. He asked the scribe about it and learned the reason. He sent the scribe to her and told him: "Tell her not to cry. She should prepare a good dinner for the third meal. I promise her that the boy will sit with us at the table."

The reason why the Besht lay on the floor with his hands and legs extended was his agreement to accept "fiery lashes"[1] for his oath to cure the boy. The soul was compelled to reenter the boy's body. His action ensured that the boy would live more than sixty years and that he would have sons, and he would earn a good living all his life. From this we see that the time for the boy's death had come, and therefore the Besht had to pray for the number of years he would live, for his livelihood, and for his having children.[2]

106] *The Magical Enkindling of a Tree*

RABBI PESAḤ TOLD ME STILL MORE. ONCE THE Besht traveled from Kamenka to his home, and Rabbi Barukh of Kamenka accompanied him and rode in a separate wagon. The scribe sat with him, and a wagon filled with flour followed after them. The Besht said: "We will pray Minhah in such and such place."

This was in the winter time and it was intensely cold. They were still a few versts from that place, and they were becoming chilled to the bone. They said: "It is impossible to reach that place. It is still far away and we will freeze." Even the Besht's servant said, "We will get very cold."

They were traveling through the forest. The Besht ordered them to stop. He touched a tree with his finger and the tree was enkindled. They warmed themselves by the fire. The servant took off his boots and dried the rag that was wrapped around his feet. Then they traveled to such and such place.

As they were leaving that spot Rabbi Barukh looked at the

tree to see what would happen to it, and the Besht scolded him and told him not to look back.

107] *The Choice*

I heard from Rabbi Falk the Cohen, that his father-in-law, Rabbi Shmeril, did not have a son. The Besht used to be his guest, and as he did not have a special house for him, he used to stay in Rabbi Falk's house. The women moved out to the neighbor's, and they cooked there and brought the food to the house at dinner time.

Once, a day before he was leaving, Rabbi Falk wanted to ask the Besht to pray for him so that he would have a son. He stayed near him, but he could not speak because of his embarrassment The following day, before the departure of the Besht, he again remained close by him in order to talk to him, but again he was too embarrassed.

Suddenly the Besht said to him: "Send for your wife."

She came and the Besht took his stick in his hand and said to her: "See to it that you give birth to a boy. If not, I will break your bones with this stick."

And so it was. That year she gave birth to a son and his name was Rabbi David. This was the Rabbi David who became head of the court in the holy community of Chechelnik.

It was the custom of Rabbi Shmeril that even when his wife gave birth to a daughter he would go to the Besht to receive an amulet from him and to give him two red coins or more, since at that time he was a merchant and he had about three thousand golden coins. When his son was born he went to the Besht to receive an amulet from him as was his custom.

The Besht said to him: "Did your wife give birth to a son?"

He said: "Yes."

The Besht said to him: "Know that you will no longer have money. They gave you a choice between having money or a son, and I made the right choice for you so that you could have a son."

And so it was. He lost money on all the merchandise that he bought until he had nothing left. After that he was accepted as a maggid in the holy community of Zwierzchowka. When I knew him he was a frequent visitor at the home of the rabbi of the holy community of Kosov. At that time he was a rabbinical judge in the holy community of Savran.[1]

108] *The Fish and the Dog*

I HEARD FROM THE RABBI OF THE HOLY COMMUNITY of Polonnoye and from the rabbi of our community that Rabbi Nahman of Kosov[1] had a relative named Rabbi Yudel of Chudnov, whose father, Rabbi Joseph, was a preacher.

It was Rabbi Yudel's way not to accept favors from other people. He enjoyed the fruit of his own labor. He was in the iron ore business.

Once he went to a mine where he wanted to keep the Sabbath. The householder said to him: "What will you eat, sir? I do not have fish, and you would not eat the meat because you did not examine the knife. I advise you to go to another mine nearby where there is a wealthy man, and he certainly will have fish and a shohet. You, sir, can go to this man." And so he did.

Near the mine the road passed through a pond. The water was not usually deep, but when it rained or when the snow melted the pond became deeper. Rabbi Yudel was not aware of this and he wanted to go across. A dog ran forward into the pond and sank in the water. The dog was drowning and it howled pitifully. Its cries stirred the heart of the Hasid and tears fell from his eyes. He saw that it was impossible to go across the water, and he returned to the mine and asked the householder to do everything possible to bring fish for the Sabbath. The householder went to urge the fishermen and they caught a large pike.

The householder said: "I have lived in this village for several years and I have never seen such a fish." They prepared several dishes from it.

On the Sabbath eve Rabbi Yudel was sitting by the table singing songs, and he fell asleep with his head on the table. His father appeared to him in his dream and said: "Know that I was reincarnated as that fish. The informer who I always condemned during my life was reincarnated as the dog that drowned. His redemption was that he drowned in order to save you. I was reincarnated as this fish because I persecuted him.² The tears that you shed when the dog drowned redeemed me. Be careful, my son, how you eat this fish."

When he came to the Besht, the Besht told him that he used to say that Rabbi Yudel was a reincarnation of Samuel the Prophet.

109] *The Dance of Rabbi Yudel*

I heard from Rabbi Shneur, the grandson of Rabbi Nahman, that Rabbi Yudel visited with Rabbi Nahman in the holy community of Ladimir. Rabbi Nahman built a beth-hamidrash there, practically on the water, and the mikveh was next to the beth-hamidrash. On the Sabbath morning they went to the mikveh. Rabbi Nahman was very diligent, whereas Rabbi Yudel was a little lazy. While Rabbi Yudel was still taking off his clothes in the mikveh, Rabbi Nahman was praying before the ark. When Rabbi Yudel got out of the mikveh, he heard Rabbi Nahman singing *ha-Aderet ve-ha-Emunah*,¹ and he became very excited. He ran to the beth-hamidrash dressed only in a shirt, and he danced in the beth-hamidrash for about two hours.

110] *Rabbi Nahman's Sigh*

I heard from my father-in-law, God bless his memory, that when Rabbi Nahman sighed during prayer, he so broke the listener's heart that it seemed cut in two.

The Besht said: "Where Rabbi Nahman has visited, people

know what prayer is; where Rabbi Naḥman has not visited, people do not know what prayer is."

111] *Rabbi Naḥman's Prayer*

I HEARD THAT ONCE RABBI NAḤMAN, GOD BLESS HIS memory, passed through the holy community of Zolroveh with merchandise at the time of the morning prayer. He stopped his wagon opposite the beth-hamidrash. He took his tallith and tefillin and entered the beth-hamidrash. He wrapped himself in the tallith, put on the tefillin, and stood before the ark to pray without asking permission.

It was irritating to those who prayed that this visitor dared to stand before the ark without first asking permission. But when they heard words sweeter than nectar and honey issuing from his mouth, they took pleasure in it and kept silent. Nevertheless, they were angry. After the kaddish of our rabbis,[1] he started "*O Give Thanks Unto the God*"[2] before "Blessed be He who spoke."[3] They were furious and they thought to pull him away from the ark; however, since they wanted to hear his words and prayers, all the people in the beth-hamidrash attacked him and said: "How did you dare to stand before the ark without permission and to change the order of prayers from that followed by our fathers and forefathers who were the leaders of their generations?"

He answered them saying: "Who says that they are in paradise?"

When they heard his answer they became even more furious. The author of the book *Toledot Ya'akov Yosef*, who was then very old, was there. He had authorized one disciple, whose name was Rabbi Zalman, to preach for him. Rabbi Zalman shouted at Rabbi Naḥman harder than anyone else. Then Rabbi Alexander, who was the disciple of Rabbi Zalman, came and said: "Leave this man alone. He is always on the side of the Almighty."

And since I have told you this story let me add something.

112] *Rabbi Jacob Joseph's Prayer*

I heard from the rabbi who used to say: "The tsaddik Jacob Joseph, God bless his memory, used to say that it was easier for him to discuss ten subtle halakic questions than to say the eighteen benedictions one time.

113] *Pure Prayers*

I heard from Rabbi Zusya of Annopol that when he left his brother Elimelekh and traveled through Zholkva, "In the beth-hamidrash I prayed in someone's place, and the prayer was pure and clear like the prayers of the Besht. I did not know the reason until they told me that this was the very place where the author of the book *Toledot Ya'akov Yosef* used to stand."

114] *The Interruption of the Besht's Vision*

I heard this from the rabbi of our community. Before his death, when he was ill, the Besht did not have to lie down on his bed. He just became thin and his voice was affected. He used to sit in his house of seclusion. He lacked the energy to call his servant when he needed him, and so he hung a bell in the big house and attached a string to it that led to his small house. The Besht would pull the string, the bell would ring, and the servant would come to him.[1]

Once Rabbi David Forkes, God bless his memory, the maggid of the holy community of Medzhibozh, came in and asked him something. I heard from a man of the holy community of Bar that the question concerned "How to pray for a sick person with tales."[2] The Besht began to tell him, and as he was talking he became very excited and his face burned like a torch. Rabbi David was struck with fear, and he wanted to escape from the house, but he could not leave because he and the Besht were alone standing face to face.

In the meantime the Besht's daughter, Edel, long may she live, came and said to her father: "The day is over and it's dinnertime."

He immediately lost his color and became pale. He lay down to rest on his bed. He said to her: "My daughter, my daughter, what have you done to me?"

Rabbi David said: "She is right. It is time to eat."

The Besht said: "You did not know who was here. On one side stood Elijah the Prophet, God bless his memory, and on the other side stood my rabbi.* They spoke to me and I passed it on to you. When she came in she confused me, and they left."

The Besht said that he had named his daughter's soul from the Torah verse "*Esh Dat Lamo*" ("*A fiery law unto them*"),³ abbreviated Edel.

115] *Rabbi Leib's Death*

I HEARD FROM THE RABBI THAT RABBI LEIB WAS ONE of the masters of calculations,** and he worked at it every day and night. On the day that he passed away he went to the mikveh. When he left the bathhouse he encountered the Besht who said to him: "Hurry up and do your works," because the Besht had heard kedusha and "Bless Ye the Lord" recited in all the synagogues. Rabbi Leib could not walk because of the mud that was common in that time of year, and so he rode on horseback from one synagogue to the other. On the very same day he passed away from this world.

116] *Rabbi Aaron in Heaven*

I HEARD FROM THE RABBI OF OUR COMMUNITY THAT there was a man in Kuty named Tektiner who always spoke against the group of Hasidim. Once, Rabbi Aaron, the Besht's

* Ahijah, the prophet of Shiloh. See tale 41.
** The masters of calculation tried to compute the time that the Messiah would come.

brother-in-law, heard him and quarreled with him. Tektiner jumped forward and plucked some hairs from Rabbi Aaron's beard. Rabbi Gershon, his brother, stood up and excommunicated him. Within a few days Tektiner died, and several years later Rabbi Aaron died.

During the seven days of mourning, Rabbi Gershon had a dream in which he saw his brother preaching and he ran to listen to him.[1] When he approached him he realized that it was a demon. He became furious and said: "Villain, how dare you take the shape of my brother?" He spat at it and it disappeared before his eyes.

Later, Rabbi Leib, the Preacher of Polonnoye, also saw Rabbi Aaron during the seven days of mourning. He recognized the signs and realized that it was Rabbi Aaron himself.[2] He asked him: "Why did a demon take your form?"

He said: "An impression of sins remained after me, and because of this impression, the demon had the power to assume my shape. Long life to my brother, Rabbi Gershon, who canceled this impression by his spittle."

He asked him: "Where are you now?"

He said to him: "In paradise."

He inquired about that man Tektiner to find out what he was doing.

He answered: "He is in paradise as well. It did not occur to me, and I did not think about it, but when he saw me in paradise, he said to me: 'I shall summon you to the Court of Heaven because you caused my death.' I was very frightened, and I took the hairs of my beard, which I had folded in a kerchief and put in my box, and brought them before the court. He only brought trouble on himself because they chased him away from paradise to Gehenna."

He asked him: "How are you and what do you do in paradise?"

He answered: "Lower paradise is still touched by corporeality. When Sabbath eve came I went to the synagogue. When I reached the door I did not see any of my acquaintances. I stood at the pulpit, and I prayed Minhah. Before we received the Sabbath, a voice was heard: 'Rabbi Aaron will receive the Sabbath before the ark.' I went before the ark and said, *"O come and let us sing unto the Lord."*[3] When I reached *A Psalm, a Song. For the sabbath day,*[4] everyone disappeared. I remained alone and I did not know where they had gone. I grieved about it the whole Sabbath because I missed the group. I ask you, sir, to pray for me so that I will be elevated with them on the following Sabbath."

The Preacher said to him: "You left your wife in great poverty, and you did not leave her enough food for even one meal."

He said: "There are two talers hidden in a box that I put away for a particular reason. Now she can take them."

When the Preacher awoke in the morning, he went to Rabbi Aaron's widow and told her to search in the box where she would find the two talers.

She answered: "There is absolutely no money there."

He urged her and she searched and found the two talers. She also found the hairs wrapped in a kerchief.

From this you can infer how clear and specific were the dreams of the Hasidim.

117] *The Sick Woman*

I HEARD THIS FROM MY FRIENDS WHO HEARD IT FROM Rabbi Nahum of Chernobyl. Once the Besht was in the holy community of Chmielnik where there was a proofreader whose wife was sick. The inn where the Besht was staying was near the house of the rabbi, the head of the court, the son-in-law of one of the elders. The proofreader went to the Besht to ask him for a remedy for his wife, but the Besht refused to give him one. Moreover, the Besht became furious with him and said some unpleasant things to him. This irritated the rabbi, the head of the court.

In the evening when everyone left, the rabbi asked the Besht why he had refused to cure the wife of the proofreader.

He answered: "She is a pious woman, and she protects this city from the robbers in the forest by her weakness. When the robbers will disappear from the forest, her health will be restored automatically."

He asked him why he had been angry with the proofreader, and he answered: "I saw an impression of charges against him. By my anger I canceled them."

118] *The Adulterer*

ONCE THAT RABBI SAW A MAN COME TO SEE THE Besht. The Besht was very fond of him and they talked together. That man was a well-known adulterer. The rabbi asked: "Why were you so friendly to that man who is famous for his adulteries?"

The Besht answered him: "Are you better than he is?"

The rabbi examined himself and searched his deeds and did not find anything.

He said: "I swear that you speak a lie." The Besht said: "I see adultery on you and tomorrow I shall inform you of the details."

The following day he said: "You took a vow of abstinence and you disregarded it. That night I heard that the *Rambam* decided that when a man denies himself his wife it is as if he said she is like a mother to him. Look it up in his work. Perhaps you will find it there."

Then the rabbi admitted that the Besht was correct, and he found the decision in the *Rambam*.

A case like that occurred to the Besht three times. (Another version follows later.)[1]

119] *The Besht Cures by Bloodletting*

I HEARD THIS FROM THE RABBI OF OUR COMMUNITY. Once the Besht started on a journey, and when he stopped for the night in a certain place, he heard a voice: "Return immediately to your home because Rabbi Joseph is very weak."

He told his servants to turn back, but they did not want to, and they said: "You, sir, have debts at home. Why should we return?" But they turned back and arrived home on Friday morning. He went to the mikveh before prayer. Following prayer he called a doctor and went with him to the sick person, who the Besht realized, was very weak and had lost the power of speech. The Besht told the doctor to let his blood, but the doctor refused, saying that it was very dangerous to do bloodletting.

The Besht said to him: "Are you certain that if you do not let his blood he will live?"

The doctor said: "No."

"So why are you afraid to let his blood?" Immediately the Besht ordered the bloodletting for Rabbi Joseph, and all the people gossiped about the Besht's actions. The Besht returned home. In about half an hour the sick person wanted them to give him a drink of water, and, thank God, he recovered.[1]

120] *The Death of Rabbi Joseph the Melamed*

I HEARD THIS FROM HIM AS WELL. ONCE, ON HIS way to Chmielnik, the Besht heard a herald's voice say that Rabbi Joseph, the melamed of that community, would die. When he came to the town, the people of the community wanted to pay the Besht to cure Rabbi Joseph, but he refused without revealing his reason. After the Besht left the town, a doctor came there, and he treated Rabbi Joseph and he recovered. The doctor was still there when the Besht returned to that community, and they told him that Rabbi Joseph had recovered by using the medication given to him by the doctor. During the time that the Besht was there, Rabbi Joseph asked the doctor to give him some ointment in a bandage to remove the lice from his head which had increased because of his illness. The doctor gave him a salve to annoint his head. He annointed his head with it and he died. Then the Besht revealed that the reason why he had refused to cure him was because of the herald's voice that he had heard.

121] *The Parable of the Dog*

I HEARD AS WELL FROM THAT RABBI THAT IN THE days of the Preacher of Polonnoye there was an informer in a certain city who caused great grief to the people of his town through his treachery. Once he became sick and then he died. The Preacher, God bless his memory, ordered the members of the burial society to tell him the time of the funeral. They told him and he dressed up in his coat and went to the funeral with Rabbi Meir Milkes of that holy community. When all the people saw the Preacher going to pay his respects, almost the entire city came, men and women. The informer's son was happy that the Preacher paid his father respect and had personally gone to the funeral.

The Preacher walked to the cemetery. When they came with the dead man, they laid the body down in the tent as usual. The Preacher approached and stood near the dead man to eulogize him. The informer's son was very pleased. Then the Preacher began his speech with a parable: "Once a master had a dog* called a brittany."

As soon as the informer's sons heard the opening of the parable they understood that his words would shame their father. They returned to the manor house to gather the master's servants and some loafers in order to disgrace or to beat the Preacher.

Rabbi Meir was very frightened. He took the Preacher by the end of his coat and whispered to him that the informer's sons had gone to the manor house to report about him. But the Preacher did not answer him, and he affectionately pushed him back four feet. He continued speaking: "This dog had a very good time with his master. He always used to catch all sorts of animals on the hunting trips taken by his master, as is the custom among the lords. One day the dog died." And the Preacher pointed to the dead man. "There was a great joy among the animals who were

* In common speech, the rich were often referred to as dogs. See Ben-zion Dinur, *Historical Writings*, Vol. 1 [*be-Mifneh ha-Dorot*] (Jerusalem, 1955), p. 100.

saved from being caught by that dog. The fox, the most clever animal, said to them: 'You fools, why are you so happy? If he had died before the rest of the hunting dogs learned to hunt from him, it would be proper to rejoice. Now that all the other dogs of the master have learned to hunt from him, it would have been better for you if this dog had remained alive. All the other dogs let him do the hunting since they knew that when they caught animals the brittany would come and snatch the game from them and bring it to the master and take credit for it.' They said to themselves, 'Why should we go to any trouble and then not receive any credit or appreciation from the master for our efforts?' So all the dogs stopped hunting. But now that this brittany is dead all the dogs will try to excel in hunting in order to gain the master's favor and reap the benefits. The result will be that several hunting dogs will be added. There is nothing to rejoice about! This is the parable, and its moral is as follows: The brittany dog is that informer who was considered highly by the master because of his reports about the people of the city. The rest of the dogs are the other informers who learned from him his slanderous ways. When the other informers realized that the master did not give them any credit because that informer snatched all the reports in his mouth and brought them to the master by himself, they stopped informing. But now that that dog has died, all the informers know that they will get credit and will be considered important by the master. You will be watched by many informers.[1]

When he finished his speech all the people realized that he was correct, and there was a great cry among those who stood there. After that the Preacher turned the face of the dead man downward. He slapped his cheek and quickly stepped back to Rabbi Meir. He went to the wagon which stood ready for him near the cemetery and fled.

On the way Rabbi Meir heard the Preacher arguing with the informer, but he did not see the dead man. The Preacher showed him that one of the wagon's wheels could not roll because the informer was holding it while telling him that he was grateful for being shamed. But he asked him not to speak against him so harshly in the future.

The Besht, God bless his memory, said that a brittany dog was standing nearby so that immediately after the informer was buried his soul would be reincarnated into this dog; however, the disgrace contained in the Preacher's eulogy saved him from that punishment.

I forgot the main point. After the Preacher finished explaining the moral of the parable, he said: "This is the meaning of the phrase *Wherefore I praise the dead that are already dead.*[2] If he had died before the rest of the informers had learned from him, his death would have been found praiseworthy. But this was no longer possible. The living could not rejoice at his death because of the other informers who were still alive."

122] *The Present Generation*

I HEARD FROM THAT RABBI THAT AFTER A WHILE, because of our many sins and the immorality of our generation, he heard that the Preacher, God bless his memory, said: "I wish that the informer were alive today. He would have been considered a Hasid in comparison with the wicked people of this generation."

123] *A Dowry*

I HEARD FROM A MAN WHO HEARD FROM RABBI TSEVI, the scribe, God bless his memory, that the Besht had arranged a marriage between two orphans whom he and the famous Rabbi Ze'ev Kotses had educated in their homes. The girl had grown up in the Besht's home, and the boy had grown up in the home of Rabbi Ze'ev.[1] The Besht pledged two hundred golden coins for her dowry.

On the wedding day before the veiling of the bride, our teacher and rabbi, Ze'ev, God bless his memory, said to the Besht, God bless his memory, that he would not go with the groom to the veiling of the bride until the Besht paid the two hundred golden coins which he had pledged.

The Besht thought he was joking and said: "Don't you trust me for that money?"

He answered him: "I assure you that I will not change my

stand. I have to maintain the groom in my home and study with him, and 'where there is no meal, there is no Torah.'[2] "

In the meantime, Rabbi Leib of Kremenets came to the Besht's house. The Besht gave him the seat of honor and ordered that a glass of wine be brought to him. Rabbi Leib said the blessing and the Besht answered: "Amen." Then Rabbi Leib told the Besht the reason for his visit. The governor of the city had sent for him and had showed him a letter from a master who lived eight versts away from the holy community of Medzhibozh. The nobleman had written that as stipulated in a note the Besht owed him a thousand golden coins for the ransom of prisoners, and he wanted the Besht to pay the debt immediately. The governor said that if the Besht would not pay the master in full at once he would send him to that master in chains. And they informed the Besht that he had to pay the debt at once.

When the Besht heard these things he shouted to his servant to harness the horses to the wagon, and he said to Rabbi Leib: "Go immediately to that master and pay him that amount and then hurry back for the veiling of the bride." And the Besht did not permit him to return home.

Rabbi Leib was surprised, but he did not question him. He immediately set out for that master. On the way he stopped at an inn whose owner he knew, and he told him the reason for his journey. He was in such a great rush that the innkeeper was surprised. Rabbi Leib continued on, and he came to the master at noontime when they were having lunch. Rabbi Leib waited until the end of the meal and then entered the master's house.

The master immediately asked him whether he brought the money from the Besht.

He answered him: "Yes."

The master respectfully offered him a place to sit and gave him mead to drink.

Rabbi Leib himself wondered how the payment would actually be made. He said to himself: "Perhaps it is the intention of the Besht to have the master admire one of the Besht's good horses and then be willing to accept one of them instead of the money." As he was thinking, something occurred to him and he said to the nobleman: "I have to talk to you about a private matter." He went with him to another room, and he said to the master: "I know that you are a righteous and a very faithful person, and you would not want even a pittance of someone else's money. Now I want to pay you that amount, but according to our calculation we do not owe you that amount for the prisoners, and if you take the money you will be committing robbery, God forbid."

The master was very grateful and answered him: "I love you very much for saving me from committing robbery and from the punishment I would receive in the next world." He immediately searched for the receipts for the *arrendators* who were ransomed. He calculated the amount and then he took the note of the Besht and threw it into the fire. He said to Rabbi Leib: "On the contrary, I owe the Besht two hundred golden coins." And he gave him eleven red coins.

Rabbi Leib said to him: "You are still short two golden coins."

The master saw that he was not being given special favor and he continued to talk with him affectionately. He loved Rabbi Leib for saving him from the sin of robbery, and he gave him the two golden coins. Rabbi Leib started on his way back. When he came to the inn he jumped from the wagon to tell the innkeeper about the wonders.

Meanwhile, the Besht, at home, was irritated: "That fool. He is stopping on his way to relate the story."

Afterwards Rabbi Leib returned to the Besht and wanted to tell him about the affair, but the Besht answered: "I know about it. Hurry and give me the money. It is already late for the veiling of the bride." He became angry with him for stopping on his way back. Then he said: "Now it is the time for the wedding." (And he acted as one of the jesters.)

124] *Rabbi Abraham and the Besht*

I HEARD FROM THE RABBI OF OUR COMMUNITY THAT once Rabbi Pinhas of Korets*[1] and the rabbi of the holy community of Rovno traveled around collecting ransom money in order

* One of the early Lithuanian Hasidim (about 1726 to about 1791).

to redeem a relative of theirs who was in prison. Rabbi Pinḥas said to the rabbi of Rovno: "I heard that the Besht observes the Sabbath in the holy community of Kamenka. Let us go to him. Perhaps he will bring us help, and we can avoid having to take a bumpy ride."

They decided to go to him, and they hurried in order to reach him before he went to the mikveh, since afterwards it was impossible to discuss anything with him. However, when they met him he had already been to the mikveh and was dressed in his Sabbath clothes.

In the beth-hamidrash his followers told them: "Let yourselves be seen by him and he will certainly know your needs even without your telling him."

And so they did. They came to the door of the beth-hamidrash, and when he saw them he motioned to them with his hand to leave.

After that Rabbi Pinḥas heard that his father, our teacher and rabbi, Abraham Aba, had arrived at the holy community of Mariupol across the river. He went to him, since he was afraid that his father would want to keep the Sabbath with the Besht even though he considered him insignificant. Rabbi Abraham always used to say to his son: "Why are you going to the Besht?" Therefore, Rabbi Pinḥas was afraid that his father would be disrespectful and impudent to the Besht in one way or another, and he would be shamed and disgraced, God forbid. Rabbi Pinḥas asked him where he would observe the Sabbath and he said: "Why should I go to the Besht? I will observe the Sabbath here and preach here."

In the morning when the Besht started the prayer of "O Give Thanks Unto the Lord," Rabbi Abraham came to the beth-hamidrash of Kamenka and stood near the holy ark before which the Besht was praying. Rabbi Pinḥas' father was praying in a loud voice, and Rabbi Pinḥas was afraid that his father would confuse the Besht and that the Besht would scold him. But the Besht did not say a word to him until after the morning prayer.

It was the Sabbath and also the first of the month, and they had to take out two scrolls of the Torah. The Besht took one of the scrolls, and Rabbi Pinḥas' father took the other one, and he followed the Besht to the reader's stand. The Besht saw him holding the Torah scroll, and he scolded him and told someone: "Take the Torah scroll from him."

Rabbi Abraham kept quiet and did not answer back. Rabbi Pinḥas was surprised. After the prayer Rabbi Abraham went to one of the elders of the town across the river. He ate there and slept a little while, and then he went to preach in the synagogue. But he returned to the Besht at the time of the third meal.

It was the custom of the people of Kamenka that when the Besht visited with them, they placed a table for themselves on the side, while the Besht and the guests sat around the main table. When they saw Rabbi Abraham coming they called him to sit with them since they knew that he was an aggressive Lithuanian,* and he might interrupt the Besht's talk and confuse him. They called to him: "Rabbi Abraham, come sit with us," and they gave him a glass of mead.

When the Besht began to say torah, Rabbi Abraham left his place. He stood in the center of the room opposite the Besht and stared at his face. Rabbi Pinḥas was afraid to tell him not to stare at the Besht's face because one must honor one's father. So Rabbi Abraham stood opposite the Besht and Rabbi Pinḥas was embarrassed. When the Besht stopped saying torah, he returned to his place. After that they lit the candles, and they ate some meat.

The Besht began speaking again: "I have to say one more thing. It was not on my mind to say it, but I heard it said in paradise in my name." The Besht began talking, and Rabbi Abraham once again left his place and stood opposite the Besht until he finished his talk. Then he returned to his place. They said the blessing for the food and prayed the evening prayer. After the prayer Rabbi Abraham said to Rabbi Pinḥas: "It is he himself and no one else, he himself and no one else."

Rabbi Pinḥas said: "What have you seen in him."

He said to him: "Do you think that I did not mind his scolding me at the reading of the Torah? But I waited until the

* Lithuania was the center for mitnaggedim, the opponents of the Hasidim.

end. Let me tell you, my son, that that night I had a dream in which I entered paradise and the Prince of the Torah entered and repeated a torah said by the Besht. When I awoke from my sleep I remembered it very well, and I came here for that reason. And what I had already heard I heard again from his holy mouth."

I did not hear from the rabbi anything about the prisoner and I forgot to ask about him.

125] *A Combat in Magic*

I HEARD THAT THERE WAS A PRIEST, ASSOCIATED with the governor of the holy community of Medzhibozh, who caused great trouble to the Jews of that town. The people of the city always urged the Besht to pray for his banishment from the city, and he used to say: "I do not want to provoke him because he is a great sorcerer: He will sense it the moment that I begin to deal with him." And he did nothing about him at all.

Once the priest severely oppressed the people of the city, and they went to the Besht with a great outcry and complained.

He answered them: "What can I do with you? I will begin to deal with him slowly and carefully so that he will not notice it."

He started with prayers, but the priest sensed it immediately. Once while ascending a mountain in a wagon, the Besht encountered the priest coming down the mountain. The Besht said that he would have a downfall. "If it were the other way around, God forbid, it would not have been good for me."

And so it was. Officials came from the governor of the city and confiscated all of the priest's property and fortune. He was dismissed from his post, and he had to pay the claims of every Jew in the town until he was ruined. He left the town in a broken-down wagon harnessed to a single horse.[1]

126] *A Combat in Magic: A Second Version*

I HEARD ANOTHER VERSION FROM RABBI LEIB OF Sinami[1] in which the priest bewitched the Besht. While the Besht was crossing the bridge near the mill, the priest began to sweep the wagon and the horses from the bridge. The Besht brought the wagon to a halt and braced the axle with boards. The people went to hire gentiles who pulled the horses and the wagon.

Then the Besht said: "Since he senses my opposition he will certainly meet with an evil end."

Rabbi Leib was a distinguished and learned man. He was the brother of Rabbi David, a scribe of Annopol.

127] *The Jewish Thief*

I ALSO HEARD FROM HIM AND LATER FROM THE RABBI of our community that once a merchant came to the city of Whitefield from Breslau with a wagon loaded with fabric. He arrived at night, but he did not want to open the store. He ordered the horses to be unharnessed from the wagon, and he said to himself: "Who could steal such a huge wagon?" He left the wagon with the merchandise outside. Later a thief came and stole it. He harnessed other horses to the wagon and escaped with the wagon and with all the merchandise. In the morning they saw that the wagon with the merchandise had been stolen. They ran to search all the streets and all the crossroads, but they found neither the wagon nor the thief.

The merchant sent a letter to the Besht. When the messenger came to the Besht he found him standing by the mezuzah about to leave to attend a berith in the holy community of Derazne, for he was being honored with the mitzvah of the berith. He received the letter from the messenger, and he told him: "Wait until I return." The messenger waited.

The Besht slept overnight on the road. In the morning he drove to the city. When the Besht reached the outskirts of the city, he saw in the distance the wagon with the merchandise approaching the city on another road. He said to Rabbi Ze'ev, the scribe: "Do you see the wagon driven by two horses?"

He said: "I do."

He said: "The messenger that they sent to me came for this wagon with the stolen merchandise in it. When we arrive at the town ask what inn he is at and tell him to give you the wagon and the merchandise because you stole it."

When they arrived in the city, Rabbi Ze'ev, the scribe, immediately went to the inn where the thief was staying, and he saw him standing and praying. He dared not confront him with those words since he was praying like an honest and innocent man. The scribe went to the Besht and told him the situation.

He said to him: "Return immediately because he will soon drive away with the merchandise and both the wagon and the merchandise will be lost."

The scribe went a second time and found him eating breakfast. He asked the innkeeper whether he drank a lot of brandy like a thief. He told him that he drank just two groschen worth as everyone does. He left again with empty hands.

The Besht said to him: "Go and tell him the following signs: that he hid for three days in the forest until all his pursuers passed by and that he slept overnight in a certain place. Name for him all the places in which he slept overnight until he came to the city of Derazne."

The scribe went and told him all the signs. Then the thief gave up and said: "Indeed, it is true. Take the wagon with the merchandise."

The scribe ordered the innkeeper to watch the wagon with the merchandise.

When it was time to eat at the berith, the thief said to himself: "Now that I am a poor man, I will go to the berith to eat like all the other beggars. When they ate and drank mead, the thief stood near the Besht and said: "I have a great and difficult question to ask you, sir. Since you, sir, know and see how thieves steal and where they sleep, you can probably see better things than these. Why do you bother with such mean things? It would be better to look at good things."

The Besht, God bless his memory, said torah about this question until Minhah, and he still had not finished.

128] *The Besht's Funeral*

I heard this from the rabbi of our community. During the Besht's funeral, Rabbi Naḥman of Horodenka was puzzled because he saw nothing at all. But when he returned from the cemetery he saw great and wonderful things, and he told Rabbi Ze'ev Kotses that undoubtedly that was the way it had to be.

129] *Rabbi Naḥman Travels to the Holy Land*

I heard this from the rabbi of our community. When Rabbi Naḥman wanted to travel to the Holy Land a second time, he went to the Besht's tomb with Rabbi Joseph of Kamenka. When he returned from the cemetery he rejoiced greatly and said: "The Besht told me to travel to our Holy Land."[1]

Rabbi Joseph was very puzzled and he said: "Where was it that he talked with you?"

Rabbi Naḥman said in wonder: "Didn't you see him standing by my side talking with me?"

During the journey he observed the Sabbath with the rabbi and the Preacher, and I was there as well. And I, the author, heard about clever exchanges between Rabbi Naḥman and the Preacher. Rabbi Naḥman said something witty to the Preacher and then laughed. The Preacher, God bless his memory, was very strict with Rabbi Naḥman, and he said: "A man cannot save himself from a wayward thought. Even though he may pray without any wayward thoughts, near the end of the prayer it will occur to him that he is about to finish the prayer, and this itself is a tiny thought. Because this is a very tiny thought, it enters a scholar and disturbs him. From each sin an accuser, God forbid, is created."

All the people of the city saw Rabbi Naḥman off. I was among them as well, and the rabbi and the Preacher were there too. The

Preacher wanted to accompany him until the town of Ladyzhin, but since he was concerned about their taking leave of each other in the proper way, he did not go. They prayed Minhah in the field, and the rabbi put on tefillin and prayed before the ark. Rabbi Nahman prayed without a tallith or tefillin. I did not see whether the Preacher prayed there, and I believe that he went to the city to pray.

One year, Rabbi Nahman, God bless his memory, died during the month of Tammuz.* He was in Nemirov that month. Rabbi Mendele of Peremyshlyany accompanied him and received from him the wisdom of the Besht, at which he marveled.

I heard that Rabbi Nahman died on the holy Sabbath. Rabbi Mendele was sitting with him. He sanctified the wine and drank a little of it. He sat dressed in Sabbath clothes. Rabbi Mendele went to eat the Sabbath dinner. While eating the dessert Rabbi Mendele sent for Rabbi Nahman and discovered that he was dying. Rabbi Nahman had been studying the Zohar at the time of the departure of his soul. He died during Minhah and went to his rest.[2]

130] *Rabbi Mendele Visits with Rabbi Jacob Joseph*

I HEARD THAT THE RABBI** HIGHLY PRAISED THE prayer of Rabbi Mendele. He traveled from the holy community of Cekinowka[1] to take leave of the rabbi before his trip,[2] and he observed the Sabbath there and remained for about five days. He arrived on Wednesday when the rabbi was praying Minhah. The wagon and horses of Rabbi Mendele remained there but nothing was carried from the wagon. I was teaching across the river some distance away and it took me a while to come, but when I arrived I asked his people why they did not carry anything from the wagon. They answered that he did not want to be the rabbi's guest. The rabbi was the one to pray before the ark, but Rabbi Mendele also wanted to pray before the ark. Therefore, he wanted

* The tenth month of the Jewish calendar which corresponds approximately to July.
** Probably Rabbi Jacob Joseph of Polonnoye.

them to provide him with quarters near the rabbi so that he would be able to see him nonetheless. They did not let me pray because Rabbi Mendele was still smoking his pipe. They did not let anyone in where they were praying because the rabbi had not yet finished his prayer. So everyone who was late was stopped so that Rabbi Mendele would have a minyan.

When the rabbi finished his prayer he left the building with his minyan and Rabbi Mendele entered it with us to pray before the ark. He stood apart as was his custom and prayed Minhah. After he finished his prayer he sat down near his place and rearranged his tefillin.

The rabbi came in and greeted him. He asked him: "Why don't they unload the wagon?"

In answering, Rabbi Mendele stuttered because he had not spoken for twelve years and he always communicated by writing. When he started speaking he would pause and sit down before uttering a word. It was impolite to give such an answer. He was stuttering and the rabbi did not hear him respond.

Finally, I could not stand it any longer and although I was embarrassed before the rabbi, I had to speak out: "It is because you, sir, have to pray before the ark in Minhah and on the Sabbath. He has to pray before the ark as well."

The rabbi answered: "This is not a cause for a delay. 'In a place where there are no men, strive thou to be a man.'³" Then the rabbi ordered the baggage to be taken from the wagon, and he let Rabbi Mendele stay in his house of seclusion, while he himself stayed in a sukkah.* It was still cold, and Rabbi Mendele came on Wednesday and left on Monday. The rabbi stayed in the cold sukkah and let Rabbi Mendele sleep in the small house where they prayed. The rabbi, God bless his memory, never slept in the small house. When Rabbi Mendele went away, Rabbi David of the holy community of Ilintsy arrived. He planned to travel to the Holy Land, but he wanted to see Rabbi Mendele first. He did not find

---

* A tabernacle in which Jews eat and many also sleep during the festival of Sukkoth, as a commemoration of the dwelling of the children of Israel in the desert after they left Egypt. The structure must be temporary: its roof is covered with the branches of trees.

him in the holy community of Nemirov and so he slept over at the rabbi's.

131] *The Prayers of Rabbi Mendele and Rabbi Fridel*

I HEARD THAT THE RABBI HIGHLY PRAISED THE prayer of Rabbi Mendele. He said the following: "I, too, became like one of the common folk and forgot the way to pray. They reminded me of the way of prayer."

He spoke about *them*, meaning Rabbi Mendele and Rabbi Fridel. Rabbi Fridel had prayed with the rabbi in front of the ark on Monday morning before the arrival of Rabbi Mendele. The rabbi said the following: "When they say 'Blessed be He and blessed be His name,' you should see how Rabbi Fridel, the householder of Brody, prays." I also heard that once he let Rabbi Pinhas of Korets pray the Sabbath prayer in the holy community of Polonnoye. The rabbi of our community was very surprised when I told him about it, and he said: "I heard him say that he would always regret that he let them pray in his place."

At that time Rabbi Mendele was thirty-six years old and the rabbi was close to sixty and perhaps even more. You can see how humbly the first tsaddikim behaved.

132] *The Heavy Load of Honor*

I HEARD THAT RABBI MENDELE COMPLAINED TO THE rabbi about the great honor that was accorded him. I heard that in the holy community of Old Konstantynow the whole city went out to welcome him, and he said to the rabbi, "The honor was like a heavy load on me."

The rabbi answered him that the Besht had always prayed that people would disparage him. Rabbi Mendele said that he had also thought about such an idea.

133] *Rabbi Nahman's Cold Mikveh*

Once I heard Rabbi Nahman of Horodenka say: "When I was a great Hasid I went every day to a cold mikveh. There is no one in this generation who could bear such a mikveh. When I went home I did not feel warm for about an hour even though it was so hot the walls were like fire. Despite this I could not rid myself of wayward thoughts until I turned to the wisdom of the Besht."

134] *Iniquities and Prayers*

I heard Rabbi Mendel of Bar say: "In my youth in the excitement of prayer the thought occurred to me, 'How dare I pray to God, blessed be He, since I am filled with iniquities?' And *my heart within me is broken.*[1] For a long time I could not rid myself of that thought, since it seemed to be right. Then I settled it in my heart, 'Why does this thought not occur in my mind and heart when I sit with a bowl to eat?' Then I rejected this thought."

135] *The Preacher's Sermon*

I heard this at the house of the rabbi in the holy community of Nemirov from Rabbi Moses, who heard it from the Preacher. Once the Preacher dreamed that he was taught a sermon. He remembered some things and he mentioned it to the Besht, who said to him: "Tell me what you remember." And the Besht told him that at first he should preach in his home using a book, and after that he would know how to preach the sermon well.

The Preacher said: "The Besht told me to go to the holy

community of Lemberg as he had ordered me in the dream. He told me to preach in the great synagogue and in no other and to be the guest of the town elder.

"I set out to travel and I preached everywhere. Once I preached in a city and my torah flowed like a fountain. There was a wealthy man from the holy community of Lemberg who heard the sermon and liked it. Afterwards, that sermon slipped from my mind.

"I traveled to another city where the boys mocked me in the street crying, 'As it is said . . . as it is said.' Then that wealthy man appeared and chided them: 'I have heard him and he is a great preacher.' And they left me alone. When I came to the holy community of Lemberg I went to the house of the town elder but he was not at home. I wanted to remain there, but the servant did not let me, and he said, 'It is the custom for the preacher to stay in the public house.' "

The Preacher pushed himself inside because he wanted to stay with the town elder. In the meantime the town elder came and saw that he insisted on staying at his house. He said: "It is not the custom here to stay with the town elder, but since you insist so vehemently I will provide you a place."

The Preacher was given a small room in the house, and he placed his belongings there and sat down. It was still broad daylight, and so he took out his Book of Psalms and recited psalms. The town elder was at home looking after his own affairs. He was pleased when he heard him reciting the Psalms, and the Preacher found favor in his eyes. He came into his room and asked him in which synagogue he wanted to preach. The Preacher said: "In the great synagogue."

He answered: "This is not the custom here." At the beginning one preaches in the *klaus*, then in the beth-hamidrash, and when the city people like one's sermons, one preaches in the great synagogue."

He said to him: "But I want to preach in the great synagogue right at the beginning."

The town elder said: "Before we allow that we have to obtain permission from the rabbi of our community."

In the meantime the wealthy man who heard him in another city came and told the town elder that he was a great preacher. He said: "I will talk with the rabbi personally to permit you to preach in the synagogue."

The Preacher did not have fine garments and he had but one coat. The town elder asked him: "What will you wear to go to synagogue to preach?"

He said: "I have only this coat. If you want to lend me some clothes I will dress up in them."

The town elder immediately took his woolen Sabbath and holiday clothes from the drawer.

The Preacher said: "I do not wear woolen clothing."

The town elder took out some silk garments and the Preacher put them on.

The town elder went to the rabbi and asked him to grant the Preacher permission to preach in the synagogue.

The rabbi said: "He may preach and I myself will go to listen to the sermon." The rabbi asked the shammash to inform him when the Preacher would go to preach. As soon as the Preacher went to preach, the shammash told the rabbi. The rabbi ran to the synagogue and he enjoyed the sermon very much. After the evening prayer the rabbi asked the Preacher to be his guest.

The Preacher said: "I am staying with someone."

The rabbi went to the home of the town elder and asked him to let the Preacher be his guest. He could not dare refuse the rabbi and he turned his guest over to him.

The rabbi asked the Preacher: "Are you a disciple of the Besht, and is your name Rabbi Leib?"

He said: "Yes."

The rabbi asked him about the appearance of the Besht and began to describe him.

He said: "Yes, that is the Besht." The Preacher asked the rabbi: "How did you know what he looked like?"

The rabbi said: "A little while before Minhah I took a nap, and in my dream I saw the Besht and he said: 'Let my disciple preach in the great synagogue.' He said that his uncle was a pillar of his generation. I believe his name was Rabbi Abraham, the rabbi's son. I forgot his name. He said: "I was at his side at the time of his death, and I heard him telling his son: 'There will be a man whose name will be Israel, the son of the midwife.[1] Know that he is true and his teaching is true and follow him.' "

The rabbi was the Preacher's host for three weeks, and he asked him to reveal to him all that he had learned from the Besht. The rabbi wanted to travel to the Besht, but he died before he could go. They gave the Preacher thirty red coins, and if he had wanted more they would have given him two hundred red coins. In the holy community of Lemberg they prepared white Sabbath clothes for him, and on his return he observed the Sabbath with the Besht.

At night when they returned from prayer the Besht stood at the table and said, "*shalom 'aleikhem.*"

The Preacher said, "*shalom 'aleikhem*" while he was strolling back and forth in the house. The Preacher saw the Besht turn back toward the door and motion with his hand. It occurred to him that the Besht was behaving as if he saw something—but the Preacher had lost his power to perceive. The Besht turned back in this manner two or three times, and the Preacher was afraid to ask him about it. At the conclusion of the Sabbath, after the Havdalah, it was the custom of the Besht to lie down to rest and to smoke his tobacco pipe while telling what he had envisioned during the Sabbath. He continued speaking.

The Preacher asked him: "Why did I see you, sir, turn back two or three times while saying "*shalom 'aleikhem?*"

The Besht said to him: "Satan wanted to carry you off from my home, and I scolded him by saying "*shalom 'aleikhem.*" When he came a second time I told him: "He will be punished, but you will not take him from me."

And so it was. On his way home the Preacher together with all the members of his household became ill, and there was much work for the Besht until the Preacher and all his family recovered. And he forgot all the sermons. The Preacher said that he had severe trials and a lot of work to do until he could preach again.

The main part of this story I heard from Rabbi Moses, the son-in-law of the sister of the rabbi of the holy community of Polonnoye. He heard it in the holy community of Nemirov from the Preacher himself. I heard other versions of the same story from Rabbi Joseph, the son of Rabbi Moses of the holy community of Polonnoye.

136] *A Madman Feigns Death*

Once Rabbi David, the maggid of the holy community of Tulchin, who was the grandson of the tsaddik Rabbi David Forkes, observed the Sabbath with the rabbi of our community, Rabbi David, told me the following story.

A man took his insane son to the Besht. When they arrived at a place about one verst from the city, his madness became more severe, and he feigned death. His father brought him to the town for burial, and he laid him down in the women's section of the synagogue.

The Besht said to the scribe: "Today we must beat a dead man." When they brought in the dead man, he said to the scribe: "Take a thick strap,[1] go to the synagogue, and chase the funeral society away." He then ordered him to beat the dead man. He did as he was told, but the dead man neither moved nor got up. The Besht ordered that the dead man be left in a certain house, and the house be locked and watched until the Passover holiday. There were three weeks until the Passover.

On Passover night he ordered that the dead man be seated at the table and kept upright with pillows. They appointed a man to put in his mouth some of their food and drink and to see that he did not escape, because, if he escaped it would be difficult to find him. At the third glass of wine he could bear it no longer. He jumped up and ran from the house and escaped. They searched for him for twenty-four hours. They found him and the Besht cured him.

137] *The Martyrs*

THERE WAS A BLOOD LIBEL IN THE HOLY community of Pavlysh.* The rabbi of the holy community of Korostyshev, whose name was Rabbi David, escaped. He wanted to flee as far as the provinces of Walachia. All the important people in the area around Pavlysh were afraid that a libel would be made against them as well. When Rabbi David arrived at the holy community of Medzhibozh, the Besht stopped him and told him several times that the people would be saved. But they were killed, and afterwards a letter reached Rabbi David telling him about the horrible and painful tortures that each of them had suffered. He brought this letter to the Besht who became grief-stricken. That day was Sabbath Eve, and the Besht went to the mikveh and cried bitterly. He prayed Minhah with great bitterness until his followers could not lift up their heads.

They said: "Perhaps when he will begin welcoming the Sabbath, he will do it joyfully."

But the Besht also prayed the Reception of the Sabbath prayer and the Maariv with a bitter heart. He sanctified the wine as he wept. He washed his hands, sat at the table, and then went to sleep. In his room he stretched himself out on the floor and lay there for a long time. The members of his household and the guests waited until the candles began to die out.

His wife went to him and said: "The candles will soon die out and the guests are waiting."

He said to her: "Let them eat, recite the blessing over the food, and go."

His wife also went to the room where the Besht was and lay

---

* In 1753 twenty-four Jews were charged with the murder of a four-year-old Christian boy. The trial took place in Zhitomir, but since most of these Jews lived in the small town of Pavlysh, it was known as the Pavlysh accusation. Twelve of the Jews were tortured and executed; the rest saved their lives by converting to Christianity. See Dubnov, [Dubnow], *History of the Jews in Russia and Poland*, I, 178.

down on her bed. The Besht was still lying down on the floor with his arms and legs outstretched.

Rabbi David stood at the door to watch what would happen, but he became weary of standing, and he took a bench and sat at the door. At about midnight he heard the Besht say to his wife: "Cover your face."

At that very moment the room became brightly lit, and the light shone through the cracks. The Besht said: "Welcome Rabbi Akiva." And he also welcomed the martyrs whose names no one knows. Rabbi David recognized Rabbi Akiva by his voice.*

The Besht said to the martyrs: "I decree that you go and take revenge on the enemy, the persecutor." The martyrs answered: "Do not let these words pass from your lips again, and let what you have said be nullified. You, sir, are not aware of your power. When you, sir, upset the Sabbath, there was a great tumult in paradise and we fled from the palaces as though we were running before the sword. Even when we reached an upper palace we found that all had to flee from there as well, though they knew not why. Finally, we came to an upper palace where they understood the cause, and they shouted at us: 'Hurry and go to quiet the Besht's tears.' Let us tell you, sir, that all the suffering man has to endure in life is like the skin of a garlic clove in comparison to the suffering we endured as martyrs for His blessed and lofty name. Nevertheless, the yetzer hara** played its role and confused our thoughts just a hair. In spite of the fact that we completely

---

* The Hebrew text does not clarify whose voice is concerned. Another possible reading could imply that the Besht called out the names of the various saints, and Rabbi David heard him pronouncing only Rabbi Akiva's name. Rabbi Akiva (about 40 to about 155) was one of the major Tannaim whose teachings and methods of interpretation served as a basis for the development of Jewish oral law as it is represented in the Mishnah and the Talmud. According to tradition, he was one of the ten martyrs executed by the Romans following the defeat of the Bar Kokhba rebellion in 135. See Louis Finkelstein, *Akiba, Scholar, Saint and Martyr,* paperback (New York and Philadelphia, 1962); Henry A. Fischel, "Martyr and Prophet," *Jewish Quarterly Review,* XXXVIII (1947), 265–80, 363–86; Saul Lieberman, "The Martyrs of Caesarea," *Philologie et d'Histoire Orientales et Slaves,* VII (1939–44), 395–446.

** Man's evil inclination.

spurned the yetzer hara, we had to suffer a half an hour in Gehenna. After we entered paradise we began to argue that we wanted to take revenge upon our enemies. They answered us: 'Since he is still living if you want to take revenge, you will have to become reincarnated.' We said, 'Thank God that we sanctified ourselves and became martyrs for His name and had to suffer the pain of Gehenna, and that half an hour in Gehenna makes all other suffering seem like the skin of a garlic clove in comparison. What would become of us if we were to be reborn again in this world? We might commit sins, God forbid, from which we would not have any redemption. It is better for us not to take revenge and not to be reincarnated.' Therefore, it is our request that you, sir, cancel what you have said."

The Besht asked them: "Why did those in heaven mislead me and not reveal to me that you were destined to be martyrs?"

They answered him: "If you had known of it you would have prayed a great deal and canceled the decree, and it could have caused great trouble, God forbid. Therefore, they did not inform you, sir."[1]

I heard from the rabbi of our community that the Besht said that in heaven they had promised him to cancel the decree, but a preacher gave a sermon in the holy community of Brody exploiting the plight of the prisoners and in so doing caused strife which resulted in the death of the prisoners because of our many sins.

138] *The Adulterous Woman*

I HEARD FROM RABBI AARON OF OUR COMMUNITY, who heard from the rabbi, the gaon, of the holy community of Shepetovka that in their area there was a deserted wife* who held the *arrendeh*. Once the Besht perceived that she had commited adultery with her gentile servant. When her two brothers, who lived in two different villages, learned of it they were ashamed

* According to Jewish religious law she is not free to remarry unless she receives a bill of divorce from her husband or his authorized representative.

and thought that she would forsake the Jewish community, God forbid. They took counsel with each other and decided that each of them would ask her to come to his village. In the evening both of them would follow her and weed her out of this world. And so they did. That night the Besht was sitting with two candles lit before him when suddenly one candle died out. He relit it with the second candle. At that moment the second candle was extinguished, and he relit it with the first candle. He heard a voice talking to him: "Murderer. How dare you interfere with these two candles?" He realized what was happening. He took a horse and rode in a great hurry to where they were meeting, and he arrived before they killed her. He saved her from their hands, and she became a thoroughly repentant sinner. After that she could be found standing in the mikveh at midnight.

139] *The Delayed Homecoming: A Second Version*

There was a cloth merchant in the holy community of Medzhibozh whose son went to Breslau and remained there for a long time. His mother was very worried, and she told her husband to go and ask the Besht where he was. Her husband did not think very highly of the Besht and he refused, but his wife nagged him so much that he had to go. He came to the Besht and said with a smile: "My wife said that you know certain things, and so I came to ask you to tell me where my son is."

The Besht answered: "To see such things I go to the synagogue." He took his pipe, and went to the synagogue. Then he returned and said: "I saw that he is still in Breslau and he is wearing a German hat." That was the custom there. When they completed their business they exchanged hats. That was the sign of the conclusion of the transaction.

The father marked the day in order to recall when the business transaction took place. When his son returned from the trip, his father asked him: "On what day did you conclude your business?"

He told him the day, and it was the same day that he had written down, the day when they had exchanged hats.

He asked him: "Why didn't you send me a letter from time to time?"

He said to him: "Because I came across a good customer on the road and I sold him merchandise. I had to deliver it to the merchant's house, and so I had to leave the road on which the mail travels. Then I bought other merchandise and went to Breslau, and because of that, I was late in returning home."[1]

140] *The Besht, the Merchant, and the Robbers*

ONCE THIS MERCHANT WANTED TO TRAVEL TO THE holy community of Whitefield with merchandise, but he was afraid to go because of the robbers who were said to be on the road. His wife said to him: "I heard that the Besht travels on the same road. Give his servant a present and he will inform you on what day the Besht goes. You will travel in his company and you will not have any fear."

He did so and he traveled in the same company with the Besht. When they arrived at the forest where the robbers were, the Besht ordered his servant to stop and permit the horses to graze. The man became very frightened. The Besht ordered that the wagons be placed opposite each other and the Besht sat in the center. He opened the Book of the Zohar and read it.

The robbers came out of the forest, but when they approached them they were seized with trembling and they fled. When they were far away the robbers said to themselves: "Let us go to them again." But when they approached they were again seized by trembling. When the company left the robbers did not want to go after them, and they said to themselves: "This is not a simple matter."

When the merchant saw what happened, he fell on the Besht's

neck and kissed him. He said: "Now I know, sir, of your greatness.

The Besht said to him: "So you think that you know? You still do not know."

I cannot recall from whom I heard this story, but I believe that I heard it from the rabbi of our community.

141] *The Besht Discharges a Shohet*

Once the Besht traveled to Kamenka and when he came near the city he heard a voice telling him to discharge the shohet of that holy community from his position. Since he was careful about cutting off anyone's livelihood, he said: "I will remove him from his position and find another way for him to earn a living."

When he came to the house of Rabbi Barukh, Rabbi Barukh prepared himself and slaughtered a few cows. One of the cows was found to be not kosher, and he hung it in the passageway. And the Besht smoked his pipe there. Rabbi Barukh came into the passageway, and the Besht told him to cut a piece of meat from that animal and roast it for him.

Rabbi Barukh thought that he was joking, and he said: "You, sir, could not eat from this animal."

He said: "I certainly will."

When Rabbi Barukh realized that he really meant it, he said: "This cow is not kosher."

The Besht said to him: "But this cow asks me to eat from it. Tell me why it became not kosher."

He sent for the shohet and asked him: "Why did this cow become not kosher?"

The shohet said to him: "There are several opinions regarding this question. Some consider it to be kosher, and some say it is not."

The Besht ordered him to cut a piece of meat and to prepare a roast. The Besht realized that this was very difficult for his followers to understand, and he asked them to send someone to

Rabbi Samuel, the judge, in the holy community of Polonnoye, and to bring a letter from him before they prepared the roast. They immediately sent a messenger riding on the back of a good horse, and he returned with a letter from the judge saying that the cow was kosher.

The Besht removed the shohet from his post and did not want to provide him another means of making a living.[1]

142] *The Optimism of Rabbi Naḥman*

It was the custom of Rabbi Naḥman of Horodenka to say about everything that he saw or everything that befell him that it is for the best. His faith was as strong as an iron pillar.

Once they drafted soldiers from among the Jews of the holy community of Medzhibozh. The Besht said to him: "Pray that they do not draft soldiers from the Jews."

He said to him that it was for the best. The Besht said to him: "It is good that you did not live in Haman's time because you would have said that his decree was good as well. The only good that came of it was that they hanged Haman—which was for the best."

Once Rabbi Naḥman and the rabbi of the holy community of Polonnoye traveled from the holy community of Nemirov to visit the Besht for the Sabbath. On Friday they came upon a master who was riding very slowly in a large carriage on the same road. They were afraid to pass him. The rabbi was wringing his hands and said: "*Oy vey, oy vey*, we will profane the Sabbath, God forbid." And he was deeply troubled.

Rabbi Naḥman said that it was for the best, and this just added to the grief of the rabbi of Polonnoye.

A little while later they encountered a long train of loaded wagons. The snow was very deep, and there was no way to pass them because they were headed in the same direction rather than coming toward them. When the gentiles with the wagons saw the master they cleared the road and so they were all able to pass the group. Then they came to a crossroads and the nobleman went his way, and they arrived at the Besht's when it was still broad daylight.

All this I heard from the rabbi of the holy community of Polonnoye.[1]

143] *Rabbi Naḥman Prays Minḥah*

I HEARD FROM THE RABBI OF OUR COMMUNITY THAT once Rabbi Naḥman traveled with the Besht and they arrived at a certain village. It was time for Minhah.: The Besht said to the gabbai: "Go to that house and see whether it is possible to pray there."

Rabbi Naḥman took his sack containing his tallith and tefillin, and he went to the house.

The gabbai said to the Besht: "The house is filled with gentiles."

The Besht said: "Go and call Rabbi Naḥman, to climb into the wagon because we will be late for Minhah."

The gabbai entered the house and found Rabbi Naḥman praying wrapped in the tallith and the tefillin. The gabbai told him to leave, but he did not hear him. The gabbai went out and told the Besht that Rabbi Naḥman was praying wrapped in his tallith and tefillin.

The Besht said: "He will probably create some trouble for the gentiles." As he said it the manor house caught fire. Some village youths came and called all the gentiles to save the manor house, and the house was left empty. Then the Besht went in to pray as well.

144] *Feeling the Tefillin*

I SAW THAT THE RABBI OF THE HOLY COMMUNITY of Polonnoye used to feel the tefillin before and after the eighteen benedictions. When he finished, "Blessed art Thou O Lord who blessest Thy people, Israel, with peace," he immediately felt the tefillin.[1] I wrote down what he did to learn to be quick in worshiping the Creator. He always read the voiced eighteen benedictions from the prayer book as well as listening to the hazan read it.[2]

145] *The Height of Prayer*

I HEARD FROM THE RABBI OF THE HOLY COMMUNITY of Polonnoye that once he traveled to the governor of the holy community of Raszkow for some purpose. He prayed while on the road. When he reached the prayer, *But He, being full of compassion*[1]—it was either on Monday or Thursday—he stated his need as if the Shekinah were praying before God for a similar need. Then he returned home and said humbly. "I can tell you now what I said because I am not at that height now."

146] *Ascension to Heaven*

I HEARD FROM THE RABBI OF OUR COMMUNITY that he heard from Rabbi Joseph of Kamenka that the Besht expected to ascend to heaven in a storm like Elijah the Prophet. And he was very sorry about it. His friends thought that he was sad about the death of his wife, and they asked him about it because they knew that it was not like him. He answered that he was sorry that his own mind would now have to rest in the ground. "I expected to ascend in a storm, but now that I am only part of a body it is impossible, and I am grieved."[1]

147] *The Besht's Second Coming*

I HEARD ALSO THAT HE SAID: "IF THE REDEEMER does not come within the next sixty years I must return to this world."

The rabbi of our community said that he had heard from his grandfather, who stayed with the Besht on the Sabbath before Shabuoth in which the Besht passed away,[1] that the Besht discussed the matter. He had a scribe. The rabbi said that he had two doubts; he did not know whether the Besht said that he would return within fifteen or fifty years, or whether within sixteen or sixty. From other people I heard that it would be definitely within sixty years. I asked Rabbi Aaron of Medzhibozh, and he told me that the Besht had said that he would certainly be reincarnated in this world, "but I will not be then as I am now." And they did not understand what he meant, since the Besht said: "Who questions the meaning of these words?"

148] *The Perpetual Error*

I HEARD FROM THE RABBI THAT IN ONE TORAH scroll they always found a mistake. They corrected it each time, but in spite of this they continued to find a mistake in it. They showed the Torah scroll to the Besht, and he said that the money given to enscribe this scroll was from debt money—that is to say, the coins collected at card games which are given to the person in whose house the game is played. This person collected the coins and used the money to have that Torah scroll enscribed.

This turned out to be the case. The Besht said that there was no way to correct it and it would be defective forever even if it were corrected over and over again.

149] *The Ring*

I HEARD A SIMILAR STORY FROM RABBI ELIMELEKH.[1] Once Rabbi Elimelekh came to his neighbor, a silversmith, and saw a ring there. He took it in his hand and immediately threw it away. He said that this ring was ordered with money gained from interest. The silversmith investigated and found it to be so.

150] *Rabbi Motil*

THERE WAS A MAN IN THE HOLY COMMUNITY OF Polonnoye who did favors for the Besht by giving him flour and fish on credit. When the time of his death approached he asked the Besht to look after his only son, Rabbi Mordecai, who was called Rabbi Motil.

Rabbi Motil had his ups and downs. Once he lost all his property and only his house remained. The Besht told him: "When the court sends for you to ask you to rent the *arrendeh* of the city, do not go. Even if they send for you several times, do not go until they send a cart for you."

And so it was. Several men came to rent the *arrendeh*, and the master could not come to an agreement with them. The master's wife sent for Rabbi Motil, but he refused to go, saying that he did not feel well and he could not walk. And indeed he had a slight pain. And so it was on the second and the third day, until she sent a cart for him. Then he said that he could not keep the *arrendeh* because he did not have the means to distill alcohol.

She said: "I will give you several hundred sacks of grain and please rent the *arrendeh*." The master's wife was filled with joy that she rented the *arrendeh* to him. In the arrangement he made a profit of about twelve hundred red coins.

The Besht said to him: "Do not trade in oxen." But he did not listen to him. He traded in oxen, and returned from a journey with an empty pocket. This happened several times.

Once he lost a lot of money. He owed about thirteen golden coins to a certain master, and he did not have enough to pay the debt.

The master said: "If he doesn't pay me, I'll shoot him."

Rabbi Motil heard this and was afraid. He went to the Besht and stayed there for all of the Days of Awe. The master summoned him to court, and he said, "I don't have any money."

After Yom Kippur, early in the morning, the Besht said to him: "Come with me to the mikveh." He went with him. After that the Besht told him: "Go home."

He asked: "What will happen when I go home?"

He told him: "*Fear not, neither be dismayed.*"[1]

He returned home and celebrated the holiday. After the holiday there were some rainy days, and as he was worried he smoked his pipe and looked through the window. He saw a group of gentiles called Haidamaks coming back from a trip. They always used to go through the city. They had searched for an inn throughout the whole city without success, since there were about forty or fifty herdsmen altogether. When they came to his house he received them and gave them rooms, and food and drink, and everything they desired. He bought two quarts of brandy from his neighbor and sold it to them, and then he bought more brandy. He profited so much from them that he could buy a liter* of brandy, and they ate and drank as much as they wanted. When they proceeded on their way they asked him to accompany them and carry some barrels of mead. They wanted to drink all the mead barrels. They returned to the city again and stayed overnight in his place. This happened several times until they had provided him with enough money to pay his debt. But he still needed two golden coins to pay off the debt completely. Then one herdsman left the group and came to his house and gave him two golden coins.

Later, the master came by riding on horseback. He called him outside and asked for the money. He said: "I have the money." He asked the master in and paid the complete sum that he owed him.

The master said to him: "It was told to me that you were not able to pay. Now that you have paid me I see it is a lie. You can have the money for as long as you want."

He refused to take the money, and he told him that "a miracle does not take place on every occasion."[2]

And the Besht said: "This nobleman was really lucky because, if you had not had the money, he would have had to die."

* The measurements referred to in the tale do not correspond to those used today.

151] *Rabbi Gershon's Enemies*

I HEARD THIS FROM THE RABBI OF THE HOLY COM-
munity of Nemirov and the holy community of Polonnoye. It is
written in the Zohar Ḥadash: "During the time of the Tannaim
and Amoraim, for whose merit the world exists, one spoke to his
friend: 'From the mishnah that you pronounced I could see what
will happen today and tomorrow.' "[1]

I heard from the Besht that when he heard someone studying
he could tell what was going to happen at the end of the year.
Once I came to the holy community of Brody, and I did not find
Rabbi Gershon at home because he was away on a trip. In the
meantime Rabbi Gershon came home.

Rabbi Gershon's son said to his mother: "I have good news for
you. They took the steward to prison."

Rabbi Gershon said to him: "Israel, my brother-in-law, said
last year that this would happen. I was studying the Mishnah after
prayer, and when I studied a certain mishnah the Besht said to me:
'Do you know what you have learned?'

"I said: 'I do.' I thought he was referring to the apparent
meaning of the mishnah.

"He said to me: 'You have learned two new things. You have
two enemies here: one of them will be reconciled with you, and
the other will suffer a great downfall.' "

And so it was. Rabbi Gershon used to go to greet the wealthy
people on the holiday. He passed by the house of one of his
enemies who sent his son-in-law to invite him into his house
where he appeased him.

152] *The Wandering Soul*

WHEN THE BESHT CAME TO THE HOLY COMMUNITY
of Medzhibozh, he was not regarded as an important man by the
Hasidim—that is to say, by Rabbi Ze'ev Kotses and Rabbi David

Forkes—because he was called the Besht, the master of a good name. This name was not considered proper for a pious man.

They had a worthy student who became sick. He was a good and pious man. His teachers paid him a visit. He wanted to ask for the Besht, but they refused. Later he became even weaker, and they consented to call the Besht, but they said to the sick man: "Be certain to tell us everything that he says to you."

When the Besht came he ordered everyone to leave the house. One boy, however, concealed himself. The Besht told the sick student that he was going to die. "You have not yet corrected one thing," and he told him what it was.

He admitted it and said: "I expected to correct it. What should I do now?"

The Besht said to him: "Do not worry. I will see to it that it will not cause you any delay, and I will help you to enter paradise. Do not reveal what I am telling you to anyone." And the Besht went away.

When his teachers returned they asked him what the Besht said to him, but he refused to reveal it. However, the boy told it to them. They asked the sick man whether it was true, and he said: "It is true. That is what he told me."

They wondered how he could have knowledge of heaven and of who would be sent to paradise. They forced the sick man to shake hands and promise to reveal to them how he would be treated after his death.

After he died he appeared to them and revealed that he was brought into paradise, but he did not see the Besht there, and he did not know who let him in. But he did not have a place in paradise. When he sat in one place somebody else came and pushed him away and sat down there. It happened with one place after another until he was pushed from every single place. "I am a wanderer. I do not have a resting place, and this causes me great sorrow. Once it happened that the people of one palace went to another palace, and I went along with them. When they arrived at that palace I immediately rushed in and sat at the table, but they pushed me from my seat. When I stood up before the table I saw the Besht sitting among them saying torah. He addressed questions to the students of the yeshivah and told them to solve them. But they failed to do so, and he answered the questions himself. Each one went to his place and I asked the Besht why I do not have a place in paradise. He said to me: 'Because you did not fulfill the promise on which you shook hands.' I immediately appeared in your dream."

He told them the content of the question, and the solution that the Besht had given in paradise. Immediately after, on the very same Sabbath, they came to the Besht for the third meal. He said this torah, and when he asked the question they gave the solution. The Besht said: "I know that the dead man told you this."

From that day on they followed the Besht.

The rabbi of our community said they did not let the dead man into paradise, although they gave him a place near the gates. But after each of the ascensions of his soul the light of paradise shone upon him.[1]

153] *Dream Teaching*

THERE WAS A MELAMED NAMED RABBI MOSES KEDS who was very learned, and he did not think highly of the Besht. It was his custom to send a messenger to the beth-hamidrash while he himself came in to pray only near the time of *Blessed ye the Lord*.[1] Once he had some difficulty understanding a commentary on the tractate Shebu'oth. He worked on the problem for about two weeks, and he could not arrive at the correct meaning.

Once he saw himself in his dreams entering a palace. The Besht saw him there and said to him: "Why didn't you know the meaning of the commentary?" And the Besht said to him: "This is the meaning."

He awoke from his sleep and recalled the interpretation. He got up and took the Gemara. In the moonlight he looked up the commentary, and it fit very well with the interpretation given him. Nevertheless, he said to himself: "Perhaps it is just a dream and the Besht does not know about it."

The Besht invited him to the third meal. When the Besht told him the commentary and its interpretation, he knew that the Besht had indeed told it to him. He began to follow him, and he became a great tsaddik.[2]

154] *The Forbidden City*

I heard this from Rabbi Moses, the son of Yakil of Medzhibozh, who was in the holy community of Nemirov. When his father took him to the Besht to be blessed by him, the Besht said to him: "Be careful not to travel to the city of Vinnitsa."

Some time later when he was on a journey he lost his way and found himself nearby that city, and he took another road. All his life Rabbi Moses was very careful not to go to Vinnitsa. When he told this to me it was only a few years before his death.

Once while he was traveling they caused him trouble over his train ticket, and they took him to the city of Vinnitsa. He begged them not to take him to Vinnitsa, but nevertheless they brought him to the city and put him in prison where he died. It was forty years or more after his marriage.

155] *The Hunchback*

I heard from Rabbi Moses, the hunchback, that the Besht had circumcised him, and he ordered that they not take him over a bridge called a *greblyeh*.* For several years they followed his advice. Once they had to go to a wedding party. They took him along and his hunchback was formed.

* *Greblyeh* does not mean a bridge in Yiddish. The writer apparently provided the wrong Hebrew equivalent to this Yiddish term. See Menashe Unger, "Yiddish Words in the *Shivhe Habesht*," Yiddish, *Yidishe Shprakh* (*The Yiddish Language*), XXI (1961), 68.

156]   *The Forbidden Country*

I HEARD THIS STORY FROM THE RABBI OF OUR community. The Besht was in the holy community of Kamenka and he said to Rabbi Barukh: "When the rabbi of the holy community of Ostrog will come here, tell him in my name that the learned rabbi, his father, Tsevi, appeared to me and asked me to tell his son not to go to the Ukraine. If he does not believe that I have seen him, describe his father's appearance, his gestures, his clothes, and say that he wore short stockings."

When that rabbi came to Kamenka, Rabbi Barukh told him what the Besht had said, and when he heard the description he believed him. He asked them to repeat some of the torah that they had heard from the Besht. Rabbi Joseph of Kamenka told him what the Besht had said about an interpretation of *Rashi* on the biblical verse, *When a ruler sinneth*.[1] I heard this interpretation from the rabbi of the holy community of Polonnoye, but I have forgotten it. But it is certainly written in his books, and you can look it up there.[2] When he heard that interpretation he liked it very much and he said: "Such an interpretation suits the rabbi of the holy community of Ostrog very well."

He returned home and avoided the Ukraine. In his old age he traveled to the Ukraine, and he died in the holy community of Fastov.

157]   *The Spiritual Cure*

THERE WAS A SICK MAN WHOM A GREAT JEWISH doctor could not cure, and the sick person could no longer speak. The Besht came to that place, and they called him to see the sick man. The Besht told them to cook meat soup for the sick person and that then he would start talking immediately. They gave him soup to eat and the Besht treated him until he recovered.

The doctor asked the Besht how he cured him: "I know that his veins were bad, and it is impossible to provide any remedy for such veins."

The Besht said to him: "You approached the sick man corporeally and I approached him spiritually. A man has 248 members in his body and 365 veins. Corresponding to them are 248 positive and 365 negative commandments. If a man commits one crime, God forbid, the corresponding member or vein becomes ill. If he does not observe many negative commandments, many veins become ill. The blood no longer flows in them and the person is in danger. I urged the soul to accept repentence and it did so. In this way all his members and veins were repaired and I could cure him."[1]

158] *The Stolen Stockings*

THE BESHT HAD A SERVANT WHOSE NAME WAS Rabbi Aaron. He married and no longer wanted to be a servant. He asked the Besht to accept Rabbi Jacob as his servant.

Once Rabbi Jacob traveled with the Besht and they slept overnight in a village. They had a small house near the *arrendator* which was vacated for them, but a pair of stockings had been left behind on a pole. When the Besht continued on his way, the servant, Rabbi Jacob, hid the stockings. They had not gone far when the Besht ordered a halt and he said to the servant: "You stole something." He denied it.

"The dog calls you a thief and you deny it?"

Nevertheless, he kept denying it. The Besht told him where the stockings were hidden and he confessed. The servant told the gentile servant to return the stockings to the inn.

The Besht said to him: "You yourself should go and return what you have stolen."

From then on he did not steal a single thing. The rabbi of our community heard it from the servant himself, and I heard it from the rabbi.

159] *Writing Down the Besht's Torah*

I HEARD THIS FROM THE RABBI OF OUR COMMUNITY.
There was a man who wrote down the torah of the Besht that he
heard from him. Once the Besht saw a demon walking and holding a book in his hand. He said to him: "What is the book that
you hold in your hand?"

He answered him: "This is the book that you have written."

The Besht then understood that there was a person who was
writing down his torah. He gathered all his followers and asked
them: "Who among you is writing down my torah?"

The man admitted it and he brought the manuscript to the
Besht. The Besht examined it and said: "There is not even a single
word here that is mine."

160] *The Besht and His Son*

ONCE WHEN HE WAS A BOY, RABBI TSEVI, THE SON
of the Besht, went with his father to greet the local rabbi. And he
observed that there were a great many pieces of silverware there.
On the way back the Besht said to his son: "You are doubtless
envious because your father does not possess any silverware."

His son said: "Yes."

The Besht said: "If your father had money for silverware, it
would be better used to provide for poor people and the rest to
give for charity."

161] *The Generosity of the Besht*

I HEARD FROM THE RABBI THAT THE BESHT NEVER
kept money overnight. When he returned from his travels he used
to pay his debts, and he would give the rest of it to charity on
the very same day. Once he returned from his travels with a great
deal of money. He paid his debts and gave charity, and he asked

his followers to provide him with a mitzvah on which he could spend the money.

Meanwhile, his wife took part of the money and said to herself: "For a few days I will not have to buy on credit."

That night he felt some hindrance in his worship. He realized what had happened, and he returned home and said: "Admit who it was who took some of my money."

His wife admitted that she had taken some of the money. That night he ordered them to gather the poor people, and he divided the money among them.

162] *The Demons*

I heard this from the rabbi, Rabbi Gedaliah. The daughter-in-law of Rabbi Moses, the rabbi of the holy community of Kuty, "experienced the pain of bringing up children,"[1] and she consulted gentile sorceresses. They performed their charms, and they put an emasculated cock under the threshold of the house.[2] From this bit of sorcery a demon came to inhabit the house.

One night Rabbi Moses saw pigs walking on the ceiling, and he left the house. The Preacher came and said to the rabbi: "Let me live in your house."

He answered him: "If I had a suitable house I would be living in it."

The Preacher said to him: "Nevertheless, I will live there. I have had trouble with my neighbors." And he moved in.

Once the Preacher was sitting in his small house, wrapped in his tallith and tefillin. The door was open and his baby was walking in the passageway. The Preacher saw that the demon was about to approach the boy, and he scolded it saying: "What are you doing here?"

The demon answered: "And what are you doing here?"

The Preacher realized that he had to leave the house, but since it was evening he said he would leave the place on the following day. He asked three friends to sleep overnight in the house, and they sat and studied. After a while the Preacher wanted to sleep a little bit, and he said to them: "I will go to sleep, but you remain awake, for the sake of heaven, and study."

When he fell asleep, all of them dozed over their books, and the candle died out. The demon poured a pile of sand from the attic on each book. When the Preacher awoke and realized that it was dark, he began to tremble. He entered the main house and the demon threw a board from the attic at him. Had he not stepped back a little into the room, he would have been injured, God forbid. He remained frozen with fear in one spot until he heard the call of the rooster. Then he took a candle and went to light it. The window was lit up in the rabbi's house, and he went there to light his candle. The rabbi realized that the Preacher was terribly frightened. He asked him about it, but the Preacher did not want to answer him until he had lit the candle in his hand, as it is written in *Sefer Hasidim.*[3] Then he told the rabbi.

The rabbi said: "Didn't I tell you?"

The Preacher entered the house and found all of them asleep with a pile of sand on each book. In the morning he left the house.

When the house was torn down each of the neighbors took a bench or a board or some other wooden parts and the Preacher took something as well. That night the demon knocked on the walls and windows of each house of the people who had taken something.

On the third night the Besht said: "I will be at your place and the demon will not knock any more. I will sleep for a while, and when you hear ringing at the window or at any other place you should say: 'Israel, son of Eliezer, is here, and it will not knock again.' " And so it was.

Then the Preacher said: "Since the name Israel, son of Eliezer, is a *name*, it means that he is a tsaddik." After that he became his close follower.[4]

163] *The Guest Who Snored*

I HEARD THAT ONCE A GUEST STAYED WITH THE Besht and slept overnight in his house. And he snored, as some people do. Rabbi Tsevi, the Besht's son, was then a small boy and the sound frightened him. He went to his father and told him. His father said to him: "Swing the door open and closed, and you will not hear any sound from him. He will sleep quietly." He did so and it helped.

The following night his son tried this remedy again by himself, but it did not help. He went to his father, who said to him: "Last night they discharged the Angel of Sleep and appointed a new one. In the interim the charm worked, but today the new angel is instated and the charm is of no avail."

164] *The Impure House*

IN THE HOLY COMMUNITY OF NEMIROV THERE WAS an impure house. They asked the Besht to examine the house. He asked the Preacher to accompany him. The Besht saw a demon standing there, but the Preacher did not see it. The Preacher asked him to enable him to see it as well. The Besht said to him: "But you will be frightened."

He said: "No."

The Besht said to him: "Close and open your eyes several times." The Preacher did so, and he saw the demon standing in the corner of the house facing the wall. The demon was as dark as a cloud. The Preacher asked the Besht: "Why does the demon turn his face away?"

The Besht answered: "He is ashamed before me." Then the Preacher began to be afraid. The Besht said to him: "Close and open your eyes as you did the first time, and you will not see it any more."

He did so and he could no longer see the demon.

The householder asked the Besht to banish the demon, but the Besht refused.

165] *The Preacher Who Spoke Evil of the Jews*

I HEARD FROM THE RABBI OF OUR COMMUNITY THAT he heard the following from the Hasid, our teacher Ze'ev of Olyka. Once the Besht observed the Sabbath in that holy community with a householder who was an elder of the community. On the Sabbath the householder went to the synagogue for Minhah to listen to a sermon of a visiting preacher, and the Besht waited to begin the third meal until he arrived from the synagogue. While waiting the Besht heard that the preacher was vilifying the Jews. The Besht became angry, and he told the gabbai to go and call the householder. The gabbai reported to a few people that the Besht was angry at the preacher. The preacher saw that the people dropped out one by one, and he stopped preaching.

The following day the preacher came to the Besht and greeted him. The Besht asked him who he was, and he replied: "I am the preacher. Why did you become angry with me?"

The Besht jumped up and tears poured from his eyes. He said: "You speak evil of the Jewish people. A Jew goes to the market every day, but toward evening, when it becomes dark, he becomes anxious. '*Oy*, I'll skip Minhah.' He goes to a house and prays the Minhah. Even if he does not know what he is saying, the seraphim and the *ofannim*[1] are stirred by it."

166] *The Dead Man in Hell*

I HEARD THIS STORY FROM RABBI MOSES, THE SON-in-law of the sister of the rabbi of the holy community of Polonnoye, who heard it himself from the Besht when he told it in the following words to the villagers in the holy community of Nemirov.

"Once in a dream I was walking in a field, and in the distance I saw mist. I went on until I arrived at one side of the place where the mist was. The sun cast light on this side and also on the road, but opposite me it was foggy. It was as if I were standing on a long slope. I went on until I came to the end of the valley. For several years I had had a gentile servant who had left me. I saw him there walking with a heavy load of wood on his shoulders. When he saw me he threw down the wood and fell at my feet, and he said: 'When I served you, sir, I used to observe the Sabbath. When I left you I served an *arrendator* who made me work on the Sabbath. He used to order me to go to the forest on the Sabbath to bring wood. Now both of us are dead, and each Sabbath I have to bring wood to Gehenna until there is enough there for the *arrendator* for every day of the week. I ask you to wait for me until I return. Since you, sir, are very important in this world, I will show you, sir, the place where you can ask them to release me from my sentence. I cannot show it to you now because the attendants are just behind me.'

"The Besht said to him: 'If I am important in this world, put down the wood and show me the place immediately.'

"He went with me and showed me a palace. I entered the palace. I pleaded for him and they released him from the sentence. When I pleaded for the gentile I appealed for the Jew as well, and they released him also from the sentence.'"[1]

167] *The Servant's Evil Thoughts*

I HEARD FROM THE RABBI OF OUR COMMUNITY THAT once the Besht traveled from the village of Chertryeh[1] and slept overnight near the village in a forest where Jewish people had been killed on several occasions. He wanted to sleep there in order to banish the demon responsible for the murders in that place. He said to his followers: "I am going to sleep, but you remain awake. Recite the Psalms because our gentile servant wants to kill us. Stay awake the whole night."

In the morning they sent the servant to the village for water so they could wash. While they were eating the Besht called the servant and gave him a glass of mead, which he drank. The Besht said to him: "Confess that you wanted to kill us last night."

He said: "It is so."

"You wanted to kill me another time near the holy community of Nemirov."

He said to him: "It is true."

He said to him: "Why did you plan to do this? Don't you know that it is impossible to trick me?"

He said, as the gentiles say: "A demon has his teeth in me."

168] *"Streams of Wisdom"*

I HEARD THIS FROM THE RABBI, THE HASID, RABBI Jehiel Mikhel of the holy community of Zolochev. When he visited here in the town of Ilintsy for the wedding of his son, our teacher Ze'ev, he said that he was ordered from heaven to accept the Besht as his rabbi and to go and learn from him. They showed him the "streams of wisdom" which led to the Besht. When the Besht passed away he was ordered to accept the Great Maggid, Rabbi Dov, as his rabbi. They showed him that the same "streams of wisdom" that formerly ran to the Besht now led to the rabbi, the Maggid, God bless his memory.

169] *Rabbi Eliezer and Rabbi Naḥman*

I HEARD FROM THE SAME RABBI THAT RABBI ELIEZER of Amsterdam went to the Holy Land for the sake of Rabbi Naḥman of Horodenka. He said: "When both of us are in the Holy Land we will bring the redeemer."

When he came to the Holy Land all the people from his town who were there welcomed him. When he saw Rabbi Samson, Rabbi Naḥman's son, he asked him: "Where is your father?"

He said to him: "He went abroad."

He said: "*Vey, Vey,* I came because of him."

When Rabbi Naḥman heard that Rabbi Eliezer had gone to the Holy Land he hastened his return, but because of our many sins, Rabbi Eliezer died just before his arrival.[1]

170] *The Contaminated Bed*

I HEARD THIS AS WELL FROM THE RABBI OF OUR community. In the holy community of Ladimir there was a rich man who had no sons. He sent for Besht and when he came they made a bed for him on which he sat down. He immediately got up and said:

"The sin of adultery was committed on this very bed."

The man said that it was not his bed. There was an informer who had harmed many people of the town. When he died they pillaged all his property, and the rich man took the bed.

The Besht remained there for the Sabbath and told the householder that he would have sons if he would agree that they be deformed. He agreed and he had three sons who were hunchbacked.

171] *Rabbi Tsevi's Dream*

I HEARD THIS FROM THE RABBI OF THE HOLY community of Polonnoye. Rabbi Tsevi, the Besht's son saw his father in his dream two years before the flight.[1] He was in great trouble because he was in debt to various noblemen, and he did not have money to pay them. He asked his father: "Did you know of my trouble?"

He said: "I knew."

He said: "Who told you?"

He said: "Those who walked by the crossroads informed me."

He asked: "Who are those who walked by the crossroads?"

He said: "Abraham, Isaac, and Jacob. They walk by the crossroads to learn the troubles of the Jews, and then they go to the tombs of the tsaddikim and inform them. They told me about your grief. But I do not have time to talk with you because I have to go and nullify plots of the thieves called Haidamaks."

This dream took place three weeks before Passover. On that Passover holiday there was a plot against the holy community of Whitefield and several people were arrested. They sent a messenger to the rabbi to pray for them. On the seventh day of the Passover he said the "Song of the Sea"[2] with great joy before the ark. During dinner my father-in-law heard him say: "I believe the Shekinah hovered above during the reciting of the 'Song of the

Sea,' and I have faith in God, blessed be He, that the decree will be nullified."

And so it was. In the last days of the Passover they were found not guilty and were released from prison. They were completely vindicated.

After the Passover, robbers attacked several villages. Afterwards, about five hundred thieves gathered. That night they attacked the city of Krasne and besieged it the entire day. All the townspeople fled into the fortress and fought from there until almost all the gunpowder in the fortress was used up. The thieves found three women. They took wagons loaded with hay. The women pulled the wagons with the hay, and they pushed them from behind. They wanted to set the fortress on fire. There was a Polish army camp near the city of Tuberig,[3] and at that moment the army arrived with their cannon. All the thieves ran away and not even a single one remained behind. And that whole summer they left us in peace.

172] *The Protective Tefillin*

I HEARD THIS FROM A MAN WHOSE NAME WAS Rabbi Ze'ev. He was the brother of Rabbi Leib, a Hasid of Ilintsy, who lived in the Holy Land for more than thirty years and passed away in the Holy City, Jerusalem. Rabbi Ze'ev was also a learned and God-fearing man whose word could be trusted. I heard another version of this from the rabbi of our community, and I will write down his view as well.

Once the Besht became so ill that he lost the power of speech. His followers stood around him, and he motioned to them to put his tefillin on him, and they did so. He lay wearing the tefillin a long while. Then he began to talk. They asked him: "What happened?"

He told them that there was a sin that he had committed in his boyhood and that an accusation had been made against him. His rabbi came and informed him about it and said: "Hurry. Put on the tefillin."

"Then the accuser came in the image of a gentile with an iron shovel in his hand to cut off my head. But because of the tefillin he could not get near me. He shouted at me in Russian: 'Throw away that leather!' But I did not pay any attention to him, and he continued shouting until the accusation was nullified."[1]

The rabbi said that he saw that the gates were closed, and they did not want to let his brother-in-law, Rabbi Gershon, in. He took a big piece of wood and knocked on the gates until they were opened. Rabbi Gershon entered and shouted angrily at the court: "Will you condemn him to death, God forbid, for such a trivial thing?"

This is what is said in the *Tikkunei Zohar:* "The commandment of *Matronita* places a man under its wings and does not expose him to the hand of the accuser. So it is with the commandment of wearing tefillin."[2]

173] *Rabbi Jehiel Mikhel*

I HEARD FROM THE RABBI OF OUR COMMUNITY THAT the Besht accompanied the rabbi, our teacher Jehiel Mikhel, to his rabbinical post in the holy community of Horodnya.[1] On Friday night they went astray, and it was so dark that they actually could not see each other. The Besht got down from the wagon to look for the road, and then the rabbi, our teacher Jehiel Mikhel, got down, too. He found the Besht lying on the ground with his arms and legs outstretched, crying bitterly and tearing at the hair on his head. He said that we will profane the Sabbath, God forbid.

Rabbi Jehiel Mikhel said: "If we had seen nothing other than his bitter weeping because of profaning the Sabbath, it would have been sufficient."

After that they came to the holy community of Horodnya and the rabbi preached there on the Sabbath. During the sermon there was a great argument in the synagogue. A great scholar named Rabbi Mikhel the Judge, who was very sharp-witted, posed difficult questions. The rabbi excused himself: "At the third meal I will answer the questions for you."

The community had a large house which was used only when they received a new rabbi. They prepared the third meal for all the people of the town. They seated each person according to his standing. The judge, Rabbi Mikhel, sat next to the rabbi, while Rabbi Ze'ev Kotses sat at the lower end of the table.

The Besht scolded him in these words: "I despise a man who prides himself on being humble. Come and sit here."

The rabbi began to answer questions in his sermon. Rabbi Mikhel presented difficult problems, and Rabbi Ze'ev argued with him until he won. Rabbi Mikhel was embarrassed, but he protested that the point was incorrect, and he refused to admit the truth. The Besht began to speak and he said: "Do not upset the gathering." Rabbi Mikhel became quiet.

After the Sabbath the Besht and the rabbi traveled to a village for a berith. Rabbi Mikhel hurried forward in order to accompany them, and they took him along in the wagon. On the way he began to talk about astrology, and Rabbi Ze'ev Kotses discussed it with him. He realized that Rabbi Ze'ev was as knowledgeable as he was about astrology, and he wondered how a Hasid came to learn about such things.

Afterwards when the Besht wanted to continue on his way, he was afraid that Rabbi Mikhel would disturb the rabbi, and so he wiped away all his knowledge so that he became an unlettered man.

It was Rabbi Mikhel's custom to get up at midnight to learn Gemara, the codifiers, and *Rambam*, but when he opened the book he did not know a single thing. He thought that his mind was not clear because he had drunk a lot of mead. He closed the book and smoked his pipe. Then he napped for a little while and lay down until the morning. In the morning after the prayer he used to study the daily portion. He took the book and opened it, and he did not know a single thing. He realized that the Besht had done this to him. He went to the Besht and said: "Rabbi, give me back my learning."

The Besht scolded him, saying: "Is it to argue and tease that we learn the Torah?" He scolded him and Rabbi Mikhel became a complete tsaddik.[2]

174] *The War Between the Greeks and the Ishmaelites*

I HEARD THIS FROM THE RABBI OF THE HOLY community of Polonnoye. In his lifetime, when there was a war between the Greeks and the Ishmaelites, the Besht said: "I perceived two rulers fighting with each other, and the Ishmaelite ruler overcame the other. I perceived the Greek ruler departing in anger. I realized that the Jews will have great trials, God forbid. I prayed that the situation be reversed, that the Greek ruler overcome the Ishmaelite. There were only two Jews whom I could not save from their hands."

175] *The Flickering Candle*

I HEARD THAT THE BESHT STAYED OVER FOR THE Sabbath with a tsaddik, and the candle began to flicker. The Besht said: "The candle tells me that you had intercourse by candle light." This was the truth but he was not guilty. The candle had gone down and he thought that it had died out completely, but then it began to cast light as a candle does at the very end.[1]

176] *The Poverty and Generosity of the Besht*

I HEARD FROM RABBI ZELIG OF THE HOLY COMmunity of Letichev that while on a journey he came to the holy community of Shpola, which was then a village, and he stayed with the shohet. They heard that the rabbi, Rabbi Meir, the district rabbi, had come to the community, and they went to welcome him.* The rabbi asked Rabbi Zelig to remain there several days until all the villagers had gathered for the court trials,

* Rabbi Meir Margaliot was elected as the Lvov regional Rabbi in 1755. According to Gelber (*The History of the Jews in Brody*, p. 43), the Rabbi expressed his admiration of the Besht in his book *Sod Yakhin ve Boaz* ["The Secret of Jachin and Boas"] (Polonnoye, 1795), p. 5.

and in the meanwhile he would keep him company. Rabbi Zelig sat with the rabbi who told this story to him:

"Once the Besht traveled to the holy community of Brody, and he passed through Horodenka. He stopped before my house and sent for me to come out. Then I was not yet the head of the court.*

"The Besht said: "Meir, sit with me in the wagon and travel with me to the holy community of Brody.'

"I took the sack with my tefillin and the tallith and an overcoat and I traveled with him. When we came to the holy community of Brody, he stayed in the inn as merchants are accustomed to do. No one came to see him except two people, one of whom was wealthy and the other of whom was not. They were important people. They greeted him and came to him often. I saw that the Besht did not have any more money—not even a single coin. I was sorry I had not taken money from my home. I heard him saying to the wagon driver: 'Prepare yourself for the journey.' I went and informed these two people that the Besht was leaving and they came to the inn. When they saw that he was not yet ready to depart they said: 'We will go to the beth-hamidrash, and when the Besht is ready to go, Rabbi Meir will send us a message, and we will return.'

"And so it was that when they were so informed they returned. When the wealthy man had come the first time that day he had given the Besht a golden red coin. When he returned the second time, the Besht took that golden red coin and gave it back to the wealthy man saying, 'Give twelve golden coins to the members of the *klaus*'—of whom the Besht thought very highly and had said that he had seen the Shekinah hovering above the *klaus*—'the remaining twelve golden coins you should distribute among the poor.' And they left the town.

"When I saw how he tossed away the golden red coin I lost my heart, as I knew that he had not a single coin. I asked him why he was doing it, since he lacked even one coin for his expenses. He answered me very clearly: 'Know without doubt that as long as I live we have nothing to worry about.'

"And so it was. When they arrived at the holy community of

Radzivilov, the people of the town began to visit him to ask for remedies. It was like this in every place, and he returned home with a sum of money."[1]

177] *The Shabbetian Shohet*

I HEARD FROM THE RABBI OF OUR COMMUNITY that the Besht notified the rabbi of the holy community of Byshev that his shohet was from the sect of Shabbetai Tsevi, may his name be blotted out, and that he made the meat not kosher. After showing the rabbi his knife, the shohet would hit it with a heavy hammer in order to disqualify it. The rabbi watched the shohet and found it to be true.

178] *The Hen Shohet*

WHEN RABBI DAVID FORKES AND THE BESHT CAME to the holy community of Konstantynow, the Besht ordered that the shohet come to show him his knife, but the shohet did not come right away. When the Besht began to pray the shohet came, but he did not want to wait. He demanded that the housewife let him slaughter the hens, and she gave in. He slaughtered them and went away.

After the prayer the Besht said: "Has the shohet not come yet?"

They answered him: "He came already and slaughtered the hens."

The hens were still lying in salt. The Besht looked at them and said that he would eat them. Rabbi David refused to eat, but the Besht was not strict about it.

179] *The Melamed's Death*

I HEARD THIS FROM THE RABBI OF OUR COMMUNITY. Once the Besht was in the Padberezye region, and he said that a tsaddik passed away nearby, and he believed that he was a melamed in the holy community of Konstantynow "because I saw the ascension of his soul, and I recognized him by his movements."

180] *The Invisibility of the Besht*

I HEARD FROM THE RABBI OF OUR COMMUNITY that a nobleman hated the Besht and said that when he saw the Besht he would kill him with a gun. Once the Besht was walking around in the yard of the manor house with the governor. That nobleman came to the manor house, and the governor left the Besht and went to talk to him, and he led him into his house. The Besht came into the house as well and said farewell to the governor and went home. The governor wondered about this since he knew that that nobleman was very angry at the Besht. During the meal the governor talked with this nobleman about the Besht, and the nobleman said that he would kill him if he saw him. The governor said to him: "But he was here when you came, and he also entered the house to take his farewell."

He said: "I did not see him." He said, "Since he is a man who is able to make himself invisible at will, I will have to become reconciled with him."

181] *Rabbi Moses' Death*

I HEARD FROM THE RABBI OF OUR COMMUNITY that once the tsitsith of the Besht's tallith was soiled with mud. He said that Rabbi Moses of Satanov had died. And he said: "I did not detain him. Why do they impress him on my tsitsith?"

182] *Rabbi Zusman*

INCIDENTALLY, I WILL WRITE DOWN WHAT I HEARD from the rabbi, our teacher Rabbi Jehiel, the head of the court in the holy community of Kovel. In that city there was a man whose name was Rabbi Zusman. He was very rich and influential in the town. Once on Sabbath Eve Rabbi Jehiel left for his home after prayer, and he heard that in the synagogue they had just welcomed the Sabbath. He sent to the shammash and asked him: "Why were you late in welcoming the Sabbath in the synagogue?"

He answered that Rabbi Zusman was in the manor house, and they had waited for him.

He said: "And if Rabbi Zusman would not have arrived until tomorrow would you have waited to welcome the Sabbath until tomorrow?"

Rabbi Zusman's wife heard this and said: "If the rabbi prays kedushah, *Bless ye the Lord*, and amen in the synagogue without waiting for my husband I will close your beth-hamidrash."

The rabbi used to pray in a special small room in the beth-hamidrash where he was able to hear the kedushah, *Bless ye the Lord*, and amen. In the morning when she got up she went to the washbasin and washed her face and hands. When she went to take the towel to dry them, she froze like a stone.

They ran to the rabbi, who was praying, and he said: "And let it *be cut off*."[1] He made a motion with his hand and she died.

183] *The Death of the* Arrendator's *Wife*

THERE IS ANOTHER STORY ABOUT THE RABBI WHO ordered the villagers to be in the city for the Passover holiday. The custom was that he appointed two students to go from house to house. The pots and dishes would be rinsed, and the matzoth would be baked in their presence.

In one village there was a learned *arrendator* who did not pay attention to the rabbi's order and did not come to the city for the Passover. His tavern keeper did not come to the city either. During the intermediary days of the holiday the *arrendator* came to the city and the rabbi sent for him. He said: "Because you have not been in the city for the first days of the Passover you will be in the city for the last days."

And so it was. When he came back to the village he found that his wife had died. He brought his wife to the city on the sixth day of the Passover. By the time that they buried her it was nightfall, and he had to stay the last day of the holiday in the city. His tavern keeper died during the kiddush of the last day of the holiday.

184] *The Bastard*

IT HAPPENED THAT WHEN THE RABBI WAS THE head of the court in the holy community of Horodnya there was a berith, and he refused to be the godfather. They insisted until he said that the boy was a bastard. The father of the baby was a member of a large family. When the family heard his words they began to shout, and there was a great tumult in the synagogue. The rabbi said to the shammash: "Take my staff in your hand. Go to the new mother and show her the staff, and she will confess immediately. If she does not she will die."

She confessed and said that she was raped. She had gone to the cellar to bring wine, and a certain master ran after her and raped her. Then all her family kept quiet.

185] *Praying Word for Word with the Besht*

I HEARD IN THE NAME OF RABBI ELIJAH OF THE holy community of Sokolov[1] that when he was young he lived in the holy community of Medzhibozh, and once he heard that the Besht said: "Anyone who wants his prayer to ascend to heaven should pray word for word with me."

Rabbi Elijah did so. When the Besht said "Lord," he said it also. When the Besht said "world," he also said "world." And he followed him through the whole prayer. They did this for a long time.

Once the Besht came across the verse, *A horse is a vain thing for safety,*[2] in the *Pesukei de Zimrah,*[3] and he kept repeating it over and over. The first time Rabbi Elijah repeated it with him he wondered what the Besht was referring to in this verse. He looked at the book *Mishnat Hasidim*,[4] and he could not find any kavvanoth. And he stopped praying with the Besht.

Once he come to the Besht's house. The Besht saw him and said to him: "Elijah, you have stopped praying with me."

He told him that the reason was that the Besht had repeated the verse several times.

The Besht answered that a Jew had been traveling when the Sabbath Eve fell. He could not reach any settlement before the Sabbath in the field. A robber learned that a Jew was observing the Sabbath in the field, and he went on horseback to find him and kill him. "By saying this verse I confused his way so that he was not able to find him."

186] *The Defective Mezuzah*

ONCE WHEN THE BESHT WAS IN THE HOLY COM-munity of Nemirov he was going from a big room to a small room, and by mistake he went to the cellar. He entered the cellar and ordered that the mezuzah be checked. A man asked him: "And if a man goes astray should he immediately attach some cause to it? Perhaps it is an accident?"

The Besht answered him: "There are no accidents so far as I am concerned."

This shows that everyone should believe that everything comes from Providence and he should not relate it to chance, God forbid.

187] *The Amulet*

THE RABBI OF THE HOLY COMMUNITY OF POLON-noye had an amulet made by the Rabbi Naphtali, and he showed it to the Besht. The Besht could tell that it was written while Rabbi Naphtali was in the mikveh and was fasting. He said:

"I could write such an amulet after eating and while sitting on a bed."[1]

188] *The Devoted Weaver*

I HEARD ALSO FROM THE RABBI OF THE HOLY community of Polonnoye that the rabbi mentioned above used to select an old woman and give her a gold coin for not speaking a word the entire time while winding four tsitsith, each with eight fringes. When they brought him tsitsith from the holy community of Kalisz for the first time, he bought them because they were very pretty. Still he was afraid to put them in his tallith for fear they were not wound with devotion.

He showed them to the Besht who said: "If you are afraid to put them in your tallith, give them to me and I will put them in my tallith."

And he realized that they were woven with devotion.

189] *The Turnip*

I HEARD THAT ONCE THEY PUT A TURNIP ON THE Besht's table, but he refused to eat it. They asked him why, and he said: "This turnip grew in a gentile cemetary."

They did not want to eat it either, and they put it at the end of the table.

190] *Two Rabbis David*

I HEARD FROM THE RABBI OF OUR COMMUNITY that in the holy community of Mikolajow there were two Hasidim and that both of them were named Rabbi David. One was an old man whom we knew, and the other died in his youth. Once they traveled together with the Besht. They asked him: "Our rabbi, tell us what we have to correct in ourselves."

He ordered each of them to read from a book, and one read—I do not know whether it was Mishnah, *Ein Ya'akov,* or the Zohar—and then he ordered the second one to read. The Besht said: "Now I know."

He told one his sin in the presence of his friend. Then he ordered the other one to get down from the wagon. He got down with him and spoke to him in secret because it was an embarrassing matter. The rabbi said that the Rabbis David loved each other, and when one of them died the other one mourned him for many days. Once he came to the Besht, who tried to console him. He said: "Do not worry about your friend. I was in the palace of King David, and I saw your friend there. I asked him whether he corrected the matter that he had to, and he said that he had done it already in his lifetime. I saw the Tanna, Rabbi Akiva, standing there on guard in a red garment and with a spear in his hand."

191] *The Angel Hadarniel*

I HEARD ALSO FROM THE RABBI MENTIONED ABOVE that the Besht saw the angel Hadarniel, who was the second angel that Moses, our teacher, may he rest in peace, encountered in his ascension on Mount Sinai, as it is said in the holy Zohar.[1]

192] *The Young Martyr*

I HEARD FROM THE RABBI OF OUR COMMUNITY that once a youth died as a martyr in the holy community of Polonnoye when a false libel was charged against him. His martyrdom was very painful.

Once the Besht came to the holy community of Polonnoye. He stopped at the house of the youth's mother, and he sent for her. When she came out he consoled her saying: "Know that at the hour of his death they opened for him the heavenly world that they had opened for Isaac at the time of his sacrifice."[1] The Besht was afraid to enter the house because it belonged to gentiles, and he said that the youth had been killed because of that house.

193] *Rabbi Gershon in the Holy Land*

I HEARD FROM THE RABBI MENTIONED ABOVE THAT once the Besht said: "I am puzzled. On Sabbath Eve during prayer I looked for Rabbi Gershon, and I did not find him in the Land of Israel. On Sabbath morning during prayer I saw him in the Land of Israel, and I do not know what happened, unless he went outside the border." Several years later Rabbi Gershon came to him, and the Besht asked him about this matter, and Rabbi Gershon did not know either. Later he recalled that they had honored him with the mitzvah of the berith in Acre, and he had kept the Sabbath there. In Acre there are two synagogues, one in the Land of Israel and one outside. "On Sabbath Eve I went to pray in the synagogue outside, but later it hurt my heart that I had not prayed in the Land of Israel, and so the following day I prayed in the synagogue in the Land of Israel."[1]

194] *Storytelling and* Ma'aseh Merkavah

WHEN THERE WAS A BERITH AT THE HOUSE OF THE head of the court of the holy community of Horodnya, I heard from the rabbi of the holy community of Polonnoye and then from the rabbi of our community that the Besht said: "When one tells stories in praise of the tsaddikim, it is though he were engaged in *Ma'aseh Merkavah*."[1]

195] *Man in the World*

I ALSO HEARD: "IN WHATEVER WORLD MAN IS, IT IS AS if the worlds were spread before him."

196] *The Demon*

Once i was in the holy community of Tulchin with a man whose name was Rabbi David. At that time there was a marriage arrangement made between the Hasid, our teacher Barukh and the Hasid Rabbi Joseph, the son of Rabbi Jehiel Mikhel, God bless his memory. Rabbi David heard this from Rabbi Joseph who heard it from the Besht.

"*And Jacob sent messengers before him.*[1] These are the angels."[2] He said that angels were at the right hand of Jacob, our Patriarch, and demons were at his left hand. Angels were also on the right side of the Besht, and demons were on his left side.[3] But he refused to use the angels because they were holy, and he refused to use the demons because they were liars.

There was a widow who lived in a certain village, and a man came to take the *arrendeh* from her. He went to the master to rent the *arrendeh*. A demon asked that he be sent to this man, but the Besht refused. A demon urged the Besht to send him, saying that he promised to do whatever the Besht would order him to. The Besht sent him and commanded him: "Be careful not to do any harm to him. But when he wants to speak before the master cover his mouth with your hand."

The demon let the man talk all that he wanted, and he waited until he took the *arrendeh* and accepted the contract. On the man's return when he arrived at a bridge, the demon tripped him, and the man fell down on the bridge. The Besht ran to the man and ordered the demon to come out of the man without harming him. The demon answered: "You see, my master, I obey your order." I do not remember, but I believe that the man remained healthy and strong.

197] *Competing for the* Arrendeh

I heard this story from my father-in-law, our teacher and rabbi, Alexander.

There was a man who wanted to take the *arrendeh* in a village away from a widow. The Besht chastised him, but he did not listen to him. He rode on horseback by the Besht's house and knocked on the window and said: "See, I am going to rent the village *arrendeh,* and let us see what God will do to me."

And the Besht shed tears.

When the man came to the village he rented the *arrendeh* by offering a great sum of money. As the master was about to write the contract, the man's head began to ache. He said to the master: "I have a terrible headache."

The master said: "Sit down, I will not delay writing the contract."

He waited for a while. He said a second time: "I have a terrible headache." He said: "Lie down on the bed."

Saliva began to flow from his mouth. The master ordered his servant to throw him among the pigs. As it is said: "They suffer not a man to be near them except it be for their own requirement, . . . but they do not stand by a man in the hour of his distress."[1]

They brought him home. His hands and legs were paralyzed, and his tongue was also paralyzed. They called the Besht to cure him, and the man began to speak a little. Meanwhile, the Besht noticed that the members of his family asked gentile sorceresses to cure him, and after that he refused to go to him. And the man was only able to speak a few words.

198] *The Imprisonment of Israel Shafir*

I HEARD FROM THE RABBI OF OUR COMMUNITY that there was a man named Rabbi Israel Shafir in the holy community of Mohilev[1] who was slandered by the governor. He went to the governor, and on his way he made a special trip to the Besht to tell him his problem and to ask him about it. The Besht said to him: "Do not be afraid. Every man has to be imprisoned once."

He went to the governor in great fear. On his arrival he found favor in the eyes of the governor, who even loaned him more money. On his return from the governor he passed through the holy community of Bar. The governor of that city put him in prison on some matter. The people of the town said to the governor, "Leave him alone because he is the kind of man who can cause you trouble." And he let him return home in peace.

199] *The Preacher Cancels the Charges Against a Rabbi*

In the holy community of bar, one of the townspeople argued with the head of the court, and then he went to the governor to complain about him. I do not know whether the matter concerned rabbinical affairs or some other business. He took a special trip to the Besht to ask him to pray that the governor fulfill his wish. After the Besht promised him that he would, he continued on his way.

At that time the Preacher was in the holy community of Medzhibozh, and he knew that the rabbi, the head of the court, was in the right in his dispute with the people of the town and that his opponent was an evil man. The Preacher was afraid to tell this to the Besht, and so what did he do? He secretly gathered a minyan. He took a Torah scroll and canceled the charges against the rabbi, the head of the court, so that they would not be able to hurt him.

Once, and I believe it was the first of the month, the Preacher and his in-law, whom I believe was Rabbi Ze'ev Kotses, sat at the Besht's table. During the meal the Besht said: "I do not understand what happened. I prayed for a man from the holy community of Bar. Sometimes they respond to my prayers and yet hang back."

The Preacher, God bless his memory, began to laugh a little.

His in-law said: "Why is it that I saw a minyan called to you?" The Preacher tried to ignore him and did not answer. The Besht pressed him to tell the story.

The Preacher answered him: "I can not deny our rabbi. That man from the holy community of Bar spoke very nicely to you, but I know the heart of the matter. The rabbi is right in his dispute with the people of the town. I gathered a minyan. I took a Torah scroll and I canceled the charges against him."

The Besht said to him: "Blessings be on your head. You have done well."

200] *The Sermon of Rabbi Moses*

I HEARD FROM RABBI YAKIL OF THE HOLY COM-munity of Medzhibozh, may he rest in peace, that in the holy community of Bar there was a hazan in the beth-hamidrash named Rabbi Moses who was a wonderful tsaddik. Once they asked him to pray on Rosh Hashanah in the beth-hamidrash. I do not know whether it was the Shaharith or the second day's Musaf. There was another hazan who had the same prayer on the first day. He asked Rabbi Moses to switch days with him so that Rabbi Moses would pray on the first day. And so he did. Rabbi Moses prayed on the first day of the holiday. During the spoken eighteen bene-dictions, Rabbi Moses turned his face toward the congregation and said to the other cantor, calling him by name: "Why did you make me a target for arrows?" He preached a moralizing sermon for about half an hour, and there was great weeping in the synagogue. Then he continued in his prayer. The learned men were upset because he had interrupted the eighteen benedictions. After Minhah, when they went to say tashlik,* Rabbi Yakil asked him why he had interrupted the eighteen benedictions, and he did not know anything about it and could not recall a single thing.

Rabbi Yakil told me: "I would not have believed it, but once I had heard that the Besht fell upon the ark and did not recall it later, and so I knew that something like that was possible."

201] *The Angels' Request*

I HEARD FROM THE RABBI OF OUR COMMUNITY that when the rabbi of the holy community of Polonnoye was the head of the court in the holy community of Raszkow, the angels

* A religious rite performed on the afternoon of the first day of Rosh Hashanah.

said to the Besht: "Why do you keep still when the rabbi of the holy community of Raszkow can not make a living?"[1]

202] *Rabbi Moses the Mohel*

I heard from the rabbi of the holy community of Polonnoye that when Rabbi Moses the cantor circumcised a Jewish infant, his face shone until the third day. The rabbi of our community said to me that his brother was a shohet in the holy community of Kuty and that Rabbi Moses was from that region also.

203] *The Besht Chokes on His Food*

I heard that once the Besht, God bless his memory, was attending a feast celebrating the redemption of the first born,* and at the end of the meal he took a piece of bread and began to chew it. His face became red and he suddenly became upset. They thought that he was choking and they wanted to save him. Rabbi Ze'ev Kotses looked at his face and said: "Leave him alone."

He was like that for a long while and then he recovered by himself. They asked him: "What was the matter?"

He answered: "When I ate the piece of bread I concentrated on the kavvanoth of eating, and through a kavvanah I attained what Moses, our teacher, may he rest in peace, had in kavvanah the first time that Zipporah gave him a meal. When I concentrated on this *yihud*, Moses, our teacher, may he rest in peace, came here. That is what happened."

---

* A service for the redemption of the first-born, which takes place when the baby boy is one month old. This custom is in accord with the biblical law. See Num. 18:14–17.

204] *A Charm for Easy Delivery*

I HEARD THIS BUT I DO NOT REMEMBER FROM WHOM.
Once, when the famous Hasid, Rabbi Jehiel Mikhel, was
visiting with the Besht, on Friday morning before the Shaharith
prayer the Besht told him to go home that day. He did not answer
him, saying in his heart: "Today is Sabbath Eve and I still do not
have a wagon." He went to the beth-hamidrash to read the
weekly portion of the Bible, twice the Hebrew text and once the
Targum in conjunction with it.*

When it was time for the meal the Besht's wife asked: "Where
is Rabbi Mikhel?"

The Besht said: "I ordered him to go home."

Nevertheless, she sent for him. They found him in the beth-
hamidrash and they called him to the meal. When he arrived, the
Besht said to him: "Sit down and eat and you will have a wagon."

After the meal he went outside, and saw a boy standing in the
market with a wagon and three horses. He asked him: "Where
are you from?"

He said: "From the town of Olyka." And indeed this was the
truth. He had left a merchant in a certain place and was returning
home with the empty wagon.

It is said that it is seventeen versts from the town of Medzhibozh to the town of Olyka. The driver of the wagon asked Rabbi
Jehiel Mikhel in what place or what settlement he would observe
the Sabbath. He answered that he did not know how far one
could travel by the Sabbath. He hired the driver of the wagon and
went to take leave of the Besht.

The Besht said to him: "Return home in peace. You will find
your wife in difficult labor surrounded by many women. Send
them out of your home. Whisper in her ear what I taught you,

---

* The Targum is the Aramaic translation of the Bible. In the post-
biblical period Aramaic became the spoken language of the Jews in
Palestine and Babylonia, and it became necessary to read the Hebrew
text in translation as well. In public worship each biblical verse was read
twice in Hebrew and once in the Aramaic.

and you will have a baby boy. Mazal tov." And so it was. He arrived home two hours before nightfall. He did as the Besht had ordered him and she gave birth to a baby boy. This boy was Rabbi Joseph of Yampol.

205] *Heavenly Garments*

I HEARD FROM THE RABBI OF THE HOLY COM-munity of Polonnoye that he asked the Besht about what is mentioned regarding garments in the upper world. How is it possible that this could also be found among men?

He said to him: "The money or torah that you give to your friend are the clothing that are given as gifts." And both the giver and the receiver partake of the gift.*

206] *The Besht in the Mikveh*

I HEARD FROM HIM FURTHER THAT THE BESHT asked him: "Why is it that you remain for so long in the mikveh, and why when I go to the mikveh do I just close my eyes and I see all the worlds?"

207] *The Kind Boy*

I HEARD FROM RABBI ABRAHAM OF THE HOLY COM-munity of Medzhibozh, who was the son-in-law of Rabbi Mikhel of the holy community of Tulchin, that Rabbi Joseph, the

---

* In Jewish tradition there is a belief that the souls in paradise have garments which are woven of the good deeds men perform upon earth. Conversely bad actions subtract from this heavenly dress. For a discussion of this tradition, particularly in the Kabbalistic literature, see Gershom Scholem, "The Paradisic Garb of Souls and the Origin of the Concept of Haluka de-Rabbanan," Hebrew, *Tarbiz*, XXIV (1955), 290–306. Metaphorically speaking, the teaching of the Torah may be, according to this tale, the earthly equivalent of the heavenly garments.

preacher of the holy community of Medzhibozh, had an intestinal disease before his death, and he did not have anyone to take proper care of him. Once a boy from the slaughter house came to him and took pity on him. He removed the sheet underneath Rabbi Joseph and cleaned him thoroughly. He washed the sheet in the river, let it dry and set it underneath him again. He did this every day until the day of the death of the preacher. Not long after that the boy became sick. The preacher appeared to the Besht and said to him: "Why do you not go to visit my friend who is sick?"

Immediately, the Besht, God bless his memory, together with his followers, went to visit the sick boy. The boy passed away, and the Besht saw that the preacher, God bless his memory, led the funeral procession.

208] *Gematria*

I HEARD FROM THE SON OF THE TSADDIK, RABBI Ḥayyim of Krasne, God bless his memory, that once Rabbi Ḥayyim asked the Besht, God bless his memory, to remember his name and his wife's name so that he could pray for them.

The Besht said to him: "In what way shall I remember your name?"

Rabbi Ḥayyim, God bless his memory, answered him: "I will give you a sign. The abbreviation of Ḥayyim ben Raḥel (Ḥayyim, son of Rachel) is *ḥaver* (a fellow scholar), and "the wife of a *ḥaver* is like a *ḥaver*."[1] The abbreviation of Ḥayyah Bat Rivkah (Ḥayyah, daughter of Rivkah) is also *ḥaver*."

The Besht said to him: "What kind of a sign is that? The letter *ḥ* could also stand for Ḥayykil or something like that, and the letter *ḥ* of her name could stand for Ḥannah or something similar?" And the Besht said: "There is, however, a gematrial sign, because Ḥayyim (חיים) and Ḥayyah (חיה) equal Lord God (הויה אדני).*

* The numerical value of the Hebrew letters of each of these pairs of words amounts to 91.

209] *Rabbi Naḥman of Kosov*

I HEARD FROM THE RABBI OF OUR COMMUNITY THAT the famous rabbi, our teacher, Naḥman of Kosov, maintained the *arrendeh* in a village. He used to send messages to the members of the holy group in the city telling each of them what sins they had to correct in this world. Every thing that he said was true, but they were very annoyed with his prophecies because they had an agreement among them not to prophesy. They wanted to send one of them to him to ask why he did this.

The rabbi of the holy community of Polonnoye * said: "I will go to him since I need to see him anyhow and I will ask him." He was teaching Rabbi Naḥman's sons, and they ate at his table, and Rabbi Naḥman used to send him flour and grain. But it had been a long time since he had done so, and so the rabbi, the Preacher, went to see him. He did not find him at home. He saw a wagon waiting and he asked about him. He was told that Rabbi Naḥman had gone to the village and so he waited for him. When Rabbi Naḥman came, the Preacher saw that Rabbi Naḥman had a heavy load of straw on his shoulder, and he said to him: "Naḥman, you crazy fool. Do you have to carry the straw? Couldn't you tell your gentile servant to carry it?"

Rabbi Naḥman answered him: "You are the crazy one. Does not the Torah say: *I will give grass in thy fields for thy cattle, and thou shalt eat and be satisfied.*[1] And you want to honor the gentile with this mitzvah."

The Preacher kept silent because it was well put.

The horses of Rabbi Naḥman, God bless his memory, were harnessed to the wagon ready to go to the town. The Preacher said to him: "Why didn't you send me flour?"

He answered him: "Look. The wagon with the flour is there and I am ready to bring it to you." Then he asked him: "Why is it that you make prophecies?"

He answered him: "*I was no prophet, neither was I a*

* Probably Rabbi Aryeh Leib, the Preacher, rather than Rabbi Jacob Joseph, whom the writer usually refers to as the rabbi of Polonnoye.

prophet's son.[2] You know what happend when I sat at the third meal with the rabbi, Rabbi Moses, the head of the court of the holy community of Kuty. They sat late into the night, and the shohet who is a member of our group was there also. A butcher, whose name is Leib and who is called Leib Glits, came and he asked the shohet to slaughter. He called him once, twice, and then three times, but the shohet did not want to go because he desired to listen to the living words of God. This was always the subject of their conversation—how to worship God.

"When the butcher saw that the shohet did not want to leave them, he said to himself: 'I will go and disturb them. They will pray the Maariv prayer, and then the shohet will go to slaughter.'

"And so he did. When he brought a candle,* the rabbi became angry at him. He excommunicated him, and the butcher died.

"I had a dream that I went to a synagogue and I heard someone saying torah, and I ran into the synagogue. But when I came to the door of the synagogue, I recognized that the speaker was a demon. The rabbi said that they had signs to tell whether it was the dead man himself or not.[3] I ran to the demon, but my father stopped me and said: 'You may embarrass someone.' He was referring to an incident when my father-in-law, God bless his memory, pulled a preacher from the pulpit.

"I freed myself from my father's grip, and I spit in the face of the demon. He remained standing there naked, with only a kerchief to cover his nakedness, and I recognized that it was the butcher. I said to him: 'Leib where did you learn this torah?'

"He answered: "Because I was excommunicated they did not judge me, and I wander around paradise and hear what they study inside. I cannot enter Gehenna nor paradise. I beg you, sir, to tell the rabbi to remove the ban from me.'

"He told me what each person had to correct, and this was what I sent to you. I asked him what I have to correct, and he led me to a certain house and showed me a gentile lying there dead. He said to me: 'This is what you have to correct.'"

* By bringing a candle the butcher indicated that the Sabbath was at an end. He thus prevented the group from prolonging their Sabbath talk.

The story was that once while Rabbi Naḥman, God bless his memory, was traveling he stayed overnight in a village. He did not want to stay with a Jew for a reason which I do not know. He gave a bottle of brandy to the gentile and stayed there. His horse was given fodder. During the night he overheard the intimacies between the husband and the wife, and he could not restrain his thoughts, and he had an accidental sexual emission, God forbid.* Because of this, he fasted from one Sabbath to the other, and he killed the demon. But the impression still remained. The butcher said that Rabbi Naḥman had to correct this matter and Rabbi Naḥman began to cry. Then it seemed to Rabbi Naḥman as if he saw a sword hanging on the wall.

"I took the sword and cut the gentile in two." He said: "In this way I corrected the matter, and I was about to leave; however, since you came to me, I do not have to go. See to it that they remove the ban from the butcher. Take the flour and go in peace."⁴

210] *The Flight of the Besht*

I heard this from my father-in-law, God bless his memory. Once before the first flight, which was before the flight that took place in our days,¹ after midnight on the eve of the holy Sabbath when everyone was cooking in honor of the Sabbath, the Besht sent word to all the people of the town that they would have to flee. And he escaped immediately so that he would be able to welcome the Sabbath early as was his custom. He had good horses and the distance was not far, just one verst to the river Dnestr. He crossed the river and welcomed the Sabbath. All the people of the town strained the soup from the meat and escaped across the Dnestr as well. However, they were a little

* Accidental sexual emissions were thought to result from the effort of demons to arouse one's passions. These accidents provided the seed from which hybrid demonic offsprings were born. See Trachtenberg, *Jewish Magic and Superstition*, pp. 51–54, *The Zohar*, I, 83, 173; III, 371; V, 81 [I, 19a, 54b; II, 130a; III, 76b], and B. *'Erubin* 18b.

late, and they had to light the Sabbath candles during the passage. Thank God that all of them were saved.

On the Sabbath the bandits came to the town and did not find the Jews. I do not know whether the incident took place in the holy community of Tlust or in the holy community of Kolomyya, because subsequently the Besht lived in the holy community of Kolomyya.

211] *The Chief* Arrendators

I HEARD THIS FROM THE RABBI OF OUR COMMUNITY, God bless his memory. The Besht was with the chief *arrendators* of the holy community of Slutsk. One was named Rabbi Samuel and the other was named Rabbi Gedaliah.* The name of Rabbi Samuel's wife was Toveleh. She had urged her husband to send for the Besht because they had built a stone house, but they were afraid to live there.[1] They sent for the Besht, but when he arrived they were not at home. He wanted to prepare dinner and he said that he had to examine the knife. The shohet had to come and show him the knife. The people of the town were very angry. How dare he examine the knife of the local shohet, especially in a big community. But they could not stop him because this wealthy

---

* Solomon Maimon describes these two brothers in his *Autobiography*, p. 12. "Two brothers from Galicia, where the Jews are much shrewder than in Lithuainia, took under the name of *Dersawzes* or farmers-general, a lease of all estates of Prince Radzivill, and, by means of greater industry as well as greater economy, they not only brought the estates into a better condition, but also enriched themselves in a short time. Disregarding the clamour of their brethren, they increased the rents, and enforced payment with the utmost stringency. They themselves exercised a direct oversight of the farms, and whenever they found a farmer who, instead of looking after his own interests and those of his landlord by improving his farm through industry and economy, spent the whole day in idleness, or lay drunk about the stove, they soon brought him to his senses, and roused him out of his indolence with a flogging. This procedure of course acquired for the farmers-general, among their own people the name of tyrants." Israel Halpern discusses a rebellion of the peasants against the Radzivills which was directed toward these Jewish farmers-general. See "The Woszczylo Revolt," Hebrew, *Zion*, XXII (1957), 56–67.

woman ordered it. At Minhah they heard him praying in the Sephardic style, and they became still angrier.

When Rabbi Samuel returned home they complained about the Besht, but Rabbi Samuel answered them: "According to our custom we cannot do anything to him without a legitimate excuse." Before Minhah the woman took him to all the new buildings, and in several places he made some motions as if he saw something. Everyone in the city was there and they suspected that he was lying.

Rabbi Samuel said to his wife that he wanted to test him on some matter, I forget what. The Besht, who was in the inn, heard him talking at home in bed with her about it. The Besht sent his servant to the woman to tell her to come to him immediately and not to worry about the guards that were standing there. She immediately rose from her bed and went out. Her husband wanted to prevent her from going, but she did not pay any attention to him. When she arrived the Besht motioned to her, saying: "The fool wants to test me."

She became very frightened, and she pacified the Besht until he was no longer angry. When she came home, she told her husband about it, and the Besht grew in importance in his eyes. The following day he prepared a great dinner for the Besht, and he talked with him about the routes to the Holy Land because the Besht wanted Rabbi Samuel to send him by land. He asked the Besht: "How much does one need for that?"

The Besht answered that one thousand was necessary for expenses.

He said to him: "It is a trivial matter for me." He promised to send him money for his livelihood every year.

The Besht answered that he was not worried about his making a living because the main object was to be in the Holy Land.[2]

The Besht remained with him about three weeks. Once during that time, the woman Toveleh asked the Besht: "For how long will our good years last?"

The Besht scolded her and told her that one does not ask about such matters. She pressed him hard, and he closed his eyes for a moment and said: "They will last twenty-two years."[3] When her husband heard this he became very angry with her.

Another thing happened during that time. The child of a wealthy man became sick. The man brought the child to the Besht, who said that he would live. Then the Besht saw that he would die. The Besht realized that they would like to disgrace him, and he left there at midnight. He traveled so swiftly that he covered fifteen versts and passed beyond their authority over the boundary to another kingdom. They would approach a village and then pass through it. While in the village or the town he traveled at the usual pace, but as soon as they left the village they immediately arrived at another village.

Rabbi Tsevi the scribe, asked him: "What is this?"

But the Besht did not answer him because he was not allowed to stop, and he simply silenced him with his hand. I heard from the rabbi of our community several times that it is not permissible to stop.[4] When they came to a border the Besht stopped to rest, and he wrote a letter: "Know without doubt that I could have found a way so that you would not have been able to harm me. I was simply afraid that I would have been vulnerable elsewhere, and therefore I turned away from you. Everything that I said will take place. In twenty-two years you will suffer a downfall which will be brought about by one of your servants." He signed at the end: "So spoke Israel Besht, the servant of God."

He sent the letter by a special messenger. Rabbi Samuel was very angry and he was embarrassed to show the letter to other people. He showed his signature only.

212] *A Tenth for a Minyan*

I HEARD FROM OTHERS THAT BY THIS SWIFT TRAVEL the Besht came home in three days even though there were heavy rains. Since this incident took place just before Rosh Hashanah, he wanted to be home for the holiday.

I heard from a man in our community who was from Bircza[1]

and whose name was Rabbi Eliezer that during the return trip the Besht observed the Sabbath a short verst from that town. He told me the name of the village, but I do not remember it. The Besht arrived at the village. When it was told at the house of the *arrendator* that the Besht had come, the *arrendator* ran outside toward him feeling happy because he had never had children and he said to himself, "Perhaps now I will have some help."

He greeted him, and the Besht asked: "Is it possible for me to stay with you for the Sabbath?"

He answered the Besht: "Certainly it is possible. I invite you, sir, to stay with me for the Sabbath."

The Besht asked: "Will you have a minyan?"

He counted those who had accompanied him, and there were but nine people. He said to the Besht: "We have only nine people with us."

The Besht answered: "There will be a minyan." He did not get off the wagon and ordered them to drive the wagon to the passageway by the house. The gate was very low and it did not have a special lintel; instead, the wooden wall of the house rested on the two columns. The arch of the wagon was high, and when the servant drove to the passageway, he stopped the horses before the arch was touched. The Besht said: "Why did you stop?"

The servant drove on and the lintel together with the whole building was uplifted, and the wagon with the arch was able to enter. I did not inquire how they got out from there later. All the people were there watching this miracle.

The *arrendator* was very happy, and he said in his heart: "If God wills it, there will be a remedy."

When it was afternoon the Besht told him to gather the minyan to stand for prayer. It was his custom on the Sabbath Eve to pray immediately after midday. He said to them: "We number ten people among us."

They answered: "There are but nine people."

He said: "I know for certain there will be a minyan." They laughed behind his back because they saw that there were not ten people there. As they talked it occurred to the *arrendator* that there was a small *arrendeh* across the river, and there was a sick man there. He had been sick for about ten years, lying like a stone, not having the use of hands, legs, or tongue. They just fed him a little bit of food. The householder said to the Besht: "Perhaps you refer to him?"

The Besht said: "Go and summon him here for a minyan." He gave them his staff to hold in his hand so that he could come. They went for him, but he neither moved nor got up, and they returned with empty hands. The Besht took his hat off his head and sent them back, saying: "Place my hat on him and put the staff in his hand and he will come."

And so it was. The man came for the minyan. He lived ten years after this event, and he was a big brute, as healthy as an ox.

Rabbi Eliezer saw that lintel twenty years later, and they showed him the sign. The lintel has not yet returned to its former position.

After the *arrendator* saw these two awesome miracles, while they sat eating he asked the Besht: "I am in my middle age and I do not have children. In a short time I will be old and I will not be able to procreate. What will become of me."

The Besht answered him: "You will have children."

He asked him whether or not to divorce his wife and the Besht answered him: "What for? You will have children."

After that he lived with his wife until he was sixty. Then his wife died and he married another woman. She gave birth to two children. I do not know whether or not they were twins.

213] *The Fall of the Chief* Arrendators

I heard from Rabbi Isaac Aizik that this was how the chief *arrendators* met their end. Radzivill was the duke of Slutsk. He borrowed money from the chief *arrendators*, and they could not collect their money from him. They were afraid that he would ask to borrow still more, and it occurred to them to move to the city of Breslau. They would ask the king to take them under his protection in the holy community of Breslau, and they would present him with the note for the debt as a gift, so that the king would be able either to collect the debt or to confiscate the duke's property. And that is what they did.

They sailed in a boat along the river until they arrived at the holy community of Slonim, which was the duke's city. They were carrying with them three barrels full of money to deposit in the holy community of Breslau. Their clerk was also traveling with them. After they landed in the port, Rabbi Samuel, who went to the inn with the clerk, dressed himself up in order to go to the governor. While he was getting dressed and adorning himself, the clerk sneaked out. Rabbi Samuel was very frightened and he hurried to the duke. When Rabbi Samuel saw the clerk next, he was standing and talking with the duke in an inner room. He came over to him and slapped the clerk on his cheek.

The duke said: "Although it was impolite, I forgive you for slapping him in my presence because of the certainty of my great love toward you. Even if you had slapped my son in my presence, I would have forgiven you. But can you explain what he has told me?"

Rabbi Samuel did not know what to say. The duke had the boat examined, and everything was found exactly as the clerk had said. He immediately put them in prison and ordered cavalry led by a major to go to the holy community of Slutsk. He ordered the major to put a seal on all their property, their money, and their possessions.

When the major received the letter from the duke he became frightened and said, "Perhaps their luck will be good again, and then they will be my enemy." He pretended he was in a drunken sleep until nightfall. When he saw that all the people in the city were asleep, the major himself went to the woman Toveleh, Rabbi Samuel's wife. He told her what was happening, and said that she had to remove all that she could because in the morning he would seal everything. She sent her son-in-law away, and he escaped with the jewelry and the ornaments. Later he became the head of the court in the holy community of Breslau. As a result he became very rich, and he was a wealthy man.

The duke caught all the members of their family that he could find because they themselves were forced to send wedding invitations to all their relatives. Those who heard what had happened while they were on their way returned home, but those who had not heard were caught.

Marat Toveleh asked the people of the town to send for the Besht, thinking that perhaps he would help them with his prayers. The townspeople hated the chief *arrendators;* nevertheless, they sent a special messenger. But they secretly told the messenger to ask the Besht not to help them.

Two or three days passed before the messenger disclosed the request of the people of the town. The Besht said: "I looked for some way in which I could help them, but since Jews ask me not to help them I will not help."

This incident took place after twenty-two years had passed, just as the Besht had written to him.[1]

214] *The Bear*

ONCE, ON THE SABBATH BEFORE THE PASSOVER, THE rabbi* prayed Shaharith, and after the prayer he took off his tallith and went outside. They thought that he had to relieve himself. When he was in the synagogue courtyard the rabbi saw a bear being led. Boys were running after the bear, and the rabbi followed also. The bear was led from the gate of the synagogue courtyard to the market. He followed it there as well, and all the people wondered about it. The bear was led until he was opposite the judge's house, and then the bear broke the rope and seemed to act crazy. All the people who had followed it ran away in fear that it might run wild throughout the town and hurt people. But the rabbi remained standing in his place. The bear ran into the judge's yard, entered his passageway, and broke into the house.

The Besht immediately went to a window to watch the bear, and most of the people also stood at windows to see what the bear would do. The bear immediately removed the table from its place and lifted up the floor. It dug in the ground until it found a dead

* The Besht.

bastard hidden in the earth. It took the bastard by its two hands and lifted it up so that all the people could see.

The rabbi cried: "You are witnesses." And then in Polish, "Protest!" There had been a plot to libel the Jews. Then the Besht went to the synagogue to complete the prayer.

215] *The Exceptional Horse*

Once, during his travels, the rabbi* stayed as a guest in a village with one of his followers who prepared a great dinner in his honor. While he was there, the rabbi talked with him about his problems as people do—whether he made a living and his standing in the community. The man told him about his good standing and every detail about himself. The rabbi said: "Do you have good horses?" And he said, "Let us go and see your horses."

They went to the stables and he favored a small horse. The rabbi asked the householder to give him the horse as a present.

He answered him: "Sir, you do not really want to ask me for that horse. That horse is dear to me. It is my favorite. Every time when three good horses cannot draw the wagon, this one horse can do it by himself. It has happened several times and I have come to love this horse."

After a while they talked again about his good situation and about the many debts that people owed him. The rabbi said: "I would like to see some of the notes for your debts." He showed him all the notes. When the rabbi saw a certain note, he asked him to give him this note as a gift.

He answered: "Why does the rabbi want this note?" It has been several years since the debtor died and nothing was left to pay his debt."

The rabbi said: "Nevertheless, I want this note."

He gave him the note as a present, and the rabbi took the note and tore it into two pieces. They both completely forgave the dead man his debt. Then the rabbi said: Please go and see how your horse fares."

* The Besht.

He went and he saw the horse lying dead. He realized that this was not an idle matter.

The rabbi said: "Because the man from whom you demanded payment was not able to pay you, he was sentenced to please you and to work the debt. He was transformed into a horse. He pleased you by doing the hard jobs, and when his enslavement was forgiven he stopped living like a horse and returned to his place in heaven. He truly died."

216] *The Death of Rabbi David Forkes*

I HEARD THIS FROM THE RABBI OF OUR COM-munity. Once the Besht was in the holy community of Polon-noye, and he traveled from that holy community to New City.[1] The road passed by the cemetery of New City, and the Besht saw a great column of fire hovering above a grave.[2] He sent his servant to look at the tombstone to see who was buried there. It was written that there was buried a pious man whose name was Moses, the servant of God.

The rabbi said that a man named Rabbi David would be buried next to him. In that town there was a man whose name was Rabbi David Tseres, and he became very frightened when he heard this, because he thought that the Besht was referring to him as the man who would die.

The rabbi said to him: "Do not be frightened. You are not the David I referred to."

About twelve years after the death of the Besht, God bless his memory, the rabbi, our teacher, David Forkes, came to the holy community of Polonnoye for the *Ḥazon* Sabbath.[3] He stopped his wagon before the house of the rabbi of that holy community to see him personally and receive his permission to observe the Sabbath in New City. He went to the rabbi's house, but he did not find him at home since the rabbi was traveling and was observing the Sabbath on the road. The whole Sabbath Rabbi David wondered to himself: "I do not know what I am doing here. The rabbi, the maggid, is not at home, and I came just to see him because he is a tsaddik. At the conclusion of the Sabbath, which was the Ninth of Av, he felt faint. He called the society of undertakers and wrote a will. He lay down on his bed and passed away on Sunday. They buried him next to the grave of Rabbi Moses.

When they were in the cemetery they saw what was written on the tomb, and they were astonished. They talked about this wonder throughout the whole city. Then the mother of the Preacher of Polonnoye, who was very old, recalled the words that the Besht had said over twenty years before, that Rabbi David would be buried next to that grave. They realized that this had been ordained by God.

217] *A Brand Plucked Out of the Fire*

ONCE THE BESHT WENT TO THE BATHHOUSE WITH Rabbi David Forkes. As they were on their way a very handsome man come toward them. His curly locks were combed and his clothes were well groomed. When the man came close to them the Besht jumped aside as far as he could. When he went by the Besht returned to the path, passed his hands over his eyes, and said: "Look who has passed us." He saw that it was a *brand plucked out of the fire.*[1] The fire glowed in his hair.

218] *The Rabbi's Tobacco Pipe*

ONCE THE RABBI* WAS TRAVELING AND ON THE WAY he smoked his pipe. The stem was so long that the pipe stuck out beyond the wagon. As they were traveling along like this, a governor and two soldiers riding on horseback came from the opposite direction and snatched the pipe from him and continued on their way. The rabbi went on as well, but after an hour the rabbi stopped and said to his servant: "Take a horse and ride until you reach the soldiers and take the pipe back from them."

* The Besht.

And so he did. When he reached the soldiers he saw them sitting on their horses asleep. He took the pipe and went on his way.

219] *The Hasid Who Prayed in the Field*

ONCE A MAN TRAVELED TO THE BESHT FOR YOM Kippur. A day before Yom Kippur Eve he traveled all day and all night in order to arrive there early. At dawn on Yom Kippur Eve he was one verst from the city of Medzhibozh. He said to himself: "I am near the town and the horse is weary from having traveled all night. I will stop here to pray and in the meantime the horse can graze."

After the prayer he was overcome by sleep. He said to himself: "It will not make any difference if I sleep here for two hours. The horse will rest from the journey, and then afterwards I will be able to travel quickly. In any case, I certainly will reach the town before midday."

He lay down on the wagon and he fell into a deep sleep. When he awoke he realized that it was twilight, and it was Yom Kippur. He was very upset. After all his efforts to reach the Besht for Yom Kippur, he had to spend Yom Kippur alone in the field near the town. And it was his own fault. He wept bitterly all night and all day. At the conclusion of Yom Kippur, very embittered, he traveled quickly to the Besht. When he arrived the Besht made fun of him. The reason was that in his prayers the man had had to elevate the prayers of the people in the fields. He had been forced to do this by heaven.

220] *The Besht Saves a Drowning Man*

ONCE IN THE MIDDLE OF A MEAL WHEN THE Besht sat with his followers, he lifted up his arms and made motions like a person swimming in a river. He said: "Fool! Do this and you will be saved."

This was a wonder in the eyes of those present. In about an hour a man came and told them how he and his wagon had fallen into the river. He did not know how to swim, but it immediately occurred to him: "I will try to do like this with my hands. And, thank God, it helped me and I managed to get out of the river."

Similarly, once during a meal the Besht shouted: "Fool! Have you not seen how many gentiles there are in the field. Take your bagel and throw it in front of them, and they will come to you."

Within an hour a man came and said that he had fallen into the river, and there was no one to save him because the gentiles were up on the mountain, and they had not seen him in the river. He recalled that he had a bagel and he threw it to the gentiles. They came at once, and with God's help they saved him.

221] *The Council of Four Lands*

ONCE DURING THE MEETING OF THE COUNCIL OF Four Lands* the first leader, the famous wealthy rabbi our teacher Abraham Aba, brought up the matter that the fame of the Besht was spreading and that word indicated that he was an unlearned man. How could he possess divine inspiration, since an ignorant man cannot be pious?[1] The assembly sent for the Besht. They asked him to appear before them immediately and he did so.[2]

When he came before them that rabbi was the main speaker. He said to the Besht: "According to your behavior, it would seem that the Holy Spirit inspires you, but there are those who say that you, sir, are an unlearned man. Well, let us hear whether or not you, sir, know something of the law." This incident took place on the first of the month. He asked him: "What is the law if a person forgets 'Rise and Come.' "[3]

* This was the chief governing body of Polish Jewry from the last quarter of the sixteenth century up to 1764. The four lands were Great Poland, Little Poland, Red Russia (Podolia and Galicia), and Volhynia. The council met periodically in Lublin and Jaroslaw alternately. A collection of documents of the Councils was published: Israel Halpern [Halperin], *Acta Congressus Generalis Judaerom Regni Polonniae* (*1580–1764*), Hebrew (Jerusalem, 1945).

The Besht answered: "Neither you, sir, nor I need this law. Even if you, sir, repeat the prayer, you will forget it again (indeed it was the truth that he had forgotten 'Rise and Come' the second time), and I certainly shall not forget it."

When the Besht told him the truth he was very frightened of the Besht's knowledge of secret things. He immediately made up his mind to return to the place where the Besht stayed ahead of the Besht in order to observe his behavior. He would hide himself in a room and look through a knothole to see what the Besht was doing. When he saw that the time of the Besht's departure approached, he went before him to the inn where the Besht would stay overnight, and he hid himself there in a secret place.

When the Besht came to the inn they offered him an upholstered bed. When the Besht came and saw the bed he cried: "*Vey!* There has been sexual intercourse with a gentile woman on this bed. How is it possible for me to sleep on it?"[4]

The innkeeper immediately came and complained greatly about his son-in-law, who slept with a gentile woman on this bed.

At once the Besht said: "Rabbi Aba, have you heard what he has said?"

Rabbi Aba immediately stepped out before him.

222] *The Blessing of a Poor Man*

ONCE ON SIMHATH TORAH THE MEMBERS OF THE holy group, the disciples of the Besht, were dancing joyfully in a circle and the Shekinah was in flames about them. During the dance the shoe of one of the lesser members of the group was torn. He was a poor man and it angered him that he was prevented from dancing with his friends and from rejoicing in the festivity of the mitzvah.

The Besht's daughter, the pious Edel, who was also in the house, was standing on the side watching their celebration of the Water Libation.[1] She said to that disciple: "If you promise me that I will give birth to a baby boy this year, I will give you good shoes immediately." She could say this because she had shoes in the store.

He promised her that she certainly would have a baby boy. And so it was that the rabbi, our rabbi and teacher, Barukh of the holy community of Tulchin, was born to her.

223] *"The Hour Has Come But Not The Man"*

In the holy community of Old Konstanty-now there was a man who did not have children. He visited the Besht several times. Once the Besht promised him that his wife would give birth to a baby boy, and he told him to let him know when she had delivered.

And so it was that his wife gave birth to a baby boy, and he went to the Besht with great joy to tell him of his wife's delivery. But when he came to the Besht and broke this news to him, the Besht restrained himself for a long while, and then he began to weep uncontrollably and his hands hung limply at his side.

The man asked him: "Why are you crying, sir?"

He said: "Because I see that on the day that the boy will be bar-mitzvahed he will be drawn into the river, God forbid." And the Besht said: "You will probably forget completely about it, but here is a sign for you to remember. On that day the boy will put two stockings on one foot and he will search for the second one. You must guard him very carefully the entire day and prevent him from seeing water. 'If the verdict is postponed overnight it comes to nought.'¹ But if you do not watch him then he certainly will be drawn into the river, God forbid."

In the course of the time the whole matter was completely forgotten.

On the day that the boy became bar-mitzvahed the man went to pray in the synagogue while the boy was still asleep. When he returned from the synagogue the boy was searching in every corner of the house. His father asked him: "What are you looking for?"

He said to him: "I lost a stocking."

His father saw that he was wearing two stockings on one foot. When he saw this he recalled the warning, and he was careful to watch the boy that day.

During the day the sun was very hot and all the people of the town ran to swim in the river. The boy sneaked out as well and ran to the river. They immediately ran after him and brought him back home. When his father realized that the boy fought to swim in the river, and it was impossible to keep him from it, he put him in a room and locked the door. All day long the boy cried bitterly: "Let me out! Where is the compassion a father should have for his children?[2] I am hot from the sun."

But they did not pay any attention to him, and they did not give him even a drop of water to drink.

After the Minhah, when all the people of the town were near the river, a creature with a head and two hands came out of the water, slapped his hands on the water and said: "The one who is mine is not here." Then it sank and disappeared.

At once the fever subsided and the boy slept. And with the help of God he grew up well, and he had a long life, as the Besht, God bless his memory, had said.[3]

224] *Jonah*

WE HEARD IN THE NAME OF THE HOLY RABBI, OUR teacher and rabbi, Menaḥem Nahum of Chernobyl, God bless his memory, that in a certain community near the holy community of Medzhibozh there was a very rich man who traded in Leipzig. For several years he had not had any children, but he refused to go to the Besht. Once he traveled to the holy community of Medzhibozh on some business affair, and he stayed there with someone who was his faithful friend. They asked each other how they were and he told him his whole problem.

The man said to him: "The whole world goes to the Besht, why do you avoid going to him? Maybe it will be a favorable time and you will have children." He could not oppose him and both of them went together to the Besht.

The Besht said to him: "My advice is that you stop your trade with Leipzig. Sell all the merchandise and the wagons, and rent an *arrendeh* from your governor. Within a year your wife will give birth to a baby boy. Mazal tov. Let me know when she delivers."

He almost fainted. He could not believe it, particularly since that governor hated Jews and for fifteen years had prevented Jews from living in his villages. When he came home he did not want to go to the governor because he thought that they were mere words. After two days the governor himself sent for him and gave him the *arrendeh* as the Besht had said. He thought it might be that the governor needed money so urgently that he changed his mind.

Within a year his wife gave birth to a baby boy, but it did not occur to him to inform the Besht, because he said to himself that it was mere chance. As the boy grew bigger he became wild. *His hand shall be against every man and every man's hand against him.*[1] It was impossible to send him to school. The man hated his life. He actually regretted that he wanted children to begin with because it would have been better for him had he not had children at all. Indeed, death would have been more pleasant than his life.

In the course of time it happened that he traveled to Medzhibozh. He stayed with his friend, and he told him all his troubles.

The friend told him: "It was stupid not to have informed the Besht immediately when your wife gave birth as you were ordered to from his holy lips. Nevertheless, let us go to him now and ask his advice."

When they came to the Besht the man began to apologize for not having informed him.

The Besht said: "My advice is that you leave the *arrendeh*. Sell all the grain and everything else for cash. Go to Leipzig and spend a year traveling. When you return home you will find that your son has become a different man, and he will be very learned in the Torah."

He acted accordingly. He sold everything that he had for cash, and then he went to Leipzig. He went about his business cautiously, and gradually he bought merchandise on good terms.

All the merchants returned to their towns and he remained there alone. He said to himself: "What can I do here, especially since I am by myself. Although only four months have passed, I have no more money." Nevertheless, he put all his merchandise in a wagon, and he went on his way with his coachman.

During their trip, on Friday, on the eve of the holy Sabbath, they lost their way. They traveled all day and could not find a place to sleep. In the late afternoon they agreed to leave the wagon on the road, and one would go to the right to search for a good place to rest and the other would go to the left. When the man had gone about a hundred feet or more from the road, he saw a small house in the forest in which candles were burning. He took courage and went there. When he entered the house he saw a man standing and praying, and another man nearby attending him. Since he had not taken anything from the wagon, the servant immediately brought him a shirt and clothes for the Sabbath and he prayed as well. After the reception of the Sabbath and Maariv, the householder said joyously: "Good Sabbath."

Grape wine was brought to them for kiddush, as well as delicacies fit for a king. After that they brought him to an upholstered bed. The guest hesitated to sleep on the bed, and when the householder realized it, he said: "Is it not true that *women have been kept from us?*"[2] Indeed he did not see any women. There were only the householder and the servant.

They arose early in the morning and prayed both Shaharith and the Musaf in accordance with the law of the Torah. They ate and drank and enjoyed themselves, and then they took their midday nap. Because he drank so much grape wine he slept until the time for Minhah. They prayed Minhah, and they ate the third meal, and they enjoyed themselves until evening. Then they prayed Maariv and made the Havdalah. After the Havdalah the householder shook hands with his guest, since earlier during the Sabbath it is not proper to shake hands. The guest was very concerned that he did not know where his coachman and his merchandise were.

The householder said to him: "If you want to, you can sell me your merchandise on these terms: I will pay cash now for half of the merchandise, and I will hold the rest on credit until the fair in Leipzig and pay you there."

Although it was very difficult for him to sell on credit to a person that he knew nothing about, he felt that he had to do it. They came to an agreement on the terms. Afterwards, he looked through the window and saw his wagon standing near the house together with the coachman and all the merchandise. He went out to him, and he was very angry with him, but he could not change anything. He wondered to himself where he was going to put the merchandise, since there was no building there except the house.

The householder said: "Give me the merchandise." They began to unload it. They opened a door to the cellar and put all the merchandise there. They calculated the amount between them, and it added up to a large sum. He paid him about eighty thousand red coins in cash and gave him a note for the other half.

As they left the place he said to himself: "The Besht told me to spend a whole year traveling, but I have sold all my merchandise. What will I do at home? I had better travel to Leipzig again and carefully buy all the merchandise that I will need."

While he was on his way he took out the note, and he saw that it was signed by Jonah. He began to inquire about him, but no one knew him. After he stayed for the fair in Leipzig and bought all his merchandise, he began to inquire after him there too. He was mocked by everyone that he met. "How can one give such a large sum on credit to a complete stranger?" When each of the merchants began to return home, he too loaded his merchandise on wagons and he went on his way. As he was approaching the city gate, he looked up and saw the man standing in front of him. He almost fainted because he did not recognize him.

The man said to him: "You, sir, have my note for the amount of eighty thousand red coins. Please give me the note, sir, and I will pay you in cash."

He asked him: "Tell me, who are you?"

He answered: "Why do you need to know who I am? Don't I pay cash?" Nevertheless, he desired to learn his true identity.

The man said to him: "If you give me my note, I will pay you the money, and if not I certainly will not pay you. Do as you like."

He gave him the note and the man paid the money to the last coin.

Then he said to him: "Give my regards to the Besht, may he live long."

He asked him: "What name shall I tell him?"

He said: "Tell him Jonah sends his regards."

He went on his way home with joy in his heart. On his return he found that his son had become like another man and studied diligently. He immediately went to the Besht and told him the whole story. The Besht asked about Jonah's welfare, and the man said: "He told me to give his regards to you."

The Besht said: "Know that this was Jonah, the son of Amittai."

That is all.[3]

225] *The Three Brothers*

IN A HOLY COMMUNITY THERE WERE THREE VERY learned, God-fearing brothers. Two of them followed the Besht, and the third one opposed him. Whenever the Besht visited this community he stayed with the two brothers, and each time he inquired about the welfare of the third brother. Once he came to that community on Thursday, and before he reached the house of the brothers he asked the people of the town about the welfare of the third brother in these words: "How is my opponent."[1]

The people thought that they would be bearing good news to him when they told him that he was lying on his deathbed and had lost the power of speech. The rabbi* said that it was necessary to go and visit him while he was sick.

On Friday, the eve of the holy Sabbath, he asked the two brothers whether it would be possible for him to pray at their brother's on the holy Sabbath.

They said: "If he were healthy he surely would not let the rabbi pray at his place, but now he cannot care since he is lying like a stone too heavy to be moved. It is certainly possible because there is a special room to pray."

* The Besht.

The holy ark and a Torah scroll were brought there, and there the Besht prayed Minhah and Maariv on Friday, the holy Sabbath Eve. The following morning he prayed Shaharith there, and he prolonged the prayer until two o'clock in the afternoon. Before reading the Torah he went into the passageway to cool himself, and he immediately heard a moan from the sick man indicating that he was dying. He said to his people: "Let us go and visit the sick man." He took a place at the sick man's side.

The sick man's mother said to her son: "Why don't you greet the rabbi?"

He did not say a word. She put his hand into the rabbi's hand. The rabbi asked the sick man whether he had studied Gemara, but he kept silent. He asked him this several times, but he kept silent until the rabbi scolded him: "Where are your manners? I am speaking to you and you do not say a word."

Then he answered him: "I studied Gemara."

He asked: "In which tractate is the saying, "Are your sufferings welcome to you?""

He said to him: "In the tractate Berakoth."

"And what is said there?"

He said to him: "Neither they nor their reward."

The rabbi asked him: "Are your sufferings welcome to you?"

He answered: "Neither they nor their reward."

The rabbi said: "Give me your hand." He gave him his hand and he sat up. Then the rabbi told him to put his feet out of the bed, and he did so. Then the rabbi told him to dress himself slowly and to wash his hands, and he did everything that he told him. After that the sick man went with the Besht to the synagogue. He prayed Musaf with the people, and with the help of God he recovered.[2]

226] *Hearing at Will*

Once the Besht praised the rabbi, our rabbi and teacher, Naḥman of Horodenka, in his presence while he was sitting some distance from him. Then Rabbi Naḥman of

Horodenka bent forward and cocked his ear to listen. The people found this very strange. They asked the rabbi about it, and he told them that the rabbi, our teacher and rabbi, Naḥman, asked God, blessed be He, to give him the gift of hearing only the things that he had to hear: "He does not hear when I praise him. When he saw my lips moving but could not hear my voice he thought that I was saying torah. He bent forward to get closer to hear it. As a sign this is true, know that when I talk about the Torah he hears even from afar."

I heard another version that the rabbi did it deliberately. Because when the Besht praised him and Rabbi Naḥman saw his lips moving without hearing his voice he bent forward to listen and every one laughed at him. The Besht did it because he did not approve of the rabbi's request to God, blessed be He, that he hear only what is necessary. He said: "If his actions merited this reward, God, blessed be He, would not deprive him of it. Consider the case of Abraham, our father, may he rest in peace, who after his circumcision could control all his five senses, hearing among them. If his actions do not merit it, why should he rise to a higher stage?"*

227] *The Sinner*

THERE WAS A MAN, ONE OF THE BESHT'S FOL-lowers, who lived in a village. The rabbi had favored him in various ways, and he used to stay with the Besht during the Days of Awe. Once when he came to the rabbi, the rabbi turned his face away. It surprised him, and he assumed that perhaps he was either preoccupied thinking about great matters or that he was angry with him. After an hour he entered the Besht's room once

---

* The patriarch's name before the circumcision corresponded to the numerical value of 243, and only with the addition of the letter ‏ה‎ = 5, which followed the covenant, did it become equivalent to the number of the members of the human body. According to the commentary of *Rashi*, Abraham gained control over his sight and hearing and could select what he chose to hear. See Ginzberg, *The Legends of the Jews*, V, 233, and *Tanḥuma* (Buber, ed.), I, 39a.

more, and again the Besht turned his face away from him. He did this three times, and the man became very depressed. Certainly it was not an empty matter. It was unusual because before the Besht had always favored him in various ways.

The man went to the rabbi, our teacher, Gershon of Kuty, and told him the whole story. The rabbi, our teacher and rabbi, Gershon, went to his brother-in-law, the Besht, and talked with him: "Why do you reject him when he has not committed any evil and all his actions are proper?"

He answered him: "Why do you want me to become involved with the people and befriend them and talk with them. I do not want it."

When this man realized that there was no solution, he went to the rabbi, our teacher and rabbi, Gershon, and cried from his bitter and broken heart: "I know that this is not an empty matter. I have no life. I will not be able to bear it much longer."

The rabbi, our rabbi and teacher, Gershon, went to the rabbi a second time, and he said that it was actually a matter of life and death. He should reveal to him what it was all about.

Then the Besht answered that the sin of adultery was written on his forehead.

The man argued that it was not true, and that he had been continent with his wife for more than sixteen years. How was it possible.

The rabbi, our teacher and rabbi, Gershon, told the Besht that it was up to him to look into the matter. "I cannot perceive it. Since you are the only one who knows it, the sin is not a physical one but is rather an intangible matter."

The Besht said to him that on Friday, Sabbath Eve, in the Minhah prayer, which is the time for the ascension of the soul to the upper palaces, he would look into it.[1] When the Besht's soul ascended to the palace of the tosaphists,* he did not find any impression of the sin that the man had committed. Then he ascended up to the *Rambam's* palace, and there he found the

* The commentators on the Talmud. See Efraim Elimelech Urbach, *The Tosaphists: Their History, Writings, and Methods,* Hebrew, 2nd ed. (Jerusalem, 1955).

man's sin impressed. The matter was that he had imposed upon himself abstinence from sexual relations with his wife, and according to the opinion of the *Rambam* it was as if he said: "You are like my mother to me." The person who takes the vow of abstinence towards his wife is forbidden to touch her jewelry. When he had needed money for a wedding, he had taken his wife's jewelry and pawned it. Thus he had enjoyed her and he had broken his vow. According to the opinion of the *Rambam* it was as if he had committed adultery with a married woman. The rabbi* argued with the *Rambam* (and I heard that he called to the *Rif*** and the *Rosh**** who argued with him also). Then the *Rambam* conceded to them and the sin was erased. Since then there is not any hint of the matter in the *Rambam's* book.[2]

(Rabbi Ḥayyim Vital wrote similarly about the phrase, "Rabbi Simeon opened. . . ."[3] Its meaning is that he opened a channel to this interpretation because a pious man is capable of opening new channels. This is not so of Elijah, who is like an angel.[4] About him is said, "It was decreed according to Elijah." That is the end.

It was said in the Besht's name† about the saying "the whole world draws its substance because of the merit of Ḥanina, my son,"[5] that the words should be "the pathway that Ḥanina prepared."[6] When Rabbi Ḥanina ben Dosa, revealed some secret it became easier for other people to understand it. As it is told, the rabbi, *Bet Yosef*,†† had difficulty understanding one saying, but after he had figured out its meaning, he heard the same

---

* The Besht.

** Alfasi, Isaac ben Jacob (1013–1103). A Talmudic scholar who lived most of his life in Fez, North Africa.

*** Asher ben Jehiel (about 1250–1327), an outstanding codifier and rabbi. He was regarded as the leader of German Jewry. In 1303 he moved to Toledo and became a leading rabbinic authority in Spain.

† Rabbi Jacob Joseph of Polonnoye quoted the Besht in that regard in *Toldot Ya'akov Yosef* (Medzhibozh, 1816), 35a.

†† Rabbi Joseph Karo (1488–1575). He is referred to by the title of his commentary on Jacob ben Asher's (died about 1340) *Arba'ah Turim Bet Yosef*, which was completed in 1542. For a recent monograph about Joseph Karo see Raphael Jehudah Zwi Werblowsky, *Joseph Karo, Lawyer and Mystic* (London, 1962).

explanation from several unlearned people. He asked the *Ari,* who answered him: "Since you opened the channel it is easier for everyone to understand. And this is what is meant by: 'Had I not lifted up the shred, would you have found the pearl beneath it?'" Therefore, when the *Rambam* conceded this decision the interpretation of the *Rambam* as it was decided in the upper world was automatically comprehended in this world. And a hint to the wise is sufficient.")

228] *Rabbi Naḥman and the Besht*

THE RABBI, OUR TEACHER AND RABBI, NAḤMAN OF Kosov, was an opponent of the Besht. (I heard that the Besht stems from the soul of King David, may he rest in peace, and the rabbi, our teacher and rabbi, Naḥman stems from the soul of King Saul, may he rest in peace. Therefore, Rabbi Naḥman always hated this David.)

Once the Besht said: "The rabbi, our teacher and rabbi, Naḥman, pursues me to kill me." (It is known that in bowing down there is the kavvanah of killing one's enemies.)[1] "But with the help of God he will not get me."

Once the disciples of our teacher and rabbi, Naḥman, went to their rabbi and said to him: "Why is it that all the world goes to the rabbi, the Besht, and everyone praises him highly? Why don't you come to an agreement and learn his true nature so that we will know where the truth lies. Why let him be a snare for us?"

He listened to their words and he went to the holy community of Medzhibozh to the rabbi, the Besht, who received him with great honor. Afterwards, both of them entered a special room, and everyone was excluded from the room save one who hid himself in a certain place. The rabbi, our teacher and rabbi, Naḥman, said: "Israel, is it true you say that you know people's thoughts?"

He said to him: "Yes."

He said to him: "Do you know what I am thinking now?"

The rabbi answered: "It is known that thought is not fixed. It wanders from one point to another and is continually transformed. If you concentrate your thought on one thing, then I will be able to know."

The rabbi, our teacher and rabbi, Naḥman, did so.

The Besht said: "The name of YAHWEH is in your thoughts."

The rabbi, our teacher and rabbi, Naḥman, said: "You would know this anyhow, for I must always keep this thought. As it is written: *I have set the Lord always before me.*² Whenever I remove all thought and concentrate on one thing, the name of the Presence is before my eyes."

The Besht said: "But there are several holy names, and you could have concentrated on any that you like."

Then the rabbi, our rabbi and teacher, admitted that it was as the Besht had said. After that they discussed the secrets of the Torah.

229] *The Besht as Rabbi Naḥman's Guest*

ONCE THE BESHT SAW THAT THE RABBI, OUR teacher and rabbi, Naḥman, went on a journey. The Besht followed him so that after our teacher and rabbi, Naḥman would arrive at an inn before the Sabbath, the Besht would arrive after him and would be his guest. The rabbi, our teacher and rabbi, Naḥman, would not be able to obtain fish for the Sabbath, and it would be embarrassing for him. When the rabbi, our teacher and rabbi, Naḥman, saw that the Besht was following him, he changed direction and took a crooked route. For two days he left the road altogether and avoided passing through any village. But the Besht knew the road and he was able to follow him anyway. On Thursday evening, the rabbi, our teacher and rabbi, Naḥman, came to a village where a Jew lived and immediately upon his arrival there he asked whether it was possible to obtain fish because he could not leave there on the eve of the holy Sabbath. The householder told him that it was utterly impossible to obtain fish, since they were about twenty versts or more in each direction from the rivers.

The rabbi, our teacher and rabbi, Naḥman, asked him: "How is it possible for a Jew to be without water for drinking, for washing one's hands, and for bathing."

He answered him that he had two ponds of water, one with clear water for drinking and the other with muddy water for washing and bathing.

He said: "If this is so I will certainly obtain fish." At once he said to his servant: "Once I saw a fisherman take a stick, tie a string on it, and throw it into the river and fish with it. Take a stick and a string and go to the pond immediately."

The servant did so and he caught a big fish in the pond.

The following day when Rabbi Naḥman saw that the Besht would soon arrive, he went toward him happily to welcome him. He greeted him: "With the help of God I have fish for the Sabbath."

The Besht answered him: "Congratulations to you for sending me Cossacks.* I had to deal with them, and because of this you obtained fish. If not, you would not have had fish by any means."

230] *The Parable of the King's Crown*

Once, the rabbi, our teacher and rabbi, Naḥman, heard our own people speaking evil about the Besht. It irritated him greatly and he told them this parable: "Once two high ministers spent a fortune making a crown for the king. When they were about to complete the crown they began to argue about where to fix the precious stone. One said, here, and the other said there. Both desired the glorification of the king. While they were quarreling about it, a simple man passed by and sided with one of them. They rebuked him: 'Why do you interfere in a quarrel that is none of your affair? Although we argue about

---

* The Yiddish word, דאנצעס (*dontses*) appears in the original text. According to Ch. Shmeruk, who suggested this translation to us, it may mean "Cossacks of the Don River."

it, we are well aware of the greatness of the king, and it has to be either this way or that way in keeping with his grandeur!' The quarrel between the Besht and myself is a very old one. It is the quarrel that was between King Saul and David, may they rest in peace, and the quarrel that was between Hillel and Shamai.* How can you dare to butt into it?"[1]

231] *The Blind Boy*

There was a very rich man in Istanbul whose only son was an exceptional boy. All of a sudden he became blind in both eyes. They asked the physicians to cure him, but none of the remedies that they prepared helped at all, and they gave up hope for a cure.

While the Besht was in that holy community,** he said to that man that he would completely cure his son. The man was very happy to hear his words, and he received him in his house with great honor. But when the wife of the wealthy man saw the Besht, she despised him in her heart because he was not well dressed, since the Besht was traveling over land and sea. She became angry with her husband and said: "Why did you bring him to me? None of the physicians could do anything. What help will that one bring by using names?" And she spoke against the holy names.[1]

The Besht became very angry because she did not believe in the active power of the holy names, and he said: "Where is the blind boy? Bring him to me and I will cure him so he will be able to see at once as well as anyone."

As he spoke she suddenly became very hopeful because a liar

---

* Hillel and Shamai were the last of the great teachers of the Oral Law who were considered as a pair (Mishnah, Aboth 1.12). They are known for their conflicting views concerning the Law and its implications. Hillel is thought to be the more moderate of the two.

** The Yiddish edition states clearly that the Besht stayed in Istanbul on his way to the Land of Israel. See Yaari, "Two Basic Recensions . . . ," *Kirjath Sepher*, XXXIX (1964), 559–61. According to Yaari the Yiddish edition is, in general, more explicit about the failure of the Besht to arrive in the Land of Israel.

promises only far off rewards[2] and the Besht said that the boy would see that very minute. "Perhaps he will make his words come true."

At once they brought the sick boy to the Besht, and he whispered something in his ear. Then he immediately ordered a Gemara brought to him and he told the boy to read. He read as every one does. The family was joyous. Then the rabbi passed his hand over the boy's eyes, and they reversed to their former condition. There was terrible weeping in the house. They begged and bowed before him, and the man wanted to give him a huge sum of money. The rabbi answered: "Wicked woman, you mocked the holy names and you must not enjoy this power. From the beginning I acted not to glorify myself, God forbid, nor for money, but simply for the sanctification of His name, blessed be He. I showed you the great power of the holiness of the name. But you will not enjoy it." And he left them so.

232] *The Paralyzed Woman*

There was a rich man who was famous in the state of Walachia, whose wife suddenly became paralyzed in both hands. She could not raise them up at all. He went with her to all the physicians, but they could not help and gave her up as hopeless. He asked for help among the Kedarites as well, but they could not find a remedy for her disease. Her husband decided to travel with her from one city to another in the hope that perhaps some physicians or a master of the name would find a remedy. On the trip he heard from afar of the reputation of the Besht, and he went to the holy community of Medzhibozh.

Upon his arrival in that holy community they went to the Besht, who told him that she should remain in that holy community. She stayed there for many days. During the course of this time they went to the rabbi several times, and he told them to remain there longer. Then after many days he ordered his wagon to be harnessed with horses, and he told that man to follow him with his sick wife. On their trip they came to a village where one of the Besht's followers lived. Upon their arrival he asked the innkeeper whether he would give him rooms. This question astonished the innkeeper because actually it was a great privilege for him to have the rabbi stay with him. The rabbi told him that during their stay he would have to lock all the windows, the gates, and the doors, and not open them to any person, no matter who he were, even if he were a great governor. If anyone forced his way in, he should be told that Rabbi Besht was there. The innkeeper promised to do so and so they stayed at his inn. They immediately followed the rabbi's instructions and prepared themselves for supper. After the meal all of them slept, except the Besht who sat at the table and studied from a book. The sick woman sat in the corner of the house.

On that day the governor who owned the inn was visited by his brother whom he had not seen for more than twelve years. There was a great celebration. They ate and drank and they became drunk. During the conversation, the governor began to brag about how he had built an excellent and very ornate inn at a particular place. He praised it very highly. The guest asked that they give him a horse so that he could ride there. They gave him an excellent horse, and since the place was nearby the governor's court, he rode there without a coat. As soon as he started out a snowstorm began and it took him several hours to ride to the inn. He knocked on the door so that they would open up for him. They answered him that it was impossible to open the door for him because the rabbi, the Besht, was there. He pleaded with them several times to open the door for him because he was very cold, but they always gave him the same answer, until at last the Besht motioned for them to open the door for him.

When the governor came into the house he walked back and forth until he warmed up a little. When he felt restored he asked: "Who is the Besht?" They pointed out the rabbi to him. He immediately became furious and he walked back and forth several more times and asked again: "Who and what is the Besht that you did not open the door for me until I almost died of the cold?" They again pointed out the rabbi to him.

The third time the fire of anger so burned in him that when

they pointed out the rabbi he drew his sword from its sheath and lifted it above the rabbi to kill him.

At once the rabbi shouted at the sick woman: "Lift up both your hands!"

She did so and the Besht made a transference. The hands of the woman were restored to their former health, and, the governor could not lower his hands and they withered. He pleaded with the rabbi, but he said: "I cannot help you. The transference has been made and it is impossible to change again."

233] *The Son Who Hit His Father*

ONCE THE BESHT WAS IN A CERTAIN COMMUNITY and he stayed in the attic of the inn. He saw a man passing in the street and immediately he ordered his servant: "Run quickly and bring that man to me." The boy ran after him and called him. At first he was surprised and did not want to go, but he did not dare refuse and he went to the rabbi.* When he came in, the rabbi said: "You have sinned today."

The man denied it and said: "What do you care, sir?"

The rabbi said: "You committed a great crime when you struck your father."

This is what happened. His father was an old man who was confined to the house. That day his father went to bring brandy up into the house and he delayed returning. The man went to see why his father took so long, and he saw him drinking brandy from a large pot placed under the barrels. The man became very angry and he took the pot and struck his father on the head. When the Besht told him the truth he immediately uttered a great cry and asked him to help him repent. As a repentance the Besht told him to fast on Mondays and Thursdays, and to stand in the mourner's place in the synagogue, and to do some other things as well. The man agreed to follow the path of repentance. The rabbi warned him that if he changed anything, God forbid, he would

* The Besht.

not live out the year. During the time that he was repentant his mother began to try to dissuade him. She mocked the rabbi until she persuaded him with her words and he abandoned the path of repentance. And so it happened that he did not live out the year. So it was told by the rabbi of Turov who witnessed this story.

234] *Charity*

THIS RABBI TOLD ANOTHER STORY. ONCE AT THE third meal the rabbi* said torah, and they remained at the table far into the night. He called his servant and told him to take several golden coins from his box and go to a certain house where a woman had delivered a child and did not have enough for a single meal. The servant immediately went there with the bag of money. The door was still closed because they had not yet cut the umbilical cord. He left the money according to the rabbi's order.

235] *The Besht Prevents a Blood Libel*

ONCE THE DISCIPLES OF THE BESHT CAME TO HIS house on the afternoon of Passover Eve to fulfill the mitzvah of baking matzoth. It was their custom to bake as a group while singing the Hallel.** The Besht was walking back and forth in the yard of the synagogue absorbed in deep thought. As the disciples had to wait for a few hours they became very upset. Meanwhile, they saw that the Besht had recognized the priest from afar and had approached him. He began to talk with him and they strolled together for a long time. Afterwards, the Besht invited him home, he offered him a seat, he treated him with Passover mead, and he continued to talk with him. Then the priest left and the Besht saw

* The Besht.
** A group of Psalms (113–18) which are recited in the synagogue on Sukkoth, Passover, Shabuoth, and Hanukkah.

him out. Afterwards, the Besht said: "Now we will soon begin to bake the matzoth. The day has begun to wane."

The disciples asked him: "Why did you have to talk with the priest for so long?"

He said that the priest had planned to throw a murdered bastard into the synagogue street on Passover night and then blame all the people of the town. By talking with him so long and by treating him well he had erased the plot from the priest's mind.

236] *The Gentile Who Blessed the Jews*

Once the Besht prayed before the ark. In the middle of the prayer he stopped praying and went to the street before the synagogue where he saw a gentile selling wood.[1] He bought a wagon load of wood from him, and the gentile followed after the Besht and carried the wood to the beth-hamidrash. The Besht told them to pay him for the wood and to give him brandy for carrying the wood to the beth-hamidrash.

The gentile said: "Blessed be the God of the Jews who has such a holy people." Had a gentile bought the wood from him he certainly would not have given him anything.

The disciples asked the Besht why he had stopped in the middle of his prayer to buy wood, and he answered that during his prayer he saw that in heaven there was an accusation made against the Jews who live in the villages that they cheated the gentiles in their accounts. He had to silence the accuser. As a result of the gentile's praise of the Jews the arguments of the accuser were silenced.

237] *The Language of the Animals*

It happened that the rabbi, the Preacher, our teacher and rabbi, Aryeh Leib of Polonnoye, wanted to learn the language of the animals, birds, and palm trees, as he thought that this knowledge was necessary for his preaching. Since his intention to learn this was for the sake of heaven, he decided to go to the Besht and ask him to teach him this knowledge. He thought that the Besht would certainly fulfill his wish, as it was for the sake of heaven. When he came to the Besht's room, he found many people present, and the Besht did not turn to him at all. Later, only after he had stood there for a long time, did the Besht greet him half-heartedly. The Preacher wondered about this because he was close to the Besht and the Besht was fond of him. Nevertheless, his desire to learn the language of the birds did not diminish, and he remained with the Besht still longer, saying to himself, "Perhaps it was just an oversight and I will find the proper time to approach him."

One day the Besht happened to take a trip to the holy community of Kamenka by way of Mariupol, and the Besht asked the Preacher to accompany him. He was filled with joy, thinking that on the way his wish would be fulfilled.

They traveled together with several other people. During the journey at an inn the Besht went to sleep in a special room in the attic. The Preacher waited until he awoke from his sleep, and then he climbed up the ladder to the attic where the Besht was. When he reached the last rung he saw the Besht seated concentrating on *yiḥudim*, and his face was aflame like a torch. He was very frightened and he almost fell from the rung in his great fear. Then the Besht scolded him and said: "Stand up. Do not be afraid. What do you want?"

He became silent from fear and he did not answer.

When they continued on their way from the inn the Besht asked the Preacher to sit with him in his wagon, and he did so. The Besht said to him: "It is known to me that the main reason that you joined my group is to learn the language of birds and so on. Come here and I will explain it to you carefully. To begin, it is known that in the upper chariot there is the face of an ox, the face of a man, the face of an eagle, and the face of a lion. The choicest one in the chariot is the face of the man, and from him the life power extends downward to lower man. From the face of the upper ox through the chain of phases, through risings and fallings and many contractions, the life power descends to all the lower animals. From the face of the lion the life power extends down to the lower beasts, and from the face of the eagle it goes to all the lower birds. This is the secret of *Perek Shirah.** Similarly, the language of each animal in the upper chariot descends to the lower animals, beasts, and birds. The wise man who can understand and examine everything in its upper source in the upper chariot will be able to comprehend the origin of all and the details and the means of the speech of the animals, beasts, and birds. This is the picture in general."

When he explained these things in detail, he revealed to the Preacher awesome and wonderful secrets until he knew the matter thoroughly.

After the Besht revealed to him the essential profundity of the secrets of this knowledge, while they were traveling he interpreted for him the sayings of the Zohar and the Tikkunim. The Preacher listened to him with one ear, while with the second ear he listened to the conversation of the birds, the animals, and the beasts. During the journey, until they came near the city, the Besht interpreted all these secrets for him. As they approached the city the Besht said to him: "Did you fully grasp this knowledge?"

He said to him: "Yes."

Then the Besht passed his hands over the Preacher's face, and he forgot all the secret details of this knowledge. Only the introduction remained in his memory. The Besht laughed and said: "If you had need of this knowledge to help you in worshiping the Creator, I would have hastened to teach it to you myself. I taught you this knowledge to satisfy your thirst, and you have forgotten it because it is not meant for your work. *Thou shalt be whole-*

---

* Literally, "Chapter of Song." This is an old *baraita* in which all parts of nature, animals, and plants praise God using scriptural phrases. It is probably referred to in B. Ḥullin 64b, Sanhedrin 95b and Ḥagigah 13a. In later periods it was highly valued and commended for daily prayer, though only very pious Jews came to recite it daily. Many kabbalist authors commented on "Chapter of Song." See J. D. Eisenstein, "Shirah Perek," *Jewish Encyclopedia* (1905), XI, 294–96.

hearted with the Lord thy God[1] and a hint to the wise is sufficient."

238] *The Loose Woman*

ONCE THE RABBI, THE BESHT, WAS SITTING AT THE
third meal, and he was deep in thought. He did not say torah at
the third meal at all which was unusual to the disciples. It was his
custom at the conclusion of every Sabbath, after the Havdalah, to
travel outside the city for about half a verst and then to return. At
the conclusion of that Sabbath he also had the wagon and horses
prepared to travel, and he said that a few of the disciples would
accompany him. He told them to prepare provisions for the
journey and to take a satchel with clothes. The members of his
household wondered at this. He did not say where he was going.
After they passed through the city gate, he ordered the disciples
to turn their faces toward him, and he told the coachman as well
to turn his face toward him and to tie the reins and let the horses
go by themselves. And that is what happened. The disciples
realized that they were traveling from one city to another. Almost
every quarter of an hour they entered another city. They journeyed like that all night until dawn. By swift travel they covered
a very long distance that night. They came to a big city, and the
horses stopped at a large, ornate house. The Besht told the coachman to direct the horses into the yard.

The householder awoke from his sleep and greeted them. He
asked them: "Where are you from?"

They said: "From Volhynia."

He told them that, if they were merchants, they would have
to stay at the inn which was especially for them, and if they were
preachers, they would have to stay with the elder of the community.

The Besht said: "Why are you concerned? I will be here for
only a few hours." The householder went away.

The Besht got down from his wagon. He took his pipe and
went into the kitchen for a burning coal to light his pipe. As he

entered, a young woman who had just gotten out of her bed also came into the kitchen half dressed. The Besht asked her to take a burning coal and put it in his pipe, and she did so. The Besht said to her: "Do you recognize me?"

She said: "No."

He said: "I am your uncle from Medzhibozh. What are you doing here?"

The woman said: "I was the householder's son's wife. My husband died and my father-in-law wants me to marry his nephew who is still a boy. I cannot oppose him, but it is against my will."

The Besht said to her: "Do not worry. I will be as a father to you, and if it is your desire, you can accompany me to my place today. There I will give you a good man that you will like for a husband."

The woman said: "Yes, I will go with you."

He said to her: "Go and prepare yourself because we will not stay here."

The woman took her clothes and jewelry and put them in a box. When her father-in-law saw her doing this, he asked her: "Why are you preparing yourself? Where are you going?"

She said to him: "This man is my uncle, and he wants to take me to his state where he will give me a husband."

The householder became angry at the Besht. He ran toward him furiously and said to him: "What are you doing to me, taking my daughter-in-law and all her clothing and jewelry without my knowledge?"

The Besht took him into a closed room and said to him: "Know that I am a Besht. Yesterday I started out from my home and I traveled swiftly on this long road. The fact is that after the death of her husband your daughter-in-law became a loose woman and slept with several Polish noblemen. In short, recently she promised an officer to change her religion and to marry him. Yesterday during the third meal, her grandfather, who was a famous tsaddik and a pillar of his generation, came to me from the upper world and asked me to correct his granddaughter, this woman, who has a lofty soul but who has fallen into demonic depths, so that she would not remain there, God forbid. I promised him. This woman planned that today, two hours from now, the officer would come with soldiers and take her by force together with all her clothing and jewelry, and she would change her religion. Therefore, I give this counsel. God will be with you and a great mitzvah will be credited to you for the saving of a soul."

The words penetrated to the heart of the householder and he believed him. The Besht promised him that he would return all the belongings that the woman took which were not hers. The Besht took the woman and brought her back with him. The disciples, who did not know anything about it, were very surprised by this sight. All the way back the Besht was kind to her, and she called him "my uncle."

Upon their arrival in the holy community of Medzhibozh the Besht arranged her engagement to a respectable, famous, and wealthy man. At the wedding, before the ceremony at the canopy, the woman came to the rabbi's room to confess and to ask repentance for her sins, since being in the rabbi's house had removed all the evil from her heart. When the Besht realized that she spoke from the depths of her heart, he said to her: "How could you imagine that I am your uncle? You should know that I am not your uncle. Because you fixed the time to convert, your grandfather asked me to save you, but if you do not make proper repentance you will die at once."

She wept great tears and asked him to tell her the way to repentance. The rabbi answered that this would be her repentance: "The marriage will be canceled because you are not worthy of this man. After you experience the bitterness in your soul, you will marry a baker and sit in the market selling bagels. You will return all the belongings that your father-in-law gave you because it is not his crime and his sin. He gave them to you in his trust for me and in order to save your soul from hell."

She accepted the repentance wholeheartedly and became completely pious. After that her grandfather appeared in the Besht's dream and said to him: "You can rest now that you have eased my mind."

239] *The Besht and the Old Priest*

Once, on the evening of Yom Kippur, before Kol Nidre, the congregation gathered in the beth-hamidrash. The Besht stood up, but he did not begin to pray. It was evident that he was greatly perplexed. There was a long delay, and the entire congregation began to cry because they realized that this was not an empty matter. Then the rabbi looked through the window and saw an old priest walking before the beth-hamidrash, and he went out to him. The rabbi began to talk with him. He asked him how he was, and they became so engrossed in conversation that he accompanied him home. The rabbi discussed with him why he did not take a wife, as *He created it* [the earth] *not a waste, He formed it to be inhabited*.[1] The priest answered him that he was not permitted to marry. The rabbi argued with him a great deal about it and urged him to resign his priesthood and perform the mitzvah of propagation at least in his old age. The priest said that according to his rank he could not marry a woman of the lower class and a woman of a worthy family would not agree to marry him. The rabbi said that a certain governor had a beautiful daughter and he would certainly be willing to give her to him as a wife. He kept talking with him until he agreed. Her beauty so appealed to him that he had an accidental emission from the excess of his desire. The rabbi immediately went to the beth-hamidrash and began to pray Kol Nidre.

After the prayer his followers came to him and he told them the story. A great accusation in heaven had blocked all the prayers from ascending because this priest had never had an accidental emission.

They asked: "How did you know that he had an accidental emission."

He said: "Because it was immediately impossible to stand near him."

With the help of God all the accusers were silenced.

240] *Rabbi Isaac of Berdichev*

I HEARD THAT THE RABBI, THE GREAT MAGGID OF the holy community of Mezhirich, did not himself blow the shofar. The holy rabbi, our teacher and rabbi, Menaḥem Mendel, who passed away in the Holy Land,* used to blow the shofar, and the Maggid, God bless his memory, used to signal the trumpets. Even before his death, when his leg troubled him for several years, he used to give the signals from his room. Once, the rabbi, our teacher and rabbi, Menaḥem Mendel, was not in that holy community for Rosh Hashanah, and the Great Maggid told the rabbi, the gaon, our teacher and rabbi, Levi Isaac, the head of the court of the holy community of Berdichev,** to blow the shofar. He approached the task with awe and fear, and, as was his custom, he made a great tumult. When the Maggid gave the signal for the first trumpet, Levi Isaac saw great flashes of light, and he fainted.

The Maggid, the rabbi, said: "I do not know what happened to him. Mendel sees much more and he is not afraid."

They had to give the trumpeting to another person who would not be able to see and so would not be frightened.

241] *Rabbi David Forkes' Dream*

ONCE, THE RABBI, OUR TEACHER DAVID FORKES, dreamed that he came to the Besht. He saw four people standing with the Besht. He knew two of them. The third one was Elijah, God bless his memory, and the fourth one was unknown to him.

---

* Rabbi Menaḥem Mendel of Vitbesk (1730–1788) immigrated to the Land of Israel in 1777.

** Rabbi Levi Isaac of Berdichev (1740–1809) was a central figure among the Hasidim in the Ukraine. He was known as "the defender of Israel" for relating the virtues of the Jewish people as a defense against the Almighty Himself.

He did not know him and he was ashamed to ask the Besht who he was.

Once, after the death of the Besht, he visited with the rabbi, the Maggid, who asked him to describe the form, appearance, and gestures of that man. When Rabbi David told him, the Maggid said that it was our teacher and rabbi, Isaac Luria,[1] God bless his memory.

Similarly, they heard from the Besht that the great rabbi, our teacher and rabbi, Hayyim Tsenzer of Brody, was a spark of Rabbi Yohanan ben Zakkai.* The Maggid said: "Why does it surprise you? He actually looked like Rabbi Yohanan ben Zakkai."[2]

242] *A Glass of Wine*

Once the Besht was in the state of Walachia where they have grape wine which is so strong that even when you mix two or three drops in a glass it is too strong to drink. The householder offered the Besht a glass of this wine. When he tasted it the Besht said: "Your wine is delicious. Why is your glass so small?"

The householder answered: "Because it is dangerous to drink a large portion."

The Besht said: "I am not afraid of that." They gave him a large glass and he drank it all. All of them stared at him in fright as his face became red, and his hair stood up as though it were on fire. But the Besht passed his hands over his face and at once he returned to normal. All of them were very surprised, but he said that our rabbis, God bless their memory, said: "Wine is strong but fear works it off."[1] When he looked at the greatness of the Blessed One, he was struck by fear and trembling, and it completely undid the effects of the wine.

* Yohanan ben Zakkai was a Tanna of the 1st century. After the destruction of the Temple he founded the Academy at Yavneh and thus insured the continuation of the learning of the oral tradition. See Jacob Neusner, *A Life of Rabban Yohanan Ben Zakkai, ca 1–80, C.E.*, Studia Post-Biblica, VI (Leiden, 1962).

243] *The Besht's Dinner*

ONCE THE BESHT TRAVELED WITH HIS DISCIPLES, AND they had to sleep overnight in the forest. The disciples said jokingly: "Let's see the meal that the rabbi can prepare for us."

The rabbi said: "Tomorrow, if God wills it, I will prepare a great meal for you with all sorts of delicacies."

The following day they came to a large city, and they stayed in the house of a wealthy man. The uncle of that wealthy man was visiting with him. This uncle was a rabbi in a community which was about eighty versts away, and they had not seen each other for more than twelve years. In his honor he prepared a great dinner to which he had invited all the people of the town. Although they had heard about the Besht, they did not regard him very highly. After the prayers at the synagogue, all the people of the town came to his house, and his uncle sat at the head of the table. The Besht was still praying in a corner of the house, and his uncle, the rabbi, asked: "Who is that who is still praying?"

The householder answered: "That is the Besht." They did not pay any attention to him, nor did they invite his holy disciples to the table.

When the Besht finished praying he came to the rabbi's seat, and he said to him: "I have a secret to tell you." They went to a secluded place and the Besht said: "You have a failing, sir."

He said: "I do not."

The Besht answered: "Each time that you want to concentrate on *Hear O Israel*,[1] Jesus stands before you."

He denied it and the Besht answered: "How could it be a lie when you have made eighty fasts for it."

He had to confess to him, and he cried before him, asking for help. The Besht told him that his cure consisted of not doubting the deeds of the great tsaddikim. He accepted it upon himself wholeheartedly to avoid returning to the stupidity of doubting the tsaddikim. The Besht said: "Today, try to concentrate on this kavvanah and you will see that you are cured."

And so it was. He immediately took the Besht by the hand and

252 · IN PRAISE OF THE BAAL SHEM TOV

seated him at the head of the table. All his disciples were also seated around at the head of the table, and they were treated with great honor.

244] *The Besht Resuscitates a Child: A Second Version*

THERE WAS A MAN LIVING IN THE HOLY COMMUNITY of Medzhibozh who had no children, and he always mentioned it to the Besht. The Besht promised him that he would surely have children. When he became old he kept bothering the Besht, and with God's help his wife gave birth to a baby boy in her old age. Not many days after he was born, the baby died. At once the man went to the Besht in terrible anger. "Why did you delude me with false hopes and give me something which was immediately taken from me. It would have been better had I not had children to begin with."

The Besht answered: "Did I not tell you that you will have children. The boy will surely live."

The man waited a long while, but the boy neither got up nor moved. He did not appear to have any life in him. He could not face the Besht again after having received his certain promise. He came to the rabbi and approached him in another way, by asking him if he should prepare himself for the berith and whom he should honor. The Besht told him to prepare himself as is the custom, and to honor a well known man as the sandek and another for the cutting, while the sucking of the blood should be reserved for the Besht. And so they did.

They brought the baby to the synagogue and had him circumcised, but the blood did not flow. It was like cutting dead flesh. The rabbi began to say the blessing following the berith. When he said the words, "Preserve this child to his mother and father," he lingered for a long time until breath was restored to the boy and the blood of the circumcision spurted highly. With God's help the boy completely revived.

245] *The Doctor*

ONCE A WELL KNOWN, GREAT DOCTOR CAME TO THE duchess of the town. The duchess praised the Besht highly, saying that he was a great man and knowledgeable in medicine.

The doctor said: "Tell him to come here."

She said: "Since he is a great man, it would be in keeping with his honor if we send a carriage for him as one does for governors." She sent for him and he appeared before them.

The doctor asked the rabbi whether it was true that he was knowledgeable about medicine.

He answered him: "It is true."

He said: "Where did you study and with what expert?"

He said: "God, blessed be He, taught me."

The doctor laughed at him.

The rabbi immediately asked him whether he could diagnose an illness from one's pulse. The rabbi said: "I have a deficiency. You try to diagnose my pulse. I will take your pulse and diagnose your condition."

The doctor took the rabbi's pulse. He could tell that there was something wrong, but he did not know what it was, because he was lovesick for God, blessed be He, and this was beyond the grasp of the doctor.

Then the rabbi took the doctor's pulse, and he turned his face to the duchess and asked her: "Were such and such precious objects stolen from you?"

She said: "Yes. It has been several years since they were stolen from me, and I do not know where they are."

The rabbi said: "Send someone to his inn and open his trunk. There you will find all of these objects."

She immediately sent someone and the objects were found there according to his holy words. The doctor left there in disgrace and contempt.

(The method the tsaddikim used was to read the word, *pulse,* backwards, like *Abba:** the letters daleth, peh, koph— דפק (pulse) backwards are koph, peh, daleth— קפד (be strict). In this way the tsaddikim could recognize sins from the pulse. So it is written in the holy Zohar and the *Tikunei ha-Zohar*.)

246] *The Careless Shohet*

ONCE, WHILE THE BESHT WAS ON A JOURNEY, HE stayed with the rabbi of the community in order to be there for the Sabbath. The rabbi said to his wife: "Accord him every honor because he is a great and famous man."

His wife said: "Did we not, with the help of God, buy meat?" Let us choose a good cut from it in honor of our guest. When she went to look for the meat she did not find it, and her heart was nearly broken. She went to her neighbor. Perhaps she could borrow something from her. But her neighbor could not find a trace of what she had prepared. She went to a second neighbor and she too did not find anything. She consulted her husband about what to do. As she was talking with him she saw the local shohet passing by the window. She told him her problem and what had happened, and he said: "It has been just two or three hours since I slaughtered a good tender calf."

The Besht said: "I like to eat the head very much. If it is possible, bring it to me whole and bore it out here."

The shohet said: "Very good." He rose, went quickly, and brought the head to the rabbi's house.

The Besht began to talk with the shohet: "People say that there is some dispute concerning the teeth. Please count the number of teeth that the calf has."

He opened the animal's mouth and put his hand into it to count the teeth. As soon as he pushed his hand inside he could not

* *Abba*, father in Hebrew, is a major symbolic concept in kabbalistic mysticism. It was thought of as having two aspects—front and back. The term used her *Aḥorayim De'Abba* (דאבא אחוריים) literally means, "the back side of *Abba*"; however, our translation provides a different interpretation of this term in this particular context.

pull it out. His hand was drawn in until he could not bear it and he cried aloud.

The Besht said to him: "Why do you cry? Is the calf not dead?" The Besht shouted at him: "Wicked man. Confess!"

He confessed his sin that he never examined the lungs. He had qualified and disqualified meat according to his whim. The Besht told him what his repentance must be.

Afterwards they went to the synagogue. The Besht passed his hands over the rabbi's face, and he saw several demons and ghosts sitting on the synagogue. The rabbi was amazed. The Besht explained that each time before his prayers the cantor had an accidental emission. They removed him from his post.

247] *The Besht's Death*

I WILL WRITE A LITTLE ABOUT HIS DEATH. HIS PASSing away was on the first day of Shabuoth. On the Passover before that, the rabbi, our teacher Pinḥas of Korets, visited with the Besht, and Rabbi Pinḥas felt a little weak. Because of this he hesitated to go to the mikveh on the eve of the last holiday of Passover, and finally he decided not to go. On the seventh day of the Passover Rabbi Pinḥas perceived within the prayer that it was decreed that the Besht would soon pass away because of his fight against the sect of Shabbetai Tsevi, as it is told above in the story when they wanted to burn the Babylonian Talmud on Yom Kippur.[1] The rabbi, our teacher and rabbi, Rabbi Pinḥas, began to strengthen his prayer, but it did not help, and he regretted that he had not gone to the mikveh. He thought that if he would have seen this while he was in the mikveh it would have helped. After the prayer the Besht asked him whether he went to the mikveh on the previous day, and he said, "No."

The Besht said: "The deed has already been done and there is nothing that can alter it."

After the Passover the Besht was sick with diarrhea, but in spite of that he gathered his strength and went to pray before the ark. He did not say anything about it to his students, who were known to have powerful prayers, and he sent them elsewhere. The rabbi, our teacher and rabbi, Pinḥas, did not return home. On the eve of Shabuoth all his followers gathered to spend the night saying prayers, such as the redemption prayer of the *Ari*, God bless his memory. The Besht said torah before them concerning the biblical portion of the week and the giving of the Torah. In the morning he sent for all his followers to gather and he told Rabbi Leib Kessler and someone else, I have forgotten his name, to handle his burial. Because they were members of the funeral society and needed to know about diseases, he showed them the signs on each of the members of his own body, and he explained how the soul emanates from this member and from that member. He told them to gather a minyan to pray with him. He told them to give him a prayer book and he said: "Soon I shall be with God, blessed be He."

After the prayer, Rabbi Naḥman of Horodenka went to the beth-hamidrash to pray for him. The Besht said: "He shouts in vain. If he could have entered in the gate where I was accustomed to enter, his prayer would have helped." At that moment the soul of a dead man came to him asking for redemption. He scolded him, saying: "For eighty years you have wandered, and you have not heard until today that I am in this world. Get out, wicked one." He immediately said to the servant: "Rush outside and shout for everyone to clear away from the road because I angered him and he may hurt someone." And so it was that he hurt a maiden, the daughter of the shammash. The servant returned and he heard the Besht saying: "I grant you these two hours. Do not torture me."

The servant said: "Who are you talking to, sir?"

He said: "Do you not see the Angel of Death who always ran from me? As people say, 'I banished him to where black peppers grow.' Now that they have given him control over me his shoulders have broadened and he feels joyous."

Then all the people of the town came to see him on the holiday, and he said torah to them. After that, during the meal, he told the servant to put mead in a large glass, but the servant put it in a small glass. The Besht said: "Man has no *power* [on] *the day of death*,[2] even the gabbai does not obey me." Then he said:

"Until now I have done favors for you. Now you will do a favor
for me." Then he went to the toilet and the servant wanted to
follow him. He asked him: "Is today different from any other day
that you want to follow me? What do you see in me?" He did not
go after him.

He also gave them a sign that when he passes away the two
clocks will stop. When he washed his hands the big clock
stopped, and his followers stood around it so that he would not
see it. He said to them: "I am not concerned about myself because
I know clearly that when I leave through this door I immediately
enter another door." He sat on his bed and he told them to
gather around him. He said torah to them about the column on
which one ascends from lower paradise to upper paradise, and
how this was so in each world. He described what it was like in
the world of the souls, and he interpreted the order of worship.
He told them to say, "Let the pleasantness of the Lord our God
be upon us."[3] He lay down and sat up several times. He concentrated on kavvanoth until they could not distinguish the syllables.
He ordered them to cover him with a sheet, and he began to
tremble as one saying the eighteen benedictions. Then slowly he
became quiet and they saw that the small clock had stopped.
They waited for a long time. Then they put a feather under his
nose and they realized that he had passed away.

I heard all this from Rabbi Jacob of the holy community of
Medzhibozh, who passed away in the Holy Land. The rabbi said
that Rabbi Leib Kessler saw the departure of his soul as a blue
flame.[4]

248] *Rabbi Leib Kessler's Offer*

ONCE, A FEW WEEKS BEFORE THE BESHT'S DEATH,
Rabbi Leib came to him, and the Besht told him that he would
soon die. Rabbi Leib said: "My head and eyes for your eyes."

But the Besht refused. He said: "They will return to me what
they took from me about a year ago." He did not want to live.
Who would want such a life?

249] *The Besht's Son*

I heard that when the Besht's wife died, his followers and those of his generation suggested that he remarry, but he replied to them in wonder: "Why do I need a wife? For the last fourteen years I refrained from sleeping with my wife, and my son Hersheleh was born by the *word*."[1]

On the day of his death, his son, Hersheleh Tsevi, was sleeping. They said to the Besht: "Why do you not give your son instructions?"

He said: "What can I do? He is asleep."

He was sleeping because he did not believe his father would die. They woke him up and said to him: "Your father said that he will surely die today."

He came to his father and began to cry. His father said to him: "I know that I gave you a holy soul for when I joined in union with my wife the heavens shook. If I had wanted to, in the secret of conception, it was in my power to bring the soul of Adam. I knew everything that was necessary, but you have a holy soul, and you did not need all that."

He asked him: "Nevertheless, tell me *something*."

He began to speak.

He said: "I do not understand what you are saying."

The Besht said: "There is nothing I can do. I cannot talk with you." He taught him a name, and he said: "Concentrate on this name, and you will be able to see me, and I will study with you."

He said to him: "And if I forget this name?"

He told him a way to remember the name, but I have forgotten what he said to him.

250] *The Fish and the Dog: A Second Version*

Once, one of the students of the holy rabbi our teacher, Jehiel Mikhel of Zolochev, traveled to his rabbi, and upon his arrival the rabbi said: "Return home immediately." He did what he was told. He was confused as he did not know the reason why the rabbi had ordered him to return to his home, especially as he had longed to spend the Sabbath with the rabbi. On his way a small, pretty, and well groomed dog accompanied him. He liked the dog and took him into his wagon and played with him all the way. When they reached a bridge over the water, the dog jumped into the river and began to swim. He could not swim well and he began to sink in the river. The dog threw out his legs and struggled a great deal until he drowned. The man felt sorrow because the dog, whom he liked, had drowned.

Meanwhile, during his delay, the fishermen caught a large fish in their net. Since he was near his home, and it was the evening of the holy Sabbath, he bought the fish from the fishermen. When he came home he prepared the fish for the Sabbath with all sorts of ingredients. When he came from the bathhouse he tasted the fish and, as our rabbis, God bless their memory, said: "Its taste is like life itself."[1] He immediately became another person. His face shone, and during the entire Sabbath his prayers were like those of a great and holy man. At every meal he revealed secrets of the Torah unheard of before. It was a wonder to everyone and to himself as well. When he finished the evening prayer and made the Havdalah he became as he was before and this surprised him.

The following day he went to the rabbi again. The rabbi called him a one-day scholar.[2] He wanted to know the reason and the rabbi told him that his father, God bless his memory, had committed a sin, and he had been reincarnated into a dog. There-fore, because the heart understands the bitterness of the soul, he loved the dog very much and grieved a great deal when it drowned. His father had been uplifted and was privileged to be reincarnated into the fish which the fishermen caught. And be-cause he had prepared it in honor of the Sabbath, they had granted him permission to absorb his father's soul. Therefore, he had wonderful experiences the entire Sabbath. After performing the ceremony of the Havdalah his father had been uplifted to his rightful place and the son remained as he was before.[3]

251] *The Burning of Rabbi Jacob Joseph's Books*

Once, the son of the holy rabbi, our teacher and rabbi, Mikhel of Zolochev, was very sick. At that moment news reached the rabbi that in a certain country they wanted to burn the holy books of the rabbi, our teacher Jacob Joseph of Polonnoye.[1] The rabbi left his home, and he told the members of his household that if, God forbid, his son should die, they should wait with the burial until he returns home. After his departure, the boy fell into a lethargy, which is called in German *hiner plet*,[2] and they thought that the boy was dead. After three days he began to perspire, and his soul returned to his body. When he recovered, he told them all that had happened.

As soon as his soul left his body an angel took him and brought him to a palace. The angel did not have permission to go into the palace, and he entered the palace alone. He stood at the door and saw that the great court was in session. He saw two messengers carrying a book containing his good deeds, but the scale was unbalanced until they brought in a third book, which was the book of the sufferings he had endured, as the rabbis, God bless their memory, say "What is the extent of man's sufferings? And so on."[3] Then, many of the sins were eliminated. Nevertheless, they wanted to sentence him to death because of what remained. They were about to pronounce the sentence. At that moment his father, the rabbi, our rabbi and teacher, Mikhel, made a noisy entrance and cried out that they wanted to burn the books of Jacob Joseph: "It is well known and revealed to the One who said 'Let the world be created' that Jacob Joseph did not do his work for his own honor, God forbid, but for God's honor and for His blessed Torah." When he saw his son standing at the door, he said to him: "My son, what are you doing here?"

He answered him: "I have been standing here for a long time and I do not know why. Please say something in my favor."

He said: "If I do not forget, I will speak well of you." And again he shouted about the books as he had done the first time.

The court answered: "This matter does not belong to our court but to the one who *higher than the high watcheth,*[4] and so on."

The rabbi departed and he did not remember to mention his son. In the meantime the holy rabbi, our teacher, the author, Jacob Joseph, ascended to this palace, and he also cried out, weeping and complaining greatly because they wanted to burn his holy books. Jacob Joseph saw him standing at the door, and he asked him: "Joseph, what are you doing here?" He answered him as he had before, and he asked him to speak in his favor. Jacob Joseph answered him as his father had: "If I do not forget, I will speak well of you." Afterwards, he went away as well, and the boy stood in despair because he had no one to support him. Immediately, a great sound was heard and all the worlds resounded, and they announced: "Clear the way. The Besht himself is coming into the palace." The Besht saw him standing at the door and asked him: "Joseph, what business do you have here?"

He answered him as he had before: "I asked my master, my father, and the rabbi of the holy community of Polonnoye to speak in my favor, but they forgot. Therefore, I ask you, your holy honor, to speak for me."

The rabbi asked the court to let the boy go in peace. He told him to return home. He wanted to stay there a little longer to see what the Besht was going to do there. At once two men came and took him with them. They found a putrid corpse lying on the floor and they told him, "Enter into that corpse," but he absolutely refused. He cried and appealed to them, but they hit him and made him enter in spite of himself. When he entered the corpse he began to perspire.

THE END. COMPLETED.
PRAISE TO GOD, THE CREATOR OF THE WORLD.

GLOSSARY

Admor: Abbreviation of the Hebrew words *adonenu morenu ve-rabbenu,* our master, teacher, and rabbi. The Hasidim addressed their tsaddikim and rabbinical authorities by this title; however, in this book it refers specifically to Rabbi Shneur Zalman of Lyady (1747–1813), the founder of the Habad Hasidism and the author of *Likutei Amarim,* Slavuta, 1796.

Amora (*pl.* Amoraim): A name given to the rabbinic teacher who discussed the Mishnaic law both in Palestine and Babylonia (third to sixth centuries). Their collective discussions comprise the Palestinian and Babylonian Talmuds.

arrendator: The leasee of a landed estate; or a feudal tax collector who pays a fee for his commission and then retains a percentage of the taxes.

arrendeh: A leased estate or revenue derived from taxation and collected on a contractual basis by other people.

Ari: Rabbi Isaac Luria (1534–72), a major Jewish mystic who lived in Safed. His teachings are recorded in the books of his disciple Hayyim Vital (1543–1620). His name, *Ari,* is an abbreviation of Ashkenazi Rabbi Isaac. In Hebrew the name also means "a lion" and hence most often his disciples referred to him as *ha-Ari ha-Kaddosh,* "the holy lion."

Ashkenazi (*pl.* Ashkenazim): A term applied to German Jews since the ninth century. At later periods it was extended to include all Yiddish speaking Jews and their descendants.

Awe, Days of: The first ten days of the year from Rosh Hashanah to Yom Kippur inclusive. It is a time devoted to repentence. Selihoth, penitential prayers, are recited in the synagogue each day before the night is completely over.

baalshem: Literally "a master of names": a person who heals the sick, exorcises demons, writes amulets, and performs miracles by using the magical power of divine names.

bagel: A small doughnut-shaped type of roll.

baraita: A traditional Jewish teaching from the Tannaic period which is not included in the Mishnah.

bar mitzvah: Literally son of commandment; Jewish adult male obligated to perform religious commandments and qualified to undertake communal and social responsibilities; the celebration of the occasion at which, at the age of thirteen, a boy becomes a member of the adult community.

berith: The circumcision of a Jewish infant boy which normally takes place eight days after birth. This is a festive occasion.

beth-hamidrash: "The House of Study." In eastern Europe this consisted of a room, a house, or a school used for study and prayer. It was equipped with a small library.

Cohen: Originally the descendants of Aaron from the tribe of Levi, whose function and privilege it was to carry out the priestly duties in the temple. These responsibilities were hereditary through the male line of descent. Later, after the destruction of the temples, the descendants of this class continued to observe many of the prohibitions and customs which their ancestors were obliged to follow.

devekut: Cleaving to God. A term which denotes a meditative as well as an ecstatic communion with God.

dybbuk: The restless soul of a dead person which possesses a living man or woman. The concept appeared in Judaism in the sixteenth and seventeenth centuries.

eighteen benedictions: The principle prayer. The worshipers, standing, first recite the benedictions silently and then repeat them aloud with the reader. This is the main part of the Shaharith, Minhah, and Maariv on weekdays as well as of Musaf on Sabbaths and Neilah on Yom Kippur. The various benedictions which constitute this prayer originated in different periods; some are from the era of the Second Temple, while others are from a later date.

elder: A high ranking leader of the Jewish community (Hebrew, *parnas*). The office holders changed on a monthly rotating system.

Erets Yisrael: The Land of Israel.

gabbai (*pl.* gabbaim): Tsaddik's assistant; a synagogue official, treasurer, or administrator of synagogue funds.

gaon (pl. geonim): The title of the head of a Babylonian academy during the period between the sixth and the twelfth centuries. An outstanding rabbinical scholar.

Gemara: The discussion and interpretation of the Mishnah in the Babylonian and Jerusalemian Talmuds.

gematria (*pl.* gematriot): The calculation of the numerical value of Hebrew words as a homlitic method to uncover any hidden meaning in biblical phrases. It had a significant role in the Kabbalah as well as in magical practices.

Gehenna: Hell. A place of punishment and torment of the wicked. The term derived from the biblical *Gei Hinnom*, a valley outside the western wall of Jerusalem where child sacrifice was offered to the pagan gods.

golden coins: Zlotys. Literally in Polish "golden." A golden coin was equivalent to thirty groschen.

Greeks: Local Russian Orthodox peasants, Ukrainians.

groschen: *Grossus, grosz,* a small coin; a golden coin equal to thirty groschen.

hafsakah, ta'anit: A type of fasting which is not supposed to be broken with a meal at the end of the day.

Haidamaks: Ukrainian bands, hostile to the Poles and the Jews, who were active chiefly in the regions of Kiev and Podolia in the eighteenth century.

hakam (*also* haham, chacham): A sage. Originally, a Pharisaic teacher and a member of the ancient rabbinic courts in Palestine and Babylonia. Later the term applied to an officiating rabbi in Sephardic communities.

Halakah: The religious, ethical, civil, and criminal Jewish laws and ordinances as they have been formulated in the Mishnah and the Babylonian and Jerusalemian Talmuds and in literature related to these main bodies of oral law.

hallah: A loaf of bread used for Sabbath and festive meals.

Hallel: A name of a group of Psalms (113–18), which are recited in the synagogue on Sukkoth, Passover, Shabuoth, and Hanukkah.

hametz: Leaven. Dough kneaded from flour and water and allowed to become sour. In commemoration of the Exodus, when the Jews could not wait until their dough had leavened, only unleavened food is allowed during Passover.

Hanukkah: A festival commemorating the rededication of the Second Temple by Judah the Maccabee on the twenty-fifth of Kislev (Dec.–Jan.) 165 B.C.E. The main feature of the festival, which lasts eight days, is the kindling of eight-branched candelabrum.

Hasid (*pl.* Hasidim): An extremely pious person. In the Hellenistic period the term referred to a member of the sect which strongly opposed the Hellenization of Jewish culture. In current usage it applies to a member of the religious mystical sect which emerged in the Ukraine and Southern Poland in the middle of the eighteenth century and later spread to other parts of eastern and central Europe. At the present time, Israel and the United States are the main centers of this sect.

Hasidism: The teaching that evolved among the Hasidim; the movement espousing Hasidic teachings.

Havdalah: A prayer which is recited at the conclusion of Sabbaths and holidays to mark the conclusion of the sacred day and the beginning of the profane time.

hazan: Cantor; the reader of the prayers in the synagogue.

heder: Elementary religious school in East European Jewish communities. Often it was situated in a single room in the teacher's house.

hitlahavut: Enthusiasm, ecstasy. A central Hasidic concept of worshiping God.

impression: According to Lurianic mysticism, a residue of divine light remains in the primeval space created by the withdrawal of God into Himself, an act necessary for Creation. In this text the term *impression* applies to any remaining traces of human past actions.

Ishmaelites: Turks, Muslems.

Kabbalah (*also* cabala, cabbala, kabala): Jewish mystical doctrines and their systems which developed in Southern France and Spain from the twelfth century on, and subsequently spread into Safed, North Africa, Yemen, and eastern Europe.

kaddish: A prayer recited by the reader before and after certain sections of the service. It is best known as the mourner's prayer.

kavvanah (*pl.* kavvanoth): Inner devotion in prayer directed toward God. Systematic meditations and other mystical means which aid in attaining a high degree of concentration in prayer.

Kedarites: Tartars.

kedushah: (*pl.* kedushoth): A prayer which consists of the verses Is. 6:3 and Ezek. 3:12. It is said by the whole congregation in two places in the service.

kiddush: A prayer and a ceremony by which the Sabbath and holidays are sanctified. The prayer is recited over wine and hallah.

kittle: A white robe worn by the officiant at the Musaf, Additional Service, on the first day of Passover, and the eighth day of Sukkoth and by members of the congregation during prayer on the High Holidays.

klaus (also *kloiz*): A place of study which also served as a synagogue. The Hasidim often referred to their synagogues by this term.

Kohen: *See* Cohen.

Kol Nidre: The opening prayer recited before the beginning of the Yom Kipper Eve services.

kosher: Food fit to eat according to the Jewish dietary laws.

lolkeh: Tobacco pipe.

Maariv: The evening service which is recited daily after nightfall.

Ma'aseh Merkavah (also *Ma'aseh Merkabah*): A term applied to the principle subject matter of Jewish mysticism in the Tannaic and post-Tannaic periods. In Hebrew it means "work of the chariot," and essentially it concerns Ezekiel's vision of the divine throne-chariot.

maggid (*pl.* maggidim): A Jewish preacher; often an itinerant preacher. Customarily, the preacher's discourse would draw upon a biblical text, which would be embellished by parables drawn from the rabbinical commentaries and folklore. The discourse was often delivered in chant.

Mar (f. *Marat*, Aramaic): In an earlier period, the title "Master" given to some Babylonian rabbis. In current usage it is equivalent to mister.

matzah (*pl.* matzoth): Unleavened bread eaten on Passover.

mazal tov: Good luck. A blessing of congratulation said at the time of birth and marriage.

melamed (*pl.* melamedim): A teacher of children in the heder.

metsitsah: The sucking of the blood from the penis after the berith, which is done by the mohel.

mezuzah (*pl.* mezuzoth): A small parchment placed in a metal or wooden case and nailed in a slanting position on the doorpost. Inscribed on one side of the parchment are Deuteronomy 6:4–9 and 11:13–21; enscribed on the other side, and visible through an aperture, is the name of God, *Shaddai*, Almighty.

Midrash: Exegetical method which provides an elaborated and not literal interpretation of biblical words and phrases. It flourished during the Tannaic and Amoraic periods and the Midrashic literature that developed at those periods contains legends and tales which supplement the biblical narrative.

mikveh (*also* mikvah): A bath or a bathing place for immersion in water for purposes of ritual purification.

Minhah: The afternoon daily prayer. It can be recited from noontime until sunset.

minyan (*pl.* minyanim): The quorum of ten adult men required for holding liturgical services.

Mishnah: The core of the oral law, compiled by Rabbi Judah ha-Nasi (about 135 to about 217) on the basis of previous collections and codified around 200 A.D. Any of the interpretations in this work is a mishnah (*pl.* mishnayoth).

mitnagged (*pl.* mitnaggedim): An opponent of the Hasidim.

mitzvah (*pl.* mitzvoth): A commandment or precept and the act of fulfilling such a commandment. It refers to charitable as well as ritualistic acts.

mohel: A circumciser.

Musaf: An additional morning service recited on the Sabbath, Rosh Hashanah, Yom Kippur, Sukkoth, Passover, Shabuoth, and the New Moon.

Neilah: The concluding prayer of the Yom Kippur service. Its name in Hebrew means "closing" and it refers to the closing of the gates of heaven.

notarikon: The abbreviation of words by writing only their initial letters; hence, the interpretation of words as if they were the initials of other words.

rabbi: The title conferred upon an ordained teacher of Jewish law authorized to issue decisions in religious and ritualistic matters and to perform marriages. Also a respectful term of address.

Rambam: Maimonides, an abbreviation of his Hebrew name, Rabbi Moses ben-Maimon (1135–1204), a medieval Jewish philosopher and codifier.

Rashi: Abbreviation of Rabbi Solomon Yitshaki (1040–1105), a

French Jewish biblical and Talmudic scholar. His commentary established him as the foremost authority in the traditional interpretation of the Talmud and the Bible.

Rebbe: A term applied to the tsaddikim and Hasidic leaders.

red coins: Popular term for currency officially known as floren, dukat, czerwony, or zloty. Their value increased from two Polish zloties per red coin at the end of the sixteenth century to eighteen zloties during the eighteenth century.

Rosh Hashanah: The Jewish New Year. A two-day holiday at the beginning of the month of Tishri (approximately September–October).

sandek: The person who holds the baby on his knees during the circumcision ceremony.

sefirah (pl. sefirot): A concept in Jewish mysticism which refers to emanations and manifestations of the Godhead. There are ten such sefirot which constitute the mystical archetypes for the existence of the world.

selihah (pl. selihoth): A penitential prayer. Liturgical poems recited on fast days and during the period proceeding the high holidays.

Sephardi (pl. Sephardim): A term applied to Spanish and Portuguese Jews and their descendants who after the expellation of the Jews from Spain in 1492 settled in Mediterranean countries and in smaller numbers in Western Europe.

Shabuoth: Literally "weeks." A holiday which takes place seven weeks after the first day of Passover to commemorate the revelation of Mount Sinai and to celebrate the beginning of the wheat harvest.

Shaharith: The morning daily prayer recited after sunrise and before the end of the first quarter of the day.

shalom 'aleikhem: Literally "peace upon you." A greeting formula.

shammash: A minor synagogue official who kept order in the synagogue.

Shekinah: Divine Presence. The manifestation of the presence of God in the life of man and the community. In the Kabbalah the Shekinah is the tenth sefirah representing the feminine aspect of divinity.

shtetl: A small Jewish town in eastern Europe.

shofar: A ram's horn blown as a trumpet in the synagogue before and during Rosh Hashanah and at the conclusion of Yom Kippur.

shohet (pl. shohetim): A ritual slaughterer of animals and poultry. Among the mitnaggedim they were licensed by the rabbis. The hasidim named their own shohetim.

Simhath Torah (*also* Simchath Torah): Literally "the rejoicing of the Torah," a holiday marking the completion of the synagogue readings of the Pentateuch, celebrated on the twenty-third of Tishri (September–October) following Sukkoth.

sixer (*Szóstak, grossus sex duplex*): Polish currency equal to six groschen. During the eighteenth century its value increased up to twelve groschen and two szelag (a small copper coin).

sukkah (*pl.* sukkoth): A tabernacle in which Jews eat and many also sleep during the festival of Sukkoth, as a commemoration of the dwelling of the children of Israel in the desert after they left Egypt. The structure must be temporary; its roof is covered with the branches of trees.

Sukkoth: Feast of Tabernacles. A seven-day holiday starting on the fifteenth day of Tishri (September–October) which both commemorates the temporary shelter the Jews had during their wandering in the desert and also celebrates the gathering of the harvest.

taler (also thaler): A German silver coin. Its value increased from thirty-five groschen at the end of the sixteenth century to eight zloties (240 groschen) during the eighteenth century.

tallith: A woolen or silk rectangular prayer shawl with fringes at the four corners and blue or black stripes at the ends. It is worn over the head or around the shoulder during Shaharith and Musaf.

Talmud: The Palestinian and Babylonian Talmuds are the two great compilations of the discussions and interpretations of the Oral Law that took place in the various academies. They were completed in the fifth and sixth centuries respectively and comprise the major source for the Jewish religious code of laws.

Tanna (*pl.* Tannaim): The Palestinian teachers of the first two centuries A.D. who interpreted biblical law and the oral tradition. Their teachings are recorded in the Mishnah, Tosaphoth, and other books.

tashlik: A religious rite performed on the afternoon of the first day of Rosh Hashanah. The worshipers assemble along a bank of running water or a seashore, recite penitential prayers and the verses of Micah 7:18–20, and shake their garments as if casting their sins into the water.

tefillin: Phylacteries: two black leather cubes fastened to leather straps and containing four passages from the Pentateuch written on parchment (Exodus 13:1–10; 13:11–16; Deuteronomy 6:4–9; 11:13–21). An error in the written text disqualifies the tefillin. They are worn on the left arm and the forehead during the weekday morning service.

third meal: In the Talmudic period people used to eat only two meals a day. In order to honor the Sabbath the rabbis demanded that three meals should be eaten during this holiday, one on the Sabbath Eve and two during the day. Among the Hasidim the third meal became a major social event imbued with religious and mystical meaning. The group used to congregate around the tsaddik to listen to his torah and to sing hymns and songs.

torah: The exegitical commentaries and teachings of the Hasidic rabbis relating to the Bible, the Oral Tradition, and to kabbalistic literature.

Torah: The Pentateuch as well as the teaching of law in the Talmudic literature and the commentaries.

tosaphoth: Additional commentary on the Talmud, printed on the outer column of all editions of the Talmuds, they were written by the tosaphists in Northern France and Germany during the twelfth to the fourteenth century.

tsaddik: (*pl.* tsaddikim): A righteous person. A leader of a Hasidic community.

tsitsith: The fringes of entwined threads worn by Jews on the four corners of the tallith in accordance with Deuteronomy 22:12 and Numbers 15:37–41.

verst: A Russian linear unit, about two-thirds of a mile. In the Hebrew text the unit of length referred to is a *parsah*. This measure is found in the Talmud, where it refers to the ancient Persian unit parasang, which is about three and a half miles.

wayward thoughts: Thoughts about immoral or profane matters which disturb a man during prayer and prevent him from obtaining the desired *devekut*. Such thoughts may turn a prayer over to the evil forces. The Hasidim considered wayward thoughts as the means by which Satan tried to obtain their prayer. A contrasting theory viewed wayward thoughts as fallen divine sparks which turn to the tsaddik so that he may elevate them to the divine sphere. The Hasidim developed methods for contemplative praying which helped them either to avoid the danger of wayward thoughts or to elevate the fallen sparks to the divine world.

yeshivah: The main institution of Jewish learning in which young men studied the Torah and the Talmud. They flourished in Palestine and Babylonia. With the spread of Jewish communities into

France, Germany, and eastern Europe, they served as centers for study and education.

yetzer hara: Man's evil inclination, considered as an integral part of human nature.

yiḥud (pl. *yiḥudim*): Special mystical formulae constituting divine names which are used in mystical contemplations to bring about the ultimate union of God and the Shekinah—the true unity of God.

Yom Kippur: The Day of Atonement. A day of continual prayer and fasting in repentence over the sins committed during the preceding year.

zloty: *See* golden coins.

A SELECTED BIBLIOGRAPHY

AEŠCOLY-WEINTRAUB, AARON Z. *Le Hassidisme: Essai Critique avec un Exposé de la Kabbale.* Paris, 1927.

BAND, ARNOLD J., Ed and trans. *Nahman of Bratslav: The Tales.* "Preface," by Joseph Dan. Classics of Western Spirituality. New York, 1978.

BARON, SALO W. "Hasidism," in *A Social and Religious History of the Jews,* New York, 1937, II, 153–63.

BAUMINGER, MORDECAI SHRAGA. "On the Besht's Letter," Hebrew, *Sinai,* LXVIII (1971), 198–200.

——————. "The Letters of our Rabbi Israel Baal Shem Tov and his Son-in-Law Yehiel Mikhal to Rabbi Abraham Gershon of Kuty," Hebrew, *Sinai,* LXXI (1972), 248–269.

——————. "More on the Besht's and His Son-in-Law Letters to Rabbi Abraham Gershon of Kuty," Hebrew, *Sinai,* LXXII (1973), 270–282.

BICHOVSKY, CHAIM ELIEZER. *Ginzay Nistaroth, in Three Parts: Or Israel, Or Naarav, Or Rav,* Hebrew. Jerusalem, 1924.

BIRNBAUM, SALOMO. *The Life and Sayings of the Baal Shem,* trans. Irene Birnbaum, ed. Maximilian Hurwitz. New York, 1933.

BUBER, MARTIN. *Hasidism,* trans. Greta Hort, and others. New York, 1948.

——————. *Hasidism and Modern Man,* ed. and trans. Maurice Friedman. New York, 1958.

——————. "Interpreting Hasidism," *Commentary,* XXXVI (1963), 218–25.

——————. *Jewish Mysticism and the Legends of the Baalshem,* trans. Lucy Cohen. London and Toronto, 1931.

——————. *The Legend of the Baal-Shem,* trans. Maurice Friedman. New York, 1955.

——————. *The Origin and Meaning of Hasidism,* ed. and trans. Maurice Friedman. New York, 1960.

——————————. *Tales of the Hasidim*, trans. Olga Marx, 2 vols. New York, 1947–48.

——————————. *The Way of Man, According to the Teachings of Hasidism*, London, 1950.

DAN JOSEPH. *The Hasidic Novella*, Hebrew, Jerusalem, 1966.

——————————. "Research Techniques for Hasidic Tales," Hebrew. *Fourth World Congress of Jewish Studies: Papers* (Jerusalem, 1968), II. Pp. 53–7.

——————————. "The Beginnings of Hebrew Hagiographic Literature," Hebrew, *Jerusalem Studies in Jewish Folklore*, I (1981), 82–100.

——————————. *The Hasidic Story—Its History and Development*, Hebrew, Jerusalem, 1975.

DINABURG, BENZION. "The Beginnings of Hassidism and its Social and Messianic Elements," Hebrew, *Zion*, VIII (1943), 107–115; 117–34; 179–200; IX (1943), 39–45; IX (1944), 89–108; 186–97; X (1944–45). 67–77; 149–86. Reprinted in Benzion Dinur. *Historical Writings; Vol.* 1 [*be-Mifneh ha-Dorot*]. Jerusalem, 1955. Pp. 83–227.

DRESNER, SAMUEL H. *The Zaddik: The Doctrine of the Zaddik According to the Writings of Rabbi Yaakov Yosef of Polnoy*. London, New York, Toronto, 1960.

DUBNOV, SEMEN MARKOVICH [DUBNOV, SIMEON]. *The History of Hasidism*, Hebrew. 2nd ed. Tel-Aviv, 1960.

——————————— [DUBNOW, S. M.]. *History of the Jews in Russia and Poland from the Earliest Times until the Present Day*, 3 vols. trans. I. Friedlaender. Philadelphia, 1916–20.

ELBAUM, YAAKOV. "The Baal Shem Tov and the Son of R. Adam— A Study of a Story in Praise of the Baal Shem Tov," Hebrew, *Jerusalem Studies in Jewish Folklore*, II (1982), 66–79.

Elbogen, Ismar. *Der jüdische Gottesdienst in seiner geschichtlichen Entwicklung*. Hildesheim, 1962.

ELIACH, YAFFA. "The Russian Dissenting Sects and Their Influence on Israel Baal Shem Tov, Founder of Hasidism," *The Proceedings of the American Academy for Jewish Research*, 36 (1968), 57–83.

FISHMAN, JUDAH LOEB, ed. *The Besht Book, Essays and Studies in the History and Thought of Hasidism*, Hebrew. Jerusalem, 1960.

GASTER, MOSES. *The Exempla of the Rabbis; Being a Collection of Exempla, Apologues and Tales Culled from Hebrew Manuscripts and Rare Hebrew Books*. London, Leipzig, 1924.

——————————, trans. *Ma'aseh Book; Book of Jewish Tales and Legends*. 2 vols. Philadelphia, 1934.

GELBER, NATHAN M. *The History of the Jews in Brody, 1584–1943*, Hebrew, in Judah Loeb Fishman, ed., *Jewish Centers and Cities*. Vol. IV. Jerusalem, 1955.

GINZBERG, LOUIS. *The Legends of the Jews.* 7 vols. (vols. I, II, IV trans. by Henrietta Szold; vol. III trans. by Paul Radin; vol. VII, index, by Boaz Cohen.) Philadelphia, 1909–38.

GÜNZIG, J. *Rabbi Israel Baal-Shem, der Stifter des Chassidismus. Sein Leben und Seine Lehr.* Brünn, 1908.

——————. *Die "Wundermänner" im jüdischen Volke. Ihr Leben Und Treiben.* Antwerpen, 1921.

GULKOWITSCH, LAZAR. *Der Hassidismus. Religionswissenschaftlich Untersucht.* Leipzig, 1927.

——————. *Das Kulturhistorische Bild des Chassidismus.* Tartu, 1938.

HALPERN, ISRAEL. "Associations for the Study of the Torah and for Good Deeds and the Spread of the Hassidic Movement," Hebrew, *Zion,* XXII (1957), 195–213.

——————. *The Hasidic Immigrations to Palestine During the Eighteenth Century,* Hebrew, Studies and Texts in Jewish Mysticism, vol. 4. Jerusalem, Tel-Aviv, 1946.

——————. "The Woszczylo Revolt," Hebrew, *Zion,* XXII (1957), 56–67.

HESCHEL, ABRAHAM J. "A Biographical Note on Rabbi Pinḥas of Korets," Hebrew, in *Alei Ayin: The Salman Schocken Jubilee Volume . . . Issued on the Occasion of His Seventieth Birthday . . .* Jerusalem, 1948–52. Pp. 213–44.

——————. "Rabbi Gershon of Kuty, His Life and Immigration to the Land of Israel," Hebrew, *Hebrew Union College Annual,* XXIII, pt. 2 (1950–51), 17–71.

——————. "Rabbi Naḥman of Kosov, the Besht's Friend," Hebrew, in *Harry Austryn Wolfson Jubilee Volume,* ed. Saul Lieberman (New York and Jerusalem, 1965), III.

——————. "Reb Pinkhes Koritser," Yiddish, *Yivo Bleter,* XXXIII (New York, 1949), 9–48.

——————. "Unknown Documents on the History of Hassidism," Yiddish, Yivo Bleter, XXXVI (New York, 1952), 113–35.

HORODEZKY, SAMUEL ABA, ed. *In Praise of the Besht,* Hebrew, by Dob Baer ben Samuel. 2nd ed. Tel-Aviv, 1960.

——————. *Hasidim and Hasidism,* Hebrew, 3rd ed. 2 vols. Tel-Aviv, 1951.

——————. Leaders of Hassidism, trans. Maria Horodezky Magasanik. London, 1928.

JACOBS, L. "The Concept of Ḥasid in the Biblical and Rabbinic Literatures," *The Journal of Jewish Studies,* VIII (1957), 143–54.

——————. *Hasidic Prayer.* The Littman Library of Jewish Civilization, New York, 1973.

KAHANA, ABRAHAM. *The Book of Hasidism,* Hebrew. Warsaw, 1922.
——————. *Rabbi Israel Baal Shem-Tov, His Life, Methods, and Deeds,* Hebrew. Zhitomir, 1901.
KATZ, JACOB. *Tradition and Crisis; Jewish Society at the End of the Middle Ages.* New York, 1961.
KHITRIK, AARON. "On the Besht's Vision of Ahijah, the Prophet of Shiloh." Hebrew, *Sinai,* LXXIII (1973), 189–190.
LACHOWER, FISCHEL, and ISAIAH TISHBY. *The Wisdom of the Zohar; Texts from the Book of Splendour,* Hebrew. 2nd ed. vol. I. Jerusalem, 1957.
MAHLER, RAPHAEL. *Hasidism and Haskalah in Galicia and the Congress Kingdom of Poland in the First Half of the Nineteenth Century,* Hebrew. Merḥavya, 1961.
MAIMON, SOLOMON. *Autobiography.* With an essay on Maimon's philosophy by Hugo Bergman; trans. J. Clark Murray. London, 1954.
MINKIN, JACOB S. *The Romance of Hassidism.* 2nd ed. New York, 1955.
MINTZ, JEROME R. *Legends of the Hasidim: An Introduction to Hasidic Culture and Oral Tradition in the New World.* Chicago, 1968.
MONDSHEIN, JOSHUA. *Shivhei Ha-Baal Shem Tov: A Facsimile of a Unique Manuscript, Variant Versions and Appendices,* Hebrew, Jerusalem, 1982.
NEWMAN, LOUIS I. " 'The Baal Shem Tov,' " in *Great Jewish Personalities in Ancient and Medieval Times,* ed. Simon Noveck. New York, 1959. Pp. 281–307.
NEWMAN, LOUIS I. and SAMUEL SPITZ. *The Hasidic Anthology; Tales and Teachings of the Hasidim.* New York. 1934.
——————. *Maggidim and Hasidim: Their Wisdom,* New York, 1962.
NIGAL, GEDALYAH. *The Hasidic Tale: Its History and Topics.* Hebrew, Jerusalem, 1981.
——————. "The Image of the Hasidic Tsaddik," Hebrew, *Molad,* N.S. Vol. 7, Nos. 35–36 (1975), 173–182.
NIGAL, GEDALYAH. *Leader and Community. Theories and Parables in the Beginning of Hasidism According to the Writings of Rabbi Jacob Joseph of Polonnoye,* Hebrew. Jerusalem, 1962.
——————. "The Mentor of Rabbi Israel Baal Shem Tov," Hebrew, *Sinai,* LXXI (1972), 150–159.
——————. "A Primary Source for the Hasidic Narrative Literature—On the Book *Keter Shem Tov* and Its Sources," Hebrew, *Sinai,* LXXIX (1976), 132–146.
——————. "Women in the Book of Shivhei Ha-Besht," Hebrew, *Molad,* N.S., Vol. 6, no. 31 (1974), 138–145.
NOY, DOV. "The Baal-Shem-Tov Legend in the Carpathian Mountains," Hebrew, *Machnayim,* No. 46 (June 1960).

PATTERSON, D. "The Portrait of Hasidism in the Nineteenth-century Hebrew Novel," *Journal of Semitic Studies*, V (1960), 359–77.

PIEKARZ, MENDEL. *The Beginning of Hasidism: Ideological Trends in Derush and Musar Literature*, Hebrew, Jerusalem, 1978.

——————. *Studies in Braslav Hasidism*, Hebrew, Jerusalem, 1972.

RABINOWITSCH, WOLF. *Lithuanian Hassidism from its Beginnings to the Present Day*, Hebrew. Jerusalem, 1961.

—————— [RABINOVICH, WOLF]. "Karlin Hasidism," *Yivo Annual of Jewish Social Science*, V (New York, 1950), 123–51.

—————— [RABINOWICZ, W.]. "Manuscripts from an Archive in Stolin," Hebrew, *Zion*, V (1940), 125–32; 244–47.

—————— [RABINOWICZ, W.]. " 'Sefer Hazoreph' by R. Joshua Heshel Zoreph," Hebrew, *Zion*, VI (1940), 80–4.

RAPHAEL I. [WERFEL ISAAC]. *The Book of Hasidism*, Hebrew. 2nd ed. Tel-Aviv, 1955.

——————. [WERFEL IZAK]. *Chassidism and Palestine*, Hebrew. Jerusalem, 1940.

——————. "Shivhe ha-Besht," Hebrew, *Aresheth, An Annual of Hebrew Booklore*, II (Jerusalem, 1960), 358–77. A bibliography of all editions of *Shivhei ha-besht*.

——————. "Shivhe ha-Besht (Supplement)," Hebrew, *Aresheth, An Annual of Hebrew Booklore*, III (Jerusalem, 1961), 440–41.

RUBINSTEIN, ABRAHAM. "The Appearance of the Besht in the "Shivhei ha-Besht," Hebrew, *Alei Sefer*, Nos. 6–7 (1979), 157–186.

——————. "The Besht's Letter to Rabbi Gershon of Kuty," Hebrew, *Sinai*, LXVII (1970), 120–139.

——————. "Commentary on the Book *Shivhei ha-Besht*," Hebrew, *Sinai*, LXXXVI (1980), 62–71.

——————. "Israel Ben Elizer Baal Shem Tov," *Encyclopaedia Judaica* (Jerusalem and New York, 1971), IX, 1049–1058.

——————. "The Manuscript of the Besht's Letter to Rabbi Gershon of Kuty," Hebrew, *Sinai*, LXXII (1973), 189–202.

——————. "The MS. 'Uiber [sic.] das Wesen der Secte Chassidim,' " Hebrew, *Kirjath Sepher*, XXXVIII (1963), 263–72, 415–24; XXXIX (1963), 117–136.

——————. "The Mentor of R. Israel Ba'al Shem Tov and the Sources of His Knowledge," Hebrew, *Tarbiz*, XLVII (1978), 146–158.

——————. "More on the Besht's Letters," Hebrew, *Sinai*, LXXII (1973), 175–180.

——————. "On Three Tales in Shivhei ha-Besht," Hebrew, *Sinai*, XC (1982), 269–279.

_____. "The Writer's Preface to *Shivhei ha-Besht*," Hebrew, *Sinai*, LXXXIX (1981), 59–68.

_____. "A Possible New Fragment of *'Shivḥey Habbesht,'*" Hebrew, *Tarbiz*, XXXV (1965), 174–91.

_____. ISAIAH TISHBY, and JOSEPH DAN. "Hasidism," Hebrew, *Encyclopaedia Hebraica* (Jerusalem, 1965), XVII, 756–821.

SCHATZ, RIVKA. *Quietistic Elements in 18th Century Hasidic Thought.* Hebrew, Jerusalem, 1940.

_____"The Commentary of R. Israel Ba'al Shem Tov to Psalm CVII–The Myth and Ritual of 'Descent to Sheol'," Hebrew, *Tarbiz*, XLVV (1972), 154–184.

_____. [SCHATZ-UFFENHEIMER, RIVKA]. "Contemplative Prayer in Hasidism," in *Studies and Religion Presented to Gershon G. Scholem on His Seventieth Birthday.* Jerusalem, 1967. Pp. 209–226.

SCHECHTER, SOLOMON. "The Chassidim," in *Studies in Judaism; A Selection.* Paperback ed. New York, 1958. Pp. 150–89.

SCHIPER, IGNACY [ISAAC]. "The Image of Rabbi Israel Baal Shem Tov in Early Hasidic Literature," Hebrew, *Hadoar*, XL (1960), 525–32; 551–52.

SCHOCHET, JACOB IMMANUEL. *Rabbi Israel Baal Shem Tov; a Monograph on the Life and Teachings of the Founder of Chassidism.* Toronto, 1961.

SCHOLEM, GERSHOM G. "Baal Shem," Hebrew, in *Encyclopaedia Hebraica,* (Jerusalem, Tel-Aviv, 1958), IX, 263–64.

_____. "Der Begriff der Kawwana in der alten Kabbala," *Monatsschrift für Geschichte und Wissenschaft des Judentums,* LXXVIII (1934), 492–518.

_____. "Chapters in Shabbatian Research," Hebrew, *Zion*, VI (1940), 85–100, esp. 89–93.

_____. "Devekuth, or Communion with God," *The Review of Religion*, XIV (1950), 115–39.

_____. "The Historical Image of Rabbi Israel Baal Shem Tov," Hebrew, *Molad*, XVIII (1960), 335–56.

_____. *Jewish Gnosticism, Merkabah Mysticism, and Talmudic Tradition.* New York, 1960.

_____. *Major Trends in Jewish Mysticism.* 3rd ed. New York, 1961.

_____. "Martin Buber's Hasidism," *Commentary*, XXXII (1961), 305–16.

_____. "New Material on Israel Loebel and His Anti-hassidic Polemics," Hebrew, *Zion*, XX (1955), 153–162.

_____. [SHOLEM, G.]. "The Polemic against Hassidism and Its Leaders in the Book Nezed Ha-Dema," Hebrew, *Zion*, XX (1955), 73–81.

——————————. *Shabbethai Tsevi and the Shabbetianic Movement in His Life Time*, Hebrew. 2 vols. Tel-Aviv, 1956–57.

——————————— [SHALOM, G.]. "The Two First Testimonies on the Relations Between Chassidic Groups and Baal-Shem-Tov," Hebrew, *Tarbiz, XX* (1949), 228–240.

——————————. "Two Letters from Palestine, 1760–1764," Hebrew, *Tarbiz, XXV* (1956), 429–440.

SHMERUK, CH. "Tales about R' Adam Baal Shem in the Versions of Shibkhei Ha'Besht," Hebrew, *Zion, XXVIII* (1963), 86–105.

——————————— [SZMERUK, CH.] "The Social Significance of the Hassidic Shekhita," *Zion,* Hebrew, XX (1955), 47–72.

——————————. *Yiddish Literature in Poland: Historical Studies and Perspectives,* Hebrew, Jerusalem, 1981.

SHOCHAT, A. "On Joy in Hassidism," Hebrew, *Zion,* XVI (1951), 30–43.

STEINMAN,. ELIEZER. *Rabbi Israel Baal Shem Tov,* Hebrew. Jerusalem, 1960.

——————————. *The Fount of Hasidism, the Besht Volume,* Hebrew. Tel-Aviv, 1957–58.

——————————. *The Garden of Hassidism,* trans. Haim Shacter. Jerusalem, 1961.

TESHIMA, JACOB YUROCH. "The Problem of 'Strange Thoughts' and its Treatment," in *Perspectives on Jews and Judaism: Essays in Honor of Wolfe Kelman,* edited by Arthur A. Chiel (New York, 1978), pp. 421–442.

TISHBY, ISAIAH. "Between Sabbetianism and Hasidism," Hebrew, Kenesset, IX (Tel-Aviv, 1945), 268–338.

——————————. *The Doctrine of Evil and the "Kelippah" in Lurianic Kabbalism,* Hebrew. Studies and Texts in Jewish Mysticism, vol. II. Jerusalem, 1942.

——————————. "The Messianic Idea and Messianic Trends in the Growth of Hasidism," Hebrew, Zion. XXXII (1967), 1–45.

——————————. *The Wisdom of the Zohar, Texts From the Book of Splendour, Systematically Arranged and Translated into Hebrew with Introductions, Explanations and Variants,* Hebrew. Vol. II. Jerusalem, 1961.

TRACHTENBERG, JOSHUA. *Jewish Magic and Superstition; A Study in Folk Religion.* New York, 1939.

UNGER, MENASHE. *Chasidus un Lebn,* Yiddish. New York, 1946.

——————————. *Reb Yisrael Baal-Shem-Tov,* Yiddish. New York, 1963.

——————————. "Yiddish Words in the Shivhe Habesht," *Yidishe Shprakh* ("The Yiddish Language"), XXI (1961), 65–73.

VERSES, SAMUEL. "The Image of Hasidism in the Haskalah Literature,"

Hebrew, *Molad*, XVIII (1960), 379–91.

WEISS, JOSEPH. "Beginnings of Hassidism," Hebrew, *Zion*, XVI (1951), 46–105.

_____. "A Circle of Pre-Hasidic Pneumatics," *The Journal of Jewish Studies*, VIII (1957), 199–213.

_____. "Contemplative Mysticism and 'Faith' in Hasidic Piety," *The Journal of Jewish Studies*, IV (1953), 19–29.

_____. "The Great Maggid's Theory of Contemplative Magic," *Hebrew Union College Annual*, XXXI (1960), 137–48.

_____. "The Kavvanoth of Prayer in Early Hasidism," *The Journal of Jewish Studies*, IX (1958), 163–92.

_____. "Via Passiva in Early Hasidism," *The Journal of Jewish Studies*, XI (1960), 137–55.

WERTHEIM, AARON. *Laws and Customs of Chassidism*, Hebrew. Jerusalem, 1960.

WILENSKY, MORDECAI L. "The Polemic of Rabbi David of Makow Against Hasidism," *American Academy for Jewish Research; Proceedings*, XXV (1956), 137–56.

_____. "Remarks Concerning the Controversy between the Hasidim and the Mitnaggedim," Hebrew, *Tarbiz*, XXX (1961), 396–404.

WOLF, MEYER. "The Language of *Shivkhey Habesht*," Yiddish, *Yidishe Shprakh*, 35 (1976), pp. 32–48.

YAARI, ABRAHAM. "Miscellaneous Bibliographical Notes, 10. Three Yiddish Translations of 'Shibhe ha-Besht,'" Hebrew, *Kirjath Sepher*, XII (1935), 129–31.

_____. "Two Basic Recensions of 'Shivḥē Ha-Besht,'" Hebrew, *Kirjath Sepher*, XXXIX (1964), 249–72; 394–407; 552–62.

YSANDER, TORSTEN. *Studien zum B'eštchen Ḥasidismus in seiner Religionsgeschichtlichen Sonderart*, trans. Ilse Meyer-Lüne. Uppsala, 1933.

ZEVIN, SHELOMOH YOSEF. *Hasidic Tales*, Hebrew. 2 vols. Tel-Aviv, 1956–57.

ZIMMELS, HIRSCH JAKOB. *Ashkenazim and Sephardim, Their Relations, Differences and Problems as Reflected in the Rabbinical Responsa*. Jew's College Publications, New Series No. 2. London, 1958.

_____. *Magicians, Theologians and Doctors; Studies in Folk-Medicine and Folk-Lore as Reflected in the Rabbinical Responsa*. London, 1952.

THE LEGENDS AND
THEIR SOURCES

*The Roman numerals refer to four unnumbered pages between pages 4 and 7.

TALE	SOURCE	PAGE NO. OF 1ST EDITION	PAGE NO. OF HORO-DEZKY'S EDITION
72. The Death of Rabbi Abraham the "Angel"	Rabbi Joel of Prot'hur as heard from Rabbi Menaḥem Nahum of Chernobyl.	10a–b	76–77
73. Rabbi Abraham as a Sandek	Rabbi Joel of Prot'hur as heard from Rabbi Menaḥem Nahum of Chernobyl	10b	77
74. Rabbi Abraham as a Mohel	Admor	10b	77–78
75. The Wife of Rabbi Abraham	Rabbi Menaḥem Nahum of Chernobyl, as heard from Rabbi Abraham's wife	10b–11b	78–80
76. The City of Adultery	——	11b	72–73
77. The Advice of the Great Maggid	——	11b–12a	73–74
78. The Prayers of the Hasidim	Rabbi Zusya of Annopol as heard from his brother, Rabbi Elimelekh	12a	92
79. The Two Brothers	——	12a–b	74–75
80. Sounding Out the Nature of the Besht	Rabbi Gedaliah	12b	128
81. The Lithuanian Jew and the Besht	Mar Mordecai, the writer's brother-in-law, as heard from Rabbi Jehiel of Kovel	12b	128–29
82. The Besht and Rabbi Sa'adyah Gaon	Rabbi Alexander Shohet as heard from the Besht	12b	108
83. The Besht's Sermon	Rabbi Gedaliah	12b	108
84. The Besht Banishes Demons	Rabbi Gedaliah and Rabbi Jacob Joseph	12b	118–19
85. The Rabbi's Wife in Labor	Rabbi Joseph of Zornisziza as told to the writer by his friends	12b–13a	75–76
86. The Church that Caught Fire	Rabbi Meir of Annopol	13a	117
87. The Hose-Maker	Rabbi Meir	13a–b	117–18
88. The Sin of Pride	Rabbi Aaron of Medzhibozh	13b	126
89. Two Hasidim Visit Hell	Rabbi Zelig of Letichev	13b	178–79
90. The Court in Heaven	Rabbi Zelig	13b–14a	179
91. The Besht and the Angel of Death	Rabbi Gedaliah	14a	110
92. The Repentant Rich Man	Rabbi Gedaliah	14a	176
93. The Defective Tefillin	Rabbi Gedaliah	14a–b	179–180

TALE	SOURCE	PAGE NO. OF 1ST EDITION	PAGE NO. OF HORO-DEZKY'S EDITION
94. The Tefillin Written by Rabbi Isaac	——	14b	180
95. The Righteous Woman	Rabbi Gedaliah	14b	180–81
96. The Righteous Woman and Her Sons	Rabbi Gedaliah	14b	181
97. The Blessing of Rabbi Pinḥas	Rabbi Samuel, the leader	14b–15a	82
98. The Besht's Combat with a Witch	Rabbi Gedaliah and Rabbi Alexander Shohet	15a	54–55
99. A Choice of Punishment	Rabbi Joel of Nemirov	15a	129
100. The Revenant	Rabbi Falk of Chechelnik	15a	129
101. The Redemptions of the Sparks	Rabbi Jacob of Smela, as heard from his father, Rabbi Meir Ḥarif	15a–b	125
102. The Reader's Stand of Rabbi Samson	Rabbi Gedaliah	15b	130
103. The Dismissed Arrendator	——	15b	136–37
104. The Besht's Devekut	Rabbi Jacob Joseph	15b	160
105. The Besht Resuscitates a Child	Rabbi Pesaḥ, son of Rabbi Jacob of Kamenka	16a	114–15
106. The Magical Enkindling of a Tree	Rabbi Pesaḥ	16a	115
107. The Choice	Rabbi Falk the Cohen	16a	115
108. The Fish and the Dog	Rabbi Gedaliah and Rabbi Jacob Joseph	16b	176–77
109. The Dance of Rabbi Yudel	Rabbi Shneur, grandson of Rabbi Naḥman	16b	95
110. Rabbi Naḥman's Sign	Rabbi Alexander Shohet	16b	95
111. Rabbi Naḥman's Prayer	——	16b	95
112. Rabbi Jacob Joseph's Prayer	Rabbi Gedaliah	16b	65
113. Pure Prayers	Rabbi Zusya of Annopol	16b	65
114. The Interruption of the Besht's Vision	Rabbi Gedaliah	16b–17a	167
115. Rabbi Leib's Death	Rabbi Gedaliah	17a	130
116. Rabbi Aaron in Heaven	Rabbi Gedaliah	17a	175–76
117. The Sick Woman	The author's friends as heard from Rabbi Nahum of Chernobyl	17a	131
118. The Adulterer	——	17a–b	131
119. The Besht Cures by Bloodletting	Rabbi Gedaliah	17b	112
120. The Death of Rabbi Joseph the Melamed	Rabbi Gedaliah	17b	112
121. The Parable of the Dog	Rabbi Gedaliah	17b–18a	88–89
122. The Present Generation	Rabbi Gedaliah	18a	89

TALE	SOURCE	PAGE NO. OF 1ST EDITION	PAGE NO. OF HORO- DEZKY'S EDITION
123. *A Dowry*	An anonymous man, as heard from Rabbi Tsevi, the scribe	18a–b	131–32
124. *Rabbi Abraham and the Besht*	Rabbi Gedaliah	18b	80–82
125. *A Combat in Magic*	——	18b	137
126. *A Combat in Magic: A Second Version*	Rabbi Leib of Sinami	19a	137
127. *The Jewish Thief*	Rabbi Leib of Sinami and Rabbi Gedaliah	19a	137–38
128. *The Besht's Funeral*	Rabbi Gedaliah	19a	169
129. *Rabbi Naḥman Travels to the Holy Land*	Rabbi Gedaliah	19a–b	170–71
130. *Rabbi Mendele Visits with Rabbi Jacob Joseph*	——	19b	95–96
131. *The Prayers of Rabbi Mendele and Rabbi Fridel*	——	19b	96–97
132. *The Heavy Load of Honor*	——	19b	97
133. *Rabbi Naḥman's Cold Mikveh*	Rabbi Naḥman of Horodenka	19b	82
134. *Iniquities and Prayers*	Rabbi Mendel of Bar	19b	98
135. *The Preacher's Sermon*	Rabbi Moses, son-in-law of Rabbi Jacob Joseph's sister, as heard from the Preacher; other versions told by Rabbi Joseph, son of Rabbi Moses of Polonnoye	19b–20a	84–86
136. *A Madman Feigns Death*	Rabbi David, the maggid of Tultchin, grandson of Rabbi David Forkes	20a–b	159–60
137. *The Martyrs*	——	20b	139–40
138. *The Adulterous Woman*	Rabbi Aaron of Ilintsy, as heard from the Rabbi of Shepetovka	20b–21a	140
139. *The Delayed Homecoming: A Second Version*	——	21a	140
140. *The Besht, the Merchant, and the Robbers*	Rabbi Gedaliah	21a	141
141. *The Besht Discharges a Shohet*	——	21a	127
142. *The Optimism of Rabbi Naḥman*	Rabbi Jacob Joseph	21a–b	82–83
143. *Rabbi Naḥman Prays Minhah*	Rabbi Gedaliah	21b	83
144. *Feeling the Tefillin*	Author's eye witnessing	21b	65
145. *The Height of Prayer*	Rabbi Jacob Joseph	21b	65

TALE	SOURCE	PAGE NO. OF 1ST EDITION	PAGE NO. OF HORO-DEZKY'S EDITION
146. *Ascension to Heaven*	Rabbi Gedaliah as heard from Rabbi Joseph of Kamenka	21b	169
147. *The Besht's Second Coming*	Rabbi Gedaliah as heard from his father or grandfather and from Rabbi Aaron of Medzhibozh	21b	169
148. *The Perpetual Error*	Rabbi Gedaliah	21b	141
149. *The Ring*	Rabbi Elimelekh	21b	141
150. *Rabbi Motil*	——	21b–22a	141–42
151. *Rabbi Gershon's Enemies*	Rabbi Jacob Joseph	22a	142–43
152. *The Wandering Soul*	——	22a–b	56–57
153. *Dream Teaching*	——	22b	97
154. *The Forbidden City*	Rabbi Moses, son of Yakil from Medzhibozh	22b	143
155. *The Hunchback*	Rabbi Moses, the hunchback	22b	143
156. *The Forbidden Country*	Rabbi Gedaliah	22b	143–44
157. *The Spiritual Cure*	——	22b–23a	113
158. *The Stolen Stockings*	Rabbi Gedaliah as heard from the Besht's servant	23a	144
159. *Writing Down the Besht's Torah*	Rabbi Gedaliah	23a	144
160. *The Besht and His Son*	——	23a	144
161. *The Generosity of the Besht*	Rabbi Gedaliah	23a	144
162. *The Demons*	Rabbi Gedaliah	23a	84
163. *The Guest Who Snored*	——	23b	144–45
164. *The Impure House*	——	23b	119
165. *The Preacher Who Spoke Evil of the Jews*	Rabbi Gedaliah as heard from *Mar* Zeev of Olyka	23b	145
166. *The Dead Man in Hell*	Rabbi Moses, son-in-law of Rabbi Jacob Joseph's sister, as heard from the Besht	23b	145
167. *The Servant's Evil Thoughts*	Rabbi Gedaliah	23b	145–46
168. *"Streams of Wisdom"*	Rabbi Jehiel Mikhel of Zolochev	24a	72
169. *Rabbi Eliezer and Rabbi Naḥman*	Rabbi Jehiel Mikhel	24a	82
170. *The Contaminated Bed*	Rabbi Gedaliah	24a	115–16
171. *Rabbi Tsevi's Dream*	Rabbi Jacob Joseph	24a	169–70

TALE	SOURCE	PAGE NO. OF 1ST EDITION	PAGE NO. OF HORODEZKY'S EDITION
240. Rabbi Isaac of Berdichev	——	35a	75
241. Rabbi David Forkes's Dream	——	35a	158
242. A Glass of Wine	——	35a	158–59
243. The Besht's Dinner	——	35a–b	159
244. The Besht Resuscitates a Child: A Second Version	——	35b	113–14
245. The Doctor	——	35b	113
246. The Careless Shohet	——	35b	127–28
247. The Besht's Death	Rabbi Jacob of Medzhibozh	35b–36a	167–68
248. Rabbi Leib Kessler's Offer	——	36a	169
249. The Besht's Son	——	36a	164, 169
250. The Fish and the Dog: A Second Version	——	36a–b	91–92
251. The Burning of Rabbi Jacob Joseph's Books	——	36b	65–66

INDEX OF MOTIFS

Motif numbers are from Stith Thompson, Motif-Index of Folk-Literature, A Classification of Narrative Elements in Folktales, Ballads, Myths, Fables, Mediaeval Romances, Exempla, Fabliaux, Jest-Books, and Local Legends. *6 vols. Rev. ed. (Copenhagen and Bloomington, Ind., 1955–58). Asterisks (*) designate new numbers.*

Motif
Number — Motif and Tale Numbers

A. MYTHOLOGICAL MOTIFS

A185.11. God rewards mortal for pious act, 3
*A472.0.2. Angel of sleep, 163
A528. Cultural hero has supernatural helpers, 10
A547. Culture hero dispenses food and hospitality, 14, 15
A661. Heaven, 18
A661.0.1. Gate of heaven, 41, 152
A661.0.3. Chairs in heaven, 152

B. ANIMALS

*B121.7. Bear with magic wisdom, 214
B134. Truth-telling dog, 158
B151.1.1. Horses determine road to be taken, 238
*B152.4. Dog indicates thief, 158
*B153.2. Bear indicates location of corpse to be taken in false accusation (*see* *K2116.6.), 214
B162.1. Supernatural knowledge from eating magic fish, 50, 108
B163.1. Wisdom from fox, 121
B171. Magic chicken (hen, cock), 162
B182.2. Magic bear, 214

Motif
Number   Motif and Tale Numbers

B215.   Animal languages, 158, 237
B215.1.   Bird language, 237
B215.2.   Dog languages, 158
B216.   Knowledge of animal languages, 158, 237
B217.   Animal language learned, 237
B435.4.   Helpful bear, 214

C. Tabu

*C119.1.7.   Tabu: sexual intercourse when light is on, 175
*C224.5.   Tabu: eating vegetable which grew in gentile's cemetery, 189
C300.   Looking tabu, 106
*C311.3.   Tabu: looking at magic fire, 106
C331.   Tabu: looking back, 106
*C401.7.   Tabu: speaking while weaving tsitsith, 188
*C416.   Tabu: asking for duration of good luck (see also C50.1; C61.1.), 211
C420.   Tabu: uttering secrets, 49
C617.   Forbidden country, 156
*C617.2.   Forbidden city, 154
C631.1.   Tabu: journeying on Sabbath, 15, 50
*C634.1.   Tabu: mourning on holidays, 72
C664.   Injunction: to marry the first woman met, 40
C770.   Tabu: overweening pride, 88
C824.   Tabu: finding name of ghost, 20
C900.   Punishment for breaking tabu, 155
C901.1.4.   Tabu imposed by host, 5
C901.1.6.   Tabu imposed by saint, 154, 155, 156
C901.2.   Tabu imposed at birth, 155

D. Magic

D102.   Transformation: devil to animal, 4
D113.1.   Transformation: man to wolf, 4
D479.8.   Hut transformed into golden palace, 5
*D482.5.3.   Gate magically enlarged for saint, 212
D610.   Repeated transformation, 4
D931.   Magic rock (stone), 16
D1050.   Magic clothes, 212
D1067.1.   Magic hat, 212
D1146.   Magic door (gate), 212

E. The Dead

Motif
Number   *Motif and Tale Numbers*

F. MARVELS

*Motif
Number*   *Motif and Tale Numbers*

Motif
Number   *Motif and Tale Numbers*

M302.8.   Prophecy from book, 33, 157
M311.   Prophecy: future greatness of unborn child, 3
M311.0.3.1. Prophecy: child to be born to childless couple, 3, 170, 212, 223, 224, 244
*M340.7.   Prophecy: good luck will terminate after a certain period, 211
M341.   Death prophesied, 24, 48, 68, 120, 154, 183, 211, 223, 248
*M341.0.1.1. Saint prophesies that certain men will faint, 27
M341.1.   Prophecy: death at (before, within) certain time, 223, 248
*M341.1.4.1.1. Prophecy: death at thirteen, 223
M341.3.   Prophecy: death in particular place, 154
M355.   Prophecy: unborn child to be blind, deformed, sickly, etc., 170
M358.1.   Evil predictions concerning journeys, 154, 155
*M359.7.1. Rich man will have a son but will lose his wealth, 107
*M364.10.1. Destruction and rebuilding of city foreseen by saint, 45
M369.7.   Prophecy about birth of children, 3, 70
M370.1.   Prophecy of death fulfilled, 24, 120, 154, 155
M391.   Fulfillment of prophecy, 24, 45, 120, 154, 155, 183, 212, 213, 216, 223
M400.   Curses, 67, 93, 125, 137
M430.   Curses on person, 67, 125
M451.   Curse: death, 67
M475.   Curse on a city, 45

N. CHANCE AND FATE

N131.4.   Luck changing after change of name, 59
*N384.0.2. Fainting from fright, 27, 46
N421.   Lucky bargain, 150
N810.1.   Invisible guardians, 10
N847.   Prophet as helper, 29
N848.   Saint (pious man) as helper, 53, 140

P. SOCIETY

*P231.5.1. Mother reveals fact that son is illegitimate, 184
*P251.5.7. Each of two brothers concede the greatness of the other, 79
P320.   Hospitality, 14, 15, 31, 105, 224
P431.   Merchant, 69, 139, 140, 150, 224

Motif
Number   *Motif and Tale Numbers*

Q. Rewards and Punishments

Motif
Number   Motif and Tale Numbers

T580.   Childbirth, 85, 204, 234
T640.   Illegitimate children, 184

V. RELIGION

V17.9.   Sacrifice by women at childbirth, 85
V20.   Confession of sins, 238
*V21.7.   Confession followed by repentance, 238
V50.   Prayers, 51, 55, 110, 111, 130, 131, 134, 137, 153, 199, 208
V52.   Miraculous power of prayer, 59, 182
*V52.8.1.   Saint's prayer brings death to his opponent, 182
*V54.   Saint trembles, being in trance, while praying, 34, 35, 36, 38, 39, 83
*V54.1.   Objects tremble around praying saint, 35, 37, 39
*V54.2.   Saint in trance, lying extending hands and feet, 105, 137
*V57.4.   Prayer for rescue from trouble, 51, 52
*V71.4.   Stealing to cover Sabbath expenses, 70
V82.   Circumcision, 73, 74, 184, 202, 244
V84.   Excommunication, 56, 116
*V213.   Elijah the prophet appears in dream or vision, 3, 29, 114
V221.   Miraculous healing by saints, 20, 22, 26, 27, 62, 91, 105, 119, 136, 157, 172, 212, 225, 231, 232, 244
V221.4.   Saint subdues madman, 20, 22, 136
V221.11.   Saint cures dumb person, 157
V221.12.   Saint cures blindness, 231
*V222.0.1.4. Pillar of fire rises above a grave of righteous person, 216
V222.1.   Marvelous light accompanying saint, 15, 31, 95
V223.   Saints have a miraculous knowledge, 60, 63, 64, 69, 103, 127, 150, 152, 175, 184, 189, 216, 221, 223, 233, 234
V223.1.   Saint gives advice, 77, 150, 224
V223.3.   Saint can perceive the thoughts of another man and reveal hidden sins, 25, 54, 76, 118, 190, 209, 227, 228, 233, 245, 246
*V223.3.1.   Saint has power to see whether the dead go to heaven or hell, 152
V223.4.   Saint helps with learning, 7
*V223.4.2.   Saint causes magic forgetfulness, 173
V224.3.   Animals stolen from saint miraculously replaced, 30
*V223.5.2.   Saint understands language of dog, 158
*V227.2.   Souls of martyrs visit saint, 137
*V229.2.5.1. Place of saint in synagogue retains particular holiness, 113

W. TRAITS OF CHARACTER

Z. MISCELLANEOUS GROUPS OF MOTIFS

NOTES

Translators' Note

1. The first edition of the tales appeared anonymously. Here the author of the manuscript refers to himself simply as "the writer," and alludes to his father-in-law, Alexander the Shohet, who was the Besht's scribe for eight years. It was not until the second edition was published a half year later in Berdichev that the writer is identified on the title page as Rabbi Dov Ber, the son of Shmuel, the Shohet of Ilintsy. The writer's relationship to Alexander, the Besht's scribe, is mentioned again, reestablishing the authenticity of the tales.

See S. M. Dubnov, *The History of Hasidism*, Hebrew, 2nd edition (Tel Aviv, 1960), pp. 411–416; Abraham Rubinstein, "Commentary on the Book *Shivhei ha-Besht*," Hebrew, *Sinai*, LXXXVI (1980), 62–71.

2. While the original manuscript for the printed edition has perished, other early manuscript versions are still extant. One such manuscript was found in 1980 in the library of the Lubavitcher Hasidim in Brooklyn, New York. It comprises more than half of the published Kopys edition, and its variant readings help clarify a few vague sentences and unclear references. Joshua Mondshein, *Shivhei Ha-Baal Shem Tov: A Facsimile of a Unique Manuscript, Variant Versions and Appendices*, Hebrew, Jerusalem, 1982.

3. *The Holy Scriptures According to the Masoretic Text, a New Translation* (Philadelphia: The Jewish Publication Society of America, 1917).

4. *The Babylonian Talmud*, general ed. Isidore Epstein (London: Soncino Publishing House, 1935–52).

5. *The Columbia Lippincott Gazetteer of the World*, ed. Leon E. Seltzer (New York: Columbia University Press, 1961).

The Printer's Preface

1. I Sam. 12:22.

2. See tale 194 and the note to this tale on p. 337.

3. Ecc. 5:7.

4. Rabbi Menahem Mendel of Vitbesk (1730–88), a disciple of Rabbi Dov Ber of Mezhirich. He immigrated to the Land of Israel in 1777 with

a group of three hundred Hasidim. See Israel Halpern, *The Hasidic Immigration to Palestine during the Eighteenth Century*, Hebrew, Studies and Texts in Jewish Mysticism, Vol. IV (Jerusalem and Tel-Aviv, 1946), pp. 20–37.

5. Compare Song 8:13.

6. At that period there existed two books by that name: one by Rabbi Shneur Zalman of Lyady (also Shneor Zalman), *Likutei Amarim* (Slavuta, 1796); and one by Rabbi Dov Ber of Mezhirich (also Dob Baer), *Maggid Devarav le-Ya'akov* or *Likutei Amarim*, ed. Shelomoh of Lutsk (Korets, 1787). Whereas Rabbi Shneur Zalman is usually identified as the *Admor*, awesome things about the greatness of the Besht are also found in the preface of the Rabbi Dov Ber's book. However, shortly before IN PRAISE OF THE BAAL SHEM TOV was first published, these two *Likutei Amarim* were issued together in Shklov in 1814. This might have led to the printer's confusing the two texts.

7. A collection of Menahem Mendel's letters from Israel was added to his book *Peri ha-Arets* ("The Fruit of the Land"), Kopys, 1814. This phrase is quoted from the second letter.

8. *In Praise of the Ari*, a book of biographical legends about Rabbi Isaac Luria (1534–72), the founder of the Safed school of mysticism. It was written by Shlomel Dresnitz and was first published in *Ta'alumot Hokhmah* ("Secrets of Wisdom") (Basel, 1629). For a critical edition see Meir Benayahu, *The Toledoth Ha-Ari and Luria's "Manner of Life"* (*Hanhagoth*), Hebrew, Studies and Texts, Publications of the Ben-Zvi Institute (Jerusalem, 1967).

9. Job 4:12.

10. Ps. 19:13.

The Writer's Preface

1. Ps. 40:8.

2. In the Hebrew text the writer quotes the biblical phrase, *with stammering lips*, בלעגי שפה, Is. 28:11. However, in this context a different translation seems to be more appropriate.

3. Prov. 3:34.

4. Ps. 19:4.

5. Ps. 89:38.

6. Ps. 131:1.

7. This spelling is according to Israel Halperin (Halpern), *Acta Congressus Generalis Judacorum Regni Poloniae (1580–1764)*, Hebrew (Jerusalem, 1945), p. 615.

8. B. Pesahim 50a.

9. Uncertain identification of the city. In the original text the name is Bershat.

10. See tale 41, n. 8.

11. Ecc. 12:3.

12. We could not determine the exact source of this saying. The initial formula "A man should forever" plus a verb is often found in Talmudic proverbs. See for example B. Berakoth 55b.

13. Ps. 78:2–6. In the original text the writer omitted and changed a few biblical phrases.

14. Dan. 4:10.

15. See tale 46.

16. 'Ets Hayyim ("Tree of Life"): The writer erred. This quotation is rather from the book Pri 'Ets Hayyim ("Fruits of the Tree Life"). Both books are by Hayyim Vital (1543–1620).

17. For a comparison between "The Writer's Preface" in the Kopys and the Berdichev editions see Abraham Rubinstein, "The Writer's Preface to Shivhei ha-Besht," Hebrew, Sinai, LXXXIX (1981), 59–68.

Tale 1. Rabbi Eliezer

1. See tale 135.

2. Gen. 39:4.

3. Gen. 40:8.

4. Exod. 15:3.

5. The term used is ta'anit hafsakah. See Isaac Lampronti, Paḥad Yitshak, ed., Samuel Ashkenazi (Jerusalem, 1962). When a person undertakes this type of fasting he cannot break it with a meal at the end of the day.

6. See Dan. 2:18–19, 28–30, 47.

7. See a discussion of dream divination in Joshua Trachtenberg, Jewish Magic and Superstition: A Study in Folk Religion (New York, 1939), pp. 241–43.

8. Dan. 2:11.

Tale 2. Rabbi Eliezer and the Viceroy's Daughter

1. Gen. 39:3. The first part of the sentence is quoted from the Bible while the remainder is only a paraphrase.

2. The biblical Joseph story (Gen. 39–41), serves as a model for the two narratives about Rabbi Eliezer. In Jewish mysticism Joseph has the role of the archetypal righteous man who resisted temptation. See Gershom G. Scholem, Major Trends in Jewish Mysticism (New York, 1961), p. 235, and references cited by Louis Ginzberg, The Legends of the Jews (Philadelphia, 1909–1938), V, 324–25. Other analogues are found in the legend of Rabbi Zadok, Aboth de Rabbi Nathan, ed. Solomon Schechter (New York, 1945), version I, ch. 16, p. 84; Moses Gaster, The Exempla of

the Rabbis (Leipzig, London, 1924), pp. 24–25, nos. 33–34. A legend about Rabbi Judah the Pious (died 1217) depicting him as an adviser to a duke in matters of war is found in Moses Gaster, ed., *Ma'aseh Book* (Philadelphia, 1934), II, pp. 373–75.

Tale 3. The Birth of the Besht

1. Similarly, Elijah the prophet announced the birth of Rabbi Isaac Luria (1534–72), the founder of the Safed kabbalism, to his father. See Shlomel Dresnitz, *Shivḥei ha-Ari*, first published in *Ta'alumot Ḥokhmah* (Basel, 1629). Ginzberg describes the various aspects of the image of Elijah in Jewish tradition in *The Legends of the Jews*, IV, 196–234; VI, 316–342. Martin Buber relates another version of this legend, taken from Jacob Gottlieb, *Raḥmei ha-Av* (Warsaw, 1874), in which Elijah the prophet promised Rabbi Eliezer he will have a son as a reward for his hospitality. See *Tales of the Hasidim* (New York, 1947), I, 35–6. Compare this version with the biblical story of the hospitality of Abraham, Gen. 18:1–15.

2. Is. 49:3.

3. B. Sukkah 56b.

4. See *The Zohar*, trans. H. Sperling and M. Simon (London, 1932), II, 189–98, [180a–82b]. Unless otherwise mentioned this edition will be cited throughout the book. The numbers in brackets refer to the pagination in the Hebrew edition of the Zohar.

Tale 4. The Besht's Education and Youth

1. Cf. with the legend about the childhood of Rabbi Judah the Pious in Gaster, *Ma'aseh Book*, II, 336–68.

2. This phrase, said by the whole congregation, is the kernel of the kaddish, a prayer said in Aramaic at the conclusion of the service or at the end of an important part of the service. See B. Berakoth 57a, Shabbath 119b. For discussions of it see David de Sola Pool, *The Kaddish*, 2nd ed. (New York, 1929), and his article "Kaddish," in *The Universal Jewish Encyclopedia* (New York, 1939–43), VI, 273–75; Ismar Elbogen, *Der jüdische Gottesdienst in seiner geschichtlichen Entwicklung*, (Hildesheim, 1962), pp. 92–98.

3. The main part of the kedushah prayer consists of the verses of Is. 6:3 and Ezek. 3:12. It is said by the whole congregation and is inserted in two different places in the service. Vigdor Aptowitzer, "La Kedouscha," *Revue des 'Etudes Juives*, LXXXVII (1939), 28–34; Julius Jarecki, "Kedusha," in *The Universal Jewish Encyclopedia*, VI, 353–54; Ismar Elbogen, *Der jüdische Gottesdienst*, pp. 63–67.

4. Job 2:1.

5. Satan's fear was that the Besht might bring the Messiah by his prayers.

Tale 5. Rabbi Adam and the King's Banquet

1. The identity of Rabbi Adam is unknown. The name Adam was rare among European Jewry. Gershom Scholem considers it to be a pseudonym for the Sabbetian kabbalist Rabbi Heshel Zoref (died 1700), whose writings circulated among the Hasidim and might have been in the possession of the Besht. See Scholem's *Major Trends in Jewish Mysticism*, pp. 331–34, and his article, "Chapters in Sabbatian Research," Hebrew, *Zion*, VI (1940), 85–100, esp. 89–93. For details concerning the secret manuscript of Rabbi Heshel Zoref see Wolf Rabinowitsch [Rabinowicz], "Manuscripts from an Archive in Stolin," Hebrew, *Zion*, V (1940), 125–32; 244–47; and his article " 'Sefer Hazoreph' by R. Joshua Heshel Zoreph," Hebrew, *Zion*, VI (1940), 80–84. Ch. Shmeruk traced these stories to a seventeenth-century chapbook about Rabbi Adam of Bingen in "Tales about R'Adam Baal Shem in the Versions of Shibkhei Ha'Besht," Hebrew, *Zion*, XXVIII (1963), 86–105. This seventeenth-century version of the legend takes place in Prague and the king is identified as Maximilian II (1567–76). Shmeruk compares this legend with a nineteenth-century tale about the great Jewish scholar and mystic Rabbi Judah Löw ben Bezalel of Prague, the *Maharal* (about 1525–1609), and Rudolf II (1576–1612), Maximilian's son. See "Tales about R'Adam," p. 89. For an English text of the legend about the *Maharal* see Chayim Bloch, *The Golem*, trans. Harry Schneiderman (Vienna, 1925), pp. 219–28.

For additional studies about this tale and the figure of R. Adam see, Yaakov Elbaum, "The Baal Shem Tov and the Son of R. Adam—A Study of a Story in Praise of the Baal Shem Tov," Hebrew, *Jerusalem Studies in Jewish Folklore*, II (1982), 66–79; Joshua Mondshein, *Shivhei Ha-Baal Shem Tov: A Facsimile of a Unique Manuscript, Variant Versions and Appendices*, Hebrew (Jerusalem, 1982), pp. 58–65; Abraham Rubinstein, "The Mentor of R. Israel Ba'al Shem-Tov and the Sources of his Knowledge," Hebrew, *Tarbiz*, LXVII (1978), 156–158; Chone Shmeruk, *Yiddish Literature in Poland: Historical Studies and Perspectives*, Hebrew (Jerusalem, 1981), pp. 119–146.

2. See tales 7, 17.

3. The transference of the palace and the episode concerning the Jew hater constitute two separate tales in the seventeenth century chapbook. See Shmeruk, "Tales about R'Adam," p. 91.

Tale 6. The New Coat of Rabbi Adam's Wife

1. He prefers that they suffer in this world rather than have their por-

tion in the next world reduced. Compare with the story about Ḥanina ben Dosa and his wife in B. Taʿanit 25a, and Moses Gaster, *The Exempla of the Rabbis* (London, 1924), pp. 157, 260, no. 409. In the first Yiddish edition of this book (Ostrog, 1815), tale 6 preceeds tale 5. In that version Rabbi Adam's wife appears in public wearing the better coat. This consequently leads to the meeting between the rabbi and the king. See Shmeruk, "Tales about R'Adam," p. 95. For a detailed comparison between the first two editions of the book, in Hebrew and Yiddish respectively, see Abraham Yaari, "Two Basic Recensions of 'Shivḥē Ha-Besht,'" Hebrew, *Kirjath Sepher*, XXXIX (1964), 249–72, 394–407, 552–61.

Tale 7. The Secret Manuscripts and Rabbi Adam's Son

1. Okopy, not listed in *The Columbia Lippincott Gazetteer of the World*, is cited in the index of Israel Halperin (Halpern), *Acta Congress-sus Generalis Judacorum Regni Poloniae* (1580–1764), Hebrew (Jerusalem, 1945), p. 611.

2. The elder (*parnas*) is a high ranking leader in the Jewish community. The office holders changed on a monthly rotating system. For further details see Jacob Katz, *Tradition and Crisis, Jewish Society at the End of the Middle Ages* (New York, 1961), p. 82.

3. B. Berakoth 6a.

4. The Divine Kabbalah (*Kabbalah ʿIyyunit* or *Elohit*) deals with contemplation of the sensual world as it sprang from the spiritual essence of the Deity. The Practical or Experimental Kabbalah (*Kabbalah Maʿasit*) deals with the talismanic use of divine names and words for the accomplishments of certain ends.

5. He is "the angel who can grant perfect knowledge of all fields of the Law, both in its exoteric and its esoteric aspects." Gershom Scholem, *Jewish Gnosticism, Merkabah Mysticism and Talmudic Tradition* (New York, 1960), pp. 12–13. See there further discussion of his place in *Merkavah* and Haggadah literature.

6. The ashes of a red heifer were required for complete purification, a necessary state for such mystical activity. For its ritualistic use in biblical and post-biblical times see Num. 19:1–14; 17–21, and the mishaic tractate Parah. For a discussion of this tradition in Hasidic literature see Gedalyah Nigal, *The Hasidic Tale: Its History and Topics*, Hebrew (Jerusalem, 1981), pp. 280–292.

7. These kavvanoth, intentions, are special concentrations on the inner meanings of the words of the prayers which have mystical and magical implications. For studies concerning this concept, see Isaiah Tishby, *The Wisdom of the Zohar*, Hebrew (Jerusalem, 1961), II, 247–306; Joseph G.

Weiss, "The Kavvanoth of Prayer in Early Hasidim," *The Journal of Jewish Studies*, IX (1958), 163–192; Gershom Scholem, "Der Begriff der Kawwana in der alten Kabbala," *Monatsschrift für Geschichte und Wissenschaft des Judentums*, LXXVIII (1934), 492–518, and his *Major Trends in Jewish Mysticism*, pp. 275–78; and Hyman G. Enelow, "Kawwana: the Struggle for Inwardness in Judaism," in *Selected Works of Hyman G. Enelow* (Kingsport, Tenn., 1935), IV, 252–88.

8. See B. Sanhedrin 95a.

9. This belief, which is directly connected with the saying "Sleep is one sixtieth part of death," B. Berakoth 57b, is found in *The Zohar*, I, 277–78 [I, 83a]; V, 170–71 [III, 119a]. For an analysis of this concept in the Kabbalah see Isaiah Tishby, *The Wisdom of the Zohar*, II, 125–46. Its place in Talmudic literature is discussed in W. Hirsch, *Rabbinic Psychology; Beliefs about the Soul in Rabbinic Literature of the Talmudic Period* (London, 1947), pp. 199–203.

Tale 8. The Besht's Marriage

1. I Sam. 21:14.
2. Jud. 5:29.
3. Probably a reference to the Talmudic decree "A man may not betroth a woman before he sees her," B. Ḳiddushin 41a.

Tale 11. The Besht's Journey to the Holy Land

1. Gen. 3:24.
2. The Yiddish edition of *In Praise of the Besht* is more explicit about the Besht's attempt to travel to the Land of Israel. See tales 47, 211, 231, and accompanying notes.

Tale 12. The Besht and the Frog

1. Mishnah Aboth 4.2.
2. Jer. 3:14.
3. Cf. Deut. R., 2:24.
4. Jer. 15:19.

Tale 13. The Besht Serves as Rabbi Gershon's Coachman

1. See tales 14, 15, 19, 20, 22, 31.
2. Jud. 5:29.

Tale 14. The Besht Reveals Himself

1. Mishnah Aboth 2.5.

Tale 15. The Besht Reveals Himself to the Sect
of the Great Hasidim

1. A prayer and a ceremony by which the Sabbath and holidays are sanctified. It is recited over wine and hallah by the master of the house.
2. The afternoon prayer. It is the second of the three daily prayers and has to be recited before nightfall. See Elbogen, *Der jüdische Gottesdienst*, pp. 98–99, 237.
3. A prayer for the Sabbath which was partially composed and institutionalized by the Safed Kabbalists at the end of the sixteenth century. The prayer consists of Ps. 95–99 and 29, and the song *Lekhah Dodi*, which is followed by Ps. 92 and 93. See Elbogen, *Der jüdische Gottesdienst*, p. 107.
4. This is the last of the three daily prayers. It can be recited from dusk till midnight. See Elbogen, *Der jüdische Gottesdienst*, pp. 97–100.
5. The term used is *devekut*. For a discussion of its implications see G. Scholem, "Devekuth, or Communion with God," *The Review of Religion*, XIV (1950), 115–39.
6. A song for the Sabbath morning. The song is a true acrostic, the initial letters of which make the sentence "I am Isaac Luria." For references see Israel Davidson, *Thesaurus of Mediaeval Hebrew Poetry* (New York, 1924), I, 313.
7. The blessing said before the meal on the Sabbath morning.
8. A blessing said at the conclusion of the Sabbath, over a glass of wine, incense, and a candle. The Havdalah signifies the separation between the holy and the profane, the light and the darkness. See Elbogen, *Der jüdische Gottesdienst*, pp. 46–47.

Tale 16. The Besht Locks up the Secret Manuscripts

1. See tales 5 and 7.
2. Rabbi Aryeh Leib. According to tale 48 he was the first follower of the Besht. He died in 1770.

Tale 17. The Beginning of the Writer's Manuscript

1. This is the opening of the manuscript obtained by the printer.
2. B. Shabbath 89b. See tale 26.
3. The name of the town Biala Cerkiew means literally White Church. In order to avoid mentioning a church in their conversation the Jews referred to it as Whitefield.

Tale 18. Fingernails

1. According to the kabbalistic notion the tree of life is exactly in the middle of paradise. See *The Zohar*, I, 132 [I, 35a]. For a study of the tree of life in Near Eastern religions see E. O. James, *The Tree of Life: An Archaeological Study*, (Leiden, 1966).

Tale 19. The Besht's Seclusion

1. Compare with tales 8, 13.

Tale 20. The Besht Exorcises a Madwoman

1. On the magical usage of angelic and demonic names see Trachtenberg, *Jewish Magic and Superstition*, pp. 73–103, and Hirsch J. Zimmels, *Magicians, Theologians and Doctors* (London, 1952), p. 35.
2. Literally, *he hath hid himself among the baggage*, I Sam. 10:22.
3. Concerning people possessed by the spirit of a dead person, a dybbuk, see Trachtenberg, *Jewish Magic and Superstition*, p. 50. Earlier stories about a dybbuk are found in Gaster, *Ma'aseh Book*, pp. 301–303; and in his *The Exempla of the Rabbis*, pp. 127–28. A dybbuk legend about a spirit that tells people their sins is also found in Hayyim Vital, *Book of Visions*, Hebrew, ed. Aaron Z. Aešcoly (Jerusalem, 1954), p. 21.
4. Compare this tale with the *Gospel of Mark* 1:23–28.

Tale 21. The Besht's Prayer Produces Rain

1. The Mishnah requires fasting in cases of drought. Tractate Ta'anit of the Mishnah consists mainly of the regulations of this ritualistic fast.
2. Special emphasis is put on the man who prays before the ark. His heart has to be wholly devoted in prayer. See Mishnah Ta'anit 2.2.
3. The miraculous power of bringing down rain by prayer is attributed to several people in Jewish tradition. In the Bible Elijah the Prophet has that power. See I Kings, 18:41–5. In the Mishnah, Honi ha-Me'aggel (Honi "the circle-drawer") performs this deed. See Ta'anith 3.8. In the Babylonian Talmud Nakdimon ben Gurion prays successfully for rain, as do the descendents of Honi ha-Me'aggel. See B. Ta'anith 20a, 23a–b. For further references see Gaster, *The Exempla of the Rabbis*, pp. 202, 264, nos. 85, 421–22. Raphael Patai discusses rain prayers in "The 'Control of Rain' in Ancient Palestine," *Hebrew Union College Annual*, XIV (1939), 251–86, and Dov Noy focuses on the character of the praying person in "Simpleton's Prayer Brings Down Rain," Hebrew, *Machnayim*, No. 51 (1960).

Tale 23. The Besht Exorcises Demons from a House

1. For a discussion of amulets and their preparation and usage, see Trachtenberg, *Jewish Magic and Superstition*, pp. 132–52.
2. *Kelippah*, literally, the shell of a nut. This is a kabbalistic metaphor for evil spirit. See Scholem, *Major Trends in Jewish Mysticism*, p. 239. For a detailed discussion of this concept in Safed mysticism, see Isaiah Tishby, *The Doctrine of Evil and the 'Kelippah' in Lurianic Kabbalism*, Hebrew, Studies and Texts in Jewish Mysticism, Vol. II (Jerusalem, 1960), pp. 62–90.
3. Demons.

Tale 24. The Innkeeper's Death

1. Rabbi Gershon's brother. The third brother in this family, Rabbi Aaron, is mentioned in tale 116.

Tale 25. The Besht Attracts Followers

1. We could not identify this town.
2. See tale 17, n. 3.
3. This phrase is said in Maariv on weekdays and at the conclusion of the Sabbath, but it is omitted from the prayer on Sabbath Eve.

Tale 26. The Besht and the Physician

1. The Hasidim insisted on sharpened and not merely tempered knives. See Wertheim, *Laws and Customs of Chassidism*, pp. 200–208. See also Ch. Shmeruk [Szmeruk], "The Social Significance of the Hassidic Shekhita," Hebrew, *Zion*, XX (1955), 47–72.
2. See tale 17.

Tale 27. The Besht Predicts a Need for Bloodletting

1. Concerning the use of bloodletting in Jewish medical practice, see Trachtenberg, *Jewish Magic and Superstition*, p. 196, and Zimmels, *Magicians, Theologians and Doctors*, pp. 154–57.

Tale 29. Elijah the Prophet Reveals Himself to the Besht

1. The revelation of Elijah in dreams or visions signifies the attainment

of a high degree of piety. See Ginzberg, *The Legends of the Jews,* VI, 333–34, 341–42, and his article "Elijah," *Jewish Encyclopedia,* V, 121–27. See also the monograph by Eliezer Margaliyot, *Elijah the Prophet in Jewish Literature,* Hebrew (Jerusalem, 1960). An issue of the Journal of the Israel Folklore Society, *Yeda-'Am,* VII (1960), is dedicated to "Elijah the Prophet in Folklore, Traditions and Folk-Life." M. Friedman brings together all the tales about the revelations of Elijah to the Talmudic rabbis in *Seder Eliahu Rabba and Seder Eliahu Zuta,* Hebrew (Jerusalem, 1960), pp. 32–40.

2. Rabbi Gershon rented the inn for the Besht. See tale 14.

Tale 30. The Stolen Horse

1. Compare this tale with the one about Pinhas ben Yair and the return of his stolen ass in *Aboth de-Rabbi Nathan,* ed. Schechter I, ch. 8, p. 38; B. Hullin 7b; Y. Demai 1.3, 21d; and see further references in Gaster, *The Exempla of the Rabbis,* p. 228, no. 235.

Tale 31. The Besht Reveals Himself to Rabbi David of Kolomyya

1. See tale 26, n. 1.

2. The Besht probably arose for the Midnight Service, *Tikkun Hatsot,* which is conducted to mourn for the destruction of the Temple. It consists of Ps. 137, 79, 42, 43, 111, 51, 126, lamentations, and petitions. The custom owes its spread primarily to the kabbalists in Isaac Luria's circle. See Wertheim, *Laws and Customs of Chassidism,* pp. 64–66.

Tale 33. The Delayed Journey

1. I Kings 18:26.

2. See B. Hagigah 12a; Gen. R., 11.2, 12.6, and Exod. R. 35.1. See Ginzberg, *The Legends of the Jews,* V, 8–9, n. 19, Compare with tale 69.

Tale 34. The Besht's Trembling in Prayer

1. This prayer consists of Ps. 113–18 and is recited on the New Moon, on Passover, Pentacost, Tabernacles, and Hanukkah. It is recited after the eighteen benedictions. See Elbogen, *Der jüdische Gottesdienst,* pp. 125, 137, and Solomon Zeitlin, "The Hallel," *Jewish Quarterly Review,* LIII (1962), 22–29.

2. The eighteen benedictions is the principle supplicatory prayer of Jewish liturgy. In the morning and the afternoon each member of the congre-

gation first prays it silently and then the cantor recites it aloud. See Elbogen, *Der jüdische Gottesdienst*, pp. 27–60. For recent studies concerning its origin and development, see Aaron Mirsky, "The Origin of the 'Eighteen Benedictions' of the Daily Prayer," Hebrew, *Tarbiz*, XXXIII (1963), 28–31, and Solomon Zeitlin, "The Tefillah, the Shemoneh Esreh: An Historical Study of the First Canonization of Hebrew Liturgy," *Jewish Quarterly Review*, LIV (1964), 208–249.

3. Bodily movements in prayer are an old custom, and are mentioned in Judah ha-Levi's (about 1075–1141), *Kitab Al Khazari*, trans. M. M. Kaplan (New York, 1927), p. 128. However, the Hasidim carried this custom to the extreme, moving and pacing in the synagogue with great enthusiasm. See Wertheim, *Laws and Customs of Chassidism*, p. 103, and Minkin, *The Romance of Hassidism*, pp. 89–92. This exaggerated manner of praying was considered a disgrace by their opponents and is mentioned contemptuously by contemporary rabbis. See Dubnov, *The History of Hasidism*, p. 77.

Tale 35. The Besht's Trembling in Prayer: A Second Version

1. Exod. 19:18.

Tale 38. A Sincere Prayer

1. According to the first printed Yiddish edition, Rabbi David Forkes had prepared himself for this public prayer long before Yom Kippur, intending to bring the Messiah by his prayer. The Besht, who perceived that thought, realized that the time was not yet ripe for the Messiah to come, and therefore he confused Rabbi David Forkes in order to prevent him from bringing the redeemer. See A. Yaari, "Two Basic Recensions of 'Shivḥē Ha-Besht,'" Hebrew, *Kirjath Sepher*, XXXIX (1964), 400–402.

Tale 39. The Besht's Trembling in Prayer: A Fifth Version

1. Exod. 19:18.

Tale 40. The Dream of Rabbi Joseph Ashkenazi

1. This is a reference to the attack of the Haidamaks on Uman in June 1768, in which more than twenty thousand Poles and Jews were killed. As the tales note, many others fled for their lives. See also tales 45, 50, 51, 171, 210, and S. Dubnov [Dubnow], *History of the Jews in Russia and Poland*,

trans. I. Friedlaender (Philadelphia, 1916), I, 180–87.

2. An acrostic prayer recited on the Eve of Yom Kippur. See Davidson, *Thesaurus of Mediaeval Hebrew Poetry*, III, 285–86.

3. These are additional verses which are not in alphabetical order.

4. In mystical literature one of the functions of the angel Michael is to sacrifice the souls in heaven. See the Hebrew edition of *The Zohar*, I, 8a. This motif appears in the mystical midrashim "Arkim" and "Gan ha-'Eden." See Judah David Eisenstein, *Ozar Midrashim: A Library of Two Hundred Minor Midrashim*, Hebrew (New York, 1915), I, 70, 88.

5. The last two verses deviate from the customary version which reads: "Refuge of our mothers, helper of the tribes."

Tale 41. The Besht in the Messiah's Heavenly Palace

1. This term usually refers to the Mishnah and the Talmudim. Among the kabbalists it also implies the Shekinah.

2. Literally, "all the vows." A prayer in Aramaic recited before the evening prayer on the Eve of Yom Kippur asking for the release of all the unfulfilled vows and promises which were made throughout the year. See Elbogen, *Der jüdische Gottesdienst*, pp. 153–54.

3. The concluding prayers of Yom Kippur. The term Neilah (closing) refers to the closing of the gates of Heaven at the end of this day.

4. These two phrases appear in two separate prayers of the Neilah service.

5. Putting one's head between one's knees is a typical body posture for mystical contemplation. See Scholem, *Major Trends in Jewish Mysticism*, p. 49–50. However, the Besht's movement is unique as he bends backwards and not forwards as is common.

6. In premedieval Jewish mystic literature, the visionary passes through heavenly palaces (*Heikhalot*). Concerning these mystical journeys, see Scholem, *Major Trends in Jewish Mysticism*, pp. 40–79, and his *Jewish Gnosticism, Merkabah Mysticism and Talmudic Tradition* (New York, 1960). See also Morton Smith, "Observations on Hekhalot Rabbati," in *Biblical and Other Studies*, ed. A. Altman (Cambridge, Mass., 1963), pp. 142–60.

7. The prayers, like the souls, pass from one palace to the other. See the Hebrew edition of *The Zohar*, II, 245, and Fischel Lachower and Isaiah Tishby, *The Wisdom of the Zohar*, I, 420–21.

8. For studies about the Besht's mentor see Aaron Knitrik, "On the Besht's Vision of Ahijah, the Prophet of Shiloh," Hebrew, *Sinai*, LXXIII (1973), 189–190; Gedalyah Nigal, "The Mentor of Rabbi Israel Baal Shem Tov," Hebrew, *Sinai*, LXXI (1972), 150–159; Abraham Rubinstein, "The

Mentor of R. Israel Ba'al Shem Tov and the Sources of his Knowledge," Hebrew, *Tarbiz*, LXVII (1978), 146–158.

9. These last incidents refer to actual historical events. The Frankists, referred to here as the "wicked sect" or the "sect of Shabbetai Tsevi" believed in the messianic qualities of Shabbetai Tsevi. Under the leadership of Jacob Frank (1726–91) the Frankist movement spread to eastern Galicia and Podolia. The Frankists challenged the Jewish rabbis to a public dispute concerning the Frankist charge that the Talmud contained heretic statements against Christianity. The debate took place in Kamenets on June 20, 1757, under the active sponsorship of the Archbishop Dembowski. The Frankists were declared the winners of the debate, and consequently the archbishop proclaimed that all copies of the Talmud were to be burned. The burning of the books of the Talmud was reported in books and pamphlets, as well as in letters and newspapers. Shortly after this event, in November 1757, Archbishop Dembowski died. A second debate between the Frankists and the Jewish rabbis took place in Lvov on July 17, 1759, in which the latter were declared the victors. A mass conversion to Christianity by the Frankists followed that dispute, in fulfillment of a promise they gave to the Christian authorities prior to the dispute. The episode about the way the bishop disgraced the Frankists might have been a Hasidic joke. They ridiculed the Frankists, who actually were reluctant to convert to Christianity, by facetiously suggesting a compromise between the two religions: shaving half a beard and one earlock. The second public debate has special significance for the history of the Besht. A report submitted by one Rabbi Abraham of Shargorod to Rabbi Jacob Emden (1697–1776) is the first document which mentions the Besht. He is described as one of the authorities who took part in the second debate between the Frankists and the rabbis. However, the historicity of the Besht's participation in this public debate is open to serious doubt. For a detailed discussion of these events, see Majer Balaban, *The History of the Frankist Movement*, Hebrew (Tel-Aviv, 1934–35), and S. M. Dubnov [Dubnow], *History of the Jews in Russia and Poland*, I, 211–20. For a discussion of the mythical and mystical significance of the tale see Joseph Dan, *The Hasidic Story—Its History and Development*, Hebrew (Jerusalem, 1975), pp. 118–123.

Tale 42. The Palace of the Bird's Nest

1. *The Zohar*, III, 20–26 [II 7b–8], V, 282 [III, 196b]. The idea of the Messiah being in the heavenly palace called the Bird's Nest is found in the earliest portion of the book of the Zohar, "Midrash ha-Ne'elam," which was written between 1275–80. See Scholem, *Major Trends in Jewish Mysticism*, p. 188.

Tale 43. The Besht and his Guests

1. Tales 41, 42, and 44 constitute a continuous narrative. This tale is an unclear interpolation. This episode might have been related to tale 137 "The Martyrs," in which the Besht neglects his guests because of his grief.

Tale 45. The Destruction of Balta

1. We could not identify this town. Cf. p. 3 note 7.
2. See tale 40, n. 1.

Tale 46. Rabbi Gershon Imitates the Besht

1. Concerning Rabbi Gershon's journey to the Land of Israel and his life there, see tales 53, 55, 56, 58, 193. Rabbi Gershon lived in the Holy Land from 1747 to 1757, and consequently his trip to Europe took place after that date. However, Abraham Heschel has attempted to reconstruct another visit of Rabbi Gershon to the Land of Israel prior to 1747, and therefore he dates this trip some time before that year. See his article "Rabbi Gershon of Kuty," Hebrew, *Hebrew Union College Annual*, XXIII, pt. 2 (1950–51), 56–62. For criticism of this conclusion, see Gershom Scholem, "Two Letters from Palestine, 1760–1764," *Tarbiz*, XXV (1956), 429–30, n. 4.
2. The appearance of the stars marks the beginning of the Sabbath.
3. According to B. Berakoth 8a, each verse of the weekly portion of the Torah was read twice in Hebrew and once in its Aramaic translation.
4. Both are phrases in the eighteen benedictions.

Tale 47. Rabbi Jacob Joseph Recognizes the Greatness of the Besht.

1. Concerning the Besht's attempt to travel to the Land of Israel, see tales 11, 211, 231. The Yiddish edition of *In Praise of the Baal Shem Tov* is more explicit about the Besht's failure to arrive at the Land of Israel. See A. Yaari, "Two Basic Recensions of 'Shivḥē Ha-Besht,' " Hebrew, *Kirjath Sepher*, XXXIX (1964), 560–61.

Tale 48. Rabbi Jacob Joseph is Expelled from Shargorod

1. Dubnov dates this event to 1748. See *History of Hasidism*, p. 94.
2. The fulfillment of this prophecy occurred around 1768–72, ibid.

3. According to Dubnov, he was the rabbi of Raszkow from 1748 to 1752, ibid.

4. He performed many acts of repentance for not following the teachings of the Besht. For other tales concerning the conversion of Rabbi Jacob Joseph to Beshtian Hasidism, see Dresner, *The Zaddik* (London, New York, Toronto, 1960), pp. 37–50.

Tale 49. The Ascetic Fasting of Rabbi Jacob Joseph

1. Dan. 4:14.
2. Judg. 6:12.
3. Is. 58:7.

Tale 51. The Protective Prayers

1. These are opening phrases of two parts of Shaharith.

2. This is a paraphrase on *Sefer Yezirah* 1.2. However, we do not follow the existing translation. Compare Isidor Kalisch, *Sepher Yezirah: A Book on Creation or the Jewish Metaphysics of Remote Antiquity* (New York, 1877), p. 11.

3. The acrostic Ps. 119.

4. In Hebrew, קרע שטן. Jewish secret magic lore included a few ineffable powerful names consisting of a fixed number of letters. This phrase consists of the seventh to twelfth letters in the magical name of forty-two letters. See Trachtenberg, *Jewish Magic and Superstitions*, pp. 90–97.

5. A prayer for captives usually said on Mondays and Thursdays before returning the Scroll of the Torah to the ark.

6. Ps. 90–17. This verse usually is said as a protective measure as the sacred Sabbath departs and the profane weekdays begin.

Tale 52. The Asceticism of Rabbi Jacob Joseph

1. Originally this phrase was taken from Mishnah Aboth 1.5, and B. Baba Mezi'a 60b. However, here it is quoted from the book Midrash Samuel, a collection of midrashic-talmudic sayings probably prepared in the eleventh century and first printed in Constantinople in 1522.

Tale 53. The Voyage of Rabbi Gershon

1. Cf. Exod. 15:9.
2. In Talmudic stories Elijah the Prophet often appears in the guise of an Arab. See Ginzberg, *The Legends of the Jews*, IV, 206, 208; VI, 327, 329.

Tale 54. Rabbi Gershon's Sin

1. See tale 41, n. 10.
2. In *The Columbia Lippincott Gazetteer of the World*, the name of this town is listed as Ladyzhinka. The present spelling is more common in Jewish literature.
3. Compare this story with tales 118, 227.

Tale 55. Prayers for Rain in Jerusalem

1. Lit., "Of the Western Country," a term used in the Babylonian Talmud to refer to the Land of Israel.
2. Penitential prayers asking for forgiveness for committed sins. See Elbogen, *Der jüdische Gottesdienst*, pp. 221–31.

Tale 56. A Quarrel in Safed

1. The language of the Sephardic community.
2. For a discussion of the procedure of excommunication in the Jewish juridical system, see Julius H. Greenstone, "Excommunication," *Jewish Encyclopedia*, V, 285–87.
3. See *Pirke de Rabbi Eliezer*, trans. and ed. Gerald Friedlander (New York, 1965), p. 236.

Tale 57. Rabbi Lipeh Quarrels with Rabbi Gedaliah

1. The name here changes from the diminutive Lipeh to Lipmann. We have retained Lipeh throughout to avoid confusion.

Tale 59. The Sick Girl

1. *Exod.* 20:14.
2. Concerning changing names as a curative or preventative procedure, see Trachtenberg, *Jewish Magic and Superstition*, pp. 204–206.
3. An additional prayer said on Sabbath, the new moon, and holidays. See Elbogen, *Der jüdische Gottesdienst*, pp. 115–17.

Tale 60. The Blood Libel

1. This is a reference to the blood accusation which took place in Zaslavl in 1747. The Besht mentions this event in his letter to his brother-in-law Rabbi Gershon of Kuty who lived in the Land of Israel at that time. This letter, in which he manifests his visions of heaven, was given to Rabbi

Jacob Joseph of Polonnoye to be delivered to Rabbi Gershon. However, the letter had never reached its destination and was printed by Rabbi Jacob Joseph at the end of his book, *Ben Porat Yosef* ("Joseph is a Fruitful Vine") (Korets, 1781). The letter is considered to be an authentic document both by scholars and by followers of the Besht. According to this letter and other historical documents this blood accusation occurred in 1747. See also Dubnov, *History of Hasidism*, pp. 60–61, and *History of the Jews in Russia and Poland*, I, 172, 177–78. Compare also with tale no. 137. A general discussion of blood libels against the Jews is found in Joshua Trachtenberg, *The Devil and the Jews* (New York, 1961), pp. 124–55.

2. About this position in service see Ernst Roth, "The Usage of the Footstool in the Jewish Rites of Shofar Blowing and Vows," Hebrew, *Yeda-'Am*, VIII, 1 (1962), 3–7.

Tale 61. The Dance of the Hasidim

1. Unlike rabbinical Judaism, the Hasidim conceive of singing and dancing as an integral part of the worship of God. See A. Shochat, "On Joy in Hassidism," Hebrew, *Zion*, XVI (1951), 30–43; Louis I. Newman and Samuel Spitz, *The Hasidic Anthology* (New York, 1963), pp. 66, 202–205; Jacob S. Minkin, *The Romance of Hassidism*, pp. 312–13; and Yaari, *Simhath Torah*, pp. 316–18, 320–23.

Tale 62. The Great Maggid and the Besht

1. One of them appears in the Yiddish version of this tale, which differs considerably from the Hebrew text. See Yaari, "Two Basic Recensions . . . ," *Kirjath Sepher*, XXXIX (1964), 403–407.

2. Deut. 10:19.

3. This is the book of Enoch of the Merkavah mystics, the text of which is reprinted in Eisenstein, *Ozar Midrashim*, II, 285–93. For an English edition, see Hugo Odeberg, *3. Enoch, or the Hebrew Book of Enoch* (London, 1928). It describes Metatron guiding Ishmael, a Tanna (second century), in the heavenly halls. Metatron is the name given to Enoch after his heavenly transformation. For additional information concerning this unique angelic figure, see Scholem, *Major Trends in Jewish Mysticism*, pp. 67–70, and *Jewish Gnosticism, Merkabah Mysticism, and Talmudic Tradition*, pp. 43–55; Reuben Margulies, *Heavenly Angels*, Hebrew (Jerusalem, 1945), pp. 73–108; and Ginzberg, *The Legends of the Jews*, V, 162–64.

4. A term applied to the principal subject matter of Jewish mysticism in Tannaic and Talmudic periods. In Hebrew it means "work of the chariot" and its basic text is Ezek. 1. See Mishnah Hagigah, 2:1. For a discussion of

the literature of these mystics, see Scholem, *Major Trends in Jewish Mysticism*, pp. 40–79.

5. The Zohar adheres to the Biblical description (Ex. 19:16–19) of the trumpet being the only musical instrument used at the time of God's giving the Torah to Israel. See *The Zohar*, III, 244–45 [II, 81].

Tale 64. The Book Ḥemdat ha-Yamim

1. Prov. 5:3.

2. This anonymous work, was first printed in Izmir, Turkey, 1731–32, but undoubtedly had circulated in manuscript form before that time. See Abraham Yaari, *The Mystery of a Book*, Hebrew (Jerusalem, 1954), for a discussion of the problems revolving around this book. Yaari concludes that the book was written by Rabbi Benjamin Hallevi of Safed. However, a textual comparison with other sources led Isaiah Tishby to conclude that the book was written at a later date, not earlier than 1712, forty years after the death of Hallevi, and less than thirty years prior to its publication. See Isaiah Tishby [Tishbi], "Sources of *Hemdath Hayyamim*," Hebrew, *Tarbiz*, XXV (1955) 66–92, and "Early 18th Century Sources in *Hemdath Yamim*," Hebrew, *Tarbiz*, XXV (1956), 202–230. This anonymous book belongs to kabbalistic literature. Its relationships to Shabbetianism was a subject of great dispute. See also Wertheim, *Laws and Customs in Chassidism*, p. 190, n. 97. Jacob Emden (1697–1776) mentioned in his book *Shvirat-ha-Luḥot* (Altona, 1756–59), p. 46, that Rabbi Eliezer quarreled with the Safed community over the book *Ḥemdat ha-Yamim*, and that this dispute led to his death. This may explain the juxtaposition of tales 63 and 64.

Tale 66. The Besht and Shabbetai Tsevi

1. Concerning the concept of *tikkun*, the restoration of the scattered sparks of God, and its development in Lurianic mysticism, see Scholem, *Major Trends in Jewish Mysticism*, pp. 273–78, 283–87.

2. According to the Kabbalah the soul has three parts, *nefesh, ruaḥ, neshamah*. All three words are synonymous terms for soul. See Tishby, *The Wisdom of the Zohar*, II, 3–67, and Scholem, *Major Trends in Jewish Mysticism*, pp. 240–41.

Tale 67. Rabbi Isaac Drabizner

1. B. Sanhedrin 7a.

Tale 69. The Oxen of Rabbi Barukh

1. Gen. 1:4.

2. See B. Hagigah 12a; Gen. R. 11.2; 12.6; and Exod. R. 35.1, and see Ginzberg, *The Legends of the Jews*, V, 8–9, n. 19. Cf. tales 33, 63, 139.
3. Cf. tale 63.

Tale 70. The Stolen Halter

1. The blessing of the new moon takes place preferably on Saturday night, or on any other day between the third and the sixteenth of the month according to the Hebrew calendar. The blessing is said in the open air. The entire ceremony has already been mentioned in the B. Sanhedrin 42a, and tractate Soferim 20.1–2.

Tale 71. The Shohet Who Was a Drunkard

1. Cf. tale 141.

Tale 72. The Death of Rabbi Abraham, the "Angel"

1. We could not identify the towns of Prot'hur and Porivosts.

Tale 75. The Wife of Rabbi Abraham

1. Meshullom Phoebus Hurwitz, *Mishnat Hakhamim*, Ostrog, 1796.
2. Est. 8:8. In the Hebrew text the biblical quotation is slightly paraphrased.
3. See Mishnah Kethuboth 5:2.
4. Cf. this last episode with Gaster, *The Exempla of the Rabbis*, pp. 98–99, 215, no. 139.
5. Compare the last episode with the story of Glaphyra's dream in Josephus, *Antiquitates Judaicae*, XVII, 13:4, and *Bellum Judaicum*, II, 7:4.

Tale 76. The City of Adultery

1. Rabbi Menaḥem Mendel of Vitbesk led a group of three hundred Hasidim who emigrated to the Land of Israel in 1777. He died in Tiberias in 1788.
2. The community to which this tale refers is Brody where accusations of adulterous behavior led to mass divorces in 1752 and 1756. The latter occurrence in 1756 was associated directly with the Frankist movement. See Gelber, *The History of the Jews in Brody*, pp. 106–107, and Balaban, *The History of the Frankist Movement*, pp. 118–27.

Tale 77. The Advice of the Great Maggid

1. B. Berakoth 61b.

Tale 78. The Prayers of the Hasidim

1. Known also as Meshulam Zusya (died 1800).

2. Rabbi Elimelekh of Lizensk (1717–1786), a small town near Jaroslav, was a disciple of Rabbi Dov Ber of Mezhirich, and after the death of the Great Maggid he became the leader of the Hasidim of Galicia and Poland. His main book is *No'am Elimelekh* ("Elimelekh's Delight") (Lvov, 1788). See Dubnov, *History of Hasidism*, pp. 178–188.

3. There are several books bearing that title. This may be a reference to the work of Abraham Azulai (1570–1643), who was born in Fez, Morocco, and emigrated to Hebron, Palestine, in the beginning of the 17th century. While residing in Gaza he wrote his kabbalistic work, *Ḥesed le-Abraham* (Amsterdam, 1685).

Tale 83. The Besht's Sermon

1. Cf. tales 34–37, 39.

Tale 84. The Besht Banishes Demons

1. "*Lekhah Dodi*," a Sabbath poem written in the form of an acrostic on the name of the author, the Safed Kabbalist, Rabbi Solomon ha-Levi Alkabetz (about 1505 to about 1584). In the poem the Sabbath is personified as a bride.

Tale 85. The Rabbi's Wife in Labor

1. This spelling follows Halpern [Halperin], *Acta Congressus Generalis Judacorum Regni Poloniae* (1580–1764), p. 616.

Tale 87. The Hose-Maker

1. The Besht meant that this man was one of the thirty-six righteous people of humble vocation upon whom the existence of the word depends. Rabbi Abbaye is quoted in the Babylonian Talmud saying that "there are in the world not less than thirty-six righteous persons in every generation upon whom the Shekinah rests." (B. Sukkah 45b; Sanhedrin 97b). This statement served to authenticate legends about the hidden saints which became widespread in Jewish popular literature. See Gershom Scholem, "Die 36 verborgenen Gerechten in der jüdischen Tradition," in *Judaica* (Frankfurt am Main, 1963), pp. 216–25.

Tale 89. Two Hasidim Visit Hell

1. Zech. 3:2.

2. Literally "[May our remembrance] rise, come [and be accepted before thee]." This is the beginning phrase of a prayer recited on the advent of the new moon and during the intermediate days of Passover and Sukkoth. The prayer is inserted in the eighteen benedictions.

3. Prince of Gehenna is known by different names and has various functions. According to Midrash Konen his name is *kipod*, and he is in charge of one of the three gates of hell. See Eisenstein, *Ozar Midrashim*, I, 256. In a manuscript of the 14th century his name is Ze'ufiel, see G. Scholem, "Ma'asseh Merkabah—An Unpublished Merkabah Text," in *Jewish Gnosticism, Merkabah Mysticism, and Talmudic Tradition*, pp. 101–117. Ze'ufiel is also the angel who takes the souls of the wicked down to hell. See Eisenstein, *Ozar Midrashim*, II, 291. According to *The Zohar*, III, 57, [II, 18a], Dumah, who was the Prince of Egypt, became Prince of Gehenna at the moment Moses said: *And against all the gods of Egypt I will execute judgement* (Exod. 12:12). His duty then became to judge the souls of the wicked.

Tale 90. The Court in Heaven

1. Spelled Vladimirets in *The Columbia Lippincott Gazetteer of the World*.

2. Rabbi Jacob Joseph of Polonnoye published three books in his lifetime: *Toldot Ya'akov Yosef* (Korets, 1780), *Ben Porat Yosef* (Korets, 1781), and *Tsofnat Pa'aneah* (Korets, 1782). A fourth book, *Ketonet Passim* (Lvov, 1866), appeared after his death. Dubnov believed that this book was falsely attributed to Rabbi Jacob Joseph (see *History of Hasidism*, p. 393). However, modern scholars question this view (see, for example, Joseph G. Weiss, "Is the Hasidic Book 'Kethoneth Passim' a Literary Forgery," *The Journal of Jewish Studies*, IX (1958), 81–83). Although this book was in manuscript form during the time *Shivhei ha-Besht* was written and published, we could not find any evidence that this story is taken from the manuscript of *Ketonet Passim*. Apparently, Rabbi Jacob Joseph had other works in manuscript form to which he repeatedly referred in his other writings. See Gedalyah Nigal, *Leader and Community*, p. 28, and Samuel H. Dresner, *The Zaddik*, p. 252.

3. For a monograph about the canine shape of Satan, see Barbara Allen Woods, *The Devil in Dog Form*, Univ. of California Folklore Studies No. 11 (Berkeley and Los Angeles, 1959).

Tale 92. The Repentant Rich Man

1. A German silver coin. Its value increased from five groschen at the

end of the sixteenth century to eight zlotys (240 groschen) during the eighteenth century.

2. *Ein Ya'akov*, ("Eye of Jacob") is a collection of haggadic passages from both Talmuds, which was prepared by Jacob ben Solomon Ibn Ḥabib (also Chabib), a Jewish Sephardic scholar (1460–1516). It was first printed in 1516 in Salonika where Ibn Ḥabib lived after the expulsion of the Jews from Spain in 1492. Other editions appeared frequently thereafter. For an English edition see Rabbi Jacob Ibn Chabib, *En Jacob Agada of the Babylonian Talmud*, rev. and trans. Samuel Hirsch Glick (New York, 1916–22).

3. About the role of study groups in the Jewish community, see Jacob Katz, *Tradition and Crisis*, pp. 157–67. Their history is discussed in Salo W. Baron, *The Jewish Community* (Philadelphia, 1942), I, 348–74. See also Israel Halpern, "Associations for the Study of the Torah and for Good Deeds and the Spread of the Hassidic Movement," Hebrew, *Zion*, XXII (1957), 195–213.

Tale 93. The Defective Tefillin

1. This is the major compilation of Jewish law which has served as the standard code for secular and religious practice. It was compiled by Joseph Karo (also Caro), (1st ed.; Venice, 1565). For an English edition see Solomon Ganzfried, *Code of Jewish Law, Kitzur Shulḥan Aruḥ*, trans. Hyman E. Goldin (New York, 1961), I–IV.

2. Cf. tales 14, 94.

Tale 95. The Righteous Woman

1. A euphemistic expression for carnal intimacy. See B. Makkoth 7a; Baba Meẓi'a 91a.

Tale 97. The Blessing of Rabbi Pinḥas

1. In Hebrew, הקצין (*ha-katsin*) also means an army officer.

Tale 98. The Besht's Combat with a Witch

1. Cf. with tales 21, 55, 125, 126.

Tale 100. The Revenant

1. See Ḥayyim Vital, *Sha'arei Kedushah*, ("Gates of Holiness") (Constantinople, 1734), p. 34a; 3:7.

Tale 104. The Besht's Devekut

1. Ps. 119:1.
2. In Kabbalistic literature wisdom, in Hebrew Hokhmah, is the name of the second sefirah or emanation of God that manifests the primordial idea of God. See Gershom G. Scholem, *Major Trends in Jewish Mysticism*, pp. 205–221; Iden, "Kabbalah," *Encyclopaedia Judaica* (1971), X, especially pp. 563–579.
3. See Gershom Scholem, "Devekuth, or Communion with God." Reprinted in *The Messianic Idea in Judaism* (New York, 1971), pp. 203–226.

Tale 105. The Besht Resuscitates a Child

1. See B. Baba Meẓi'a 85b.
2. Compare with the Biblical stories about reviving children by Elijah and Elisha, I Kings 17:17–24 and II Kings 4:8–37. A similar story is told about Jesus in Luke 7:11–17. Parallels to this tale in the Hellenistic tradition are quoted in Rudolf Bultman, *The History of the Synoptic Tradition*, trans. J. Marsh (New York and Evanston, 1963), pp. 233–34.

Tale 107. The Choice

1. Cf. with tales 97, 170, 223.

Tale 108. The Fish and the Dog

1. See tale 209 for further details concerning Rabbi Naḥman.
2. Motif E.617, "Reincarnation as fish," is found also in the dybbuk legend in Ḥayyim Vital, *A Book of the Visions* (Hebrew), ed. Aaron Aešcoly-Weintraub (Jerusalem, 1954), pp. 20, 27. Cf. also tale 250.

Tale 109. The Dance of Rabbi Yudel

1. An acrostic prayer taken from "Heikhalot Rabbathi," see Eisenstein, *Oẓar Midrashim*, I, 120. For further references see Davidson, *Thesaurus of Mediaeval Hebrew Poetry*, II, 116.

Tale 111. Rabbi Naḥman's Prayer

1. A kaddish prayer which is said after a haggadic sermon or a Talmudic-Midrashic discourse. See Elbogen, *Der jüdische Gottesdienst*, p. 96.
2. A part of Shaharit consists of I Chron. 16:8–36.

3. A benediction said before the morning recitation of Psalms. See Elbogen, *Der jüdische Gottesdienst*, pp. 82–84. Rabbi Naḥman followed the Lurianic Sephardic liturgy, which was adopted by the Hasidim. For a discussion of the differences between this and the Ashkenazic rite, see Hirsch J. Zimmels, *Ashkenazim and Sephardim*, Jews' College Publications, New Series, No. 2 (London, 1958), p. 120.

Tale 114. The Interruption of the Besht's Vision

1. For another tale about the last days of the Besht see tale 247.
2. Compare with tale 194 where the mystical value of storytelling is noted.
3. Deut. 33:2. The Torah is the worldly embodiment of the divine worlds. Thus, as each soul has its particular place in heaven, so each name, the earthly form of the soul, has its particular "place" in the Torah.

Tale 116. Rabbi Aaron in Heaven

1. Concerning the appearance of the dead in dreams, see Trachtenberg, *Jewish Magic and Superstition*, pp. 61–68, 234.
2. Instructions for distinguishing between the spirit of a dead man and a demon are given by Judah ben Samuel the Hasid, *The Book of Hasidim*, ed. Reuben Margulies (Jerusalem, 1960), p. 445. A dead man could not pronounce the name of God even when the living person induced him to do so. See also tale 209.
3. Ps. 95:1. This prayer six Psalms (95–99, 29) recited on the Sabbath Eve before "*Lekhah Dodi.*" It was institutionalized by the mystic Moses Cordovero of Safed (1522–70).
4. Ps. 92:1. This verse appears in the continuation of the Sabbath Eve service.

Tale 118. The Adulterer

1. Cf. tales 54, 227.

Tale 119. The Besht Cures by Bloodletting

1. See tale 27.

Tale 121. The Parable of the Dog

1. Compare this parable with the Aesopic fable of "The Fox and the Hedgehog," in which Aesop used the same reasoning in addressing the people of Samos when a demagogue was being tried for his life. See

Ben Edwin Perry, "An Analytical Survey of Greek and Latin Fables in the Aesopic Tradition," in *Babrius and Phaedrus*, The Loeb Classical Library (Cambridge, Mass., and London, 1965), p. 504, No. 427.

2. Ecc. 4:2.

Tale 123. A Dowry

1. Raising orphans in one's home was recommended in B. Megillah 13a; Sanhedrin 19b.

2. Mishnah Aboth 3.17.

Tale 124. Rabbi Abraham and the Besht

1. See Abraham J. Heschel, "A Biographical Note on Rabbi Pinḥas of Korets," Hebrew, in *Alei Ayin: The Salman Schocken Jubilee Book* (Jerusalem, 1948–52), pp. 213–14, and a Yiddish version of this essay, "Reb Pinkhes Koritser," Yiddish, *Yivo Bleter*, XXXIII (1949), pp. 9–48.

Tale 125. A Combat in Magic

1. Cf. tale 98.

Tale 126. A Combat in Magic: A Second Version

1. We could not identify this town.

Tale 129. Rabbi Nahman Travels to the Holy Land

1. Rabbi Nahman of Horodenka traveled to the Land of Israel together with Rabbi Mendele of Peremyshlyany and a small group of Hasidim in 1764. See Dubnov, *History of Hasidism*, pp. 103–104, and Halpern, *The Hasidic Immigrations to Palestine During the Eighteenth Century*, pp. 16–17. However, according to the present text this was his second trip. The first time he visited Palestine must have been before 1740, since according to tale 169, Rabbi Eliezer Rokeaḥ traveled to meet him there, and his trip took place in June 1740. See Halpern, pp. 17–18.

2. According to Horodezky, *Hasidism and Hasidim*, Hebrew (Tel-Aviv, 1951), I–II, 162, Rabbi Naḥman died in Tiberias about ten years after his arrival in the Land of Israel. Halpern suggests the date of his death as 1772. See ibid. p. 19, n. 49. The last phrase of this tale is a pun in Hebrew. "*Met be-Minhah ve-yatsa le-menuhah.*"

Tale 130. Rabbi Mendele Visits with Rabbi Jacob Joseph

1. Abraham Rubinstein suggests that Cekinowka is a small town across the river from Soroki. See following note.
2. About the year 1764 Rabbi Mendele of Peremyshlyany visited with Rabbi Jacob Joseph of Polonnoye before starting off on his trip to the Holy Land. For a newly reported document concerning Rabbi Mendele's stay in Cekinowka and a new interpretation of the motivation for his immigration to the Holy Land, see Abraham Rubinstein, "A Possible New Fragment of 'Shivḥey Habbesht,'" Hebrew, *Tarbiz*, XXXV (1965), pp. 174–91.
3. Mishnah Aboth 2:5.

Tale 134. Iniquities and Prayers

1. Jer. 23:9.

Tale 135. The Preacher's Sermon

1. See tale 1.

Tale 136. A Madman Feigns Death

1. In the Talmudic context these words designate a shoe strap. See B. Sanhedrin 74b.

Tale 137. The Martyrs

1. Cf. tale 60. The mystical ascent to heaven to challenge the necessity of martyrdom is found also in the midrash "Eleh Ezkerah," see Eisenstein, *Oẓar Midrashim*, Hebrew, II, 441.

Tale 139. The Delayed Homecoming: A Second Version

1. Cf. tales 33, 69.

Tale 141. The Besht Discharges a Shohet

1. Cf. tales 71, 246.

Tale 142. The Optimism of Rabbi Naḥman

1. Compare the character of Rabbi Naḥman with that of the Talmudic

Rabbi Nahum of Gamzu, who reacted similarly to the difficulties he encountered. See B. Ta'anit 21a.

Tale 144. Feeling the Tefillin

1. A similar practice is recommended in B. Shabbat 12a.
2. Customarily, one only listens to the hazan.

Tale 145. The Height of Prayer

1. A prayer recited during the morning service on Mondays and Thursdays. It consists of various biblical fragments starting with the verse of Ps. 78:38. See Elbogen, *Der jüdische Gottesdienst*, pp. 77–78.

Tale 146. Ascension to Heaven

1. The Kabbalah conceives of marriage as a complete human unit modeled after the divine man who was created *male and female* (Gen. 5:2). Thus a man or a woman alone is only half of the human unit. See *The Zohar*, IV, 338 [III, 7b], and traditional editions, III, 109b, 296a. For a discussion of this concept see Tishby, *The Wisdom of the Zohar*, II, 607–626.

Tale 147. The Besht's Second Coming

1. Cf. tale 247.

Tale 149. The Ring

1. See tale 78, n. 2.

Tale 150. Rabbi Motil

1. Deut. 1:21.
2. Cf. B. Megillah 7b.

Tale 151. Rabbi Gershon's Enemies

1. Zohar Ḥadash contains those parts of the Zohar and the Tikkunei Zohar which the publisher of the Mantua edition of these books missed. The material was collected chiefly by Abraham Halevi Berokhim from a manuscript found in Safed. See Scholem, *Major Trends in Jewish Mysticism*, p. 386. We could not verify and complete the writer's reference.

Tale *152. The Wandering Soul*

1. Cf. tale 92.

Tale *153. Dream Teaching*

1. Ps. 135:19. This phrase is used as an opening formula for the morning and evening prayers in the synagogue.
2. Cf. tale 32.

Tale *156. The Forbidden Country*

1. Lev. 4:22. *Rashi's* commentary is based on a philological analogy. He relates the words *asher* (when) and *osher* (happiness) and thus states that happy is that generation whose ruler (king) takes care to provide an atonement sacrifice for even an inadvertent act on his part, since it is more certain that he will do penance for his willful sins.

2. In his book *Toldot Ya'akov Yosef* (Medzhibozh, 1817), p. 576, Rabbi Jacob Joseph offers an exegesis for Lev. 4:22. He considers the sin of the ruler as the means for elevating lowly sinners. This idea is in keeping with Rabbi Jacob Joseph's general ideas about the function of the tsaddik among his people. See Gedalyah Nigal, *Leader and Community*, Hebrew (Jerusalem, 1962), pp. 65–81 and Dresner, *The Zaddik*, pp. 148–90.

Tale *157. The Spiritual Cure*

1. The conception of the human body and the positive and negative commandments corresponding to its parts, which is expressed here, follows the Talmud. See B. Makkoth 23b.

Tale *162. The Demons*

1. B. Shabbath 89b.

2. The slaughtering of a cock in magical rites was not limited to non-Jewish people. Rather, the Jews used it on various occasions as a *Kappara*—a symbolic substitution of animals for a sick or sinful person. See H. J. Zimmels, *Magicians, Theologians and Doctors* (London, 1952), pp. 144–46.

3. As a protective measure from demons one should keep silent until the candle catches fire. See Judah ben Samuel ha-Hasid, *The Book of the Hasidim*, Hebrew, ed. Reuben Margulies (Jerusalem, 1960) p. 209, no. 235.

4. For another version which tells how the Preacher became a follower of the Besht, see tale 48.

Tale 165. The Preacher Who Spoke Evil of the Jews

1. A class of angels. They are one of the constituents of the throne world. See Scholem, *Major Trends in Jewish Mysticism*, pp. 71, 73.

Tale 166. The Dead Man in Hell

1. Compare this tale with the story about Rabbi Yoḥanan ben Zakkai in M. Friedmann, "Pseudo-Seder Eliahu Zuta," Hebrew, in *Seder Eliahu Rabba and Seder Eliahu Zuta*, 2nd printing (Jerusalem, 1960), pp. 22–25. This story is told more frequently about Rabbi Akiva. It first appeared in the extra-canonical talmudic tractate Kallah Rabbathi 2.9. Later it was incorporated in such collections as Gaster, *The Exempla of the Rabbis*, pp. 92–93, no. 134; Gaster, *Ma'aseh Book* (Philadelphia, 1934), I, 286–89; Nissim ben Jacob ben Nissim ibn Shahim, *Ḥibur Yafeh me-ha-Yeshu'ah*, ed. Joachim Wilhelm Hirschberg (Jerusalem, 1954), pp. 104–105; Israel ben Joseph Alnakawa, *Menorat ha-Maor*, ed. Hyman Gerson Enelow (New York, 1932), IV, 127–28. A version of this story was found in the Cairo Geniza as well. See Louis Ginzberg, *Ginze Schechter*, (*Genizah Studies in Memory of Solomon Schechter*), (New York, 1928–29), I, 238–40. The recurrent appearance of the tale attests to its popularity in the Middle Ages.

Tale 167. The Servant's Evil Thoughts

1. We could not identify this village.

Tale 169. Rabbi Eliezer and Rabbi Naḥman

1. Rabbi Eliezer's journey took place in June 1740, and he died in Safed shortly after his arrival in Palestine in 1741. See Gelber, *The History of the Jews in Brody*, pp. 50–54 and Halpern, *The Hasidic Immigrations to Palestine*, pp. 17–18. See also tale 129 in which the text refers to the 1764 immigration of Rabbi Naḥman to Palestine as his second trip there. Also see tale 63 in which it is assumed that Rabbi Eliezer Rokeaḥ died in Amsterdam.

Tale 171. Rabbi Tsevi's Dream

1. See tales 40, 45, 50, 51, 210.
2. Exod. 15:1–19.
3. We could not identify this place.

Tale 172. The Protective Tefillin

1. Concerning the magical protective power of the tefillin, see Trachtenberg, *Jewish Magic and Superstition*, pp. 145, 158.

2. According to the Kabbalah, *Matronita* is the lowest of the ten *Sefirot* and is usually conceived of as a divine female figure synonymous with the Shekinah. *Tikkunei Zohar* is a part of the zoharic literature. It consists of a new commentary on the first section of the Torah, divided into seventy chapters, each of which begins with a new interpretation of the first words of the Torah, *Bereshit*. It was first printed in Mantua in 1558. As far as we could determine, this is not a direct quotation but is rather a paraphrase of an idea expressed in the tenth and eleventh chapters of *Tikkunei Zohar*. For a comparative study of its image in the Kabbalah and analogous figures in Near Eastern religions, see Raphael Patai, "Matronit The Goddess of the Kabbala," *History of Religions*, I (1964), 53–68.

Tale 173. Rabbi Jehiee Mikhel

1. Also spelled Gorodnya.

2. The tale points out that the Besht's prestige in Lithuania was great enough to influence the election of a rabbi. Wolf Rabinowitsch denies that this story has any historical validity. See *Lithuanian Hassidism* (Jerusalem, 1967), p. 8.

Tale 175. The Flickering Candle

1. See B. Niddah 16b: "He who has intercourse in the light of a lamp is contemptible."

Tale 176. The Poverty and Generosity of the Besht

1. Cf. tale 161.

Tale 182. Rabbi Zusman

1. In Hebrew, *karot*. This term refers to untimely death as punishment by heaven. See Num. 15:31 and B. Sanhedrin 64b, Shabbath 25a, and Kerithoth 1a.

Tale 185. Praying Word for Word with the Besht

1. In the original text the name of this town is Sokolovki. We suggest

it may have been the village of Sokolov near Zhitomir.

2. Ps. 33:17.

3. A group of biblical hymns, mainly Ps. 145–50 and Exod. 15, which are recited in the morning service. See Elbogen, *Der jüdische Gottesdienst*, pp. 81–87, and Leon J. Liebreich, "The *Pesuke De-Zimra* Benedictions," *Jewish Quarterly Review*, XLI (1950), 195–206.

4. This book is a popular kabbalistic work written by the Italian kabbalist and Talmudist Immanuel Ḥay ben Abraham Ricchi (about 1688–1743). It was first published in Amsterdam in 1727.

Tale 187. The Amulet

1. For discussion of the preparation of amulets, see Trachtenberg, *Jewish Magic and Superstition*, pp. 143–45, and Zimmels, *Magicians, Theologians and Doctors*, pp. 135–37.

Tale 191. The Angel Hadarniel

1. See the Hebrew edition of *The Zohar*, II, 58a, and also Ginzberg, *The Legends of the Jews*, III, p. 110.

Tale 192. The Young Martyr

1. When Isaac was on the altar God opened the heavens, and Isaac beheld the chambers of the *Merkavah*. See Ginzberg, *The Legends of the Jews*, V, p. 285, n. 101.

Tale 193. Rabbi Gershon in the Holy Land

1. In the Talmudic period Acre was considered as the northern boundary of the Land of Israel. See Y. Shebi'ith 6.1, 36b, and B. Giṭṭin 7b, 76b. For references to the juridical implications of this notion in past talmudic commentaries, see *Talmudic Encyclopedia*, Hebrew (Jerusalem, 1956), II, p. 210.

Tale 194. Storytelling and Ma'aseh Merkavah

1. One of the innovations of Hasidism has been the employment of tales as well as prayers for mystical purposes. At first *merkavah* mysticism consisted of attempts to perceive God's appearance on the throne and to learn the mysteries of the celestial world. In later developments, the goal of Jewish mystics was to participate in the attempts of the Divinity to purify the upper sphere by means of prayers and mystical contemplative methods. In Hasidism narratives were used for the same purpose. Tales, like prayers,

had meanings beyond their literal interpretation. This belief was one of the factors which contributed to the development of the rich Hasidic folklore. For a discussion of the Hasidic attitudes to narratives and story-telling and their place in Hasidic thought and culture see Joseph Dan, "Research Techniques for Hasidic Tales," Hebrew, *Fourth World Congress of Jewish Studies, Papers* vol. II (Jerusalem, 1968), II, pp. 53–57, and Jerome R. Mintz, *Legends of the Hasidim* (Chicago, 1968), pp. 3–8.

Tale 196. The Demons

1. Gen. 32:4.
2. This is a pun on the word, *malaakhim,* which means both messengers and angels in Hebrew.
3. The *left side* is a term used to designate demonic and evil powers. See, for example, *The Zohar,* V 16 [III, 48b].

Tale 197. Competing for the Arrendeh

1. Mishnah Aboth 2.3. In his quotation the Besht omitted four words from the original text.

Tale 198. The Imprisonment of Israel Shafir

1. Also spelled Mogilev.

Tale 201. The Angels' Request

1. See tale 48.

Tale 208. Gematria

1. B. 'Abodah Zarah 39a, Shebu'oth 30b.

Tale 209. Rabbi Naḥman of Kosov

1. Deut. 11:15.
2. Amos 7:14.
3. See tale 116, n. 2.
4. For a discussion of the significance of this story to the history of the Hasidic movement, see Joseph G. Weiss, "A Circle of Pre-Hasidic Pneumatics," *The Journal of Jewish Studies,* VIII (1957), 199–213. For a biographical sketch of Rabbi Naḥman see Abraham J. Heschel, "Rabbi

Naḥman of Kosov, the Besht's Friend," Hebrew, in *Harry Austryn Wolfson's Jubilee Volume,* ed. Saul Lieberman (New York and Jerusalem, 1965) III.

Tale 210. The Flight of the Besht

1. Cf. tales 40, 45, 50, 51, 171.

Tale 211. The Chief Arrendators

1. Concerning the danger of demons in a new house, see Trachtenberg, *Jewish Magic and Superstition,* pp. 33, 110.
2. See tales 11, 47, 231.
3. See the end of tale 213.
4. For references to this miracle in the Talmudic tradition, see Ginzberg, *The Legends of the Jews,* V, 260, n. 287. For a tale about how the Besht received the power to travel at miraculous speed, see Jerome R. Mintz, *Legends of the Hasidim, An Introduction to Their Culture and Oral Tradition in the New World* (Chicago, 1968), tale (H8).

Tale 212. A Tenth for a Minyan

1. This spelling follows the map of *The National Geographic Magazine* (1958), Atlas Plate no. 38.

Tale 213. The Fall of the Chief Arrendators

1. An allusion to the narrative, which comprises tales 211 and 213, is found in a polemic manuscript against the Hasidic movement written by David of Makow between 1810 to 1814. This document, however, mentions twelve years as the time limit that the Besht prophesied for the downfall of the *arrendators.* See Mordecai L. Wilensky, "The Polemic of Rabbi David of Makow Against Hasidism," *Proceedings of the American Academy for Jewish Research,* XXV (1956), 141, 148. Their temporary downfall is verified by an indirect report in the newspaper *Hildesheimer Relations Courier* (November, 1751). See Halpern, "The Woszczylo Revolt," Hebrew, *Zion,* XXII (1957), p. 60.

Tale 216. The Death of Rabbi David Forkes

1. Probably Novograd Volynski. There were several towns by that name.

2. A column of light also distinguishes the grave of Rabbi Akiva. See S. Buber ed. *Midrash Mishlei* (Wilna, 1893), p. 62.

3. The weekly portion of the Torah which is read in the synagogue usually denotes the name of each Sabbath. However, the Sabbath prior to the Ninth of Av (July), the day of mourning in commemoration of the destruction of the Temple, derives its name from the weekly portion of Is. 1:1–27, which starts with the word *Hazon*, "vision."

Tale 217. A Brand Plucked Out of the Fire

1. Zech. 3:2. This designation refers to Joshua, the high priest. For Talmudic Midrashic legends concerning Joshua, see Ginzberg, *The Legends of the Jews*, IV, 336–67; VI, 426–27, note 108.

Tale 221. The Council of Four Lands

1. See Mishnah Aboth 2.5.

2. The appearance of the Besht before the Council has not been verified. Israel Halpern suggests the possible identification of Rabbi Abraham Aba with either Rabbi Abraham Joski of Leszno or Rabbi Abraham Halperin, two well known elders at that time. Halpern, *Acta Congressus*, p. 532.

3. A prayer inserted into the eighteen benedictions on the New Moon. Discussion of this question resulted in a vast rabbinic literature, thorough knowledge of which the Besht was asked to demonstrate.

4. See B. Pesahim 112b, where the Talmudic sage forbids sitting on such a bed.

Tale 222. The Blessing of a Poor Man

1. In ancient times, probably biblical as well as post-biblical, the festivity of water drawing and libation took place in Jerusalem during the holiday of Sukkoth. See B. Sukkah 51a. Thus, the writer refers to the celebration of Simhath Torah with this mishnaic term.

Tale 223. "The Hour Has Come But Not The Man"

1. B. Sanhedrin 95a.

2. Cf. Ps. 103:13.

3. See Reidar Th. Christiansen, *The Migratory Legends*, FFC, 175 (Helsinki, 1958), p. 66, no. 4050. For a study of its European versions, see Robert Wildhaber, " 'Die Stunde ist da, aber der Mann nicht' Ein europaisehes Sagenmotiv," *Rheinisehes Jahrbuch für Volkskunde*, IX

(1958), 65–88. For Scottish versions of this legend see *Sir Walter Scott's Minstrelsy of the Scottish Border*, ed. T. F. Henderson (Edinburgh and London, 1902) IV, pp. 334–46.

Tale 224. Jonah

1. Gen. 16:12.
2. I Sam. 21:6.
3. The role of the anonymous helper played by the prophet Jonah in this story is similar to the part Elijah the Prophet takes in many Jewish legends. Concerning the traditional affinity between these two figures, see Ginzberg, *The Legends of the Jews*, VI, 350–351.

Tale 225. The Three Brothers

1. In the text this phrase is in Yiddish.
2. In this episode the Besht imitates the way Rabbi Yoḥanan and Rabbi Ḥanina cured sick rabbis as told in the source of the sayings, B. Berakoth 5b.

Tale 227. The Sinner

1. Concerning the significance of Minhah on Sabbath Eve, see Tishby, *The Wisdom of the Zohar*, II, 262, 269.
2. Compare this story with tales 54, 118.
3. A common opening formula of paragraphs in the Heikhalot literature is "Rabbi Ishmael said. . . ." The verb *opened* (*pataḥ*), however, is used in the midrashic literature to designate the beginning of a sermon. We could find neither the source of this quotation in Ḥayyim Vital's writings, nor the exact paragraph opening cited here.
4. Concerning the likeness of Elijah to an angel, see B. Berakoth 4b and *The Zohar*, II, 290 [I, 209a].
5. B. Ta'anith 24b.
6. This exegesis is based upon a Hebrew pun, בִּשְׁבִיל (*bishvil*) "for" and בַּשְׁבִיל (*bashvil*) "in the path."
7. B. Yebamoth 92b.

Tale 228. Rabbi Naḥman and the Besht

1. For other mystical connotations of this motion, see Tishby, *The Wisdom of the Zohar*, II, 275b.
2. Ps. 16:8.

Tale 230. The Parable of the King's Crown

1. In the Yiddish edition this parable is told at greater length; however, the conclusion which contains the comparison with the historic disputes between Hillel and Shamai is missing. See A. Yaari, "Two Basic Recensions of Shivḥē Ha-Besht," Hebrew, *Kirjath Sepher*, XXXIX (1964), 554–55.

Tale 231. The Blind Boy

1. Concerning the use of holy names in magic, see Trachtenberg, *Jewish Magic and Superstition*, pp. 52–53.
2. See commentary on the Talmud of Rabbi Asher ben Jehiel, *Rosh*, on *Shebu'oth*, 6:13.

Tale 236. The Gentile who Blessed the Jews

1. By ceasing to pray the Besht breached a severe religious prohibition which is stated in Mishnah Berakoth 5:1: "Even if a king greets him [while praying] he should not answer him; even if a snake is wound round his heel he should not break off." Hence the Besht's act had a great effect upon the audience in the synagogue.

Tale 237. The Language of the Animals

1. Deut. 18:13.

Tale 239. The Besht and the Old Priest

1. Is. 45:18.

Tale 241. Rabbi David Forkes' Dream

1. The major figure in the Safed school of mysticism (1534–1572). See G. Scholem, *Major Trends in Jewish Mysticism*, pp. 244–86.
2. A similar statement was found in the Brody community record. See Gelber, *The History of the Jews in Brody*, Hebrew, p. 334. See also tale 60.

Tale 242. A Glass of Wine

1. This is a paraphrase of the saying which originally reads: "Fright is strong, but wine banishes it. Wine is strong, but sleep works it off." B. Baba Bathra 10a.

Tale 243. The Besht's Dinner

1. The first words of an obligatory recitation, said twice a day, which consists of Deut. 6:4–9; 11:13–21 and Num. 15:13–41.

Tale 245. The Doctor

1. We could not verify nor complete the writer's reference.

Tale 247. The Besht's Death

1. See tale 47.
2. Ecc. 8:8, in the biblical context this phrase means that man has "no power over the day of death."
3. The prayer, which consists mainly of Ps. 91, asks for the protection of God from various dangers. It is usually said at the conclusion of the Sabbath.
4. The sickness of which the Besht dies conforms with the idea expressed in the Babylonian Talmud by Rabbi Jose, who said: "May my lot be of those who die with bowel trouble, for a Master said, the majority of righteous die of trouble in the bowels." B. Shabbath 118b. The Besht died surrounded by his disciples like Hillel, *Aboth de Rabbi Nathan*, ed. Schecter, Version II, ch. 28, p. 51, and Rabbi Judah the Prince, B. Kethuboth 103b–104a; Y. Kilayim 9:3. The Yiddish edition varies somewhat. See Yaari, "Two Basic Recensions . . . ," *Kirjath Sepher*, XXXIX (1964), pp. 557–59.

Tale 249. The Besht's Son

1. This statement was omitted from the second edition of the book printed in. Berdichev, 1815. Instead, the following story was inserted at the end of the book:

"A preacher came to the holy community of Chudnov and stayed there with the community elder. He preached there for several days and then he fell sick. He lay in bed unable to speak or move his hands and feet. The community elder felt pity for him. At that time the Besht was in the holy community of Polonnoye. The elder sent for the Besht to come to the holy community of Chudnov. He came and said that the preacher must die. 'But let me show you the power of the Torah.' He told them to bring him sweet water. He took ashes from the oven and put them into the water. Then he read him the biblical portion "Metsora" [Lev. 14:1–15:33] over him, and the sick man sat up and began to talk. The Besht spoke with him as much as needed. Then the preacher lay down again and passed away."

Tale 250. The Fish and the Dog: A Second Version

1. It is customary to taste the Sabbath dish on Friday afternoon. The phrase can be found in Zedekiah ben Abraham, *Sefer Shibalei ha-Leket ha-Shalem*, ed. Sh. Buber (Vilna, 1886), p. 30b.
2. B. Hagigah 5b.
3. For another version of this story see tale 108.

Tale 251. The Burning of Rabbi Jacob Joseph's Books

1. As part of the persecution of the Hasidim by their opponents, the mitnaggedim, following a Jewish court decision, burned the book *Toldot Ya'akov Yosef* publically in Brody in 1781. According to the testimony of Joseph Perl, the fire was set in front of the house of Rabbi Mikhel of Zolochev. See Dubnov, *History of Hasidism*, p. 165.
2. Yiddish.
3. B. 'Arakin 16b.
4. Ecc. 5:7.

INDEX

About the Editors

Dan Ben-Amos is a professor and the department chair of the Department of Folklore and Folklife at the University of Pennsylvania.

Jerome R. Mintz is professor of anthropology and of Jewish studies at Indiana University. He is the author of *Hasidic People: A Place in the New World* and *The Legends of the Hasidim: An Introduction to Hasidic Culture and Oral Tradition in the New World*.